*The Right Rev. George Berkeley, S. T. P.*

*Lord Bishop of Cloyne in Ireland*

THE FIVE-FOOT SHELF OF BOOKS
"THE HARVARD CLASSICS"
EDITED BY CHARLES W ELIOT LL D

# ENGLISH PHILOSOPHERS

## OF THE SEVENTEENTH AND EIGHTEENTH CENTURIES

### LOCKE · BERKELEY · HUME

WITH INTRODUCTIONS AND NOTES

VOLUME 37

P F COLLIER & SON
NEW YORK

Designed, Printed, and Bound at
The Collier Press, New York

# CONTENTS

PAGE

SOME THOUGHTS CONCERNING EDUCATION . . . . . . 9

BY JOHN LOCKE

THREE DIALOGUES BETWEEN HYLAS AND PHILONOUS IN OP-
POSITION TO SCEPTICS AND ATHEISTS . . . . . . . . 201

BY GEORGE BERKELEY

AN ENQUIRY CONCERNING HUMAN UNDERSTANDING . . 305

BY DAVID HUME

I. Of the different Species of Philosophy . . . . . 305
II. Of the Origin of Ideas . . . . . . . . . . 316
III. Of the Association of Ideas . . . . . . . . 322
IV. Sceptical Doubts concerning the Operations of the
Understanding . . . . . . . . . . . . . 324
V. Sceptical Solution of these Doubts . . . . . . 337
VI. Of Probability . . . . . . . . . . . . . 351
VII. Of the Idea of necessary Connexion . . . . . . 354
VIII. Of Liberty and Necessity . . . . . . . . . 371
IX. Of the Reason of Animals . . . . . . . . 392
X. Of Miracles . . . . . . . . . . . . . 396
XI. Of a particular Providence and of a future State . 416
XII. Of the academical or sceptical Philosophy . . . . 431

# INTRODUCTORY NOTE

JOHN LOCKE *was born near Bristol, England, on August 29, 1632; and was educated at Westminster School, where Dryden was his contemporary, and at Christ Church, Oxford. Of the discipline then in vogue in either institution, the future educational theorist had no high opinion, as may be gathered from allusions in the present treatise; yet, after taking his master's degree in 1658, he became tutor of his college, and lecturer in Greek and rhetoric. After a visit to the Continent in 1665, as secretary to an embassy, he returned to Oxford and took up the study of medicine. He became attached, as friend and physician, to Lord Ashley, afterward the first Earl of Shaftesbury; and while this nobleman was Lord Chancellor, Locke held the office of Secretary of Presentations.*

*Shaftesbury went out of office in 1673, and two years later Locke went to France in search of health, supporting himself by acting as tutor to the son of Sir John Banks, and as physician to the wife of the English Ambassador at Paris. In 1679, Shaftesbury, being again in power, recalled Locke to England. He reluctantly obeyed, and remained in attendance on his patron, assisting him in political matters and superintending the education of his grandson, the future author of "Characteristics," till Shaftesbury's political fortunes finally collapsed, and both men took refuge in Holland.*

*Locke's first two years in Holland were spent in traveling and in intercourse with scholars; but in 1685 the Dutch Government was asked to deliver him up to the English as a traitor, and he was forced to go into hiding till a pardon was granted by James II in 1686, though there is no evidence of his having been guilty of any crime beyond his friendship with Shaftesbury.*

*It was not till now, at the age of fifty-four, that Locke began to publish the results of a lifetime of study and thought. An epitome of his great "Essay Concerning Human Understanding" was printed in his friend Le Clerc's "Bibliothèque Universelle," and the work was finally published in full in 1690. It was from Holland also that he wrote, as advice to a friend on the bringing up of his son, those letters which were later printed as "Thoughts Concerning Education."*

3

*During his exile Locke had come into friendly relations with his future sovereigns, William and Mary; and when the Revolution was accomplished he came back to England with the Princess in 1689. He was offered the Ambassadorship to Prussia, but declined on account of his weak health and because he thought he was not valiant enough in strong drink to be Ambassador at the court of the Elector of Brandenburg; so he stayed at home and published his "Essay."*

*The remainder of his life was spent chiefly at the home of his friends, the Cudworths and Mashams, at Oates in Essex. He held the office of Commissioner of Appeals, and was for some years a member of the Council of Trade and Plantations, a position which led to his occupying himself with problems of economics. At Oates he had the opportunity of putting his educational theories into practise in the training of the grandson of his host, and the results confirmed his belief in his methods. He died at Oates, October 27, 1704.*

*It has been noted that while at school and at the university Locke disapproved the educational methods employed; and this independence of judgment marked him through life. In medicine he denounced the scholasticism which still survived and which in various branches of learning had already been attacked by Bacon and Hobbes; and he advocated the experimental methods adopted by his friend Sydenham, the great physician of the day. In educational theory and method he held advanced opinions, insisting especially on the importance of guarding the formation of habits, and on training in wisdom and virtue rather than on information as the main object of education. Many of his ideas are still among the objects aimed at, rather than achieved, by educational reformers. It will be observed from the following "Thoughts" that they bear the mark of their original purpose, the individual education of a gentleman's son, not the formation of a school system.*

*But it is as a philosopher that Locke's fame is greatest. He was the ancestor of the English empirical school, and he exercised a profound influence on philosophic thought throughout Europe. Almost all the main lines of the intellectual activity of the eighteenth century in England lead back to Locke, and the skepticism of Hume is the logical development of the principles laid down in the "Essay Concerning Human Understanding."*

# DEDICATION

To Edward Clarke, of Chipley, Esq.

Sir:

These *thoughts concerning education,* which now come abroad into the world, do of right belong to you, being written several years since for your sake, and are no other than what you have already by you in my letters. I have so little vary'd any thing, but only the order of what was sent you at different times, and on several occasions, that the reader will easily find, in the familiarity and fashion of the stile, that they were rather the private conversation of two friends, than a discourse design'd for publick view.

The importunity of friends is the common apology for publications men are afraid to own themselves forward to. But you know I can truly say, that if some, who having heard of these papers of mine, had not press'd to see them, and afterwards to have them printed, they had lain dormant still in that privacy they were design'd for. But those, whose judgment I defer much to, telling me, that they were persuaded, that this rough draught of mine might be of some use, if made more publick, touch'd upon what will always be very prevalent with me: for I think it every man's indispensable duty, to do all the service he can to his country; and I see not what difference he puts between himself and his cattle, who lives without that thought. This subject is of so great concernment, and a right way of education is of so general advantage, that did I find my abilities answer my wishes, I should not have needed exhortations or importunities from others. However, the meanness of these papers, and my just distrust of them, shall not keep me, by the shame of doing so little, from contributing my mite, when there is no more requir'd of me than my throwing it into the publick receptacle. And if there be any more of their size and notions, who lik'd them so well, that they thought them worth printing, I may flatter myself they will not be lost labour to every body.

5

I myself have been consulted of late by so many, who profess themselves at a loss how to breed their children, and the early corruption of youth is now become so general a complaint, that he cannot be thought wholly impertinent, who brings the consideration of this matter on the stage, and offers something, if it be but to excite others, or afford matter of correction: for errors in education should be less indulg'd than any. These, like faults in the first concoction, that are never mended in the second or third, carry their afterwards incorrigible taint with them thro' all the parts and stations of life.

I am so far from being conceited of any thing I have here offer'd, that I should not be sorry, even for your sake, if some one abler and fitter for such a task would in a just treatise of education, suited to our *English* gentry, rectify the mistakes I have made in this; it being much more desirable to me, that young gentlemen should be put into (that which every one ought to be solicitous about) the best way of being form'd and instructed, than that my opinion should be receiv'd concerning it. You will, however, in the mean time bear me witness, that the method here propos'd has had no ordinary effects upon a gentleman's son it was not design'd for. I will not say the good temper of the child did not very much contribute to it; but this I think you and the parents are satisfy'd of, that a contrary usage, according to the ordinary disciplining of children, would not have mended that temper, nor have brought him to be in love with his book, to take a pleasure in learning, and to desire, as he does, to be taught more than those about him think fit always to teach him.

But my business is not to recommend this treatise to you, whose opinion of it I know already; nor it to the world, either by your opinion or patronage. The well educating of their children is so much the duty and concern of parents, and the welfare and prosperity of the nation so much depends on it, that I would have every one lay it seriously to heart; and after having well examin'd and distinguish'd what fancy, custom, or reason advises in the case, set his helping hand to promote every where that way of training up youth, with regard to their several conditions, which is the easiest, shortest, and likeliest to produce virtuous, useful, and able men in their distinct callings; tho' that most to be taken care of is the gentleman's calling. For if those of that rank are by their education once set right, they will quickly bring all the rest into order.

I know not whether I have done more than shewn my good wishes towards it in this short discourse; such as it is, the world now has it, and if there be any thing in it worth their acceptance, they owe their thanks to you for it. My affection to you gave the first rise to it, and I am pleas'd, that I can leave to posterity this mark of the friendship that has been between us. For I know no greater pleasure in this life, nor a better remembrance to be left behind one, than a long continued friendship with an honest, useful, and worthy man, and lover of his country. I am, Sir,

> Your most humble and most faithful servant,

> JOHN LOCKE.

March 7, 1692 [i. e. 169⅔].

# SOME THOUGHTS
# CONCERNING EDUCATION

§ 1. A SOUND mind in a sound body, is a short, but full
description of a happy state in this world. He
that has these two, has little more to wish for;
and he that wants either of them, will be but little the better
for any thing else. Men's happiness or misery is most part
of their own making. He, whose mind directs not wisely, will
never take the right way; and he, whose body is crazy and
feeble, will never be able to advance in it. I confess, there
are some men's constitutions of body and mind so vigorous,
and well fram'd by nature, that they need not much assistance from others; but by the strength of their natural genius,
they are from their cradles carried towards what is excellent; and by the privilege of their happy constitutions,
are able to do wonders. But examples of this kind are
but few; and I think I may say, that of all the men we meet
with, nine parts of ten are what they are, good or evil,
useful or not, by their education. 'Tis that which makes
the great difference in mankind. The little, or almost
insensible impressions on our tender infancies, have very
important and lasting consequences: and there 'tis, as in
the fountains of some rivers, where a gentle application of
the hand turns the flexible waters in channels, that make
them take quite contrary courses; and by this direction
given them at first in the source, they receive different
tendencies, and arrive at last at very remote and distant
places.

§ 2. I imagine the minds of children as easily turn'd this
or that way, as water it self: and though this be the principal
part, and our main care should be about the inside, yet the
clay-cottage is not to be neglected. I shall therefore begin

with the case, and consider first the *health* of the body, as that which perhaps you may rather expect from that study I have been thought more peculiarly to have apply'd my self to; and that also which will be soonest dispatch'd, as lying, if I guess not amiss, in a very little compass.

§ 3. How necessary *health* is to our business and happiness; and how requisite a strong constitution, able to endure hardships and fatigue, is to one that will make any figure in the world, is too obvious to need any proof.

§ 4. The consideration I shall here have of *health,* shall be, not what a physician ought to do with a sick and crazy child; but what the parents, without the help of physick, should do for the *preservation and improvement of an healthy,* or at least *not sickly constitution* in their children. And this perhaps might be all dispatch'd in this one short rule, *viz.* That gentlemen should use their children, as the honest farmers and substantial yeomen do theirs. But because the mothers possibly may think this a little too hard, and the fathers too short, I shall explain my self more particularly; only laying down this as a general and certain observation for the women to consider, *viz.* That most children's constitutions are either spoil'd, or at least harm'd, by *cockering* and *tenderness.*

§ 5. The first thing to be taken care of, is, that children be not too *warmly clad or cover'd,* winter or summer. The face when we are born, is no less tender than any other part of the body. 'Tis use alone hardens it, and makes it more able to endure the cold. And therefore the *Scythian* philosopher gave a very significant answer to the *Athenian,* who wonder'd how he could go naked in frost and snow. *How,* said the *Scythian, can you endure your face expos'd to the sharp winter air? My face is us'd to it,* said the *Athenian. Think me all face,* reply'd the *Scythian.* Our bodies will endure any thing, that from the beginning they are accustom'd to.

An eminent instance of this, though in the contrary excess of heat, being to our present purpose, to shew what use can do, I shall set down in the author's words, as I meet with it in a late ingenious voyage.

" The heats, says he, are more violent in *Malta,* than in any

" part of *Europe:* they exceed those of *Rome* itself, and are
" perfectly stifling; and so much the more, because there are
" seldom any cooling breezes here. This makes the common
" people as black as gypsies: but yet the peasants defy the
" sun; they work on in the hottest part of the day, without
" intermission, or sheltering themselves from his scorching
" rays. This has convinc'd me, that nature can bring itself
" to many things, which seem impossible, provided we ac-
" custom ourselves from our infancy. The *Malteses* do so,
" who harden the bodies of their children, and reconcile
" them to the heat, by making them go stark naked, without
" shirt, drawers, or any thing on their heads, from their
" cradles till they are ten years old."

Give me leave therefore to advise you not to fence too
carefully against the cold of this our climate. There are
those in *England,* who wear the same clothes winter and
summer, and that without any inconvenience, or more sense
of cold than others find. But if the mother will needs
have an allowance for frost and snow, for fear of harm, and
the father, for fear of censure, be sure let not his winter-
clothing be too warm: And amongst other things, remember,
that when nature has so well covered his head with hair,
and strengthen'd it with a year or two's age, that he can run
about by day without a cap, it is best that by night a child
should also lie without one; there being nothing that more
exposes to headachs, colds, catarrhs, coughs, and several
other diseases, than keeping the *head warm.*

§ 6. I have said *he* here, because the principal aim of my
discourse is, how a young gentleman should be brought up
from his infancy, which in all things will not so perfectly
suit the education of *daughters;* though where the difference
of sex requires different treatment, 'twill be no hard matter
to distinguish.

§ 7. I will also advise his *feet to be wash'd* every day
in cold water, and to have his *shoes* so thin, that they might
leak and *let in water,* whenever he comes near it. Here, I
fear I shall have the mistress and maids too against me.
One will think it too filthy, and the other perhaps too much
pains, to make clean his stockings. But yet truth will have
it, that his health is much more worth than all such consid-

erations, and ten times as much more. And he that considers
how mischievous and mortal a thing taking *wet in the feet* is,
to those who have been bred nicely, will wish he had, with
the poor people's children, gone *bare-foot,* who, by that means,
come to be so reconcil'd by custom to wet in their feet,
that they take no more cold or harm by it, than if they
were wet in their hands. And what is it, I pray, that
makes this great difference between the hands and the feet
in others, but only custom? I doubt not, but if a man from
his cradle had been always us'd to go bare-foot, whilst his
hands were constantly wrapt up in warm mittins, and cover'd
with *hand-shoes,* as the *Dutch* call *gloves;* I doubt not, I
say, but such a custom would make taking wet in his hands
as dangerous to him, as now taking wet in their feet is to
a great many others. The way to prevent this, is, to have
his shoes made so as to leak water, and his feet wash'd
constantly every day in cold water. It is recommendable for
its cleanliness; but that which I aim at in it, is health; and
therefore I limit it not precisely to any time of the day. I
have known it us'd every night with very good success, and
that all the winter, without the omitting it so much as one
night in extreme cold weather; when thick ice cover'd the
water, the child bathed his legs and feet in it, though he
was of an age not big enough to rub and wipe them himself,
and when he began this custom was puling and very tender.
But the great end being to harden those parts by a frequent
and familiar use of cold water, and thereby to prevent the
mischiefs that usually attend accidental taking wet in the
feet in those who are bred otherwise, I think it may be
left to the prudence and convenience of the parents, to
chuse either night or morning. The time I deem indifferent,
so the thing be effectually done. The health and hardiness
procured by it, would be a good purchase at a much dearer
rate. To which if I add the preventing of corns, that to
some men would be a very valuable consideration. But
begin first in the spring with luke-warm, and so colder and
colder every time, till in a few days you come to perfectly
cold water, and then continue it so winter and summer. For
it is to be observed in this, as in all other *alterations* from
our ordinary way of living, the changes must be made by

gentle and insensible degrees; and so we may bring our bodies to any thing, without pain, and without danger.

How fond mothers are like to receive this doctrine, is not hard to foresee. What can it be less, than to murder their tender babes, to use them thus? What! put their feet in cold water in frost and snow, when all one can do is little enough to keep them warm? A little to remove their fears by examples, without which the plainest reason is seldom hearken'd to: *Seneca* tells us of himself, *Ep.* 53, and 83, that he used to bathe himself in cold spring-water in the midst of winter. This, if he had not thought it not only tolerable, but healthy too, he would scarce have done, in an exorbitant fortune, that could well have borne the expence of a warm bath, and in an age (for he was then old) that would have excused greater indulgence. If we think his stoical principles led him to this severity, let it be so, that this sect reconciled cold water to his sufferance. What made it agreeable to his health? For that was not impair'd by this hard usage. But what shall we say to *Horace,* who warm'd not himself with the reputation of any sect, and least of all affected stoical austerities? yet he assures us, he was wont in the winter season to bathe himself in cold water. But, perhaps, *Italy* will be thought much warmer than *England,* and the chillness of their waters not to come near ours in winter. If the rivers of *Italy* are warmer, those of *Germany* and *Poland* are much colder, than any in this our country, and yet in these, the *Jews,* both men and women, bathe all over, at all seasons of the year, without any prejudice to their health. And every one is not apt to believe it is miracle, or any peculiar virtue of St. *Winifred's* Well, that makes the cold waters of that famous spring do no harm to the tender bodies that bathe in it. Every one is now full of the miracles done by cold baths on decay'd and weak constitutions, for the recovery of health and strength; and therefore they cannot be impracticable or intolerable for the improving and hardening the bodies of those who are in better circumstances.

If these examples of grown men be not thought yet to reach the case of children, but that they may be judg'd still to be too tender, and unable to bear such usage, let them examine what the *Germans* of old, and the *Irish* now, do to them, and they will find, that infants too, as tender as they are thought, may, without any danger, endure bathing, not only of their feet, but of their whole bodies, in cold water. And there are, at this day, ladies in the Highlands of *Scotland* who use this discipline to their children in the midst of winter, and find that cold water does them no harm, even when there is ice in it.

§ 8. I shall not need here to mention *swimming,* when he is of an age able to learn, and has any one to teach him. 'Tis that saves many a man's life; and the *Romans* thought it so necessary, that they rank'd it with letters; and it was the common phrase to mark one ill-educated, and good for nothing, that he had neither learnt to read nor to swim: *Nec literas didicit nec natare.* But, besides the gaining a skill which may serve him at need, the advantages to health by often *bathing in cold water* during the heat of summer, are so many, that I think nothing need be said to encourage it; provided this one caution be us'd, that he never go into the water when exercise has at all warm'd him, or left any emotion in his blood or pulse.

§ 9. Another thing that is of great advantage to every one's health, but especially children's, is to be much in the *open air,* and as little as may be by the fire, even in winter. By this he will accustom himself also to heat and cold, shine and rain; all which if a man's body will not endure, it will serve him to very little purpose in this world; and when he is grown up, it is too late to begin to use him to it. It must be got early, and by degrees. Thus the body may be brought to bear almost any thing. If I should advise him to play in the *wind and sun without a hat,* I doubt whether it could be borne. There would a thousand objections be made against it, which at last would amount to no more, in truth, than being sun-burnt. And if my young master be to be kept always in the shade, and never expos'd to the sun and wind for fear of his complexion, it may be a good way to make him a *beau,* but not a man of business. And altho' greater regard be to be had to beauty in the daughters; yet I will take the liberty to say, that the more they are in the *air,* without prejudice to their faces, the stronger and healthier they will be; and the nearer they come to the hardships of

their brothers in their education, the greater advantage
will they receive from it all the remaining part of their
lives.

§ 10. Playing in the *open air* has but this one danger
in it, that I know; and that is, that when he is hot with
running up and down, he should sit or lie down on the cold
or moist earth. This I grant; and drinking cold drink, when
they are hot with labour or exercise, brings more people
to the grave, or to the brink of it, by fevers, and other
diseases, than anything I know. These mischiefs are easily
enough prevented whilst he is little, being then seldom out
of sight. And if, during his childhood, he be constantly and
rigorously kept from sitting on the ground, or drinking any
cold liquor whilst he is hot, the custom of forbearing, grown
into *habit,* will help much to preserve him, when he is no
longer under his maid's or tutor's eye. This is all I think
can be done in the case: for, as years increase, liberty must
come with them; and in a great many things he must be
trusted to his own conduct, since there cannot always be
a guard upon him, except what you have put into his own
mind by good principles, and establish'd habits, which is
the best and surest, and therefore most to be taken care of.
For, from repeated cautions and rules, never so often
inculcated, you are not to expect any thing either in this, or
any other case, farther than practice has establish'd them into
habits.

§ 11. One thing the mention of the girls brings into my
mind, which must not be forgot; and that is, that your son's
*clothes* be *never* made *strait,* especially about the breast.
Let nature have scope to fashion the body as she thinks
best. She works of herself a great deal better and exacter
than we can direct her. And if women were themselves
to frame the bodies of their children in their wombs, as
they often endeavour to mend their shapes when they are
out, we should as certainly have no perfect children born,
as we have few well-shap'd that are *strait-lac'd,* or much
tamper'd with. This consideration should, methinks, keep
busy people (I will not say ignorant nurses and bodice-
makers) from meddling in a matter they understand not;
and they should be afraid to put nature out of her way in

fashioning the parts, when they know not how the least and meanest is made. And yet I have seen so many instances of children receiving great harm from *strait-lacing*, that I cannot but conclude there are other creatures as well as monkeys, who, little wiser than they, destroy their young ones by senseless fondness, and too much embracing.

§ 12. Narrow breasts, short and stinking breath, ill lungs, and crookedness, are natural and almost constant effects of *hard bodice*, and *clothes that pinch*. That way of making slender wastes, and fine shapes, serves but the more effectually to spoil them. Nor can there indeed but be disproportion in the parts, when the nourishment prepared in the several offices of the body cannot be distributed as nature designs. And therefore what wonder is it, if, it being laid where it can, on some part not so *braced*, it often makes a shoulder or hip higher or bigger than its just proportion? 'Tis generally known, that the women of *China*, (imagining I know not what kind of beauty in it) by bracing and binding them hard from their infancy, have very little feet. I saw lately a pair of *China* shoes, which I was told were for a grown woman: they were so exceedingly disproportion'd to the feet of one of the same age among us, that they would scarce have been big enough for one of our little girls. Besides this, 'tis observ'd, that their women are also very little, and short-liv'd; whereas the men are of the ordinary stature of other men, and live to a proportionable age. These defects in the female sex in that country, are by some imputed to the unreasonable binding of their feet, whereby the free circulation of the blood is hinder'd, and the growth and health of the whole body suffers. And how often do we see, that some small part of the foot being injur'd by a wrench or a blow, the whole leg or thigh thereby lose their strength and nourishment, and dwindle away? How much greater inconveniences may we expect, when the *thorax*, wherein is placed the heart and seat of life, is unnaturally *compress'd*, and hinder'd from its due expansion?

§ 13. As for his *diet*, it ought to be very plain and simple; and, if I might advise, flesh should be forborne as long as he is in coats, or at least till he is two or three years old. But whatever advantage this may be to his present and

future health and strength, I fear it will hardly be consented
to by parents, misled by the custom of eating too much
flesh themselves, who will be apt to think their children, as
they do themselves, in danger to be starv'd, if they have
not flesh at least twice a-day. This I am sure, children would
breed their teeth with much less danger, be freer from diseases whilst they were little, and lay the foundations of an
healthy and strong constitution much surer, if they were
not cramm'd so much as they are by fond mothers and foolish
servants, and were kept wholly from flesh the first three or
four years of their lives.

But if my young master must needs have flesh, let it be
but once a day, and of one sort at a meal. Plain beef,
mutton, veal, &c. without other sauce than hunger, is best;
and great care should be used, that he eat *bread* plentifully,
both alone and with every thing else; and whatever he eats
that is solid, make him chew it well. We *English* are often
negligent herein; from whence follow indigestion, and other
great inconveniences.

§ 14. For *breakfast* and *supper, milk, milk-pottage, water-
gruel, flummery,* and twenty other things, that we are wont
to make in *England,* are very fit for children; only, in all
these, let care be taken that they be plain, and without much
mixture, and very sparingly season'd with sugar, or rather
none at all; especially *all spice,* and other things that may
heat the blood, are carefully to be avoided. Be sparing
also of *salt* in the seasoning of all his victuals, and use him
not to high-season'd meats. Our palates grow into a relish
and liking of the seasoning and cookery which by custom
they are set to; and an over-much use of salt, besides that
it occasions thirst, and over-much drinking, has other ill
effects upon the body. I should think that a good piece of
well-made and well-bak'd *brown bread,* sometimes with, and
sometimes without *butter* or *cheese,* would be often the best
breakfast for my young master. I am sure 'tis as wholesome,
and will make him as strong a man as greater delicacies;
and if he be used to it, it will be as pleasant to him. If
he at any time calls for victuals between meals, use him to
nothing but dry *bread*. If he be hungry more than wanton,
*bread* alone will down; and if he be not hungry, 'tis not

fit he should eat.  By this you will obtain two good effects:
1. That by custom he will come to be in love with *bread;*
for, as I said, our palates and stomachs too are pleased with
the things we are used to.  2. Another good you will gain
hereby is, that you will not teach him to eat more nor oftener
than nature requires.  I do not think that all people's appetites are alike; some have naturally stronger, and some
weaker stomachs.  But this I think, that many are made *gor-
mands* and *gluttons* by custom, that were not so by nature:
and I see in some countries, men as lusty and strong, that eat
but two meals a-day, as others that have set their stomachs
by a constant usage, like larums, to call on them for four
or five.  The *Romans* usually fasted till supper, the only
set meal even of those who eat more than once a-day; and
those who us'd breakfast, as some did, at eight, some at
ten, others at twelve of the clock, and some later, neither
eat flesh, nor had any thing made ready for them.  *Augustus,*
when the greatest monarch on the earth, tells us, he took a
bit of dry bread in his chariot.  And *Seneca,* in his 83rd
*Epistle,* giving an account how he managed himself, even
when he was old, and his age permitted indulgence, says,
that he used to eat a piece of dry bread for his dinner,
without the formality of sitting to it, tho' his estate would as
well have paid for a better meal (had health requir'd it)
as any subject's in *England,* were it doubled.  The masters
of the world were bred up with this spare diet; and the young
gentlemen of *Rome* felt no want of strength or spirit, because
they eat but once a day.  Or if it happen'd by chance, that
any one could not fast so long as till supper, their
only set meal, he took nothing but a bit of dry bread,
or at most a few raisins, or some such slight thing with
it, to stay his stomach.  This part of temperance was found
so necessary both for health and business, that the custom
of only one meal a day held out against that prevailing
luxury which their *Eastern* conquests and spoils had brought
in  amongst them; and those who had given up their old
frugal eating, and made feasts, yet began them not till the
evening.  And more than one set meal a-day was thought
so monstrous, that it was a reproach as low down as *Cæsar's*
time, to make an entertainment, or sit down to a full table,

till towards sun-set; and therefore, if it would not be thought too severe, I should judge it most convenient that my young master should have nothing but *bread* too for *breakfast.* You cannot imagine of what force custom is; and I impute a great part of our diseases in *England,* to our eating too much *flesh,* and too little *bread.*

§ 15. As to his *meals,* I should think it best, that as much as it can be conveniently avoided, they should not be kept constantly to an hour: for when custom has fix'd his eating to certain stated periods, his stomach will expect victuals at the usual hour, and grow peevish if he passes it; either fretting itself into a troublesome excess, or flagging into a downright want of appetite. Therefore I would have no time kept constantly to for his breakfast, dinner and supper, but rather vary'd almost every day. And if betwixt these, which I call *meals,* he will eat, let him have, as often as he calls for it, good dry bread. If any one think this too hard and sparing a diet for a child, let them know, that a child will never starve nor dwindle for want of nourishment, who, besides flesh at dinner, and spoon-meat, or some such other thing, at supper, may have good bread and beer as often as he has a stomach. For thus, upon second thoughts, I should judge it best for children to be order'd. The morning is generally design'd for study, to which a full stomach is but an ill preparation. Dry bread, though the best nourishment, has the least temptation; and no body would have a child cramm'd at breakfast, who has any regard to his mind or body, and would not have him dull and unhealthy. Nor let any one think this unsuitable to one of estate and condition. A gentleman in any age ought to be so bred, as to be fitted to bear arms, and be a soldier. But he that in this, breeds his son so, as if he design'd him to sleep over his life in the plenty and ease of a full fortune he intends to leave him, little considers the examples he has seen, or the age he lives in.

§ 16. His *drink* should be only small beer; and that too he should never be suffer'd to have between meals, but after he had eat a piece of bread. The reasons why I say this are these.

§ 17. 1. More fevers and surfeits are got by people's

drinking when they are hot, than by any one thing I know. Therefore, if by play he be hot and dry, bread will ill go down; and so if he cannot have *drink* but upon that condition, he will be forced to forbear; for, if he be very hot, he should by no means *drink;* at least a good piece of bread first to be eaten, will gain time to warm the beer *blood-hot,* which then he may drink safely. If he be very dry, it will go down so warm'd, and quench his thirst better; and if he will not drink it so warm'd, abstaining will not hurt him. Besides, this will teach him to forbear, which is an habit of greatest use for health of body and mind too.

§ 18. 2. Not being permitted to *drink* without eating, will prevent the custom of having the cup often at his nose; a dangerous beginning, and preparation to *good-fellowship.* Men often bring habitual hunger and thirst on themselves by custom. And if you please to try, you may, though he be wean'd from it, bring him by use to such a necessity again of *drinking* in the night, that he will not be able to sleep without it. It being the lullaby used by nurses to still crying children, I believe mothers generally find some difficulty to wean their children from *drinking* in the night, when they first take them home. Believe it, custom prevails as much by day as by night; and you may, if you please, bring any one to be thirsty every hour.

I once liv'd in a house, where, to appease a froward child, they gave him *drink* as often as he cry'd; so that he was constantly bibbing. And tho' he could not speak, yet he drank more in twenty-four hours than I did. Try it when you please, you may with small, as well as with strong beer, drink your self into a drought. The great thing to be minded in education is, what *habits* you settle; and therefore in this, as all other things, do not begin to make any thing *customary,* the practice whereof you would not have continue and increase. It is convenient for health and sobriety, to *drink* no more than natural thirst requires; and he that eats not salt meats, nor drinks strong drink, will seldom thirst between meals, unless he has been accustom'd to such unseasonable *drinking.*

§ 19. Above all, take great care that he seldom, if ever, taste any *wine* or *strong drink.* There is nothing so ordi-

narily given children in *England,* and nothing so destructive
to them. They ought never to *drink* any *strong liquor* but
when they need it as a cordial, and the doctor prescribes it.
And in this case it is, that servants are most narrowly to be
watch'd and most severely to be reprehended when they
transgress. Those mean sort of people, placing a great part
of their happiness in *strong drink,* are always forward to
make court to my young master by offering him that which
they love best themselves: and finding themselves made
merry by it, they foolishly think 'twill do the child no harm.
This you are carefully to have your eye upon, and restrain
with all the skill and industry you can, there being nothing
that lays a surer foundation of mischief, both to body and
mind than children's being us'd to *strong drink,* especially
to drink in private *with the servants.*

§ 20. *Fruit* makes one of the most difficult chapters in
the government of health, especially that of children. Our
first parents ventur'd *Paradise* for it; and 'tis no wonder
our children cannot stand the temptation, tho' it cost them
their health. The regulation of this cannot come under any
one general rule; for I am by no means of their mind, who
would keep children almost wholly from *fruit,* as a thing
totally unwholesome for them: by which strict way, they
make them but the more ravenous after it, and to eat good
or bad, ripe or unripe, all that they can get, whenever they
come at it. *Melons, peaches,* most sorts of *plums,* and all
sorts of *grapes* in *England,* I think children should be *wholly
kept from,* as having a very tempting taste, in a very unwholesome juice; so that if it were possible, they should
never so much as see them, or know there were any such
thing. But *strawberries, cherries, gooseberries,* or *currants,*
when thorough ripe, I think may be very safely allow'd
them, and that with a pretty liberal hand, if they be eaten
with these cautions: 1. Not after meals, as we usually do,
when the stomach is already full of other food: but I think
they should be eaten rather before or between meals, and
children should have them for their breakfast. 2. Bread
eaten with them. 3. Perfectly ripe. If they are thus eaten,
I imagine them rather conducing than hurtful to our health.
*Summer-fruits,* being suited to the hot season of the year

they come in, refresh our stomachs, languishing and faint-ing under it; and therefore I should not be altogether so strict in this point, as some are to their children; who being kept so very short, instead of a moderate quantity of well-chosen *fruit,* which being allow'd them would con-tent them, whenever they can get loose, or bribe a servant to supply them, satisfy their longing with any trash they can get, and eat to a surfeit.

*Apples* and *pears* too, which are thorough ripe, and have been gather'd some time, I think may be safely eaten at any time, and in pretty large quantities, especially *apples;* which never did any body hurt, that I have heard, after *October.*

*Fruits* also dry'd without sugar, I think very wholesome. But *sweet-meats* of all kinds are to be avoided; which whether they do more harm to the maker or eater, is not easy to tell. This I am sure, it is one of the most inconve-nient ways of expence that vanity hath yet found out; and so I leave them to the ladies.

§ 21. Of all that looks soft and effeminate, nothing is more to be indulg'd children, than *sleep.* In this alone they are to be permitted to have their full satisfaction; nothing contributing more to the growth and health of children, than *sleep.* All that is to be reguiated in it, is, in what part of the twenty-four hours they should take it; which will easily be resolved, by only saying that it is of great use to accus-tom 'em to rise early in the morning. It is best so to do, for health; and he that, from his childhood, has, by a settled custom, made *rising betimes* easy and familiar to him, will not, when he is a man, waste the best and most useful part of his life in drowsiness, and lying a-bed. If children there-fore are to be call'd up early in the morning, it will follow of course, that they must go to bed betimes; whereby they will be accustom'd to avoid the unhealthy and unsafe hours of debauchery, which are those of the evenings; and they who keep good hours, seldom are guilty of any great dis-orders. I do not say this, as if your son, when grown up, should never be in company past eight, nor ever chat over a glass of wine 'till midnight. You are now, by the accustom-ing of his tender years, to indispose him to those inconve-niences as much as you can; and it will be no small advantage, that contrary practice having made sitting up uneasy to him, it will make him often avoid, and very seldom propose midnight-revels. But if it should not reach so far, but fashion and company should prevail, and make him live as others do above twenty, 'tis worth the while to accustom him to *early rising* and early going to bed, between this and that, for the present improvement of his health and other advantages.

Though I have said, a large allowance of *sleep,* even as much as they will take, should be made to children when they are little; yet I do not mean, that it should always be continued to them in so large a proportion, and they suffer'd to indulge a drowsy laziness in their bed, as they grow up bigger. But whether they should begin to be restrained at seven or ten years old, or any other time, is impossible to be precisely determined. Their tempers, strength, and constitutions, must be consider'd. But some time between seven and fourteen, if they are too great lovers of their beds, I think it may be seasonable to begin to reduce them by degrees to about eight hours, which is generally rest enough for healthy grown people. If you have accustom'd him, as you should do, to rise constantly very early in the morning, this fault of being too long in bed will easily be reform'd, and most children will be forward enough to shorten that time themselves, by coveting to sit up with the company at night; tho' if they be not look'd after, they will be apt to take it out in the morning, which should by no means be permitted. They should constantly be call'd up and made to rise at their early hour; but great care should be taken in waking them, that it be not done hastily, nor with a loud or shrill voice, or any other sudden violent noise. This often affrights children, and does them great harm; and sound *sleep* thus broke off, with sudden alarms, is apt enough to discompose any one. When children are to be waken'd out of their *sleep,* be sure to begin with a low call, and some gentle motion, and so draw them out of it by degrees, and give them none but kind words and usage, 'till they are come perfectly to themselves, and being quite dress'd, you are sure they are thoroughly awake. The being forc'd from their *sleep,* how gently soever you do it, is

pain enough to them; and care should be taken not to add
any other uneasiness to it, especially such that may terrify
them.

§ 22. Let his *bed* be *hard,* and rather quilts than feathers.
Hard lodging strengthens the parts; whereas being bury'd
every night in feathers melts and dissolves the body, is often
the cause of weakness, and forerunner of an early grave.
And, besides the stone, which has often its rise from this
warm wrapping of the reins, several other indispositions,
and that which is the root of them all, a tender weakly
constitution, is very much owing to *down-beds.* Besides, he
that is used to hard lodging at home, will not miss his sleep
(where he has most need of it) in his travels abroad, for
want of his soft bed, and his pillows laid in order. And
therefore, I think it would not be amiss, to *make his bed*
after different fashions, sometimes lay his head higher,
sometimes lower, that he may not feel every little change
he must be sure to meet with, who is not design'd to lie
always in my young master's bed at home, and to have his
maid lay all things in print, and tuck him in warm. The
great cordial of nature is *sleep.* He that misses that, will
suffer by it; and he is very unfortunate, who can take his
cordial only in his mother's fine gilt cup, and not in a wooden
dish. He that can sleep soundly, takes the cordial; and it
matters not whether it be on a soft *bed* or the hard boards.
'Tis *sleep* only that is the thing necessary.

§ 23. One thing more there is, which has a great influence upon the health, and that is, *going to stool* regularly:
people that are very *loose,* have seldom strong thoughts, or
strong bodies. But the cure of this, both by diet and medicine,
being much more easy than the contrary evil, there needs
not much to be said about it: for if it come to threaten,
either by its violence or duration, it will soon enough, and
sometimes too soon, make a physician be sent for; and if
it be moderate or short, it is commonly best to leave it to
nature. On the other side, *costiveness* has too its ill effects,
and is much harder to be dealt with by physick; purging
medicines, which seem to give relief, rather increasing them
than removing the evil.

§ 24. It being an indisposition I had a particular reason

to enquire into, and not finding the cure of it in books, I set my thoughts on work, believing that greater changes than that might be made in our bodies, if we took the right course, and proceeded by rational steps.

1. Then I consider'd, that *going to stool,* was the effect of certain motions of the body; especially of the peristaltick motion of the guts.

2. I consider'd, that several motions, that were not perfectly voluntary, might yet, by use and constant application, be brought to be habitual, if by an unintermitted custom they were at certain seasons endeavour'd to be constantly produced.

3. I had observ'd some men, who by taking after supper a pipe of tobacco, never fail'd of a *stool,* and began to doubt with myself, whether it were not more custom, than the tobacco, that gave them the benefit of nature; or at least, if the tobacco did it, it was rather by exciting a vigorous motion in the guts, than by any purging quality; for then it would have had other effects.

Having thus once got the opinion that it was possible to make it habitual, the next thing was to consider what way and means was the likeliest to obtain it.

4. Then I guess'd, that if a man, after his first eating in the morning, would presently solicit nature, and try whether he could strain himself so as to obtain a *stool,* he might in time, by constant application, bring it to be habitual.

§ 25. The reasons that made me chuse this time, were,

1. Because the stomach being then empty, if it receiv'd any thing grateful to it (for I would never, but in case of necessity, have any one eat but what he likes, and when he has an appetite) it was apt to embrace it close by a strong constriction of its fibres; which constriction, I suppos'd, might probably be continu'd on in the guts, and so increase their peristaltick motion, as we see in the *Ileus,* that an inverted motion, being begun any where below, continues itself all the whole length, and makes even the stomach obey that irregular motion.

2. Because when men eat, they usually relax their thoughts, and the spirits then, free from other employments,

are more vigorously distributed into the lower belly, which thereby contribute to the same effect.

3. Because, whenever men have leisure to eat, they have leisure enough also to make so much court to Madam *Cloacina,* as would be necessary to our present purpose; but else, in the variety of human affairs and accidents, it was impossible to affix it to any hour certain, whereby the custom would be interrupted. Whereas men in health seldom failing to eat once a day, tho' the hour chang'd, the custom might still be preserv'd.

§ 26. Upon these grounds the experiment began to be try'd, and I have known none who have been steady in the prosecution of it, and taken care to go constantly to the necessary-house, after their first eating, whenever that happen'd, whether they found themselves call'd on or no, and there endeavoured to put nature upon her duty, but in a few months they obtain'd the desired success, and brought themselves to so regular an habit, that they seldom ever fail'd of a *stool* after their first eating, unless it were by their own neglect: for, whether they have any motion or no, if they go to the place, and do their part, they are sure to have nature very obedient.

§ 27. I would therefore advise, that this course should be taken with a child every day presently after he has eaten his breakfast. Let him be set upon the stool, as if disburthening were as much in his power as filling his belly; and let not him or his maid know any thing to the contrary, but that it is so; and if he be forc'd to endeavour, by being hinder'd from his play or eating again 'till he has been effectually at *stool,* or at least done his utmost, I doubt not but in a little while it will become natural to him. For there is reason to suspect, that children being usually intent on their play, and very heedless of any thing else, often let pass those motions of nature, when she calls them but gently; and so they, neglecting the seasonable offers, do by degrees bring themselves into an habitual costiveness. That by this method costiveness may be prevented, I do more than guess; having known by the constant practice of it for some time, a child brought to have a *stool* regularly after his breakfast every morning.

§ 28. How far any grown people will think fit to make trial of it, must be left to them; tho' I cannot but say, that considering the many evils that come from that defect, of a requisite easing of nature, I scarce know any thing more conducing to the preservation of health, than this is. Once in four and twenty hours, I think is enough; and no body, I guess, will think it too much. And by this means it is to be obtain'd without physick, which commonly proves very ineffectual in the cure of a settled and habitual costiveness.

§ 29. This is all I have to trouble you with concerning his management in the ordinary course of his health. Perhaps it will be expected from me, that I should give some directions of *physick,* to prevent diseases; for which I have only this one, very sacredly to be observ'd, never to give children any *physick* for prevention. The observation of what I have already advis'd, will, I suppose, do that better than the ladies' diet-drinks or apothecaries' medicines. Have a great care of tampering that way, lest, instead of preventing, you draw on diseases. Nor even upon every little indisposition is *physick* to be given, or the physician to be call'd to children, especially if he be a busy man, that will presently fill their windows with gally-pots, and their stomachs with drugs. It is safer to leave them wholly to nature, than to put 'em into the hands of one forward to tamper, or that thinks children are to be cur'd, in ordinary distempers, by any thing but diet, or by a method very little distant from it: it seeming suitable both to my reason and experience, that the tender constitutions of children should have as little done to them as is possible, and as the absolute necessity of the case requires. A little cold-still'd red *poppy-water,* which is the true surfeit-water with ease, and abstinence from flesh, often puts an end to several distempers in the beginning, which, by too forward applications, might have been made lusty diseases. When such a gentle treatment will not stop the growing mischief, nor hinder it from turning into a form'd disease, it will be time to seek the advice of some sober and discreet physician. In this part, I hope, I shall find an easy belief; and no body can have a pretence to doubt the advice of one who has spent some time in the study of physick, when he counsels you not to be too forward in making use of *physick* and *physicians.*

§ 30. And thus I have done with what concerns the body and health, which reduces itself to these few and easy observable rules: plenty of *open air, exercise,* and *sleep,* plain *diet,* no *wine* or *strong drink,* and very little or no *physick,* not too warm and strait *clothing,* especially the *head* and *feet* kept cold, and the *feet* often us'd to cold water, and expos'd to wet.

§ 31. Due care being had to keep the body in strength and vigour, so that it may be able to obey and execute the orders of the *mind;* the next and principal business is, to set the *mind* right, that on all occasions it may be dispos'd to consent to nothing but what may be suitable to the dignity and excellency of a rational creature.

§ 32. If what I have said in the beginning of this discourse be true, as I do not doubt but it is, *viz.* That the difference to be found in the manners and abilities of men is owing more to their *education* than to any thing else, we have reason to conclude, that great care is to be had of the forming children's *minds,* and giving them that seasoning early, which shall influence their lives always after: For when they do well or ill, the praise and blame will be laid there; and when any thing is done awkwardly, the common saying will pass upon them, that it's suitable to their *breeding.*

§ 33. As the strength of the body lies chiefly in being able to endure hardships, so also does that of the mind. And the great principle and foundation of all virtue and worth is plac'd in this: that a man is able to *deny himself* his own desires, cross his own inclinations, and purely follow what reason directs as best, tho' the appetite lean the other way.

§ 34. The great mistake I have observ'd in people's breeding their children, has been, that this has not been taken care enough of in its *due season;* that the mind has not been made obedient to discipline, and pliant to reason, when at first it was most tender, most easy to be bow'd. Parents being wisely ordain'd by nature to love their children, are very apt, if reason watch not that natural affection very warily, are apt, I say, to let it run into fondness. They love their little ones and it is their duty; but they often, with them, cherish their faults too. They must not be cross'd, forsooth; they must be permitted to have their wills in all things; and they being in their infancies not capable of great vices, their parents think they may safe enough indulge their irregularities, and make themselves sport with that pretty perverseness which they think well enough becomes that innocent age. But to a fond parent, that would not have his child corrected for a perverse trick, but excus'd it, saying it was a small matter, *Solon* very well reply'd, *aye, but custom is a great one.*

§ 35. The fondling must be taught to strike and call names, must have what he cries for, and do what he pleases. Thus parents, by humouring and cockering them when *little,* corrupt the principles of nature in their children, and wonder afterwards to taste the bitter waters, when they themselves have poison'd the fountain. For when their children are grown up, and these ill habits with them; when they are now too big to be dandled, and their parents can no longer make use of them as play-things, then they complain that the brats are untoward and perverse; then they are offended to see them wilful, and are troubled with those ill humours which they themselves infus'd and fomented in them; and then, perhaps too late, would be glad to get out those weeds which their own hands have planted, and which now have taken too deep root to be easily extirpated. For he that hath been us'd to have his will in every thing, as long as he was in coats, why should we think it strange, that he should desire it, and contend for it still, when he is in breeches? Indeed, as he grows more towards a man, age shews his faults the more; so that there be few parents then so blind as not to see them, few so insensible as not to feel the ill effects of their own indulgence. He had the will of his maid before he could speak or go; he had the mastery of his parents ever since he could prattle; and why, now he is grown up, is stronger and wiser than he was then, why now of a sudden must he be restrain'd and curb'd? Why must he at seven, fourteen, or twenty years old, lose the privilege, which the parents' indulgence 'till then so largely

allow'd him? Try it in a dog or an horse or any other creature, and see whether the ill and resty tricks they have
learn'd when young, are easily to be mended when they are
knit; and yet none of those creatures are half so wilful and
proud, or half so desirous to be masters of themselves and
others, as man.

§ 36. We are generally wise enough to begin with them
when they are *very young,* and discipline *betimes* those other
creatures we would make useful and good for somewhat.
They are only our own offspring, that we neglect in this
point; and having made them ill children, we foolishly expect they should be good men. For if the child must have
grapes or sugar-plums when he has a mind to them, rather
than make the poor baby cry or be out of humour; why,
when he is grown up, must he not be satisfy'd too, if his
desires carry him to wine or women? They are objects as
suitable to the longing of one of more years, as what he
cry'd for, when little, was to the inclinations of a child.
The having desires accommodated to the apprehensions and
relish of those several ages, is not the fault; but the not
having them subject to the rules and restraints of reason:
the difference lies not in having or not having appetites,
but in the power to govern, and deny ourselves in them.
He that is not us'd to submit his will to the reason of others
*when* he is *young,* will scarce hearken to submit to his own
reason when he is of an age to make use of it. And what
kind of a man such an one is like to prove, is easy to foresee.

§ 37. These are oversights usually committed by those
who seem to take the greatest care of their children's education. But if we look into the common management of
children, we shall have reason to wonder, in the great dissoluteness of manners which the world complains of, that
there are any footsteps at all left of virtue. I desire to
know what vice can be nam'd, which parents, and those
about children, do not season them with, and drop into 'em
the seeds of, as soon as they are capable to receive them?
I do not mean by the examples they give, and the patterns
they set before them, which is encouragement enough; but
that which I would take notice of here is, the downright
teaching them vice, and actual putting them out of the

way of virtue. Before they can go, they principle 'em with violence, revenge, and cruelty. *Give me a blow, that I may beat him,* is a lesson which most children every day hear; and it is thought nothing, because their hands have not strength to do any mischief. But I ask, does not this corrupt their mind? Is not this the way of force and violence, that they are set in? And if they have been taught when little, to strike and hurt others by proxy, and encourag'd to rejoice in the harm they have brought upon them, and see them suffer, are they not prepar'd to do it when they are strong enough to be felt themselves, and can strike to some purpose?

The coverings of our bodies which are for modesty, warmth and defence, are by the folly or vice of parents recommended to their children for other uses. They are made matters of vanity and emulation. A child is set a-longing after a new suit, for the finery of it; and when the little girl is trick'd up in her new gown and commode, how can her mother do less than teach her to admire herself, by calling her, *her little queen* and *her princess?* Thus the little ones are taught to be *proud* of their clothes before they can put them on. And why should they not continue to value themselves for their outside fashionableness of the taylor or tirewoman's making, when their parents have so early instructed them to do so?

*Lying* and equivocations, and excuses little different from lying, are put into the mouths of young people, and commended in apprentices and children, whilst they are for their master's or parents' advantage. And can it be thought, that he that finds the straining of truth dispens'd with, and encourag'd, whilst it is for his godly master's turn, will not make use of that privilege for himself, when it may be for his own profit?

Those of the meaner sort are hinder'd, by the straitness of their fortunes, from encouraging *intemperance* in their children by the temptation of their diet, or invitations to eat or drink more than enough; but their own ill examples, whenever plenty comes in their way, shew, that 'tis not the dislike of drunkenness or gluttony, that keeps them from excess, but want of materials. But if we look into the houses of those who are a little warmer in their fortunes, their eating and drinking are made so much the great business and happiness of life, that children are thought neglected, if they have not their share of it. Sauces and ragoos, and food disguis'd by all the arts of cookery, must tempt their palates, when their bellies are full; and then, for fear the stomach should be overcharg'd, a pretence is found for t'other glass of wine to help digestion, tho' it only serves to increase the surfeit.

Is my young master a little out of order, the first question is, *What will my dear eat? What shall I get for thee?* Eating and drinking are instantly press'd; and every body's invention is set on work to find out something luscious and delicate enough to prevail over that want of appetite, which nature has wisely order'd in the beginning of distempers, as a defence against their increase; that being freed from the ordinary labour of digesting any new load in the stomach, she may be at leisure to correct and master the peccant humours.

And where children are so happy in the care of their parents, as by their prudence to be kept from the excess of their tables, to the sobriety of a plain and simple diet, yet there too they are scarce to be preserv'd from the contagion that poisons the mind; though, by a discreet management whilst they are under tuition, their healths perhaps may be pretty well secure, yet their desires must needs yield to the lessons which every where will be read to them upon this part of *epicurism*. The commendation that *eating well* has every where, cannot fail to be a successful incentive to natural appetites, and bring them quickly to the liking and expence of a fashionable table. This shall have from every one, even the reprovers of vice, the title of *living well*. And what shall sullen reason dare to say against the publick testimony? Or can it hope to be heard, if it should call that *luxury,* which is so much own'd and universally practis'd by those of the best quality?

This is now so grown a vice, and has so great supports, that I know not whether it do not put in for the name of virtue; and whether it will not be thought folly, or want of knowledge of the world, to open one's mouth against it?

(1) HC XXXVII

And truly I should suspect, that what I have here said of it, might be censur'd as a little satire out of my way, did I not mention it with this view, that it might awaken the care and watchfulness of parents in the education of their children, when they see how they are beset on every side, not only with temptations, but instructors to vice, and that, perhaps, in those they thought places of security.

I shall not dwell any longer on this subject, much less run over all the particulars that would shew what pains are us'd to corrupt children, and instil principles of vice into them: but I desire parents soberly to consider, what irregularity or vice there is which children are not visibly taught, and whether it be not their duty and wisdom to provide them other instructions.

§ 38. It seems plain to me, that the principle of all virtue and excellency lies in a power of denying ourselves the satisfaction of our own desires, where reason does not authorize them. This power is to be got and improv'd by custom, made easy and familiar by an *early* practice. If therefore I might be heard, I would advise, that, contrary to the ordinary way, children should be us'd to submit their desires, and go without their longings, even *from their very cradles*. The first thing they should learn to know, should be, that they were not to have anything because it pleas'd them, but because it was thought fit for them. If things suitable to their wants were supply'd to them, so that they were never suffer'd to have what they once cry'd for, they would learn to be content without it, would never, with bawling and peevishness, contend for mastery, nor be half so uneasy to themselves and others as they are, because *from the first* beginning they are not thus handled. If they were never suffer'd to obtain their desire by the impatience they express'd for it, they would no more cry for another thing, than they do for the moon.

§ 39. I say not this, as if children were not to be indulg'd in anything, or that I expected they should in hanging-sleeves have the reason and conduct of counsellors. I consider them as children, who must be tenderly us'd, who must play, and have play-things. That which I mean, is, that whenever they crav'd what was not fit for them to have or

(2) HC XXXVII

do, they should not be permitted it because they were *little*, and desir'd it: nay, whatever they were importunate for, they should be sure, for that very reason, to be deny'd. I have seen children at a table, who, whatever was there, never ask'd for anything, but contentedly took what was given them: and at another place, I have seen others cry for everything they saw; must be serv'd out of every dish, and that first too. What made this vast difference but this? that one was accustom'd to have what they call'd or cry'd for, the other to go without it. The *younger* they are, the less I think are their unruly and disorderly appetites to be comply'd with; and the less reason they have of their own, the more are they to be under the absolute power and restraint of those in whose hands they are. From which I confess it will follow, that none but discreet people should be about them. If the world commonly does otherwise, I cannot help that. I am saying what I think should be; which if it were already in fashion, I should not need to trouble the world with a discourse on this subject. But yet I doubt not, but when it is consider'd, there will be others of opinion with me, that the *sooner* this way is begun with children, the easier it will be for them and their governors too; and that this ought to be observ'd as an inviolable maxim, that whatever once is deny'd them, they are certainly not to obtain by crying or importunity, unless one has a mind to teach them to be impatient and troublesome, by rewarding them for it when they are so.

§ 40. Those therefore that intend ever to govern their children, should begin it whilst they are *very little,* and look that they perfectly comply with the will of their parents. Would you have your son obedient to you when past a child; be sure then to establish the authority of a father *as soon* as he is capable of submission, and can understand in whose power he is. If you would have him stand in awe of you, imprint it in his *infancy;* and as he approaches more to a man, admit him nearer to your familiarity; so shall you have him your obedient subject (as is fit) whilst he is a child, and your affectionate friend when he is a man. For methinks they mightily misplace the treatment due to their children, who are indulgent and familiar when they are little, but severe to them, and keep them at a distance, when they are grown up: for liberty and indulgence can do no good to *children;* their want of judgment makes them stand in need of restraint and discipline; and on the contrary, imperiousness and severity is but an ill way of treating men, who have reason of their own to guide them; unless you have a mind to make your children, when grown up, weary of you, and secretly to say within themselves, *When will you die, father?*

§ 41. I imagine every one will judge it reasonable, that their children, *when little,* should look upon their parents as their lords, their absolute governors, and as such stand in awe of them; and that when they come to riper years, they should look on them as their best, as their only sure friends, and as such love and reverence them. The way I have mention'd, if I mistake not, is the only one to obtain this. We must look upon our children, when grown up, to be like ourselves, with the same passions, the same desires. We would be thought rational creatures, and have our freedom; we love not to be uneasy under constant rebukes and brow-beatings, nor can we bear severe humours and great distance in those we converse with. Whoever has such treatment when he is a man, will look out other company, other friends, other conversation, with whom he can be at ease. If therefore a strict hand be kept over children *from the beginning,* they will in that age be tractable, and quietly submit to it, as never having known any other: and if, as they grow up to the use of reason, the rigour of government be, as they deserve it, gently relax'd, the father's brow more smooth'd to them, and the distance by degrees abated, his former restraints will increase their love, when they find it was only a kindness to them, and a care to make them capable to deserve the favour of their parents, and the esteem of everybody else.

§ 42. Thus much for the settling your authority over your children in general. Fear and awe ought to give you the first power over their minds, and love and friendship in riper years to hold it: for the time must come, when they will be past the rod and correction; and then, if the love of you make them not obedient and dutiful, if the love of virtue and reputation keep them not in laudable courses, I ask, what hold will you have upon them to turn them to it? Indeed, fear of having a scanty portion if they displease you, may make them slaves to your estate, but they will be nevertheless ill and wicked in private; and that restraint will not last always. Every man must some time or other be trusted to himself and his own conduct; and he that is a good, a virtuous, and able man, must be made so within. And therefore what he is to receive from education, what is to sway and influence his life, must be something put into him betimes; habits woven into the very principles of his nature, and not a counterfeit carriage, and dissembled outside, put on by fear, only to avoid the present anger of a father who perhaps may disinherit him.

§ 43. This being laid down in general, as the course that ought to be taken, 'tis fit we now come to consider the parts of the discipline to be us'd, a little more particularly. I have spoken so much of carrying a *strict hand* over children, that perhaps I shall be suspected of not considering enough, what is due to their tender age and constitutions. But that opinion will vanish, when you have heard me a little farther: for I am very apt to think, that *great severity* of punishment does but very little good, nay, great harm in education; and I believe it will be found that, *cæteris paribus,* those children who have been most *chastis'd,* seldom make the best men. All that I have hitherto contended for, is, that whatsoever *rigor* is necessary, it is more to be us'd, the younger children are; and having by a due application wrought its effect, it is to be relax'd, and chang'd into a milder sort of government.

§ 44. A compliance and suppleness of their wills, being by a steady hand introduc'd by parents, before children have memories to retain the beginnings of it, will seem natural to them, and work afterwards in them as if it were so, preventing all occasions of struggling or repining. The only care is, that it be begun early, and inflexibly kept to 'till *awe* and *respect* be grown familiar, and there appears not the least reluctancy in the submission, and ready obedience of their minds. When this *reverence* is once thus established, (which it must be early, or else it will cost pains and blows to recover it, and the more the longer it is deferr'd) 'tis by it, still mix'd with as much indulgence as they make not an ill use of, and not by *beating, chiding,* or other *servile punishments,* they are for the future to be govern'd as they grow up to more understanding.

§ 45. That this is so, will be easily allow'd, when it is but consider'd, what is to be aim'd at in an ingenuous education; and upon what it turns.

1. He that has not a mastery over his inclinations, he that knows not how to *resist* the importunity of *present pleasure or pain,* for the sake of what reason tells him is fit to be done, wants the true principle of virtue and industry, and is in danger never to be good for anything. This temper therefore, so contrary to unguided nature, is to be got betimes; and this habit, as the true foundation of future ability and happiness, is to be wrought into the mind as early as may be, even from the first dawnings of knowledge or apprehension in children, and so to be confirm'd in them, by all the care and ways imaginable, by those who have the oversight of their education.

§ 46. 2. On the other side, if the *mind* be curb'd, and *humbled* too much in children; if their *spirits* be abas'd and *broken* much, by too strict an hand over them, they lose all their vigour and industry, and are in a worse state than the former. For extravagant young fellows, that have liveliness and spirit, come sometimes to be set right, and so make able and great men; but *dejected minds,* timorous and tame, and *low spirits,* are hardly ever to be rais'd, and very seldom attain to any thing. To avoid the danger that is on either hand, is the great art; and he that has found a way how to keep up a child's spirit easy, active, and free, and yet at the same time to restrain him from many things he has a mind to, and to draw him to things that are uneasy to him; he, I say, that knows how to reconcile these seeming contradictions, has, in my opinion, got the true secret of education.

§ 47. The usual lazy and short way by chastisement and the rod, which is the only instrument of government that tutors generally know, or ever think of, is the most unfit of any to be us'd in education, because it tends to both those mischiefs; which, as we have shewn, are the *Scylla* and *Charybdis,* which on the one hand or the other ruin all that miscarry.

§ 48. 1. This kind of punishment contributes not at all to the mastery of our natural propensity to indulge corporal and present pleasure, and to avoid pain at any rate, but rather encourages it, and thereby strengthens that in us, which is the root from whence spring all vicious actions, and the irregularities of life. For what other motive, but of sensual pleasure and pain, does a child act by, who drudges at his book against his inclination, or abstains from eating unwholesome fruit, that he takes pleasure in, only out of fear of *whipping?* He in this only prefers the greater *corporal pleasure,* or avoids the greater *corporal pain.* And what is it, to govern his actions, and direct his conduct by such motives as these? What is it, I say, but to cherish that principle in him, which it is our business to root out and destroy? And therefore I cannot think any correction useful to a child, where the shame of suffering for having done amiss, does not work more upon him than the pain.

§ 49. 2. This sort of correction naturally breeds an aversion to that which 'tis the tutor's business to create a liking to. How obvious is it to observe, that children come to hate things which were at first acceptable to them, when they find themselves *whipp'd,* and *chid,* and teas'd about them? And it is not to be wonder'd at in them, when grown men would not be able to be reconcil'd to any thing by such ways. Who is there that would not be disgusted with any innocent recreation, in itself indifferent to him, if he should with *blows* or ill language be *haled* to it, when he had no mind? Or be constantly so treated, for some circumstances in his application to it? This is natural to be so. Offensive circumstances ordinarily infect innocent things which they are join'd with; and the very sight of a cup wherein any one uses to take nauseous physick, turns his stomach, so that nothing will relish well out of it, tho' the cup be never so clean and well-shap'd, and of the richest materials.

§ 50. 3. Such a sort of *slavish discipline* makes a *slavish temper.* The child submits, and dissembles obedience, whilst the fear of the rod hangs over him; but when that is remov'd, and by being out of sight, he can promise himself impunity, he gives the greater scope to his natural inclination; which by this way is not at all alter'd, but, on the contrary, heighten'd and increas'd in him; and after such restraint, breaks out usually with the more violence; or,

§ 51. 4. If *severity* carry'd to the highest pitch does prevail, and works a cure upon the present unruly distemper, it often brings in the room of it a worse and more dangerous disease, by breaking the mind; and then, in the place of a disorderly young fellow, you have a *low spirited moap'd* creature, who, however with his unnatural sobriety he may please silly people, who commend tame unactive children, because they make no noise, nor give them any trouble; yet at last, will probably prove as uncomfortable a thing to his friends, as he will be all his life an useless thing to himself and others.

§ 52. Beating them, and all other sorts of slavish and corporal punishments, are not the discipline fit to be used in the education of those we would have wise, good, and ingenuous men; and therefore very rarely to be apply'd, and that only in great occasions, and cases of extremity. On the other side, to flatter children by *rewards* of things that are pleasant to them, is as carefully to be avoided. He that will give to his son *apples* or *sugar-plumbs,* or what else of this kind he is most delighted with, to make him learn his book, does but authorize his love of pleasure, and cocker up that dangerous propensity, which he ought by all means to subdue and stifle in him. You can never hope to teach him to master it, whilst you compound for the check you gave his inclination in one place, by the satisfaction you propose to it in another. To make a good, a wise, and a virtuous man, 'tis fit he should learn to cross his appetite, and deny his inclination to *riches, finery,* or *pleasing his palate,* &c. whenever his reason advises the contrary, and his duty requires it. But when you draw him to do any thing that is fit by the offer of *money,* or reward the pains of learning his book by the pleasure of a luscious morsel; when you promise him a *lace-cravat* or a *fine new suit,* upon performance of some of his little tasks; what do you by proposing these as *rewards,* but allow them to be the good things he should aim at, and thereby encourage his longing for 'em, and accustom him to place his happiness in them? Thus people, to prevail with children to be industrious about their grammar, dancing, or some other such matter, of no great moment to the happiness or usefulness of their lives, by misapply'd *rewards* and *punishments,* sacrifice their virtue, invert the order of their education, and teach them luxury, pride, or covetousness, &c. For in this way, flattering those wrong inclinations which they should restrain and suppress, they lay the foundations of those future vices, which cannot be avoided but by curbing our desires and accustoming them early to submit to reason.

§ 53. I say not this, that I would have children kept from the conveniences or pleasures of life, that are not injurious to their health or virtue. On the contrary, I would have their lives made as pleasant and as agreeable to them as may be, in a plentiful enjoyment of whatsoever might innocently delight them; provided it be with this caution, that they have those enjoyments, only as the consequences of the state of esteem and acceptation they are in with their parents and governors; but they should never be offer'd or bestow'd on them, as the *rewards of this or that particular performance,* that they shew an aversion to, or to which they would not have apply'd themselves without that temptation.

§ 54. But if you take away the rod on one hand, and these little encouragements which they are taken with, on the other, how then (will you say) shall children be govern'd? Remove hope and fear, and there is an end of all discipline. I grant that good and evil, *reward* and *punishment,* are the only motives to a rational creature: these are the spur and reins whereby all mankind are set on work, and guided, and therefore they are to be made use of to children too. For I advise their parents and governors always to carry this in their minds, that children are to be treated as rational creatures.

§ 55. *Rewards,* I grant, and *punishments* must be proposed to children, if we intend to work upon them. The mistake I imagine is, that those that are generally made use of, are *ill chosen.* The pains and pleasures of the body are, I think, of ill consequence, when made the rewards and punishments whereby men would prevail on their children; for, as I said before, they serve but to increase and strengthen those inclinations, which 'tis our business to subdue and master. What principle of virtue do you lay in a child, if you will redeem his desires of one pleasure, by the proposal of another? This is but to enlarge his appetite, and instruct it to wander. If a child cries for an unwholesome and dangerous fruit, you purchase his quiet by giving him a less hurtful sweet-meat. This perhaps may preserve his health, but spoils his mind, and sets that farther out of order. For here you only change the object, but flatter still his *appetite,* and allow that must be satisfy'd, wherein, as I have shew'd, lies the root of the mischief; and till you bring him to be able to bear a denial of that satisfaction, the child may at present be quiet and orderly, but the disease is not cured. By this way of proceeding, you foment and cherish in him that which is the spring from whence all the evil flows, which will be sure on the next occasion to break out again with more violence, give him stronger longings, and you more trouble.

§ 56. The *rewards* and *punishments* then, whereby we should keep children in order, are quite of another kind, and of that force, that when we can get them once to work, the business, I think, is done, and the difficulty is over. *Esteem* and *disgrace* are, of all others, the most powerful incentives to the mind, when once it is brought to relish them. If you can once get into children a love of credit, and an apprehension of shame and disgrace, you have put into 'em the true principle, which will constantly work and incline them to the right. But it will be ask'd, How shall this be done?

I confess it does not at first appearance want some difficulty; but yet I think it worth our while to seek the ways (and practise them when found) to attain this, which I look on as the great secret of education.

§ 57. *First,* children (earlier perhaps than we think) are very sensible of *praise* and commendation. They find a pleasure in being esteem'd and valu'd, especially by their parents and those whom they depend on. If therefore the father *caress and commend them when they do well, shew a cold and neglectful countenance to them upon doing ill,* and this accompany'd by a like carriage of the mother and all others that are about them, it will, in a little time, make them sensible of the difference; and this, if constantly observ'd, I doubt not but will of itself work more than threats or blows, which lose their force when once grown common, and are of no use when shame does not attend them; and therefore are to be forborne, and never to be us'd, but in the case hereafter-mention'd, when it is brought to extremity.

§ 58. But *secondly,* to make the sense of *esteem* or *disgrace* sink the deeper, and be of the more weight, *other agreeable or disagreeable things should constantly accompany these different states;* not as particular rewards and punishments of this or that particular action, but as necessarily belonging to, and constantly attending one, who by his carriage has brought himself into a state of disgrace or commendation. By which way of treating them, children may as much as possible be brought to conceive, that those that are commended, and in esteem for doing well, will necessarily be belov'd and cherish'd by every body, and have all other good things as a consequence of it; and on the other side, when any one by miscarriage falls into disesteem, and cares not to preserve his credit, he will unavoidably fall under neglect and contempt; and in that state, the want of whatever might satisfy or delight him will follow. In this way the objects of their desires are made assisting to virtue, when a settled experience from the beginning teaches children that the things they delight in, belong to, and are to be enjoy'd by those only who are in a state of reputation. If by these means you can come once to shame them out of their faults, (for besides that, I would willingly have no punishment) and make them in love with the pleasure of being well thought on, you may turn them as you please, and they will be in love with all the ways of virtue.

§ 59. The great difficulty here is, I imagine, from the folly and perverseness of servants, who are hardly to be hinder'd from crossing herein the design of the father and mother. Children discountenanc'd by their parents for any fault, find usually a refuge and relief in the caresses of those foolish flatterers, who thereby undo whatever the parents endeavour to establish. When the father or mother looks sowre on the child, everybody else should put on the same coldness to him, and nobody give him countenance, 'till forgiveness ask'd, and a reformation of his fault has set him right again, and restor'd him to his former credit. If this were constantly observ'd, I guess there would be little need of blows or chiding: their own ease and satisfaction would quickly teach children to court commendation, and avoid doing that which they found everybody condemn'd and they were sure to suffer for, without being chid or beaten. This would teach them modesty and shame; and they would quickly come to have a natural abhorrence for that which they found made them slighted and neglected by every body. But how this inconvenience from servants is to be remedy'd, I must leave to parents' care and consideration. Only I think it of great importance; and that they are very happy who can get discreet people about their children.

§ 60. Frequent *beating* or *chiding* is therefore carefully *to be avoided:* because this sort of correction never produces any good, farther than it serves to raise *shame* and abhorrence of the miscarriage that brought it on them. And if the greatest part of the trouble be not the sense that they have done amiss, and the apprehension that they have drawn on themselves the just displeasure of their best friends, the pain of whipping will work but an imperfect cure. It only patches up for the present, and skins it over, but reaches not to the bottom of the sore; ingenuous *shame*, and the apprehensions of displeasure, are the only true restraint. These alone ought to hold the reins, and keep the child in order. But corporal punishments must necessarily lose that effect, and wear out the sense of *shame*, where they frequently return. Shame in children has the same place that modesty has in women, which cannot be kept and often transgress'd against. And as to the apprehension of *displeasure in the parents,* that will come to be very insignificant, if the marks of that displeasure quickly cease, and a few blows fully expiate. Parents should well consider what faults in their children are weighty enough to deserve the declaration of their anger: but when their displeasure is once declar'd to a degree that carries **any** punishment with it, they ought not presently to lay by the severity of their brows, but to restore their children to their former grace with some difficulty, and delay a full reconciliation, 'till their conformity and more than ordinary merit, make good their amendment. If this be not so order'd, *punishment* will, by familiarity, become a mere thing of course, and lose all its influence; offending, being chastised, and then forgiven, will be thought as natural and necessary, as noon, night, and morning following one another.

§ 61. Concerning *reputation,* I shall only remark this one thing more of it, that though it be not the true principle and measure of virtue, (for that is the knowledge of a man's duty, and the satisfaction it is to obey his maker, in following the dictates of that light God has given him, with the hopes of acceptation and reward) yet it is that which comes nearest to it: and being the testimony and applause that other people's reason, as it were by a common consent, gives to virtuous and well-order'd actions, it is the proper guide and encouragement of children, 'till they grow able to judge for themselves, and to find what is right by their own reason.

§ 62. This consideration may direct parents how to manage themselves in reproving and commending their children. The rebukes and chiding, which their faults will sometimes make hardly to be avoided, should not only be in sober, grave, and unpassionate words, but also alone and in private: but the commendations children deserve, they should receive before others. This doubles the reward, by spreading their praise; but the backwardness parents shew in divulging their faults, will make them set a greater value on their credit themselves, and teach them to be the more careful to preserve the good opinion of others, whilst they think they have it: but when being expos'd to shame by publishing their miscarriages, they give it up for lost, that check upon them is taken off, and they will be the less careful to preserve others' good thoughts of them, the more they suspect that their reputation with them is already blemish'd.

§ 63. But if a right course be taken with children, there will not be so much need of the application of the common rewards and punishments as we imagine, and as the general practice has establish'd. For all their innocent folly, playing and *childish actions, are to be left perfectly free and unrestrain'd,* as far as they can consist with the respect due to those that are present; and that with the greatest allowance. If these faults of their age, rather than of the children themselves, were, as they should be, left only to time and imitation and riper years to cure, children would escape a great deal of misapply'd and useless correction, which either fails to overpower the natural disposition of their childhood, and so by an ineffectual familiarity, makes correction in other necessary cases of less use; or else if it be of force to restrain the natural gaiety of that age, it serves only to spoil the temper both of body and mind. If the noise and bustle of their play prove at any time inconvenient, or unsuitable to the place or company they are in, (which can only be where their parents are) a look or a word from the father or mother, if they have establish'd the authority they should, will be enough either to remove or quiet them for that time. But this gamesome humour, which is wisely adapted by nature to their age and temper, should rather be encourag'd to keep up their spirits, and improve their strength and health, than curb'd and restrain'd; and the chief art is to make all that they have to do, sport and play too.

§ 64. And here give me leave to take notice of one thing I think a fault in the ordinary method of education; and that is, the charging of children's memories, upon all occasions, with *rules* and precepts, which they often do not understand, and constantly as soon forget as given. If it be some action you would have done, or done otherwise, whenever they forget, or do it awkwardly, make them do it over and over again, 'till they are perfect, whereby you will get these two advantages. *First,* to see whether it be an action they can do, or is fit to be expected of them: for sometimes children are bid to do things which upon trial they are found not able to do, and had need be taught and exercis'd in before they are requir'd to do them. But it is much easier for a tutor to command than to teach. *Secondly,* another thing got by it will be this, that by repeating the same action 'till it be grown habitual in them, the performance will not depend on memory or reflection, the concomitant of prudence and age, and not of childhood, but will be natural in them. Thus bowing to a gentleman, when he salutes him, and looking in his face, when he speaks to him, is by constant use as natural to a well-bred man, as breathing; it requires no thought, no reflection. Having this way cured in your child any fault, it is cured for ever: and thus one by one you may weed them out all, and plant what habits you please.

§ 65. I have seen parents so heap *rules* on their children, that it was impossible for the poor little ones to remember a tenth part of them, much less to observe them. However, they were either by words or blows corrected for the breach of those multiply'd and often very impertinent precepts. Whence it naturally follow'd that the children minded not what was said to them, when it was evident to them that no attention they were capable of was sufficient to preserve them from transgression, and the rebukes which follow'd it.

Let therefore your *rules* to your son be as few as possible, and rather fewer than more than seem absolutely necessary. For if you burden him with many *rules,* one of these two things must necessarily follow; that either he must be very often punish'd, which will be of ill consequence, by making punishment too frequent and familiar; or else you must let the transgressions of some of your rules go unpunish'd, whereby they will of course grow contemptible, and your authority become cheap to him. Make but few *laws,* but see they be well observ'd when once made. Few years require but few laws, and as his age increases, when one rule is by practice well establish'd, you may add another.

§ 66. But pray remember, children are *not* to be *taught by rules* which will be always slipping out of their memories. What you think necessary for them to do, settle in them by an indispensable practice, as often as the occasion returns; and if it be possible, make occasions. This will beget *habits* in them which being once establish'd, operate of themselves easily and naturally, without the assistance of the memory.

But here let me give two cautions. 1. The one is, that you keep them to the practice of what you would have grow into a habit in them, by kind words, and gentle admonitions, rather as minding them of what they forget, than by harsh rebukes and chiding, as if they were wilfully guilty. 2. Another thing you are to take care of, is, not to endeavour to settle too many *habits* at once, lest by variety you confound them, and so perfect none. When constant custom has made any one thing easy and natural to 'em, and they practise it without reflection, you may then go on to another.

This method of teaching children by a repeated *practice*, and the same action done over and over again, under the eye and direction of the tutor, 'till they have got the habit of doing it well, and not by relying on *rules* trusted to their memories, has so many advantages, which way soever we consider it, that I cannot but wonder (if ill customs could be wondered at in any thing) how it could possibly be so much neglected. I shall name one more that comes now in my way. By this method we shall see whether what is requir'd of him be adapted to his capacity, and any way suited to the child's natural genius and constitution; for that too much be consider'd in a right education. We must not hope wholly to change their original tempers, nor make the gay pensive and grave, nor the melancholy sportive, without spoiling them. God has stamp'd certain characters upon men's minds, which like their shapes, may perhaps be a little mended, but can hardly be totally alter'd and transform'd into the contrary.

He therefore that is about children should well study their natures and aptitudes, and see by often trials what turn they easily take, and what becomes them; observe what their native stock is, how it may be improv'd, and what it is fit for: he should consider what they want, whether they be capable of having it wrought into them by industry, and incorporated there by practice; and whether it be worth while to endeavour it. For in many cases, all that we can do, or should aim at, is, to make the best of what nature has given, to prevent the vices and faults to which such a constitution is most inclin'd, and give it all the advantages it is capable of. Every one's natural genius should be carry'd as far as it could; but to attempt the putting another upon him, will be but labour in vain; and what is so plaister'd on, will at best sit but untowardly, and have always hanging to it the ungracefulness of constraint and affectation.

*Affectation* is not, I confess, an early fault of childhood, or the product of untaught nature. It is of that sort of weeds which grow not in the wild uncultivated waste, but in garden-plots, under the negligent hand or unskilful care of a gardener. Management and instruction, and some sense of the necessity of breeding, are requisite to make any one capable of *affectation,* which endeavours to correct natural defects, and has always the laudable aim of pleasing, though it always misses it; and the more it labours to put on grace-fulness, the farther it is from it. For this reason, it is the more carefully to be watch'd, because it is the proper fault of education; a perverted education indeed, but such as young people often fall into, either by their own mistake, or the ill conduct of those about them.

He that will examine wherein that gracefulness lies, which always pleases, will find it arises from that natural coherence which appears between the thing done and such a temper of mind as cannot but be approv'd of as suitable to the occasion. We cannot but be pleas'd with an humane, friendly, civil temper wherever we meet with it. A mind free, and master of itself and all its actions, not low and narrow, not haughty and insolent, not blemish'd with any great defect, is what every one is taken with. The actions which naturally flow from such a well-form'd mind, please us also, as the genuine marks of it; and being as it were natural emanations from the spirit and disposition within, cannot but be easy and unconstrain'd. This seems to me to be that beauty which shines through some men's actions, sets off all that they do, and takes all they come near; when by a constant practice, they have fashion'd their carriage, and made all those little expressions of civility and respect, which nature or custom has establish'd in conversation, so easy to them-selves, that they seem not artificial or studied, but naturally to follow from a sweetness of mind and a well-turn'd dis-position.

On the other side, *affectation* is an awkward and forc'd

imitation of what should be genuine and easy, wanting the beauty that accompanies what is natural; because there is always a disagreement between the outward action, and the mind within, one of these two ways: 1. Either when a man would outwardly put on a disposition of mind, which then he really has not, but endeavours by a forc'd carriage to make shew of; yet so, that the constraint he is under discovers itself: and thus men affect sometimes to appear sad, merry, or kind, when in truth they are not so.

2. The other is, when they do not endeavour to make shew of dispositions of mind, which they have not, but to express those they have by a carriage not suited to them. And such in conversation are all constrain'd motions, actions, words, or looks, which, though design'd to shew either their respect or civility to the company, or their satisfaction and easiness in it, are not yet natural nor genuine marks of the one or the other, but rather of some defect or mistake within. Imitation of others, without discerning what is graceful in them, or what is peculiar to their characters, often makes a great part of this. But *affectation* of all kinds, whencesoever it proceeds, is always offensive; because we naturally hate whatever is counterfeit, and condemn those who have nothing better to recommend themselves by.

Plain and rough nature, left to itself, is much better than an artificial ungracefulness, and such study'd ways of being illfashion'd. The want of an accomplishment, or some defect in our behaviour, coming short of the utmost gracefulness, often escapes observation and censure. But *affectation* in any part of our carriage is lighting up a candle to our defects, and never fails to make us be taken notice of, either as wanting sense, or wanting sincerity. This governors ought the more diligently to look after, because, as I above observ'd, 'tis an acquir'd ugliness, owing to mistaken education, few being guilty of it but those who pretend to breeding, and would not be thought ignorant of what is fashionable and becoming in conversation; and, if I mistake not, it has often its rise from the lazy admonitions of those who give rules, and propose examples, without joining practice with their instructions and making their pupils repeat the action in their sight, that they may correct what is indecent or constrain'd in it, till it be perfected into an habitual and becoming easiness.

§ 67. *Manners,* as they call it, about which children are so often perplex'd, and have so many goodly exhortations made them by their wise maids and governesses, I think, are rather to be learnt by example than rules; and then children, if kept out of ill company, will take a pride to behave themselves prettily, after the fashion of others, perceiving themselves esteem'd and commended for it. But if by a little negligence in this part, the boy should not pull off his hat, nor make legs very gracefully, a dancing-master will cure that defect, and wipe off all that plainness of nature, which the a-la-mode people call clownishness. And since nothing appears to me to give children so much becoming confidence and behaviour, and so to raise them to the conversation of those above their age, as *dancing,* I think they should be taught to dance as soon as they are capable of learning it. For tho' this consist only in outward gracefulness of motion, yet, I know not how, it gives children manly thoughts and carriage, more than any thing. But otherwise, I would not have little children much tormented about punctilio's or niceties of breeding.

Never trouble your self about those faults in them, which you know age will cure: and therefore want of well-fashion'd civility in the carriage, whilst *civility* is not wanting in the mind, (for there you must take care to plant it early) should be the parents' least care, whilst they are young. If his tender mind be fill'd with a veneration for his parents and teachers, which consists of love and esteem, and a fear to offend them; and with *respect and good will* to all people; that respect will of itself teach those ways of expressing it, which he observes most acceptable. Be sure to keep up in him the principles of good nature and kindness; make them as habitual as you can, by credit and commendation, and the good things accompanying that state: and when they have taken root in his mind, and are settled there by a continued practice, fear not, the ornaments of conversation, and the outside of fashionable manners, will come in their due time; if when they are remov'd out of their maid's care, they are put into the hands of a well-bred man to be their governor.

Whilst they are very young, any *carelessness* is to be borne with in children, that carries not with it the marks of pride or ill nature; but those, whenever they appear in any action, are to be corrected immediately by the ways abovemention'd. What I have said concerning manners, I would not have so understood, as if I meant that those who have the judgment to do it, should not gently fashion the motions and carriage of children, when they are very young. It would be of great advantage, if they had people about them from their being first able to go, that had the skill, and would take the right way to do it. That which I complain of, is the wrong course that is usually taken in this matter. Children, who were never taught any such thing as behaviour, are often (especially when strangers are present) chid for having some way or other fail'd in good manners, and have thereupon reproofs and precepts heap'd upon them, concerning putting off their hats, or making of legs, &c. Though in this, those concern'd pretend to correct the child, yet in truth, for the most part, it is but to cover their own shame; and they lay the blame on the poor little ones, sometimes passionately enough, to divert it from themselves, for fear the by-standers should impute to their want of care and skill the child's ill behaviour.

For, as for the children themselves, they are never one jot better'd by such occasional lectures. They at other times should be shewn what to do, and by reiterated actions be fashion'd beforehand into the practice of what is fit and becoming, and not told and talk'd to do upon the spot, of what they have never been accustom'd nor know how to do as they should. To hare and rate them thus at every turn, is not to teach them, but to vex and torment them to no purpose. They should be let alone, rather than chid for a fault which is none of theirs, nor is in their power to mend for speaking to. And it were much better their natural childish negligence or plainness should be left to the care of riper years, than that they should frequently have rebukes misplac'd upon them, which neither do nor can give them graceful motions. If their minds are well-dispos'd, and principled with inward civility, a great part of the roughness which sticks to the outside for want of better teaching, time

and observation will rub off, as they grow up, if they are
bred in good company; but if in ill, all the rules in the world,
all the correction imaginable, will not be able to polish them.
For you must take this for a certain truth, that let them have
what instructions you will, and ever so learned lectures of
breeding daily inculcated into them, that which will most
influence their carriage will be the company they converse
with, and the fashion of those about them. Children (nay,
and men too) do most by example. We are all a sort of
camelions, that still take a tincture from things near us;
nor is it to be wonder'd at in children, who better understand what they see than what they hear.

§ 68. I mention'd above one great mischief that came by
servants to children, when by their flatteries they take off
the edge and force of the parents' rebukes, and so lessen
their authority: and here is another great inconvenience
which children receive from the ill examples which they
meet with amongst the meaner servants.

They are wholly, if possible, to be kept from such conversation; for the contagion of these ill precedents, both
in civility and virtue, horribly infects children, as often as
they come within reach of it. They frequently learn from
unbred or debauch'd servants such language, untowardly
tricks and vices, as otherwise they possibly would be ignorant
of all their lives.

§ 69. 'Tis a hard matter wholly to prevent this mischief.
You will have very good luck, if you never have a clownish
or vicious servant, and if from them your children never
get any infection: but yet as much must be done towards
it as can be, and the children kept as much as may be *in
the company of their parents,* and those to whose care they
are committed. To this purpose, their being in their presence should be made easy to them; they should be allow'd
the liberties and freedoms suitable to their ages, and not
be held under unnecessary restraints, when in their parents'
or governor's sight. If it be a prison to them, 'tis no wonder
they should not like it. They must not be hinder'd from
being children, or from playing, or doing as children, but

---

[1] *How much the* Romans *thought the education of their children a business that properly belong'd to the parents themselves, see in* Suetonius,
*August.* § 64. Plutarch *in vita Catonis Censoris,* Diodorus Siculus, *l. 2, cap. 3.*

from doing ill; all other liberty is to be allow'd them. Next, to make them in love with the *company of their parents,* they should receive all their good things there, and from their hands. The servants should be hinder'd from making court to them by giving them strong drink, wine, fruit, play-things, and other such matters, which may make them in love with their conversation.

§ 70. Having nam'd *company,* I am almost ready to throw away my pen, and trouble you no farther on this subject: for since that does more than all precepts, rules and in-structions, methinks 'tis almost wholly in vain to make a long discourse of other things, and to talk of that almost to no purpose. For you will be ready to say, what shall I do with my son? If I keep him always at home, he will be in danger to be my young master; and if I send him abroad, how is it possible to keep him from the contagion of rude-ness and vice, which is every where so in fashion? In my house he will perhaps be more innocent, but more ignorant too of the world; wanting there change of company, and being us'd constantly to the same faces, he will, when he comes abroad, be a sheepish or conceited creature.

I confess both sides have their inconveniences. Being abroad, 'tis true, will make him bolder, and better able to bustle and shift among boys of his own age; and the emu-lation of school-fellows often puts life and industry into young lads. But still you can find a school, wherein it is possible for the master to look after the manners of his scholars, and can shew as great effects of his care of form-ing their minds to virtue, and their carriage to good breed-ing, as of forming their tongues to the learned languages, you must confess, that you have a strange value for words, when preferring the languages of the antient *Greeks* and *Romans* to that which made 'em such brave men, you think it worth while to hazard your son's innocence and virtue for a little *Greek* and *Latin.* For, as for that boldness and spirit which lads get amongst their play-fellows at school, it has ordinarily such a mixture of rudeness and ill-turn'd confidence, that those misbecoming and disingenuous ways of shifting in the world must be unlearnt, and all the tinc-ture wash'd out again, to make way for better principles, and such manners as make a truly worthy man. He that considers how diametrically opposite the skill of living well, and managing, as a man should do, his affairs in the world, is to that mal-pertness, tricking, or violence learnt amongst school-boys, will think the faults of a privater education infinitely to be preferr'd to such improvements, and will take care to preserve his child's innocence and modesty at home, as being nearer of kin, and more in the way of those qualities which make an useful and able man. Nor does any one find, or so much as suspect, that that retirement and bashfulness which their daughters are brought up in, makes them less knowing, or less able women. Conversation, when they come into the world, soon gives them a becoming assurance; and whatsoever, beyond that, there is of rough and boisterous, may in men be very well spar'd too; for courage and steadiness, as I take it, lie not in roughness and ill breeding.

Virtue is harder to be got than a knowledge of the world; and if lost in a young man, is seldom recover'd. Sheepishness and ignorance of the world, the faults imputed to a private education, are neither the necessary consequences of being bred at home, nor if they were, are they incurable evils. Vice is the more stubborn, as well as the more dangerous evil of the two; and therefore in the first place to be fenced against. If that sheepish softness which often enervates those who are bred like fondlings at home, be carefully to be avoided, it is principally so for virtue's sake; for fear lest such a yielding temper should be too susceptible of vicious impressions, and expose the novice too easily to be corrupted. A young man before he leaves the shelter of his father's house, and the guard of a tutor, should be fortify'd with resolution, and made acquainted with men, to secure his virtues, lest he should be led into some ruinous course, or fatal precipice, before he is sufficiently acquainted with the dangers of conversation, and has steadiness enough not to yield to every temptation. Were it not for this, a young man's bashfulness and ignorance in the world, would not so much need an early care. Conversation would cure it in a great measure; or if that will not do it early enough, it is only a stronger reason for a good tutor at home. For if pains be to be taken to give him a manly air and assurance betimes, it is chiefly as a fence to his virtue when he goes into the world under his own conduct.

It is preposterous therefore to sacrifice his innocency to the attaining of confidence and some little skill of bustling for himself among others, by his conversation with illbred and vicious boys; when the chief use of that sturdiness, and standing upon his own legs, is only for the preservation of his virtue. For if confidence or cunning come once to mix with vice, and support his miscarriages, he is only the surer lost; and you must undo again, and strip him of that he has got from his companions, or give him up to ruin. Boys will unavoidably be taught assurance by conversation with men, when they are brought into it; and that is time enough. Modesty and submission, till then, better fits them for instruction; and therefore there needs not any great care to stock them with confidence beforehand. That which requires most time, pains, and assiduity, is, to work into them the principles and practice of virtue and good breeding. This is the seasoning they should be prepar'd with, so as not easily to be got out again. This they had need to be well provided with, for conversation, when they come into the world, will add to their knowledge and assurance, but be too apt to take from their virtue; which therefore they ought to be plentifully stor'd with, and have that tincture sunk deep into them.

How they should be fitted for conversation, and enter'd into the world, when they are ripe for it, we shall consider in another place. But how any one's being put into a mix'd herd of unruly boys, and there learning to wrangle at trap, or rook at span-farthing, fits him for civil conversation or business, I do not see. And what qualities are ordinarily to be got from such a troop of play-fellows as schools usually assemble together from parents of all kinds, that a father should so much covet, is hard to divine. I am sure, he who is able to be at the charge of a tutor at home, may there give his son a more genteel carriage, more manly thoughts, and a sense of what is worthy and becoming, with a greater proficiency in learning into the bargain,

and ripen him up sooner into a man, than any at school
can do.  Not that I blame the schoolmaster in this, or think
it to be laid to his charge.  The difference is great between
two or three pupils in the same house, and three or four
score boys lodg'd up and down: for let the master's industry and skill be never so great, it is impossible he should
have fifty or an hundred scholars under his eye, any longer
than they are in the school together: Nor can it be expected, that he should instruct them successfully in any
thing but their books; the forming of their minds and manners requiring a constant attention, and particular application to every single boy, which is impossible in a numerous
flock, and would be wholly in vain (could he have time to
study and correct every one's particular defects and wrong
inclinations) when the lad was to be left to himself, or the
prevailing infection of his fellows, the greatest part of the
four and twenty hours.

But fathers, observing that fortune is often most successfully courted by bold and bustling men, are glad to see
their sons pert and forward betimes; take it for an happy
omen that they will be thriving men, and look on the tricks
they play their school-fellows, or learn from them, as a
proficiency in the art of living, and making their way
through the world.  But I must take the liberty to say, that
he that lays the foundation of his son's fortune in virtue
and good breeding, takes the only sure and warrantable way.
And 'tis not the waggeries or cheats practis'd amongst
school-boys, 'tis not their roughness one to another, nor the
well-laid plots of robbing an orchard together, that make
an able man; but the principles of justice, generosity, and
sobriety, join'd with observation and industry, qualities
which I judge school-boys do not learn much of one another.  And if a young gentleman bred at home, be not
taught more of them than he could learn at school, his
father has made a very ill choice of a tutor.  Take a boy
from the top of a grammar-school, and one of the same
age bred as he should be in his father's family, and bring
them into good company together, and then see which of the
two will have the more manly carriage, and address himself with the more becoming assurance to strangers.  Here

I imagine the school-boy's confidence will either fail or discredit him; and if it be such as fits him only for the conversation of boys, he were better to be without it.

Vice, if we may believe the general complaint, ripens so fast now-a-days, and runs up to seed so early in young people, that it is impossible to keep a lad from the spreading contagion, if you will venture him abroad in the herd, and trust to chance or his own inclination for the choice of his company at school. By what fate has Vice so thriven amongst us these years past, and by what hands it has been nurs'd up into so uncontroul'd a dominion, I shall leave to others to enquire. I wish that those who complain of the great decay of Christian piety and virtue every where, and of learning and acquir'd improvements in the gentry of this generation, would consider how to retrieve them in the next. This I am sure, that if the foundation of it be not laid in the education and principling of the youth, all other endeavours will be in vain. And if the innocence, sobriety, and industry of those who are coming up, be not taken care of and preserv'd, 'twill be ridiculous to expect, that those who are to succeed next on the stage, should abound in that virtue, ability, and learning, which has hitherto made *England* considerable in the world. I was going to add courage too, though it has been look'd on as the natural inheritance of *Englishmen.* What has been talk'd of some late actions at sea, of a kind unknown to our ancestors, gives me occasion to say, that debauchery sinks the courage of men; and when dissoluteness has eaten out the sense of true honour, bravery seldom stays long after it. And I think it impossible to find an instance of any nation, however renown'd for their valour, who ever kept their credit in arms, or made themselves redoubtable amongst their neighbours, after corruption had once broke through and dissolv'd the restraint of discipline, and vice was grown to such an head, that it durst shew itself barefac'd without being out of countenance.

'Tis *virtue* then, direct *virtue,* which is the hard and valuable part to be aim'd at in education, and not a forward pertness, or any little arts of shifting. All other considerations and accomplishments should give way and be post-

pon'd to this. This is the solid and substantial good which
tutors should not only read lectures, and talk of, but the
labour and art of education should furnish the mind with,
and fasten there, and never cease till the young man had
a true relish of it, and plac'd his strength, his glory, and his
pleasure in it.

The more this advances, the easier way will be made
for other accomplishments in their turns. For he that
is brought to submit to virtue, will not be refractory, or
resty, in any thing that becomes him; and therefore I cannot
but prefer breeding of a young gentleman at home in his
father's sight, under a good governour, as much the best
and safest way to this great and main end of education,
when it can be had, and is order'd as it should be. Gentlemen's houses are seldom without variety of company.
They should use their sons to all the strange faces that
come here, and engage them in conversation with men of
parts and breeding, as soon as they are capable of it. And
why those who live in the country should not take them with
them, when they make visits of civility to their neighbours, I know not. This I am sure, a father that breeds
his son at home, has the opportunity to have him more in
his own company, and there give him what encouragement
he thinks fit, and can keep him better from the taint of
servants and the meaner sort of people, than is possible
to be done abroad. But what shall be resolv'd in the case,
must in great measure be left to the parents, to be de-
termin'd by their circumstances and conveniences; only I
think it the worst sort of good husbandry for a father not
to strain himself a little for his son's breeding; which,
let his condition be what it will, is the best portion he can
leave him. But if, after all, it shall be thought by some,
that the breeding at home has too little company, and that
at ordinary schools, not such as it should be for a young
gentleman, I think there might be ways found out to avoid
the inconveniences on the one side and the other.

§ 71. Having under consideration how great the influence
of *company* is, and how prone we are all, especially children, to imitation, I must here take the liberty to mind
**parents** of this one thing, *viz.* That he that will have his

son have a respect for him and his orders, must himself have a great reverence for his son. *Maxima debetur pueris reverentia.* You must do nothing before him, which you would not have him imitate. If any thing escape you, which you would have pass for a fault in him, he will be sure to shelter himself under your example, and shelter himself so as that it will not be easy to come at him, to correct it in him the right way. If you punish him for what he sees you practise yourself, he will not think that severity to proceed from kindness in you, careful to amend a fault in him; but will be apt to interpret it the peevishness and arbitrary imperiousness of a father, who, without any ground for it, would deny his son the liberty and pleasures he takes himself. Or if you assume to yourself the liberty you have taken, as a privilege belonging to riper years, to which a child must not aspire, you do but add new force to your example, and recommend the action the more powerfully to him. For you must always remember, that children affect to be men earlier than is thought; and they love breeches, not for their cut or ease, but because the having them is a mark or step towards manhood. What I say of the father's carriage before his children, must extend itself to all those who have any authority over them, or for whom he would have them have any respect.

§ 72. But to return to the business of *rewards* and *punishments*. All the actions of childishness, and unfashionable carriage, and whatever time and age will of itself be sure to reform, being (as I have said) exempt from the discipline of the rod, there will not be so much need of beating children as is generally made use of. To which if we add learning to read, write, dance, foreign language, &c. as under the same privilege, there will be but very rarely an occasion for blows or force in an ingenuous education. The right way to teach them those things, is, to give them a liking and inclination to what you suppose to them to be learn'd, and that will engage their industry and application. This I think no hard matter to do, if children be handled as they should be, and the rewards and punishments above-mention'd be carefully apply'd, and with them these few rules observ'd in the method of instructing them.

§ 73. 1. None of the things they are to learn, should ever be made a burthen to them, or impos'd on them as a *task*. Whatever is so propos'd, presently becomes irksome; the mind takes an aversion to it, though before it were a thing of delight or indifferency. Let a child but be order'd to whip his top at a certain time every day, whether he has or has not a mind to it; let this be but requir'd of him as a duty, wherein he must spend so many hours morning and afternoon, and see whether he will not soon be weary of any play at this rate. Is it not so with grown men? What they do chearfully of themselves, do they not presently grow sick of, and can no more endure, as soon as they find it is expected of them as a duty? Children have as much a mind to shew that they are free, that their own good actions come from themselves, that they are absolute and independent, as any of the proudest of you grown men, think of them as you please.

§ 74. 2. As a consequence of this, they should seldom be put about doing even those things you have got an inclination in them to, but when they have a mind and *disposition* to it. He that loves reading, writing, musick, &c. finds yet in himself certain seasons wherein those things have no relish to him; and if at that time he forces himself to it, he only pothers and wearies himself to no purpose. So it is with children. This change of temper should be carefully observ'd in them, and the favourable *seasons of aptitude and inclination* be heedfully laid hold of: and if they are not often enough forward of themselves, a good disposition should be talk'd into them, before they be set upon any thing. This I think no hard matter for a discreet tutor to do, who has study'd his pupil's temper, and will be at a little pains to fill his head with suitable ideas, such as may make him in love with the present business. By this means a great deal of time and tiring would be sav'd: for a child will learn three times as much when he is *in tune,* as he will with double the time and pains when he goes awkwardly or is dragg'd unwillingly to it. If this were minded as it should, children might be permitted to weary themselves with play, and yet have time enough to learn what is suited to the capacity of each age. But no such thing is consider'd in the ordinary way of education, nor can it well be. That rough discipline of the rod is built upon other principles, has no attraction in it, regards not what humour children are in, nor looks after favourable seasons of inclination. And indeed it would be ridiculous, when compulsion and blows have rais'd an aversion in the child to his task, to expect he should freely of his own accord leave his play, and with pleasure court the occasions of learning; whereas, were matters order'd right, learning anything they should be taught might be made as much a recreation to their play, as their play is to their learning. The pains are equal on both sides. Nor is it that which troubles them; for they love to be busy, and the change and variety is that which naturally delights them. The only odds is, in that which we call play they act at liberty, and employ their pains (whereof you may observe them never sparing) freely; but what they are to learn is forc'd upon them, they are call'd, compell'd, and driven to it. This is that, that at first entrance balks and cools them; they want their liberty. Get them but to ask their tutor to teach them, as they do often their play-fellows, instead of his calling upon them to learn, and they being satisfy'd that they act as freely in this as they do in other things, they will go on with as much pleasure in it, and it will not differ from their other sports and play. By these ways, carefully pursu'd, a child may be brought to desire to be taught any thing you have a mind he should learn. The hardest part, I confess, is with the first or eldest; but when once he is set right, it is easy by him to lead the rest whither one will.

§ 75. Though it be past doubt, that the fittest time for children to learn any thing, is, when their *minds* are *in tune, and well dispos'd* to it; when neither flagging of spirit, nor intentness of thought upon something else, makes them awkward and averse; yet two things are to be taken care of: 1. That these seasons either not being warily observ'd, and laid hold on as often as they return, or else, not returning as often as they should, the improvement of the child be not thereby neglected, and so he be let grow into an habitual idleness, and confirm'd in this disposition: 2. That though other things are ill learn'd, when the mind is either indispos'd, or otherwise taken up; yet it is of great moment, and worth our endeavours, to teach the mind to get the mastery over itself, and to be able, upon choice, to take itself off from the hot pursuit of one thing, and set itself upon another with facility and delight, or at any time to shake off its sluggishness, and vigorously employ itself about what reason, or the advice of another shall direct. This is to be done in children, by trying them sometimes, when they are by laziness unbent, or by avocation bent another way, and endeavouring to make them buckle to the thing propos'd. If by this means the mind can get an habitual dominion over itself, lay by *ideas* or business as occasion requires, and betake itself to new and less acceptable employments without reluctancy or discomposure, it will be an advantage of more consequence than Latin or logick or most of those things children are usually requir'd to learn.

§ 76. Children being more active and busy in that age, than in any other part of their life, and being indifferent to any thing they can do, so they may be but doing, *dancing* and *Scotch-hoppers* would be the same thing to them, were the encouragements and discouragements equal. But to things we would have them learn, the great and only discouragement I can observe, is, that they are call'd to it, 'tis *made their business,* they are *teas'd* and *chid* about it, and do it with trembling and apprehension; or, when they come willingly to it, are kept too long at it, till they are quite tir'd: all which intrenches too much on that natural freedom they extremely affect. And it is that liberty alone which gives the true relish and delight to their ordinary play-games. Turn the tables, and you will find they will soon change their application; especially if they see the examples of others whom they esteem and think above themselves. And if the things which they observe others to do, be order'd so, that they insinuate themselves into them as the privilege of an age or condition above theirs; then ambition, and the desire still to get forward and higher, and to be like those above them, will set them on work, and make them go on with vigour and pleasure; pleasure in what they have begun by their own desire, in which way the enjoyment of their dearly beloved freedom will be no small encouragement to them. To all which, if there be added the satisfaction of credit and reputation, I am apt to think there will need no other spur to excite their application and assiduity, as much as is necessary. I confess, there needs patience and skill, gentleness and attention, and a prudent conduct to attain this at first. But why have you a tutor, if there needed no pains? But when this is once establish'd, all the rest will follow, more easily than in any more severe and imperious discipline. And I think it no hard matter to gain this point; I am sure it will not be, where children have no ill examples set before them. The great danger therefore, I apprehend, is only from servants, and other ill-order'd children, or such other vicious or foolish people, who spoil children both by the ill pattern they set before them in their own ill manners, and by giving them together the two things they should never have at once; I mean vicious pleasures and commendation.

§ 77. As children should very seldom be corrected by blows, so I think frequent, and especially passionate *chiding* of almost as ill consequence. It lessens the authority of the parents, and the respect of the child; for I bid you still remember, they distinguish early betwixt passion and reason: and as they cannot but have a reverence for what comes from the latter, so they quickly grow into a contempt of the former; or if it causes a present terror, yet it soon wears off, and natural inclination will easily learn to slight such scare-crows which make a noise, but are not animated by reason. Children being to be restrain'd by the parents only in vicious (which, in their tender years, are only a few) things, a look or nod only ought to correct them when they do amiss; or, if words are sometimes to be us'd, they ought to be grave, kind, and sober, representing the ill or unbecomingness of the faults, rather than a *hasty rating* of the child for it; which makes him not sufficiently distinguish, whether your dislike be not more directed to him than his fault. Passionate chiding usually carries rough and ill language with it, which has this farther ill effect, that it teaches and justifies it in children: and the names that their parents or præceptors give them, they will not be asham'd or backward to bestow on others, having so good authority for the use of them.

§ 78. I foresee here it will be objected to me, what then, will you have children never beaten nor chid for any fault? This will be to let loose the reins to all kind of disorder. Not so much, as is imagin'd, if a right course has been taken in the first seasoning of their minds, and implanting that awe of their parents above mentioned. For beating, by constant observation, is found to do little good, where the smart of it is all the punishment is fear'd or felt in it; for the influence of that quickly wears out, with the memory of it. But yet there is one, and but one fault, for which, I think, children should be beaten, and that is, *obstinacy* or *rebellion*. And in this too, I would have it order'd so, if it can be, that the shame of the whipping, and not the pain, should be the greatest part of the punishment. Shame of doing amiss, and deserving chastisement, is the only true restraint belonging to virtue. The smart of the rod, if shame accompanies it not, soon ceases, and is forgotten, and will quickly by use lose its terror. I have known the children of a person of quality kept in awe by the fear of having their shoes pull'd off, as much as others by apprehensions of a rod hanging over them. Some such punishment I think better than beating; for 'tis shame of the fault, and the disgrace that attends it, that they should stand in fear of, rather than pain, if you would have them have a temper truly ingenuous. But *stubbornness,* and an *obstinate disobedience,* must be master'd with force and blows; for this there is no other remedy. Whatever particular action you bid him do, or forbear, you must be sure to see your self obey'd; no quarter in this case, no resistance: for when once it comes to be a trial of skill, a contest for mastery betwixt you, as it is if you command and he refuses, you must be sure to carry it, whatever blows it costs, if a nod or words will not prevail; unless, for ever after, you intend to live in obedience to your son. A prudent and kind mother of my acquaintance, was, on such an occasion, forc'd to whip her little daughter, at her first coming home from nurse, eight times successively the same morning, before she could master her *stubbornness,* and obtain a compliance in a very easy and indifferent matter. If she had left off sooner, and stopp'd at the seventh whipping, she had spoil'd the child for ever, and, by her unprevailing blows, only confirm'd her refractoriness, very hardly afterwards to be cur'd: but wisely persisting till she had bent her mind, and suppled her will, the only end of correction and chastisement, she establish'd her authority thoroughly in the very first occasions, and had ever after a very ready compliance and obedience in all things from her daughter; for as this was the first time, so I think it was the last too she ever struck her.

The pain of the rod, *the first* occasion that requires it, continu'd and increas'd, without leaving off till it has throughly prevail'd, should first bend the mind, and settle the parent's authority; and then gravity, mix'd with kindness, should for ever after keep it.

This, if well reflected on, would make people more wary in the use of the rod and the cudgel, and keep them from being so apt to think beating the safe and universal remedy to be apply'd at random on all occasions. This is certain, however, if it does no good, it does great harm; if it reaches not the mind, and makes not the will supple, it hardens the offender; and whatever pain he has suffer'd for it, does but endear him to his beloved *stubbornness,* which has got him this time the victory, and prepares him to contest, and hope for it for the future. This I doubt not but by ill-order'd correction many have been taught to be *obstinate* and *refractory* who otherwise would have been very pliant and tractable. For if you punish a child so, as if it were only to revenge the past fault, which has rais'd your choler, what operation can this have upon his mind, which is the part to be amended? If there were no *sturdy humor* or *wilfulness* mix'd with his fault, there was nothing in it that requir'd the severity of blows. A kind or grave admonition is enough to remedy the slips of frailty, forgetfulness, or inadvertency, and is as much as they will stand in need of. But if there were a *perverseness* in the will, if it were a design'd, resolv'd disobedience, the punishment is not to be measur'd by the greatness or smallness of the matter wherein it appear'd, but by the opposition it carries, and stands in, to that respect and submission is due to the father's orders; which must always be rigorously exacted, and the blows by pauses laid on, till they reach the mind, and you

(3) HC XXXVII

perceive the signs of a true sorrow, shame, and purpose of
obedience.

This, I confess, requires something more than setting
children a task, and whipping them without any more a-do
if it be not done, and done to our fancy. This requires
care, attention, observation, and a nice study of children's
tempers, and weighing their faults well, before we come to
this sort of punishment. But is not that better than always
to have the rod in hand as the only instrument of government? And by frequent use of it on all occasions, misapply
and render inefficacious' this last and useful remedy, where
there is need of it? For what else can be expected, when
it is promiscuously us'd upon every little slip? When a mistake in *concordance,* or a wrong *position* in verse, shall have
the severity of the lash, in a well-temper'd and industrious
lad, as surely as a wilful crime in an obstinate and perverse
offender; how can such a way of correction be expected to
do good on the mind, and set that right? Which is the only
thing to be look'd after; and when set right, brings all the
rest that you can desire along with it.

§ 79. Where a *wrong bent of the will* wants not amendment, there can be no need of blows. All other faults,
where the mind is rightly dispos'd, and refuses not the government and authority of the father or tutor, are but mistakes,
and may often be overlook'd; or when they are taken
notice of, need no other but the gentle remedies of advice,
direction, and reproof, till the repeated and wilful neglect
of those, shews the fault to be in the mind, and that a manifest *perverseness* of the will lies at the root of their disobedience. But whenever *obstinacy,* which is an open defiance, appears, *that* cannot be wink'd at or neglected, but
must, in the first instance, be subdu'd and master'd; only care
must be had, that we mistake not and we must be sure
it is obstinacy and nothing else.

§ 80. But since the occasions of punishment, especially
beating, are as much to be avoided as may be, I think it
should not be often brought to this point. If the awe I
spoke of be once got, a look will be sufficient' in most cases.
Nor indeed should the same carriage, seriousness, or application be expected from young children as from those of

riper growth. They must be permitted, as I said, the foolish and childish actions suitable to their years, without taking notice of them. Inadvertency, carelessness, and gayety, is the character of that age. I think the severity I spoke of is not to extend itself to such unseasonable restraints. Nor is that hastily to be interpreted obstinacy or wilfulness, which is the natural product of their age or temper. In such miscarriages they are to be assisted, and help'd towards an amendment, as weak people under a natural infirmity; which, though they are warn'd of, yet every relapse must not be counted a perfect neglect, and they presently treated as obstinate. Faults of frailty, as they should never be neglected, or let pass without minding, so, unless the will mix with them, they should never be exaggerated, or very sharply reprov'd; but with a gentle hand set right, as time and age permit. By this means, children will come to see what 'tis in any miscarriage that is chiefly offensive, and so learn to avoid it. This will encourage them to keep their wills right; which is the great business, when they find that it preserves them from any great displeasure, and that in all their other failings they meet with the kind concern and help, rather than the anger and passionate reproaches of their tutor and parents. Keep them from vice and vicious dispositions, and such a kind of behaviour in general will come with every degree of their age, as is suitable to that age and the company they ordinarily converse with; and as they grow in years, they will grow in attention and application. But that your words may always carry weight and authority with them, if it shall happen, upon any occasion, that you bid him leave off the doing of any even childish things, you must be sure to carry the point, and not let him have the mastery. But yet, I say, I would have the father seldom interpose his authority and command in these cases, or in any other, but such as have a tendency to vicious habits. I think there are better ways of prevailing with them: and a gentle persuasion in reasoning, (when the first point of submission to your will is got) will most times do much better.

§81. It will perhaps be wonder'd, that I mention *reasoning* with children; and yet I cannot but think that the true way of dealing with them. They understand it as early as

they do language; and, if I misobserve not, they love to be
treated as rational creatures, sooner than is imagin'd. 'Tis
a pride should be cherish'd in them, and, as much as can
be, made the greatest instrument to turn them by.

But when I talk of *reasoning,* I do not intend any other
but such as is suited to the child's capacity and apprehension. No body can think a boy of three or seven years
old should be argu'd with as a grown man. Long discourses, and philosophical reasonings, at best, amaze and
confound, but do not instruct children. When I say, therefore, that they must be *treated as rational creatures,* I mean
that you should make them sensible, by the mildness of your
carriage, and the composure even in your correction of them,
that what you do is reasonable in you, and useful and necessary for them; and that it is not out of *caprichio,* passion
or fancy, that you command or forbid them any thing. This
they are capable of understanding; and there is no virtue
they should be excited to, nor fault they should be kept from,
which I do not think they may be convinced of; but it must
be by such *reasons* as their age and understandings are capable of, and those propos'd always *in* very *few and plain
words.* The foundations on which several duties are built,
and the fountains of right and Wrong from which they
spring, are not perhaps easily to be let into the minds of
grown men, not us'd to abstract their thoughts from common receiv'd opinions. Much less are children capable of
*reasonings* from remote principles. They cannot conceive
the force of long deductions. The *reasons* that move them
must be *obvious,* and level to their thoughts, and such as may
(if I may so say) be felt and touch'd. But yet, if their
age, temper, and inclination be consider'd, there will never
want such motives as may be sufficient to convince them.
If there be no other more particular, yet these will always
be intelligible, and of force, to deter them from any fault
fit to be taken notice of in them, (*viz.*) That it will be a
discredit and disgrace to them, and displease you.

§ 82. But of all the ways whereby children are to be instructed, and their manners formed, the plainest, easiest, and
most efficacious, is, to set before their eyes the *examples* of
those things you would have them do, or avoid; which, when

they are pointed out to them, in the practice of persons within their knowledge, with some reflections on their beauty and unbecomingness, are of more force to draw or deter their imitation, than any discourses which can be made to them. Virtues and vices can by no words be so plainly set before their understandings as the actions of other men will shew them, when you direct their observation, and bid them view this or that good or bad quality in their practice. And the beauty or uncomeliness of many things, in good and ill breeding, will be better learnt, and make deeper impressions on them, in the *examples* of others, than from any rules or instructions can be given about them.

This is a method to be us'd, not only whilst they are young, but to be continu'd even as long as they shall be under another's tuition or conduct; nay, I know not whether it be not the best way to be us'd by a father, as long as he shall think fit, on any occasion, to reform any thing he wishes mended in his son; nothing sinking so gently, and so deep, into men's minds, as *example*. And what ill they either overlook or indulge in themselves, they cannot but dislike and be asham'd of, when it is set before them in another.

§ 83. It may be doubted, concerning *whipping,* when as the last remedy, it comes to be necessary, at what times, and by whom it should be done; whether presently upon the committing the fault, whilst it is yet fresh and hot; and whether parents themselves should beat their children. As to the first, I think it should *not* be done *presently,* lest passion mingle with it; and so, though it exceed the just proportion, yet it lose of its due weight: for even children discern when we do things in passion. But, as I said before, that has most weight with them, that appears sedately to come from their parents' reason; and they are not without this distinction. Next, if you have any discreet servant capable of it, and has the place of governing your child (for if you have a tutor, there is no doubt) I think it is best the *smart* should come immediately *from another's hand,* though by the parent's order, who should see it done; whereby the parent's authority will be preserv'd, and the child's aversion, for the pain it suffers, rather to be turn'd on the person that immediately inflicts. For I would have a *father seldom strike his child,* but upon very urgent necessity, and as the last remedy; and then perhaps it will be fit to do it so that the child should not quickly forget it.

§ 84. But, as I said before, *beating* is the worst, and therefore the last means to be us'd in the correction of children, and that only in cases of extremity, after all gentle ways have been try'd, and prov'd unsuccessful; which, if well observ'd, there will be very seldom any need of blows. For, it not being to be imagin'd that a child will often, if ever, dispute his father's present command in any particular instance, and the father not interposing his absolute authority, in peremptory rules, concerning either childish or indifferent actions, wherein his son is to have his liberty, or concerning his learning or improvement, wherein there is no compulsion to be us'd: there remains only the prohibition of some vicious actions, wherein a child is capable of *obstinacy,* and consequently can deserve beating; and so there will be but very few occasions of that discipline to be us'd by any one who considers well and orders his child's education as it should be. For the first seven years, what vices can a child be guilty of, but lying or some ill-natur'd tricks; the repeated commission whereof, after his father's direct command against it, shall bring him into the condemnation of *obstinacy,* and the chastisement of the rod? If any vicious inclination in him be, in the first appearance and instances of it, treated as it should be, first with your wonder, and then, if returning again, a second time discountenanc'd with the severe brow of a father, tutor, and all about him, and a treatment suitable to the state of discredit before-mention'd; and this continu'd till he be made sensible and asham'd of his fault, I imagine there will be no need of any other correction, nor ever any occasion to come to blows. The necessity of such chastisement is usually the consequence only of former indulgences or neglects: If vicious inclinations were watch'd from the beginning, and the first irregularities which they cause, corrected by those gentler ways, we should seldom have to do with more than one disorder at once; which would be easily set right without any stir or noise, and not require so harsh a discipline as beating. Thus one by one as they appear'd, they might all be weeded out, without any signs or memory that ever they had been there. But we letting their faults (by indulging and humouring our little ones) grow up, till they are sturdy and numerous, and the deformity of them makes us asham'd and uneasy, we are fain to come to the plough and the harrow; the spade and the pick-ax must go deep to come at the roots; and all the force, skill, and diligence we can use, is scarce enough to cleanse the vitiated seed-plat, overgrown with weeds, and restore us the hopes of fruits, to reward our pains in its season.

§ 85. This course, if observ'd, will spare both father and child the trouble of repeated injunctions, and multiply'd rules of doing and forbearing. For I am of opinion, that of those actions which tend to vicious habits, (which are those alone that a father should interpose his authority and commands in) none should be forbidden children till they are found guilty of them. For such untimely prohibitions, if they do nothing worse, do at least so much towards teaching and allowing 'em, that they suppose that children may be guilty of them, who would possibly be safer in the ignorance of any such faults. And the best remedy to stop them, is, as I have said, to shew *wonder* and *amazement* at any such action as hath a vicious tendency, when it is first taken notice of in a child. For example, when he is first found in a lie, or any ill-natur'd trick, the first remedy should be, to talk to him of it as a *strange monstrous matter,* that it could not be imagin'd he would have done, and so shame him out of it.

§ 86. It will be ('tis like) objected, that whatsoever I fancy of the tractableness of children, and the prevalency of those softer ways of shame and commendation; yet there are many who will never apply themselves to their books, and to what they ought to learn, unless they are scourg'd to it. This, I fear, is nothing but the language of ordinary schools and fashion, which have never suffer'd the other to be try'd as it should be, in places where it could be taken notice of. *Why,* else, *does the learning of* Latin *and* Greek *need the rod, when* French *and* Italian *need it not?* Children learn to dance and fence without whipping; nay, Arithmetick, drawing, &c. they apply themselves well enough to without beating: which would make one suspect, that there is something strange, unnatural, and disagreeable to that Age, in the things required in grammar-schools, or in the methods us'd there, that children cannot be brought to, without the severity of the lash, and hardly with that too; or else, that it is a mistake, that those tongues could not be taught them without beating.

§ 87. But let us suppose some so negligent or idle, that they will not be brought to learn by the gentle ways pro- pos'd, (for we must grant, that there will be children found of all tempers,) yet it does not thence follow, that the rough discipline of the cudgel is to be us'd to all. Nor can any one be concluded unmanageable by the *milder methods* of government, till they have been *throughly try'd* upon him; and if they will not prevail with him to use his en- deavours, and do what is in his power to do, we make no excuses for the obstinate. Blows are the proper remedies for those; but blows laid on in a way different from the ordinary. He that wilfully neglects his book, and stub- bornly refuses any thing he can do, requir'd of him by his father, expressing himself in a positive serious command, should not be corrected with two or three angry lashes, for not performing his task, and the same punishment repeated again and again upon every the like default; but when it is brought to that pass, that wilfulness evidently shews itself, and makes blows necessary, I think the chastisement should be a little more sedate, and a little more severe, and the whipping (mingled with admonition between) so continu'd, till the impressions of it on the mind were found legible in the face, voice, and submission of the child, not so sensible of the smart as of the fault he has been guilty of, and melting in true sorrow under it. If such a correction as this, try'd some few times at fit distances, and carry'd to the utmost severity, with the visible displeasure of the father all the while, will not work the effect, turn the mind, and pro- duce a future compliance, what can be hop'd from *blows,* and to what purpose should they be any more us'd?   *Beating,* when you can expect no good from it, will look more like the fury of an enrag'd enemy, than the good-will of a compassionate friend; and such chastisement carries with it only provocation, without any prospect of amendment. If it be any father's misfortune to have a son thus perverse and untractable, I know not what more he can do but pray for him. But, I imagine, if a right course be taken with children from the beginning, very few will be found to be such; and when there are any such instances, they are not to be the rule for the education of those who are better natur'd, and may be manag'd with better usage.

§ 88. If a *tutor* can be got, that, thinking himself in the father's place, charg'd with his care, and relishing these things, will at the beginning apply himself to put them in practice, he will afterwards find his work very easy; and you will, I guess, have your son in a little time a greater proficient in both learning and breeding than perhaps you imagine. But let him by no means beat him at any time without your consent and direction; at least till you have experience of his discretion and temper. But yet, to keep up his authority with his pupil, besides concealing that he has not the power of the rod, you must be sure to use him with great respect yourself, and cause all your family to do so too: for you cannot expect your son should have any regard for one whom he sees you, or his mother, or others slight. If you think him worthy of contempt, you have chosen amiss; and if you shew any contempt of him, he will hardly escape it from your son: and whenever that happens, whatever worth he may have in himself, and abilities for this employment, they are all lost to your child, and can afterwards never be made useful to him.

§ 89. As the father's example must teach the child respect for his tutor, so the tutor's example must lead the child into those actions he would have him do. His practice must by no means cross his precepts, unless he intend to set him wrong. It will be to no purpose for the tutor to talk of the restraint of the passions whilst any of his own are let loose; and he will in vain endeavour to reform any vice or indecency in his pupil, which he allows in himself. Ill patterns are sure to be follow'd more than good rules; and therefore he must always carefully preserve him from the influence of ill precedents, especially the most dangerous of all, the examples of the servants; from whose company he is to be kept, not by prohibitions, for that will but give him an itch after it, but by other ways I have mention'd.

§ 90. In all the whole business of education, there is nothing like to be less hearken'd to, or harder to be well observ'd, than what I am now going to say; and that is, that children should, from their first beginning to talk, have some *discreet, sober,* nay, *wise* person about them, whose care it should be to fashion them aright, and keep them from all ill, especially the infection of bad company. I think this province requires great *sobriety, temperance, tenderness, diligence,* and *discretion;* qualities hardly to be found united in persons that are to be had for ordinary salaries, nor easily to be found any where. As to the charge of it, I think it will be the money best laid out that can be, about our children; and therefore, though it may be expensive more than is ordinary, yet it cannot be thought dear. He that at any rate procures his child a good mind, well-principled, temper'd to virtue and usefulness, and adorn'd with civility and good breeding, makes a better purchase for him than if he laid out the money for an addition of more earth to his former acres. Spare it in toys and play-games, in silk and ribbons, laces, and other useless expenses, as much as you please; but be not sparing in so necessary a part as this. 'Tis not good husbandry to make his fortune rich, and his mind poor. I have often with great admiration seen people lavish it profusely in tricking up their children in fine clothes, lodging and feeding them sumptuously, allowing them more than enough of useless servants, and yet at the same time starve their minds, and not take sufficient care to cover that which is the most shameful nakedness, *viz.* their natural wrong inclinations and ignorance. This I can look on as no other than a sacrificing to their own vanity, it shewing more their pride than true care of the good of their children; whatsoever you employ to the advantage of your son's mind, will shew your true kindness, tho' it be to the lessening of his estate. A wise and good man can hardly want either the opinion or reality of being great and happy; but he that is foolish or vicious, can be neither great nor happy, what estate soever you leave him: and I ask you, whether there be not men in the world, whom you had rather have your son be with five hundred pounds *per annum,* than some other you know with five thousand pounds.

§ 91. The consideration of charge ought not therefore to deter those who are able. The great difficulty will be where to find a *proper person:* for those of small age, parts, and virtue, are unfit for this employment, and those that have greater, will hardly be got to undertake such a charge. You must therefore look out early, and enquire every where; for the world has people of all sorts. And I remember, *Montaigne* says in one of his essays, that the learned *Castalio* was fain to make trenchers at *Basle,* to keep himself from starving, when his father would have given any money for such a tutor for his son, and *Castalio* have willingly embrac'd such an employment upon very reasonable terms; but this was for want of intelligence.

§ 92. If you find it difficult to meet with such a tutor as we desire, you are not to wonder. I only can say, spare no care nor cost to get such an one. All things are to be had that way: and I dare assure you, that if you can get a good one, you will never repent the charge; but will always have the satisfaction to think it the money of all other the best laid out. But be sure take no body upon friends, or charity, no, nor upon great commendations. Nay, if you will do as you ought, the reputation of a sober man, with a good stock of learning, (which is all usually requir'd in a tutor) will not be enough to serve your turn. In this choice be as curious as you would be in that of a wife for him; for you must not think of trial or changing afterwards: This will cause great inconvenience to you, and greater to your son. When I consider the scruples and cautions I here lay in your way, methinks it looks as if I advis'd you to something which I would have offer'd at, but in effect not done. But he that shall consider how much the business of a tutor, rightly employ'd, lies out of the road, and how remote it is from the thoughts of many, even of those who propose to themselves this employment, will perhaps be of my mind, that one fit to educate and form the mind of a young gentleman is not every where to be found, and that more than ordinary care is to be taken in the choice of him, or else you may fail of your end.

§ 93. The character of a sober man and a scholar is, as I have above observ'd, what every one expects in a tutor. This generally is thought enough, and is all that parents commonly look for: But when such an one has empty'd out into his pupil all the Latin and logick he has brought from the university, will that furniture make him a fine gentleman? Or can it be expected, that he should be better bred, better skill'd in the world, better principled in the grounds and foundations of true virtue and generosity, than his young *tutor* is?

To form a young gentleman as he should be, 'tis fit his *governor* should himself be well-bred, understanding the ways of carriage and measures of civility in all the variety of persons, times, and places; and keep his pupil, as much as his age requires, constantly to the observation of them. This is an art not to be learnt nor taught by books. Nothing can give it but good company and observation join'd together. The taylor may make his clothes modish, and the dancing-master give fashion to his motions; yet neither of these, tho' they set off well, make a well-bred gentleman: no, tho' he have learning to boot, which, if not well manag'd, makes him more impertinent and intolerable in conversation. Breeding is that which sets a gloss upon all his other good qualities, and renders them useful to him, in procuring him the esteem and good-will of all that he comes near. Without good breeding his other accomplishments make him pass but for proud, conceited, vain, or foolish.

Courage in an ill-bred man has the air and escapes not the opinion of brutality: Learning becomes pedantry; wit, buffoonery; plainness, rusticity; good nature, fawning. And there cannot be a good quality in him, which want of breeding will not warp and disfigure to his disadvantage. Nay, virtue and parts, though they are allow'd their due commendation, yet are not enough to procure a man a good reception, and make him welcome wherever he comes. No body contents himself with rough diamonds, and wears them so, who would appear with advantage. When they are polish'd and set, then they give a lustre. Good qualities are the substantial riches of the mind, but 'tis good breeding sets them off: and he that will be acceptable, must give beauty, as well as strength, to his actions. Solidity, or even usefulness, is not enough: a graceful way and fashion in every thing, is that which gives the ornament and liking. And in most cases, the manner of doing is of more consequence than the thing done; and upon that depends the satisfaction or disgust wherewith it is receiv'd. This therefore, which lies not in the putting off the hat, nor making of compliments, but in a due and free composure of language, looks, motion, posture, place, &c. suited to persons and occasions, and can be learn'd only by habit and use, though it be above the capacity of children, and little ones should not be perplex'd about it, yet it ought to be begun and in a good measure learn'd by a young gentleman whilst he is under a tutor, before he comes into the world upon his own legs: for then usually it is too late to hope to reform several habitual indecencies, which lie in little things. For the carriage is not as it should be, till it is become natural in every part, falling, as skilful musicians' fingers do, into harmonious order without care and without thought. If in conversation a man's mind be taken up with a solicitous watchfulness about any part of his behaviour; instead of being mended by it, it will be constrain'd, uneasy, and ungraceful.

Besides, this part is most necessary to be form'd by the hand and care of a *governor*, because, though the errors committed in breeding are the first that are taken notice of by others, yet they are the last that any one is told of; not but that the malice of the world is forward enough to tattle of them; but it is always out of his hearing, who should make profit of their judgment and reform himself by their censure. And indeed, this is so nice a point to be meddled with, that even those who are friends, and wish it were mended, scarce ever dare mention it, and tell those they love that they are guilty in such or such cases of ill breeding. Errors in other things may often with civility be shewn another; and 'tis no breach of good manners or friendship to set him right in other mistakes; but good breeding itself allows not a man to touch upon this, or to

insinuate to another that he is guilty of want of breeding.
Such information can come only from those who have
authority over them; and from them too it comes very
hardly and harshly to a grown man; and however soften'd,
goes but ill down with any one who has liv'd ever so little
in the world. Wherefore it is necessary that this part
should be the *governor's* principal care, that an habitual
gracefulness, and politeness in all his carriage, may be
settled in his charge, as much as may be, before he goes
out of his hands; and that he may not need advice in this
point when he has neither time nor disposition to receive
it, nor has any body left to give it him. The *tutor* therefore
ought in the first place to be well-bred: and a young gentleman, who gets this one qualification from his *governor,*
sets out with great advantage, and will find that this one
accomplishment will more open his way to him, get him
more friends, and carry him farther in the world, than all
the hard words or real knowledge he has got from the
liberal arts, or his *tutor's* learned *encyclopaedia:* not that
those should be neglected, but by no means preferr'd, or
suffer'd to thrust out the other.

§ 94. Besides being well-bred, the *tutor* should know
the world well; the ways, the humours, the follies, the
cheats, the faults of the age he is fallen into, and particularly
of the country he lives in. These he should be able to
shew to his pupil, as he finds him capable; teach him skill
in men, and their manners; pull off the mask which their
several callings and pretences cover them with, and make
his pupil discern what lies at the bottom under such appearances, that he may not, as unexperienc'd young men are
apt to do if they are unwarn'd, take one thing for another,
judge by the outside, and give himself up to shew, and the in-
sinuation of a fair carriage, or an obliging application. A
governor should teach his scholar to guess at and beware
of the designs of men he hath to do with, neither with too
much suspicion, nor too much confidence; but as the young
man is by nature most inclin'd to either side, rectify him,
and bend him the other way. He should accustom him to
make, as much as is possible, a true judgment of men by
those marks which serve best to shew what they are, and

give a prospect into their inside, which often shows itself in little things, especially when they are not in parade, and upon their guard. He should acquaint him with the true state of the world, and dispose him to think no man better or worse, wiser or foolisher, than he really is. Thus, by safe and insensible degrees, he will pass from a boy to a man; which is the most hazardous step in all the whole course of life. This therefore should be carefully watch'd, and a young man with great diligence handed over it; and not as now usually is done, be taken from a *governor's* conduct, and all at once thrown into the world under his own, not without manifest dangers of immediate spoiling; there being nothing more frequent than instances of the great looseness, extravagancy, and debauchery, which young men have run into as soon as they have been let loose from a severe and strict education: Which I think may be chiefly imputed to their wrong way of breeding, especially in this part; for having been bred up in a great ignorance of what the world truly is, and finding it a quite other thing, when they come into it, than what they were taught it should be, and so imagin'd it was, are easily persuaded, by other kind of tutors, which they are sure to meet with, that the discipline they were kept under, and the lectures read to them, were but the formalities of education and the restraints of childhood; that the freedom belonging to men is to take their swing in a full enjoyment of what was before forbidden them. They shew the young novice the world full of fashionable and glittering examples of this every where, and he is presently dazzled with them. My young master failing not to be willing to shew himself a man, as much as any of the sparks of his years, lets himself loose to all the irregularities he finds in the most debauch'd; and thus courts credit and manliness in the casting off the modesty and sobriety he has till then been kept in; and thinks it brave, at his first setting out, to signalize himself in running counter to all the rules of virtue which have been preach'd to him by his tutor.

The shewing him the world as really it is, before he comes wholly into it, is one of the best means, I think, to prevent this mischief. He should by degrees be informed of the vices in fashion, and warned of the applications and designs of those who will make it their business to corrupt him. He should be told the arts they use, and the trains they lay; and now and then have set before him the tragical or ridiculous examples of those who are ruining or ruin'd this way. The age is not like to want instances of this kind, which should be made land-marks to him, that by the disgraces, diseases, beggary, and shame of hopeful young men thus brought to ruin, he may be precaution'd, and be made see, how those join in the contempt and neglect of them that are undone, who, by pretences of friendship and respect, lead them to it, and help to prey upon them whilst they were undoing; that he may see, before he buys it by a too dear experience, that those who persuade him not to follow the sober advices he has receiv'd from his *governors,* and the counsel of his own reason, which they call being govern'd by others, do it only that they may have the government of him themselves; and make him believe, he goes like a man of himself, by his own conduct, and for his own pleasure, when in truth he is wholly as a child led by them into those vices which best serve their purposes. This is a knowledge which, upon all occasions, a *tutor* should endeavour to instil, and by all methods try to make him comprehend, and thoroughly relish.

I know it is often said, that to discover to a young man the vices of the age is to teach them him. That, I confess, is a good deal so, according as it is done; and therefore requires a discreet man of parts, who knows the world, and can judge of the temper, inclination, and weak side of his pupil. This farther is to be remember'd, that it is not possible now (as perhaps formerly it was) to keep a young gentleman from vice by a total ignorance of it, unless you will all his life mew him up in a closet, and never let him go into company. The longer he is kept thus hoodwink'd, the less he will see when he comes abroad into open daylight, and be the more expos'd to be a prey to himself and others. And an old boy, at his first appearance, with all the gravity of his ivy-bush about him, is sure to draw on him the eyes and chirping of the whole town volery; amongst which there will not be wanting some birds of prey, that will presently be on the wing for him.

The only fence against the world, is, a thorough knowledge of it, into which a young gentleman should be enter'd by degrees, as he can bear it; and the earlier the better, so he be in safe and skilful hands to guide him. The scene should be gently open'd, and his entrance made step by step, and the dangers pointed out that attend him from the several degrees, tempers, designs, and clubs of men. He should be prepar'd to be shock'd by some, and caress'd by others; warn'd who are like to oppose, who to mislead, who to undermine him, and who to serve him. He should be instructed how to know and distinguish them; where he should let them see, and when dissemble the knowledge of them and their aims and workings. And if he be too forward to venture upon his own strength and skill, the perplexity and trouble of a misadventure now and then, that reaches not his innocence, his health, or reputation, may not be an ill way to teach him more caution.

This, I confess, containing one great part of wisdom, is not the product of some superficial thoughts, or much reading; but the effect of experience and observation in a man who has liv'd in the world with his eyes open, and convers'd with men of all sorts. And therefore I think it of most value to be instill'd into a young man upon all occasions which offer themselves, that when he comes to launch into the deep himself, he may not be like one at sea without a line, compass or sea-chart; but may have some notice before-hand of the rocks and shoals, the currents and quicksands, and know a little how to steer, that he sink not before he get experience. He that thinks not this of more moment to his son, and for which he more needs a governor, than the languages and learned sciences, forgets of how much more use it is to judge right of men, and manage his affairs wisely with them, than to speak *Greek* and *Latin,* or argue in mood and figure; or to have his head fill'd with the abstruse speculations of natural philosophy and metaphysicks; nay, than to be well vers'd in *Greek* and *Roman* writers, though that be much better for a gentleman than to be a good Peripatetick or Cartesian, because those antient authors observ'd and painted mankind well, and give the best light into that kind of knowledge. He that goes into the eastern parts of *Asia,* will find able and acceptable men without any of these; but without virtue, knowledge of the world, and civility, an accomplish'd and valuable man can be found no where.

A great part of the learning now in fashion in the schools of *Europe,* and that goes ordinarily into the round of education, a gentleman may in a good measure be unfurnish'd with, without any great disparagement to himself or prejudice to his affairs. But prudence and good breeding are in all the stations and occurrences of life necessary; and most young men suffer in the want of them, and come rawer and more awkward into the world than they should, for this very reason, because these qualities, which are of all other the most necessary to be taught, and stand most in need of the assistance and help of a teacher, are generally neglected and thought but a slight or no part of a *tutor's* business. *Latin* and learning make all the noise; and the main stress is laid upon his proficiency in things a great part whereof belong not to a gentleman's calling; which is to have the knowledge of a man of business, a carriage suitable to his rank, and to be eminent and useful in his country, according to his station. Whenever either spare hours from that, or an inclination to perfect himself in some parts of knowledge, which his *tutor* did but just enter him in, set him upon any study, the first rudiments of it, which he learn'd before, will open the way enough for his own industry to carry him as far as his fancy will prompt, or his parts enable him to go. Or, if he thinks it may save his time and pains to be help'd over some difficulties by the hand of a master, he may then take a man that is perfectly well skilled in it, or chuse such an one as he thinks fittest for his purpose. But to initiate his pupil in any part of learning, as far as is necessary for a young man in the ordinary course of his studies, an ordinary skill in the *governor* is enough. Nor is it requisite that he should be a thorough scholar, or possess in perfection all those sciences which 'tis convenient a young gentleman should have a taste of in some general view, or short system. A gentleman that would penetrate deeper must do it by his own genius and industry afterwards: For no body ever went far in knowledge, or became eminent in any of the sciences, by the discipline and constraint of a master.

The great work of a *governor*, is to fashion the carriage, and form the mind; to settle in his pupil good habits and the principles of virtue and wisdom; to give him by little and little a view of mankind, and work him into a love and imitation of what is excellent and praise-worthy; and, in the prosecution of it, to give him vigour, activity, and industry. The studies which he sets him upon, are but as it were the exercises of his faculties, and employment of his time, to keep him from sauntering and idleness, to teach him application, and accustom him to take pains, and to give him some little taste of what his own industry must perfect. For who expects, that under a *tutor* a young gentleman should be an accomplish'd critick, orator, or logician? go to the bottom of metaphysicks, natural philosophy, or mathematicks? or be a master in history or chronology? though something of each of these is to be taught him: But it is only to open the door, that he may look in, and as it were begin an acquaintance, but not to dwell there: And a *governor* would be much blam'd that should keep his pupil too long, and lead him too far in most of them. But of good breeding, knowledge of the world, virtue, industry, and a love of reputation, he cannot have too much: And if he have these, he will not long want what he needs or desires of the other.

And since it cannot be hop'd he should have time and strength to learn all things, most pains should be taken about that which is most necessary; and that principally look'd after which will be of most and frequentest use to him in the world.

*Seneca* complains of the contrary practice in his time; and yet the *Burgursdicius's* and the *Scheiblers* did not swarm in those days as they do now in these. What would he have thought if he had liv'd now, when the *tutors* think it their great business to fill the studies and heads of their pupils with such authors as these? He would have had much more reason to say, as he does, *non vitæ sed scholæ discimus,* we learn not to live, but to dispute; and our education fits us rather for the university than the world. But 'tis no wonder if those who make the fashion suit it to what they have, and not to what their pupils want. The fashion being once establish'd, who can think it strange, that in this, as well as in all other things, it should prevail? And that the greatest part of those, who find their account in an easy submission to it, should be ready to cry out, *Heresy,* when any one departs from it? 'Tis nevertheless matter of astonishment that men of quality and parts should suffer themselves to be so far misled by custom and implicit faith. Reason, if consulted with, would advise, that their children's time should be spent in acquiring what might be useful to them when they come to be men, rather than to have their heads stuff'd with a deal of trash, a great part whereof they usually never do ('tis certain they never need to) think on again as long as they live; and so much of it as does stick by them they are only the worse for. This is so well known, that I appeal to parents themselves, who have been at cost to have their young heirs taught it, whether it be not ridiculous for their sons to have any tincture of that sort of learning, when they come abroad into the world? whether any appearance of it would not lessen and disgrace them in company? And that certainly must be an admirable acquisition, and deserves well to make a part in education, which men are asham'd of where they are most concern'd to shew their parts and breeding.

There is yet another reason why politeness of manners, and knowledge of the world should principally be look'd after in a *tutor;* and that is, because a man of parts and years may enter a lad far enough in any of those sciences, which he has no deep insight into himself. Books in these will be able to furnish him, and give him light and precedency enough to go before a young follower: but he will never be able to set another right in the knowledge of the world, and above all in breeding, who is a novice in them himself.

This is a knowledge he must have about him, worn into him by use and conversation and a long forming himself

by what he has observ'd to be practis'd and allow'd in the
best company. This, if he has it not of his own, is no
where to be borrowed for the use of his pupil; or if he
could find pertinent treatises of it in books that would
reach all the particulars of an *English* gentleman's behaviour, his own ill-fashion'd example, if he be not well-bred
himself, would spoil all his lectures; it being impossible,
that any one should come forth well-fashion'd out of un-
polish'd, ill-bred company.

I say this, not that I think such a *tutor* is every day to
be met with, or to be had at the ordinary rates; but that
those who are able, may not be sparing of enquiry or cost
in what is of so great moment; and that other parents,
whose estates will not reach to greater salaries, may yet
remember what they should principally have an eye to in
the choice of one to whom they would commit the education of their children; and what part they should chiefly
look after themselves, whilst they are under their care, and
as often as they come within their observation; and not
think that all lies in *Latin* and *French* or some dry systems
of logick and philosophy.

§ 95. But to return to our method again. Though I
have mention'd the severity of the father's brow, and the
awe settled thereby in the mind of children when young,
as one main instrument whereby their education is to be
manag'd; yet I am far from being of an opinion that it
should be continu'd all along to them, whilst they are under
the discipline and government of pupilage; I think it should
be relax'd, as fast as their age, discretion and good behaviour could allow it; even to that degree, that a father
will do well, as his son grows up, and is capable of it,
to *talk familiarly* with him; nay, *ask his advice, and consult*
with him about those things wherein he has any knowledge
or understanding. By this, the father will gain two things,
both of great moment. The one is, that it will put serious
considerations into his son's thoughts, better than any rules
or advices he can give him. The sooner you *treat him as
a man,* the sooner he will begin to be one: and if you admit
him into serious discourses sometimes with you, you will
insensibly raise his mind above the usual amusements of

youth, and those trifling occupations which it is commonly wasted in. For it is easy to observe, that **many** young men continue longer in the thought and conversation of school-boys than otherwise they would, because their parents keep them at that distance, and in that low rank, by all their carriage to them.

§ 96. Another thing of greater consequence, which you will obtain by such a way of treating him, will be *his friendship*. Many fathers, though they proportion to their sons liberal allowances, according to their age and condition, yet they keep the knowledge of their estates and concerns from them with as much reservedness as if they were guarding a secret of state from a spy or an enemy. This, if it looks not like jealousy, yet it wants those marks of kindness and intimacy which a father should shew to his son, and no doubt often hinders or abates that chearfulness and satisfaction wherewith a son should address himself to and rely upon his father. And I cannot but often wonder to see fathers who love their sons very well, yet so order the matter by a constant stiffness and a mien of authority and distance to them all their lives, as if they were never to enjoy, or have any comfort from those they love best in the world, till they had lost them by being remov'd into another. Nothing cements and establishes friendship and good-will so much as *confident communication* of concernments and affairs. Other kindnesses, without this, leave still some doubts: but when your son sees you open your mind to him, when he finds that you interest him in your affairs, as things you are willing should in their turn come into his hands, he will be concern'd for them as for his own, wait his season with patience, and love you in the mean time, who keep him not at the distance of a stranger. This will also make him see, that the enjoyment you have, is not without care; which the more he is sensible of, the less will he envy you the possession, and the more think himself happy under the management of so favourable a friend and so careful a father. There is scarce any young man of so little thought, or so void of sense, that would not be glad of a *sure friend*, that he might have recourse to, and freely consult on occasion. The reservedness and distance that fathers keep, often deprive their sons of that refuge which would be of more advantage to them than an hundred rebukes and chidings. Would your son engage in some frolick, or take a vagary, were it not much better he should do it with, than without your knowledge? For since allowances for such things must be made to young men, the more you know of his intrigues and designs, the better will you be able to prevent great mischiefs; and by letting him see what is like to follow, take the right way of prevailing with him to avoid less inconveniences. Would you have him open his heart to you, and ask your advice? you must begin to do so with him first, and by your carriage beget that confidence.

§ 97. But whatever he consults you about, unless it lead to some fatal and irremediable mischief, be sure you advise only as a friend of more experience; but with your advice mingle nothing of command or authority, nor more than you would to your equal or a stranger. That would be to drive him for ever from any farther demanding, or receiving advantage from your counsel. You must consider that he is a young man, and has pleasures and fancies which you are pass'd. You must not expect his inclination should be just as yours, nor that at twenty he should have the same thoughts you have at fifty. All that you can wish, is, that since youth must have some liberty, some outleaps, they might be with the ingenuity of a son, and *under the eye of a father,* and then no very great harm can come of it. The way to obtain this, as I said before, is (according as you find him capable) to talk with him about your affairs, propose matters to him *familiarly,* and ask his advice; and when he ever lights on the right, follow it as his; and if it succeed well, let him have the commendation. This will not at all lessen your authority, but increase his love and esteem of you. Whilst you keep your estate, the staff will be in your own hands; and your authority the surer, the more it is strengthen'd with *confidence* and *kindness.* For you have not that power you ought to have over him, till he comes to be more afraid of offending so good a friend than of losing some part of his future expectation.

§ 98. Familiarity of discourse, if it can become a father to his son, may much more be condescended to by a tutor to his pupil. All their time together should not be spent in reading of lectures, and magisterially dictating to him what he is to observe and follow. Hearing him in his turn, and using him to reason about what is propos'd, will make the rules go down the easier and sink the deeper, and will give him a liking to study and instruction: And he will then begin to value knowledge, when he sees that it enables him to discourse, and he finds the pleasure and credit of bearing a part in the conversation, and of having his reasons sometimes approv'd and hearken'd to; particularly in morality, prudence, and breeding, cases should be put to him, and his judgment ask'd. This opens the understanding better than maxims, how well soever explain'd, and settles the rules better in the memory for practice. This way lets things into the mind which stick there, and retain their evidence with them; whereas words at best are faint representations, being not so much as the true shadows of things, and are much sooner forgotten. He will better comprehend the foundations and measures of decency and justice, and have livelier, and more lasting impressions of what he ought to do, by giving his opinion on cases propos'd, and reasoning with his tutor on fit instances, than by giving a silent, negligent, sleepy audience to his tutor's lectures; and much more than by captious logical disputes, or set declamations of his own, upon any question. The one sets the thoughts upon wit and false colours, and not upon truth; the other teaches fallacy, wrangling, and opiniatry; and they are both of them things that spoil the judgment, and put a man out of the way of right and fair reasoning; and therefore carefully to be avoided by one who would improve himself, and be acceptable to others.

§ 99. When by making your son sensible that he depends on you, and is in your power, you have established your authority; and by being inflexibly severe in your carriage to him when obstinately persisting in any illnatur'd trick which you have forbidden, especially lying, you have imprinted on his mind that awe which is necessary; and, on the other side, when (by permitting him the full liberty due to his age, and laying no restraint in your presence to those childish actions and gaiety of carriage, which, whilst he is very young, is as necessary to him as meat or sleep) you have reconcil'd him to your company, and made him sensible of your care and love of him, by indulgence and tenderness, especially caressing him on all occasions wherein he does any thing well, and being kind to him after a thousand fashions suitable to his age, which nature teaches parents better than I can: When, I say, by these ways of tenderness and affection, which parents never want for their children, you have also planted in him a particular affection for you; he is then in the state you could desire, and you have form'd in his mind that true *reverence* which is always afterwards carefully to be continu'd, and maintain'd in both parts of it, *love,* and *fear,* as the great principles whereby you will always have hold upon him, to turn his mind to the ways of virtue and honour.

§ 100. When this foundation is once well lay'd, and you find this reverence begin to work in him, the next thing to be done, is carefully to consider his *temper,* and the particular constitution of his mind. Stubbornness, lying, and ill-natur'd actions, are not (as has been said) to be permitted in him from the beginning, whatever his temper be. Those seeds of vices are not to be suffer'd to take any root, but must be carefully weeded out, as soon as ever they begin to shew themselves in him; and your authority is to take place and influence his mind, from the very dawning of any knowledge in him, that it may operate as a natural principle, whereof he never perceiv'd the beginning, never knew that it was, or could be otherwise. By this, if the *reverence* he owes you be establish'd early, it will always be sacred to him, and it will be as hard for him to resist as the principles of his nature.

§ 101. Having thus very early set up your authority, and by the gentler applications of it sham'd him out of what leads towards an immoral habit, as soon as you have observ'd it in him, (for I would by no means have chiding us'd, much less blows, till obstinacy and incorrigibleness make it absolutely necessary) it will be fit to consider which

way the natural make of his *mind inclines* him. Some
men by the unalterable frame of their constitutions, are
*stout,* others *timorous,* some *confident,* others *modest,
tractable,* or *obstinate, curious* or *careless, quick* or *slow.*
There are not more differences in men's faces, and the outward lineaments of their bodies, than there are in the makes
and tempers of their minds; only there is this difference,
that the distinguishing characters of the face, and the
lineaments of the body, grow more plain and visible with
time and age; but the peculiar *physiognomy of the mind* is
most discernible in children, before art and cunning have
taught them to hide their deformities, and conceal their ill
inclinations under a dissembled outside.

§ 102. Begin therefore betimes nicely to observe your
son's *temper;* and that, when he is under least restraint,
in his play, and as he thinks out of your sight. See what
are his *predominate passions* and *prevailing inclinations;*
whether he be fierce or mild, bold or bashful, compassionate
or cruel, open or reserv'd, &c. For as these are different in
him, so are your methods to be different, and your authority must hence take measures to apply itself different
ways to him. These *native propensities,* these prevalencies
of constitution, are not to be cur'd by rules, or a direct
contest, especially those of them that are the humbler
and meaner sort, which proceed from fear, and lowness of
spirit; though with art they may be much mended, and
turn'd to good purposes. But this, be sure, after all is
done, the byass will always hang on that side that nature
first plac'd it: And if you carefully observe the characters of his mind, now in the first scenes of his life, you
will ever after be able to judge which way his thoughts
lean, and what he aims at even hereafter, when, as he
grows up, the plot thickens, and he puts on several shapes
to act it.

§ 103. I told you before, that children love *liberty;* and
therefore they should be brought to do the things are fit
for them, without feeling any restraint laid upon them.
I now tell you, they love something more; and that is
*dominion*: And this is the first original of most vicious
habits, that are ordinary and natural. This love of *power*

and dominion shews itself very early, and that in these two things.

§ 104. 1. We see children, as soon almost as they are born (I am sure long before they can speak) cry, grow peevish, sullen, and out of humour, for nothing but to have their *wills*. They would have their desires submitted to by others; they contend for a ready compliance from all about them, especially from those that stand near or beneath them in age or degree, as soon as they come to consider others with those distinctions.

§ 105. 2. Another thing wherein they shew their love of dominion, is, their desire to have things to be theirs: They would have *propriety* and possession, pleasing themselves with the power which that seems to give, and the right they thereby have, to dispose of them as they please. He that has not observ'd these two humours working very betimes in children, has taken little notice of their actions: And he who thinks that these two roots of almost all the injustice and contention that so disturb human life, are not early to be weeded out, and contrary habits introduc'd, neglects the proper season to lay the foundations of a good and worthy man. To do this, I imagine these following things may somewhat conduce.

§ 106. 1. That a child should never be suffer'd to have what he *craves,* much less what he *cries for,* I had said, *or so much as speaks for*: But that being apt to be misunderstood, and interpreted as if I meant a child should never speak to his parents for any thing, which will perhaps be thought to lay too great a curb on the minds of children, to the prejudice of that love and affection which should be between them and their parents; I shall explain my self a little more particularly. It is fit that they should have liberty to declare their wants to their parents, and that with all tenderness they should be hearken'd to, and supply'd, at least whilst they are very little. But 'tis one thing to say, I am hungry, another to say, I would have roast-meat. Having declar'd their wants, their natural wants, the pain they feel from hunger, thirst, cold, or any other necessity of nature, 'tis the duty of their parents and those about them to relieve them: But children must leave

it to the choice and ordering of their parents, what they
think properest for them, and how much; and must not
be permitted to chuse for themselves, and say, I would
have wine, or white-bread; the very naming of it should
make them lose it.

§ 107. That which parents should take care of here, is
to distinguish between the wants of fancy, and those of
nature; which *Horace* has well taught them to do in this
verse:

> *Queis humana sibi doleat natura negatis.*

Those are truly natural wants, which reason alone, without some other help, is not able to fence against, nor
keep from disturbing us. The pains of sickness and hurts,
hunger, thirst, and cold, want of sleep and rest or relaxation of the part weary'd with labour, are what all men
feel and the best dispos'd minds cannot but be sensible of
their uneasiness; and therefore ought, by fit applications, to
seek their removal, though not with impatience, or over
great haste, upon the first approaches of them, where delay
does not threaten some irreparable harm. The pains that
come from the necessities of nature, are monitors to us to
beware of greater mischiefs, which they are the forerunners
of; and therefore they must not be wholly neglected, nor
strain'd too far. But yet the more children can be inur'd
to hardships of this kind, by a wise care to make them
stronger in body and mind, the better it will be for them.
I need not here give any caution to keep within the bounds
of doing them good, and to take care, that what children
are made to suffer, should neither break their spirits, nor
injure their health, parents being but too apt of themselves to incline more than they should to the softer side.

But whatever compliance the necessities of nature may
require, the wants of fancy children should never be gratify'd in, nor suffered to *mention*. The very *speaking* for
any such thing should make them lose it. Clothes, when
they need, they must have; but if they *speak* for this stuff
or that colour, they should be sure to go without it. Not
that I would have parents purposely cross the desires of
their children in matters of indifferency; on the contrary,

where their carriage deserves it, and one is sure it will not corrupt or effeminate their minds, and make them fond of trifles, I think all things should be contriv'd, as much as could be, to their satisfaction, that they may find the ease and pleasure of doing well. The best for children is that they should not place any pleasure in such things at all, nor regulate their delight by their fancies, but be indifferent to all that nature has made so. This is what their parents and teachers should chiefly aim at; but till this be obtain'd, all that I oppose here, is the liberty of *asking,* which in these things of conceit ought to be restrain'd by a constant forfeiture annex'd to it.

This may perhaps be thought a little too severe by the natural indulgence of tender parents; but yet it is no more than necessary: For since the method I propose is to banish the rod, this restraint of their tongues will be of great use to settle that awe we have elsewhere spoken of, and to keep up in them the respect and reverence due to their parents. Next, it will teach to keep in, and so master their inclinations. By this means they will be brought to learn the art of stifling their desires, as soon as they rise up in them, when they are easiest to be subdu'd. For giving vent, gives life and strength to our appetites; and he that has the confidence to turn his wishes into demands, will be but a little way from thinking he ought to obtain them. This, I am sure, every one can more easily bear a denial from himself, than from any body else. They should therefore be accustom'd betimes to consult, and make use of their reason, before they give allowance to their inclinations. 'Tis a great step towards the mastery of our desires, to give this stop to them, and shut them up in silence. This habit got by children, of staying the forwardness of their fancies, and deliberating whether it be fit or no, before they *speak,* will be of no small advantage to them in matters of greater consequence, in the future course of their lives. For that which I cannot too often inculcate, is, that whatever the matter be about which it is conversant, whether great or small, the main (I had almost said only) thing to be consider'd in every action of a child, is, what influence it will have upon his mind; what habit it tends

to, and is like to settle in him; how it will become him when
he is bigger; and if it be encourag'd, whither it will lead
him when he is grown up.

My meaning therefore is not, that children should purposely be made uneasy. This would relish too much of
inhumanity and ill nature, and be apt to infect them with
it. They should be brought to deny their appetites; and
their minds, as well as bodies, be made vigorous, easy,
and strong, by the custom of having their inclinations in
subjection, and their bodies exercis'd with hardships: But
all this, without giving them any mark or apprehension
of ill will towards them. The constant loss of what they
*crav'd* or *carv'd* to themselves, should teach them modesty,
submission, and a power to forbear: But the rewarding
their modesty, and silence, by giving them what they
lik'd, should also assure them of the love of those who
rigorously exacted this obedience. The contenting themselves now in the want of what they wish'd for, is a virtue
that another time should be rewarded with what is suited
and acceptable to them; which should be bestow'd on them
as if it were a natural consequence of their good behaviour,
and not a bargain about it. But you will lose your labour,
and what is more, their love and reverence too, if they
can receive from others what you deny them. This is
to be kept very staunch, and carefully to be watch'd. And
here the servants come again my way.

§ 108. If this be begun betimes, and they accustom themselves early to silence their desires, this useful habit will
settle them; and as they come to grow up in age and discretion, they may be allow'd greater liberty, when reason
comes to speak in 'em, and not passion: For whenever
reason would speak, it should be hearken'd to. But as
they should never be heard, when they speak for any particular thing they would *have,* unless it be first propos'd
to them; so they should always be heard, and fairly and
kindly answer'd, when they ask after any thing they would
*know,* and desire to be inform'd about. *Curiosity* should be
as carefully *cherish'd* in children, as other appetites suppress'd.

However strict an hand is to be kept upon all desires

of fancy, yet there is one case wherein fancy must be permitted to speak, and be hearken'd to also. *Recreation* is as necessary as labour or food. But because there can be no *recreation* without delight, which depends not always on reason, but oftner fancy, it must be permitted children not only to divert themselves, but to do it after their own fashion, provided it be innocently, and without prejudice to their health; and therefore in this case they should not be deny'd, if they proposed any particular kind of *recreation*. Tho' I think in a well-order'd education, they will seldom be brought to the necessity of asking any such liberty. Care should be taken, that what is of advantage to them, they should always do with delight; and before they are weary'd with one, they should be timely *diverted* to some other useful employment. But if they are not yet brought to that degree of perfection, that one way of improvement can be made a recreation to them, they must be let loose to the childish play they fancy; which they should be wean'd from by being made to surfeit of it: But from things of use, that they are employ'd in, they should always be sent away with an appetite; at least be dismiss'd before they are tir'd, and grow quite sick of it, that so they may return to it again, as to a pleasure that diverts them. For you must never think them set right, till they can find delight in the practice of laudable things; and the useful exercises of the body and mind, taking their turns, make their lives and improvement pleasant in a continu'd train of *recreations*, wherein the weary'd part is constantly reliev'd and refresh'd. Whether this can be done in every temper, or whether tutors and parents will be at the pains, and have the discretion and patience to bring them to this, I know not; but that it may be done in most children, if a right course be taken to raise in them the desire of credit, esteem, and reputation, I do not at all doubt. And when they have so much true life put into them, they may freely be talk'd with about what most *delights* them, and be directed or let loose to it; so that they may perceive that they are belov'd and cherish'd, and that those under whose tuition they are, are not enemies to their satisfaction. Such a management will make them in love with the hand that directs them, and the virtue they are directed to.

This farther advantage may be made by a free liberty permitted them in their *recreations,* that it will discover their natural tempers, shew their inclinations and aptitudes, and thereby direct wise parents in the choice both of the course of life and employment they shall design them for, and of fit remedies, in the mean time, to be apply'd to whatever bent of nature they may observe most likely to mislead any of their children.

§ 109. 2. Children who live together, often strive for mastery, whose wills shall carry it over the rest: whoever begins the *contest,* should be sure to be cross'd in it. But not only that, but they should be taught to have all the *deference, complaisance,* and *civility* one for the other imaginable. This, when they see it procures them respect, love and esteem, and that they lose no superiority by it, they will take more pleasure in, than in insolent domineering; for so plainly is the other.

The accusations of children one against another, which usually are but the clamours of anger and revenge desiring aid, should not be favourably received, nor hearken'd to. It weakens and effeminates their minds to suffer them to *complain;* and if they endure sometimes crossing or pain from others without being permitted to think it strange or intolerable, it will do them no harm to learn sufferance, and harden them early. But though you give no countenance to the *complaints* of the *querulous,* yet take care to curb the insolence and ill nature of the injurious. When you observe it your self, reprove it before the injur'd party: but if the *complaint* be of something really worth your notice, and prevention another time, then reprove the offender by himself alone, out of sight of him that complain'd and make him go and ask pardon, and make reparation: which coming thus, as it were from himself, will be the more chearfully performed, and more kindly receiv'd, the love strengthen'd between them, and a custom of civility grow familiar amongst your children.

§ 110. 3. As to the having and possessing of things, teach them to part with what they have, easily and freely to their friends, and let them find by experience that the most *liberal* has always the most plenty, with esteem and commendation to boot, and they will quickly learn to practise it. This I imagine, will make brothers and sisters kinder and civiller to one another, and consequently to others, than twenty rules about good manners, with which children are ordinarily perplex'd and cumber'd. Covetousness, and the desire of having in our possession, and under our dominion, more than we have need of, being the root of all evil, should be early and carefully weeded out, and the contrary quality of a readiness to impart to others, implanted. This should be encourag'd by great commendation and credit, and constantly taking care that he loses nothing by his *liberality*. Let all the instances he gives of such freeness be always repay'd, and with interest; and let him sensibly perceive, that the kindness he shews to others, is no ill husbandry for himself; but that it brings a return of kindness both from those that receive it, and those who look on. Make this a contest among children, who shall out-do one another this way: and by this means, by a constant practice, children having made it easy to themselves to part with what they have, good nature may be settled in them into an habit, and they may take pleasure, and pique themselves in being *kind, liberal and civil*, to others.

If liberality ought to be encourag'd certainly great care is to be taken that children transgress not the rules of *Justice:* and whenever they do, they should be set right, and if there be occasion for it, severely rebuk'd.

Our first actions being guided more by self-love than reason or reflection, 'tis no wonder that in children they should be very apt to deviate from the just measures of right and wrong; which are in the mind the result of improv'd reason and serious meditation. This the more they are apt to mistake, the more careful guard ought to be kept over them; and every the least slip in this great social virtue taken notice of, and rectify'd; and that in things of the least weight and moment, both to instruct their ignorance, and prevent ill habits; which from small beginnings in pins and cherry-stones, will, if let alone, grow up to higher frauds, and be in danger to end at last in down-right harden'd dishonesty. The first tendency to any *in-justice* that appears, must be suppress'd with a shew of wonder and abhorrence in the parents and governors. But because children cannot well comprehend what *injustice* is, till they understand property, and how particular persons come by it, the safest way to secure *honesty,* is to lay the foundations of it early in liberality, and an easiness to part with to others whatever they have or like themselves. This may be taught them early, before they have language and understanding enough to form distinct notions of prop-erty, and to know what is theirs by a peculiar right ex-clusive of others. And since children seldom have any thing but by gift, and that for the most part from their parents, they may be at first taught not to take or keep any thing but what is given them by those, whom they take to have power over it. And as their capacities enlarge, other rules and cases of *justice,* and rights concerning *Meum* and *Tuum,* may be propos'd and inculcated. If any act of *injustice* in them appears to proceed, not from mis-take, but a perverseness in their wills, when a gentle re-buke and shame will not reform this irregular and covetous inclination, rougher remedies must be apply'd: And 'tis but for the father and tutor to take and keep from them some-thing that they value and think their own, or order some-body else to do it; and by such instances, make them sensible what little advantage they are like to make by possessing themselves *unjustly* of what is another's, whilst there are in the world stronger and more men than they. But if an ingenuous detestation of this shameful vice be but carefully and early instill'd into 'em, as I think it may, that is the true and genuine method to obviate this crime, and will be a better guard against dishonesty than any con-siderations drawn from interest; habits working more con-stantly, and with greater facility, than reason, which, when we have most need of it, is seldom fairly consulted, and more rarely obey'd.

§ 111. *Crying* is a fault that should not be tolerated in children; not only for the unpleasant and unbecoming noise it fills the house with, but for more considerable reasons, in reference to the children themselves; which is to be our aim in education.

Their *crying* is of two sorts; either *stubborn* and *domineering,* or *querulous* and *whining.*

1. Their *crying* is very often a striving for mastery, and an open declaration of their insolence or obstinacy; when they have not the power to obtain their desire, they will, by their *clamour* and *sobbing,* maintain their title and right to it. This is an avow'd continuing their claim, and a sort of remonstrance against the oppression and injustice of those who deny them what they have a mind to.

§ 112. 2. Sometimes their *crying* is the effect of pain, or true sorrow, and a *bemoaning* themselves under it.

These two, if carefully observ'd, may, by the mien, looks, actions, and particularly by the tone of their crying be easily distinguished; but neither of them must be suffer'd, much less encourag'd.

1. The obstinate or *stomachful crying* should by no means be permitted, because it is but another way of flattering their desires, and encouraging those passions which 'tis our main business to subdue: and if it be, as often it is, upon the receiving any correction, it quite defeats all the good effects of it; for any chastisement which leaves them in this declar'd opposition, only serves to make them worse. The restraints and punishments laid on children are all misapply'd and lost, as far as they do not prevail over their wills, teach them to submit their passions, and make their minds supple and pliant to what their parents' reason advises them now, and so prepare them to obey what their own reason shall advise hereafter. But if in any thing wherein they are cross'd, they may be suffer'd to go away crying, they confirm themselves in their desires, and cherish the ill humour, with a declaration of their right, and a resolution to satisfy their inclination the first opportunity. This therefore is another argument against the frequent use of blows: for, whenever you come to that extremity, 'tis not enough to whip or beat them, you must do it, till you find you have subdu'd their minds, till with submission and patience they yield to the correction; which you shall best discover by their *crying,*

and their ceasing from it upon your bidding. Without this, the beating of children is but a passionate tyranny over them, and it is mere cruelty, and not correction, to put their bodies in pain, without doing their minds any good. As this gives us a reason why children should seldom be corrected, so it also prevents their being so. For if, whenever they are chastis'd, it were done thus without passion, soberly, and yet effectually too, laying on the blows and smart not furiously, and all at once, but slowly, with reasoning between, and with observation how it wrought, stopping when it had made them pliant, penitent and yielding; they would seldom need the like punishment again, being made careful to avoid the fault that deserv'd it. Besides, by this means, as the punishment would not be lost for being too little, and not effectual, so it would be kept from being too much, if we gave off as soon as we perceiv'd that it reach'd the mind, and that was better'd. For since the chiding or beating of children should be always the least that possibly may be, that which is laid on in the heat of anger, seldom observes that measure, but is commonly more than it should be, though it prove less than enough.

§ 113. 2. Many children are apt to *cry*, upon any little pain they suffer, and the least harm that befalls them puts them into *complaints* and *bawling*. This few children avoid: for it being the first and natural way to declare their sufferings or wants, before they can speak, the compassion that is thought due to that tender age foolishly encourages, and continues it in them long after they can speak. 'Tis the duty, I confess, of those about children, to compassionate them, whenever they suffer any hurt; but not to shew it in pitying them. Help and ease them the best you can, but by no means bemoan them. This softens their minds, and makes them yield to the little harms that happen to them; whereby they sink deeper into that part which alone feels, and makes larger wounds there, than otherwise they would. They should be harden'd against all sufferings, especially of the body, and have no tenderness but what rises from an ingenuous shame, and a quick sense of reputation. The many inconveniences this life is expos'd to, require we should not be too sensible of every little hurt. What our minds yield not to, makes but a slight impression, and does us but very little harm. 'Tis the suffering of our spirits that gives and continues the pain. This brawniness and insensibility of mind, is the best armour we can have against the common evils and accidents of life; and being a temper that is to be got by exercise and custom, more than any other way, the practice of it should be begun betimes; and happy is he that is taught it early. That effeminacy of spirit, which is to be prevented or cured, as nothing that I know so much increases in children as *crying;* so nothing, on the other side, so much checks and restrains, as their being hinder'd from that sort of *complaining*. In the little harms they suffer from knocks and falls, they should not be pitied for falling, but bid do so again; which besides that it stops their *crying,* is a better way to cure their heedlessness, and prevent their tumbling another time, than either chiding or bemoaning them. But, let the hurts they receive be what they will, stop their *crying,* and that will give them more quiet and ease at present, and harden them for the future.

§ 114. The former sort of *crying* requires severity to silence it; and where a look, or a positive command will not do it, blows must: for it proceeding from pride, obstinacy, and stomach, the will, where the fault lies, must be bent, and made to comply, by a rigour sufficient to master it. But this latter being ordinarily from softness of mind, a quite contrary cause, ought to be treated with a gentler hand. Persuasion, or diverting the thoughts another way, or laughing at their *whining,* may perhaps be at first the proper method: but for this, the circumstances of the thing, and the particular temper of the child, must be considered. No certain unvariable rules can be given about it; but it must be left to the prudence of the parents or tutor. But this, I think, I may say in general, that there should be a constant discountenancing of this sort of *crying* also; and that the father, by his authority, should always stop it, mixing a greater degree of roughness in his looks or words, proportionately as the child is of a greater age, or a sturdier temper: But always let it be enough to silence their *whimpering,* and put an end to the disorder.

§ 115. *Cowardice* and *courage* are so nearly related to the foremention'd tempers, that it may not be amiss here to take notice of them. Fear is a passion that, if rightly governed, has its use. And though self-love seldom fails to keep it watchful and high enough in us, yet there may be an excess on the daring side; *fool-hardiness* and insensibility of danger being as little reasonable, as trembling and shrinking at the approach of every little evil. Fear was given us as a monitor to quicken our industry, and keep us upon our guard against the approaches of evil; and therefore to have no apprehension of mischief at hand, not to make a just estimate of the danger, but heedlessly to run into it, be the hazard what it will, without considering of what use or consequence it may be, is not the resolution of a rational creature, but brutish fury. Those who have children of this temper, have nothing to do, but a little to awaken their reason, which self-preservation will quickly dispose them to hearken to, unless (which is usually the case) some other passion hurries them on head-long, without sense and without consideration. A dislike of evil is so natural to mankind, that nobody, I think, can be without fear of it: fear being nothing but an uneasiness under the apprehension of that coming upon us, which we dislike. And therefore, whenever any one runs into danger, we may say, 'tis under the conduct of ignorance, or the command of some more imperious passion, nobody being so much an enemy to himself, as to come within the reach of evil, out of free choice, and court danger for danger's sake. If it be therefore pride, vain-glory, or rage, that silences a child's fear, or makes him not hearken to its advice, those are by fit means to be abated, that a little consideration may allay his heat, and make him bethink himself, whether this attempt be worth the venture. But this being a fault that children are not so often guilty of, I shall not be more particular in its cure. Weakness of spirit is the more common defect, and therefore will require the greater care.

*Fortitude* is the guard and support of the other virtues; and without courage a man will scarce keep steady to his duty, and fill up the character of a truly worthy man.

*Courage,* that makes us bear up against dangers that we

fear and evils that we feel, is of great use in an estate, as ours is in this life, expos'd to assaults on all hands: and therefore it is very advisable to get children into this armour as early as we can. Natural temper, I confess, does here a great deal: but even where that is defective, and the heart is in itself weak and timorous, it may, by a right management, be brought to a better resolution. What is to be done to prevent breaking children's spirits by frightful apprehensions instill'd into them when young, or bemoaning themselves under every little suffering, I have already taken notice; how to harden their tempers, and raise their *courage*, if we find them too much subject to fear, is farther to be consider'd.

True fortitude, I take to be the quiet possession of a man's self, and an undisturb'd doing his duty, whatever evil besets, or danger lies in his way. This there are so few men attain to, that we are not to expect it from children. But yet something may be done: and a wise conduct by insensible degrees may carry them farther than one expects.

The neglect of this great care of them, whilst they are young, is the reason, perhaps, why there are so few that have this virtue in its full latitude when they are men. I should not say this in a nation so naturally brave, as ours is, did I think that true fortitude required nothing but courage in the field, and a contempt of life in the face of an enemy. This, I confess, is not the least part of it, nor can be denied the laurels and honours always justly due to the valour of those who venture their lives for their country. But yet this is not all. Dangers attack us in other places besides the field of battle; and though death be the king of terrors, yet pain, disgrace and poverty, have frightful looks, able to discompose most men whom they seem ready to seize on: and there are those who contemn some of these, and yet are heartily frighted with the other. True fortitude is prepar'd for dangers of all kinds, and unmoved, whatsoever evil it be that threatens. I do not mean unmoved with any fear at all. Where danger shews it self, apprehension cannot, without stupidity, be wanting; where danger is, sense of danger should be; and so much fear as should keep us awake, and excite our attention, industry, and vigour; but not disturb the calm use of our reason, nor hinder the execution of what that dictates.

The first step to get this noble and manly steadiness, is, what I have above mentioned, carefully to keep children from frights of all kinds, when they are young. Let not any fearful apprehensions be talk'd into them, nor terrible objects surprise them. This often so shatters and discomposes the spirits, that they never recover it again; but during their whole life, upon the first suggestion or appearance of any terrifying idea, are scatter'd and confounded; the body is enervated, and the mind disturb'd, and the man scarce himself, or capable of any composed or rational action. Whether this be from an habitual motion of the animal spirits, introduc'd by the first strong impression, or from the alteration of the constitution by some more unaccountable way, this is certain, that so it is. Instances of such who in a weak timorous mind, have borne, all their whole lives through, the effects of a fright when they were young, are every where to be seen, and therefore as much as may be to be prevented.

The next thing is by gentle degrees to accustom children to those things they are too much afraid of. But here great caution is to be used, that you do not make too much haste, nor attempt this cure too early, for fear lest you increase the mischief instead of remedying it. Little ones in arms may be easily kept out of the way of terrifying objects, and till they can talk and understand what is said to them, are scarce capable of that reasoning and discourse which should be used to let them know there is no harm in those frightful objects, which we would make them familiar with, and do, to that purpose by gentle degrees bring nearer and nearer to them. And therefore 'tis seldom there is need of any application to them of this kind, till after they can run about and talk. But yet, if it should happen that infants should have taken offence at any thing which cannot be easily kept out of their way, and that they shew marks of terror as often as it comes in sight; all the allays of fright, by diverting their thoughts, or mixing pleasant and agreeable appearances with it, must be used, till it be grown familiar and inoffensive to them.

I think we may observe, that, when children are first
born, all objects of sight that do not hurt the eyes, are indifferent to them; and they are no more afraid of a blacka-
moor or a lion, than of their nurse or a cat. What is it
then, that afterwards, in certain mixtures of shape and
colour, comes to affright them? Nothing but the apprehensions of harm that accompanies those things. Did a
child suck every day a new nurse, I make account it would
be no more affrighted with the change of faces at six
months old, than at sixty. The reason then why it will not
come to a stranger, is, because having been accustomed to
receive its food and kind usage only from one or two that
are about it, the child apprehends, by coming into the arms
of a stranger, the being taken from what delights and feeds
it and every moment supplies its wants, which it often feels,
and therefore fears when the nurse is away.

The only thing we naturally are afraid of is pain, or loss
of pleasure. And because these are not annexed to any
shape, colour, or size of visible objects, we are frighted
with none of them, till either we have felt pain from them,
or have notions put into us that they will do us harm. The
pleasant brightness and lustre of flame and fire so delights
children, that at first they always desire to be handling of
it: but when constant experience has convinced them, by
the exquisite pain it has put them to, how cruel and
unmerciful it is, they are afraid to touch it, and carefully
avoid it. This being the ground of fear, 'tis not hard to
find whence it arises, and how it is to be cured in all mistaken objects of terror. And when the mind is confirm'd
against them, and has got a mastery over it self and its
usual fears in lighter occasions, it is in good preparation
to meet more real dangers. Your child shrieks, and runs
away at the sight of a frog; let another catch it, and lay it
down at a good distance from him: at first accustom him
to look upon it; when he can do that, then to come nearer
to it, and see it leap without emotion; then to touch it
lightly, when it is held fast in another's hand; and so on,
till he can come to handle it as confidently as a butterfly
or a sparrow. By the same way any other vain terrors
may be remov'd; if care be taken, that you go not too fast,

and push not the child on to a new degree of assurance, till he be thoroughly confirm'd in the former. And thus the young soldier is to be train'd on to the warfare of life; wherein care is to be taken, that more things be not represented as dangerous than really are so; and then, that whatever you observe him to be more frighted at than he should, you be sure to tole him on to by insensible degrees, till he at last, quitting his fears, masters the difficulty, and comes off with applause. Successes of this kind, often repeated, will make him find, that evils are not always so certain or so great as our fears represent them; and that the way to avoid them, is not to run away, or be discompos'd, dejected, and deterr'd by fear, where either our credit or duty requires us to go on.

But since the great foundation of fear in children is pain, the way to harden and fortify children against fear and danger is to accustom them to suffer pain. This 'tis possible will be thought, by kind parents, a very unnatural thing towards their children; and by most, unreasonable, to endeavour to reconcile any one to the sense of pain, by bringing it upon him. 'Twill be said: 'It may perhaps give the child an aversion for him that makes him suffer; but can never recommend to him suffering itself. This is a strange method. You will not have children whipp'd and punish'd for their faults, but you would have them tormented for doing well, or for tormenting sake.' I doubt not but such objections as these will be made, and I shall be thought inconsistent with my self, or fantastical, in proposing it. I confess, it is a thing to be managed with great discretion, and therefore it falls not out amiss, that it will not be receiv'd or relish'd, but by those who consider well, and look into the reason of things. I would not have children much beaten for their faults, because I would not have them think bodily pain the greatest punishment: and I would have them, when they do well, be sometimes put in pain, for the same reason, that they might be accustom'd to bear it, without looking on it as the greatest evil. How much education may reconcile young people to pain and sufference, the examples of *Sparta* do sufficiently shew: and they who have once brought themselves not to think bodily

pain the greatest of evils, or that which they ought to stand
most in fear of, have made no small advance towards virtue.
But I am not so foolish to propose the *Lacedæmonian* discipline in our age or constitution. But yet I do say, that in-
uring children gently to suffer some degrees of pain without shrinking, is a way to gain firmness to their minds,
and lay a foundation for courage and resolution in the
future part of their lives.

Not to bemoan them, or permit them to bemoan themselves,
on every little pain they suffer, is the first step to be made.
But of this I have spoken elsewhere.

The next thing is, sometimes designedly to put them in
pain: but care must be taken that this be done when the
child is in good humour, and satisfied of the good-will and
kindness of him that hurts him, at the time that he
does it. There must no marks of anger or displeasure on
the one side, nor compassion or repenting on the other, go
along with it: and it must be sure to be no more than the
child can bear without repining or taking it amiss, or for a
punishment. Managed by these degrees, and with such circumstances, I have seen a child run away laughing with
good smart blows of a wand on his back, who would have
cried for an unkind word, and have been very sensible of
the chastisement of a cold look, from the same person.
Satisfy a child by a constant course of your care and kindness, that you perfectly love him, and he may by degrees
be accustom'd to bear very painful and rough usage from
you, without flinching or complaining: and this we see
children do every day in play one with another. The
softer you find your child is, the more you are to seek occasions, at fit times, thus to harden him. The great art in
this is, to begin with what is but very little painful, and to
proceed by insensible degrees, when you are playing, and
in good humour with him, and speaking well of him: and
when you have once got him to think himself made amends
for his suffering by the praise is given him for his courage;
when he can take a pride in giving such marks of his manliness, and can prefer the reputation of being brave and
stout, to the avoiding a little pain, or the shrinking under
it; you need not despair in time and by the assistance of

his growing reason, to master his timorousness, and mend the weakness of his constitution. As he grows bigger, he is to be set upon bolder attempts than his natural temper carries him to; and whenever he is observ'd to flinch from what one has reason to think he would come off well in, if he had but courage to undertake, *that* he should be assisted in at first, and by degrees sham'd to, till at last practice has given more assurance, and with it a mastery; which must be rewarded with great praise, and the good opinion of others, for his performance. When by these steps he has got resolution enough not to be deterr'd from what he ought to do, by the apprehension of danger; when fear does not, in sudden or hazardous occurrences, discompose his mind, set his body a-trembling, and make him unfit for action, or run away from it, he has then the courage of a rational creature: and such an hardiness we should endeavour by custom and use to bring children to, as proper occasions come in our way.

§ 116. One thing I have frequently observ'd in children, that when they have got possession of any poor creature, they are apt to use it ill: they often *torment,* and treat very roughly, young birds, butterflies, and such other poor animals which fall into their hands, and that with a seeming kind of pleasure. This I think should be watched in them, and if they incline to any such cruelty, they should be taught the contrary usage. For the custom of tormenting and killing of beasts, will, by degrees, harden their minds even towards men; and they who delight in the suffering and destruction of inferior creatures, will not be apt to be very compassionate or benign to those of their own kind. Our practice takes notice of this in the exclusion of *butchers* from juries of life and death. Children should from the beginning be bred up in an abhorrence of *killing* or tormenting any living creature; and be taught not to *spoil* or destroy any thing, unless it be for the preservation or advantage of some other that is nobler. And truly, if the preservation of all mankind, as much as in him lies, were every one's persuasion, as indeed it is every one's duty, and the true principle to regulate our religion, politicks and morality by, the world would be much quieter, and better natur'd than it is. But to return to our present business; I cannot but commend both the kindness and prudence of a mother I knew, who was wont always to indulge her daughters, when any of them desired dogs, squirrels, birds, or any such things as young girls use to be delighted with: but then, when they had them, they must be sure to keep them well, and look diligently after them, that they wanted nothing, or were not ill used. For if they were negligent in their care of them, it was counted a great fault, which often forfeited their possession, or at least they fail'd not to be rebuked for it; whereby they were early taught diligence and good nature. And indeed, I think people should be accustomed, from their cradles, to be tender to all sensible creatures, and to spoil or *waste* nothing at all.

This delight they take in *doing of mischief,* whereby I mean spoiling of any thing to no purpose, but more especially the pleasure they take to put any thing in pain, that is capable of it; I cannot persuade my self to be any other than a foreign and introduced disposition, an habit borrowed from custom and conversation. People teach children to strike, and laugh when they hurt or see harm come to others: and they have the examples of most about them, to confirm them in it. All the entertainment and talk of history is nothing almost but fighting and killing: and the honour and renown that is bestowed on conquerors (who for the most part are but the great butchers of mankind) farther mislead growing youth, who by this means come to think slaughter the laudable business of mankind, and the most heroick of virtues. By these steps unnatural cruelty is planted in us; and what humanity abhors, custom reconciles and recommends to us, by laying it in the way to honour. Thus, by fashion and opinion, that comes to be a pleasure, which in itself neither is, nor can be any. This ought carefully to be watched, and early remedied; so as to settle and cherish the contrary and more natural temper of benignity and *compassion* in the room of it; but still by the same gentle methods which are to be applied to the other two faults before mention'd. It may not perhaps be unreasonable here to add this farther caution, *viz.,* That the mischiefs or harms that come by play, inadvertency, or ignorance, and were not known to be harms, or design'd for mischief's sake, though they may perhaps be sometimes of considerable damage, yet are not at all, or but very gently, to be taken notice of.  For this, I think, I cannot too often inculcate, that whatever miscarriage a child is guilty of, and whatever be the consequence of it, the thing to be regarded in taking notice of it, is only what root it springs from, and what habit it is like to establish: and to that the correction ought to be directed, and the child not to suffer any punishment for any harm which may have come by his play or inadvertency.  The faults to be amended lie in the mind; and if they are such as either age will cure, or no ill habits will follow from, the present action, whatever displeasing circumstances it may have, is to be passed by without any animadversion.

§ 117. Another way to instill sentiments of humanity, and to keep them lively in young folks, will be, to accustom them to civility in their language and deportment towards their inferiors and the meaner sort of people, particularly servants.  It is not unusual to observe the children in gentlemen's families treat the servants of the house with domineering words, names of contempt, and an imperious carriage; as if they were of another race and species beneath them.  Whether ill example, the advantage of fortune, or their natural vanity, inspire this haughtiness, it should be prevented, or weeded out; and a gentle, courteous, affable carriage towards the lower ranks of men, placed in the room of it.  No part of their superiority will be hereby lost; but the distinction increased, and their authority strengthen'd; when love in inferiors is join'd to outward respect, and an esteem of the person has a share in their submission: and domesticks will pay a more ready and chearful service, when they find themselves not spurn'd because fortune has laid them below the level of others at their master's feet.  Children should not be suffer'd to lose the consideration of human nature in the shufflings of outward conditions.  The more they have, the better humor'd they should be taught to be, and the more compassionate and gentle to those of their brethren who are placed lower, and have scantier portions.  If they are suffer'd from their cradles to treat men ill and rudely, because, by their father's title, they think they have a little power over them, at best it is ill-bred; and if care be not taken, will by degrees nurse up their natural pride into an habitual contempt of those beneath them. And where will that probably end but in oppression and cruelty?

§ 118. Curiosity in children (which I had occasion just to mention § 108) is but an appetite after knowledge; and therefore ought to be encouraged in them, not only as a good sign, but as the great instrument nature has provided to remove that ignorance they were born with; and which, without this busy *inquisitiveness*, will make them dull and useless creatures. The ways to encourage it, and keep it active and busy, are, I suppose, these following:

1. Not to check or discountenance any *enquiries* he shall make, nor suffer them to be laugh'd at; but to *answer* all his *questions*, and *explain* the matter he desires to know, so as to make them as much intelligible to him as suits the capacity of his age and knowledge. But confound not his understanding with explications or notions that are above it; or with the variety or number of things that are not to his present purpose. Mark what 'tis his mind aims at in the *question*, and not what words he expresses it in: and when you have informed and satisfied him in that, you shall see how his thoughts will enlarge themselves, and how by fit answers he may be led on farther than perhaps you could imagine. For knowledge is grateful to the understanding, as light to the eyes: children are pleased and delighted with it exceedingly, especially if they see that their *enquiries* are regarded, and that their desire of knowing is encouraged and commended. And I doubt not but one great reason why many children abandon themselves wholly to silly sports, and trifle away all their time insipidly, is, because they have found their *curiosity* baulk'd, and their *enquiries* neglected. But had they been treated with more kindness and respect, and their *questions* answered, as they should, to their satisfaction; I doubt not but they would have taken more pleasure in learning, and improving their knowledge, wherein there would be still newness and variety, which is what they

are delighted with, than in returning over and over to the same play and play-things.

§ 119. 2. To this serious answering their *questions,* and informing their understandings, in what they desire, as if it were a matter that needed it, should be added some peculiar ways of *commendation.* Let others whom they esteem, be told before their faces of the knowledge they have in such and such things; and since we are all, even from our cradles, vain and proud creatures, let their vanity be flatter'd with things that will do them good; and let their pride set them on work on something which may turn to their advantage. Upon this ground you shall find, that there cannot be a greater spur to the attaining what you would have the eldest learn, and know himself, than to set him upon *teaching* it *his younger brothers* and *sisters.*

§ 120. 3. As children's *enquiries* are not to be slighted; so also great care is to be taken, that they *never* receive *deceitful* and *eluding answers.* They easily perceive when they are slighted or deceived; and quickly learn the trick of neglect, dissimulation and falsehood, which they observe others to make use of. We are not to intrench upon truth in any conversation, but least of all with children; since if we play false with them, we not only deceive their expectation, and hinder their knowledge, but corrupt their innocence, and teach them the worst of vices. They are travellers newly arrived in a strange country, of which they know nothing; we should therefore make conscience not to mislead them. And though their *questions* seem sometimes not very material, yet they should be seriously answer'd: for however they may appear to us (to whom they are long since known) *enquiries* not worth the making; they are of moment to those who are wholly ignorant. Children are strangers to all we are acquainted with; and all the things they meet with, are at first unknown to them, as they once were to us: and happy are they who meet with civil people, that will comply with their ignorance, and help them to get out of it.

If you or I now should be set down in *Japan,* with all our prudence and knowledge about us, a conceit whereof makes us, perhaps, so apt to slight the thoughts and *en-*

*quiries* of children; should we, I say, be set down in *Japan,*
we should, no doubt (if we would inform our selves of
what is there to be known) ask a thousand questions, which,
to a supercilious or inconsiderate *Japaner,* would seem very
idle and impertinent; though to us they would be very
material and of importance to be resolved; and we should
be glad to find a man so complaisant and courteous, as
to satisfy our demands, and instruct our ignorance.

When any new thing comes in their way, children usually
ask the common *question* of a stranger: *What is it?*
Whereby they ordinarily mean nothing but the name; and
therefore to tell them how it is call'd, is usually the proper
answer to that demand. And the next question usually
is, *What is it for?* And to this it should be answered truly
and directly: The use of the thing should be told, and the
way explained, how it serves to such a purpose, as far as
their capacities can comprehend it. And so of any other
circumstances they shall ask about it; not turning them
going, till you have given them all the satisfaction they are
capable of; and so leading them by your answers into
farther questions. And perhaps to a grown man, such conversation will not be altogether so idle and insignificant
as we are apt to imagine. The native and untaught suggestions of inquisitive children do often offer things, that may
set a considering man's thoughts on work. And I think
there is frequently more to be learn'd from the unexpected
questions of a child, than the discourses of men, who talk
in a road, according to the notions they have borrowed, and
the prejudices of their education.

§ 121. 4. Perhaps it may not sometimes be amiss to excite their curiosity by bringing strange and new things in
their way, on purpose to engage their enquiry, and give
them occasion to inform themselves about them: and if by
chance their curiosity leads them to ask what they should
not know, it is a great deal better to tell them plainly, that
it is a thing that belongs not to them to know, than to pop
them off with a falsehood of a frivolous answer.

§ 122. *Pertness,* that appears sometimes so early, proceeds from a principle that seldom accompanies a strong
constitution of body, or ripens into a strong judgment of

mind. If it were desirable to have a child a more brisk
talker, I believe there might be ways found to make him
so: But I suppose a wise father had rather that his son
should be able and useful, when a man, than pretty company,
and a diversion to others, whilst a child: though if that
too were to be consider'd, I think I may say, there is not so
much pleasure to have a child prattle agreeably, as to
reason well. Encourage therefore his *inquisitiveness* all you
can, by satisfying his demands, and informing his judgment,
as far as it is capable. When his reasons are any way tolerable, let him find the credit and commendation of it: and
when they are quite out of the way, let him, without being
laugh'd at for his mistake, be gently put into the right; and
if he shew a forwardness to be reasoning about things that
come in his way, take care, as much as you can, that no
body check this inclination in him, or mislead it by captious
or fallacious ways of talking with him. For when all is
done, this, as the highest and most important faculty of
our minds, deserves the greatest care and attention in cultivating it: the right improvement, and exercise of our
reason being the highest perfection that a man can attain
to in this life.

§ 123. Contrary to this busy inquisitive temper, there is
sometimes observable in children, a *listless carelessness,* a
want of regard to any thing, and a sort of *trifling* even at
their business. This *sauntring* humour I look on as one of
the worst qualities can appear in a child, as well as one of
the hardest to be cured, where it is natural. But it being
liable to be mistaken in some cases, care must be taken to
make a right judgment concerning that trifling at their
books or business, which may sometimes be complained of
in a child. Upon the first suspicion a father has, that his
son is of a *sauntring* temper, he must carefully observe him,
whether he be *listless* and *indifferent* in all in his actions,
or whether in some things alone he be slow and sluggish,
but in others vigorous and eager. For tho' we find that he
does loiter at his book, and let a good deal of the time he
spends in his chamber or study, run idly away; he must not
presently conclude, that this is from a *sauntring* humour in
his temper. It may be childishness, and a preferring some-

thing to his study, which his thoughts run on: and he dislikes his book, as is natural, because it is forced upon him as a task. To know this perfectly, you must watch him at play, when he is out of his place and time of study, following his own inclination; and see there whether he be stirring and active; whether he designs any thing, and with labour and eagerness pursues it, till he has accomplished what he aimed at, or whether he *lazily* and *listlessly dreams away his time.* If this sloth be only when he is about his book, I think it may be easily cured. If it be in his temper, it will require a little more pains and attention to remedy it.

§ 124 If you are satisfied by his earnestness at play, or any thing else he sets his mind on, in the intervals between his hours of business, that he is not of himself inclined to *laziness,* but that only want of relish of his book makes him negligent and *sluggish* in his application to it; the first step is to try by talking to him kindly of the folly and inconvenience of it, whereby he loses a good part of his time, which he might have for his diversion: but be sure to talk calmly and kindly, and not much at first, but only these plain reasons in short. If this prevails, you have gain'd the point in the most desirable way, which is that of reason and kindness. If this softer application prevails not, try to shame him out of it, by laughing at him for it, asking every day, when he comes to table, if there be no strangers there, how long he was that day about his business: And if he has not done it in the time he might be well supposed to have dispatched it, expose and turn him into ridicule for it; but mix no chiding, only put on a pretty cold brow towards him, and keep it till he reform; and let his mother, tutor, and all about him do so too. If this work not the effect you desire, then tell him he shall be no longer troubled with a tutor to take care of his education, you will not be at the charge to have him spend his time idly with him; but since he prefers this or that [whatever play he delights in] to his book, that only he shall do; and so in earnest set him to work on his beloved play, and keep him steadily, and in earnest, to it morning and afternoon, till he be fully surfeited, and would, at any rate, change it for some hours at his book again. But when you thus set him his task of play, you must be sure to look after him your self, or set somebody else to do it, that may constantly see him employed in it, and that he be not permitted to be idle at that too. I say, your self look after him; for it is worth the father's while, whatever business he has, to bestow two or three days upon his son, to cure so great a mischief as his *sauntring* at his business.

§ 125. This is what I propose, if it be *idleness,* not from his general temper, but a peculiar or acquir'd aversion to learning, which you must be careful to examine and distinguish. But though you have your eyes upon him, to watch what he does with the time which he has at his own disposal, yet you must not let him perceive that you or any body else do so; for that may hinder him from following his own inclination, which he being full of, and not daring, for fear of you, to prosecute what his head and heart are set upon, he may neglect all other things, which then he relishes not, and so may seem to be idle and listless, when in truth it is nothing but being intent on that, which the fear of your eye or knowledge keeps him from executing. To be clear in this point, the observation must be made when you are out of the way, and he not so much as under the restraint of a suspicion that any body has an eye upon him. In those seasons of perfect freedom, let some body you can trust mark how he spends his time, whether he unactively loiters it away, when without any check he is left to his own inclination. Thus, by his employing of such times of liberty, you will easily discern, whether it be *listlessness* in his temper, or aversion to his book, that makes him *saunter* away his time of study.

§ 126. If some defect in his constitution has cast a damp on his mind, and he be naturally listless and dreaming, this unpromising disposition is none of the easiest to be dealt with, because, generally carrying with it an unconcernedness for the future, it wants the two great springs of action, *foresight* and *desire;* which how to plant and increase, where nature has given a cold and contrary temper, will be the question. As soon as you are satisfied that this is the case, you must carefully enquire whether

there be nothing he delights in; Inform your self what it
is he is most pleased with; and if you can find any particular
tendency his mind hath, increase it all you can, and make
use of that to set him on work, and to excite his industry.
If he loves praise, or play, or fine clothes, &c. or, on the
other side, dreads pain, disgrace, or your displeasure, &c.,
whatever it be that he loves most, except it be sloth (for
that will never set him on work) let that be made use of
to quicken him, and make him bestir himself. For in this
*listless temper,* you are not to fear an excess of appetite
(as in all other cases) by cherishing it. 'Tis that which
you want, and therefore must labour to raise and increase;
for where there is no desire, there will be no industry.

§ 127. If you have not hold enough upon him this way,
to stir up vigour and activity in him, you must employ him
in some constant bodily labour, whereby he may get an
habit of doing something. The keeping him hard to some
study were the better way to get him an habit of exercising
and applying his mind. But because this is an invisible
attention, and no body can tell when he is or is not idle
at it, you must find bodily employments for him, which
he must be constantly busied in, and kept to; and if they
have some little hardship and shame in them, it may not be
the worse, that they may the sooner weary him, and make
him desire to return to his book. But be sure, when you
exchange his book for his other labour, set him such a task,
to be done in such a time as may allow him no opportunity
to be idle. Only after you have by this way brought him
to be attentive and industrious at his book, you may, upon
his dispatching his study within the time set him, give him
as a reward some respite from his other labour; which you
may diminish as you find him grow more and more steady
in his application, and at last wholly take off when his *sauntring* at his book is cured.

§ 128. We formerly observed, that variety and freedom
was that that delighted children, and recommended their
plays to them; and that therefore their book or any thing
we would have them learn, should not be enjoined them as
*business.* This their parents, tutors, and teachers are apt to
forget; and their impatience to have them busied in what

is fit for them to do, suffers them not to deceive them into it: but by the repeated injunctions they meet with, children quickly distinguish between what is required of them, and what not. When this mistake has once made his book uneasy to him, the cure is to be applied at the other end. And since it will be then too late to endeavour to make it a play to him, you must take the contrary course: observe what play he is most delighted with; enjoin that, and make him play so many hours every day, not as a punishment for playing, but as if it were the business required of him. This, if I mistake not, will in a few days make him so weary of his most beloved sport, that he will prefer his book, or any thing to it, especially if it may redeem him from any part of the task of play is set him, and he may be suffered to employ some part of the time destined to his *task of play* in his book, or such other exercise as is really useful to him.    This I at least think a better cure than that forbidding, (which usually increases the desire) or any other punishment should be made use of to remedy it: for when you have once glutted his appetite (which may safely be done in all things but eating and drinking) and made him surfeit of what you would have him avoid, you have put into him a principle of aversion, and you need not so much fear afterwards his longing for the same thing again.

§ 129. This I think is sufficiently evident, that children generally hate to be idle. All the care then is, that their busy humour should be constantly employ'd in something of use to them; which, if you will attain, you must make what you would have them do a recreation to them, and not a *business*. The way to do this, so that they may not perceive you have any hand in it, is this proposed here; *viz.* To make them weary of that which you would not have them do, by enjoining and making them under some pretence or other do it, till they are surfeited. For example: Does your son play at top and scourge too much? Enjoin him to play so many hours every day, and look that he do it; and you shall see he will quickly be sick of it, and willing to leave it. By this means making the recreations you dislike a *business* to him, he will of himself with delight betake himself to those things you would have him do, especially if they be proposed as rewards for having performed his *task* in that play which is commanded him. For if he be ordered every day to whip his top so long as to make him sufficiently weary, do you not think he will apply himself with eagerness to his book, and wish for it, if you promise it him as a reward of having whipped his top lustily, quite out all the time that is set him? Children, in the things they do, if they comport with their age, find little difference so they may be doing: the esteem they have for one thing above another they borrow from others; so that what those about them make to be a reward to them, will really be so. By this art it is in their governor's choice, whether *scotchhoppers* shall reward their *dancing,* or *dancing* their *scotchhoppers;* whether peg-top, or reading; playing at trap, or studying the globes, shall be more acceptable and pleasing to them; all that they desire being to be busy, and busy, as they imagine, in things of their own choice, and which they receive as favours from their parents or others for whom they have respect and with whom they would be in credit. A set of children thus ordered and kept from the ill example of others, would all of them, I suppose, with as much earnestness and delight, learn to read, write, and what else one would have them, as others do their ordinary plays: and the eldest being thus entered, and this made the fashion of the place, it would be as impossible to hinder them from learning the one, as it is ordinarily to keep them from the other.

§ 130. Play-things, I think, children should have, and of divers sorts; but still to be in the custody of their tutors or some body else, whereof the child should have in his power but one at once, and should not be suffered to have another but when he restored that. This teaches them betimes to be careful of not losing or spoiling the things they have; whereas plenty and variety in their own keeping, makes them wanton and careless, and teaches them from the beginning to be squanderers and wasters. These, I confess, are little things, and such as will seem beneath the care of a governor; but nothing that may form children's minds is to be overlooked and neglected, and whatsoever introduces habits, and settles customs in them, deserves the care and attention of their governors, and is not a small thing in its consequences.

One thing more about children's play-things may be worth their parents' care. Though it be agreed they should have of several sorts, yet, I think, they should have none bought for them. This will hinder that great variety they are often overcharged with, which serves only to teach the mind to wander after change and superfluity, to be unquiet, and perpetually stretching itself after something more still, though it knows not what, and never to be satisfied with what it hath. The court that is made to people of condition in such kind of presents to their children, does the little ones great harm. By it they are taught pride, vanity and covetousness, almost before they can speak: and I have known a young child so distracted with the number and variety of his play-games, that he tired his maid every day to look them over; and was so accustomed to abundance, that he never thought he had enough, but was always asking, What more? What more? What new thing shall I have? A good introduction to moderate desires, and the ready way to make a contented happy man!

"How then shall they have the play-games you allow them, if none must be bought for them?" I answer, they should make them themselves, or at least endeavour it, and set themselves about it; till then they should have none, and till then they will want none of any great artifice. A smooth pebble, a piece of paper, the mother's bunch of keys, or any thing they cannot hurt themselves with, serves as much to divert little children as those more chargeable and curious toys from the shops, which are presently put out of order and broken. Children are never dull, or out of humour, for want of such play-things, unless they have been used to them; when they are little, whatever occurs serves the turn; and as they grow bigger, if they are not stored by the expensive folly of others, they will make them themselves. Indeed, when they once begin to set themselves to work about any of their inventions, they should be taught and assisted; but should have nothing whilst they lazily sit still, expecting to be furnish'd from other hands, without employing their own. And if you help them where they are at a stand, it will more endear you to them than any chargeable toys you shall buy for them. Play-things which are above their skill to make, as tops, gigs, battledores, and the like, which are to be used with labour, should indeed be procured them. These 'tis convenient they should have, not for variety but exercise; but these too should be given them as bare as might be. If they had a top, the scourge-stick and leather-strap should be left to their own making and fitting. If they sit gaping to have such things drop into their mouths, they should go without them. This will accustom them to seek for what they want, in themselves and in their own endeavours; whereby they will be taught moderation in their desires, application, industry, thought, contrivance, and good husbandry; qualities that will be useful to them when they are men, and therefore cannot be learned too soon, nor fixed too deep. All the plays and diversions of children should be directed towards good and useful habits, or else they will introduce ill ones. Whatever they do, leaves some impression on that tender age, and from thence they receive a tendency to good or evil: and whatever hath such an influence, ought not to be neglected.

§ 131. *Lying* is so ready and cheap a cover for any miscarriage, and so much in fashion among all sorts of people, that a child can hardly avoid observing the use is made of it on all occasions, and so can scarce be kept without great care from getting into it. But it is so ill a quality, and the mother of so many ill ones that spawn from it, and take shelter under it, that a child should be brought up in the greatest abhorrence of it imaginable. I should be always (when occasionally it comes to be mention'd) spoke of before him with the utmost detestation, as a quality so wholly inconsistent with the name and character of a gentleman, that no body of any credit can bear the imputation of a lie; a mark that is judg'd the utmost disgrace, which debases a man to the lowest degree of a shameful meanness, and ranks him with the most contemptible part of mankind and the abhorred rascality; and is not to be endured in any one who would converse with people of condition, or have any esteem or reputation in the

world. The first time he is found in a *lie*, it should rather
be wondered at as a monstrous thing in him, than reproved
as an ordinary fault. If that keeps him not from relapsing,
the next time he must be sharply rebuked, and fall into
the state of great displeasure of his father and mother and
all about him who take notice of it. And if this way work
not the cure, you must come to blows; for after he has
been thus warned, a premeditated *lie* must always be looked
upon as obstinacy, and never be permitted to escape un-
punished.

§ 132. Children, afraid to have their faults seen in their
naked colours, will, like the rest of the sons of *Adam*, be
apt to make *excuses*. This is a fault usually bordering upon,
and leading to untruth, and is not to be indulged in them;
but yet it ought to be cured rather with shame than roughness. If therefore, when a child is questioned for any
thing, his first answer be an *excuse*, warn him soberly to
tell the truth; and then if he persists to shuffle it off with
a *falsehood*, he must be chastised; but if he directly confess,
you must commend his ingenuity, and pardon the fault, be
it what it will; and pardon it so, that you never so much
as reproach him with it, or mention it to him again: for
if you would have him in love with ingenuity, and by a
constant practice make it habitual to him, you must take
care that it never procure him the least inconvenience;
but on the contrary, his own confession bringing always
with it perfect impunity, should be besides encouraged by
some marks of approbation. If his *excuse* be such at any
time that you cannot prove it to have any falsehood in it,
let it pass for true, and be sure not to shew any suspicion
of it. Let him keep up his reputation with you as high
as is possible; for when once he finds he has lost that,
you have lost a great, and your best hold upon him. Therefore let him not think he has the character of a liar with
you, as long as you can avoid it without flattering him in
it. Thus some slips in truth may be over-looked. But after
he has once been corrected for a *lie*, you must be sure never
after to pardon it in him, whenever you find and take
notice to him that he is guilty of it: for it being a fault
which he has been forbid, and may, unless he be wilful, avoid,

the repeating of it is perfect perverseness, and must have the chastisement due to that offence.

§ 133. This is what I have thought concerning the general method of educating a young gentleman; which, though I am apt to suppose may have some influence on the whole course of his education, yet I am far from imagining it contains all those particulars which his growing years or peculiar temper may require. But this being premised in general, we shall in the next place, descend to a more particular consideration of the several parts of his education.

§ 134. That which every gentleman (that takes any care of his education) desires for his son, besides the estate he leaves him, is contain'd (I suppose) in these four things, *virtue, wisdom, breeding* and *learning*. I will not trouble my self whether these names do not some of them sometimes stand for the same thing, or really include one another. It serves my turn here to follow the popular use of these words, which, I presume, is clear enough to make me be understood, and I hope there will be no difficulty to comprehend my meaning.

§ 135. I place *virtue* as the first and most necessary of those endowments that belong to a man or a gentleman; as absolutely requisite to make him valued and beloved by others, acceptable or tolerable to himself. Without that, I think, he will be happy neither in this nor the other world.

§ 136. As the foundation of this, there ought very early to be imprinted on his mind a true notion of *God,* as of the independent Supreme Being, Author and Maker of all things, from Whom we receive all our good, Who loves us, and gives us all things. And consequent to this, instil into him a love and reverence of this Supreme Being. This is enough to begin with, without going to explain this matter any farther; for fear lest by talking too early to him of spirits, and being unseasonably forward to make him understand the incomprehensible nature of that Infinite Being, his head be either fill'd with false, or perplex'd with unintelligible notions of Him. Let him only be told upon occasion, that *God* made and governs all things, hears and sees every thing, and does all manner of good to those that love and obey Him; you will find, that being told of such a *God,* other thoughts will be apt to rise up fast enough in his mind about Him; which, as you observe them to have any mistakes, you must set right. And I think it would be better if men generally rested in such an idea of *God,* without being too curious in their notions about a Being which all must acknowledge incomprehensible; whereby many, who have not strength and clearness of thought to distinguish between what they can, and what they cannot know, run themselves in superstitions or atheism, making *God* like themselves, or (because they cannot comprehend any thing else) none at all. And I am apt to think, the keeping children constantly morning and evening to acts of devotion to God, as to their Maker, Preserver and Benefactor, in some plain and short form of prayer, suitable to their age and capacity, will be of much more use to them in religion, knowledge, and virtue, than to distract their thoughts with curious enquiries into His inscrutable essence and being.

§ 137. Having by gentle degrees, as you find him capable of it, settled such an idea of God in his mind, and taught him to *pray* to Him, and *praise* Him as the Author of his being, and of all the good he does or can enjoy; forbear any discourse of other *spirits,* till the mention of them coming in his way, upon occasion hereafter to be set down, and his reading the scripture-history, put him upon that enquiry.

§ 138. But even then, and always whilst he is young, be sure to preserve his tender mind from all impressions and notions of *spirits* and *goblins,* or any fearful apprehensions in the dark. This he will be in danger of from the indiscretion of servants, whose usual method is to awe children, and keep them in subjection, by telling them of *raw-head and bloody-bones,* and such other names as carry with them the ideas of something terrible and hurtful, which they have reason to be afraid of when alone, especially in the dark. This must be carefully prevented: for though by this foolish way, they may keep them from little faults, yet the remedy is much worse than the disease; and there are stamped upon their imaginations ideas that follow them with terror and affrightment. Such *bug-bear* thoughts once got into the tender minds of children, and being set on with a strong impression from the dread that accompanies such apprehensions, sink deep, and fasten themselves so as not easily, if ever, to be got out again; and whilst they are there, frequently haunt them with strange visions, making children dastards when alone, and afraid of their shadows and darkness all their lives after. I have had those complain to me, when men, who had been thus used when young; that though their reason corrected the wrong ideas they had taken in, and they were satisfied that there was no cause to fear invisible beings more in the dark than in the light, yet that these notions were apt still upon any occasion to start up first in their prepossessed fancies, and not to be removed without some pains. And to let you see how lasting and frightful images are, that take place in the mind early, I shall here tell you a pretty remarkable but true story. There was in a town in the *west* a man of a disturbed brain, whom the boys used to teaze when he came in their way: this fellow one day seeing in the street one of those lads, that used to vex him, stepped into a *cutler's* shop he was near, and there seizing on a naked sword, made after the boy; who seeing him coming so armed, betook himself to his feet, and ran for his life, and by good luck had strength and heels enough to reach his father's house before the mad-man could get up to him. The door was only latch'd; and when he had the latch in his hand, he turn'd about his head, to see how near his pursuer was, who was at the entrance of the porch, with his sword up ready to strike; and he had just time to get in, and clap to the door to avoid the blow, which, though his body escaped, his mind did not. This frightening idea made so deep an impression there, that it lasted many years, if not all his life after. For, telling this story when he was a man, he said, that after that time till then, he never went in at that door (that he could remember) at any time without looking back, whatever business he had in his head, or how little soever before he came thither he thought of this mad-man.

If children were let alone, they would be no more

afraid in the dark, than in broad sun-shine: they would in their turns as much welcome the one for sleep as the other to play in. There should be no distinction made to them by any discourse of more danger or *terrible things* in the one than the other: but if the folly of any one about them should do them this harm, and make them think there is any difference between being in the dark and winking, you must get it out of their minds as soon as you can; and let them know, that God, who made all things good for them, made the night that they might sleep the better and the quieter; and that they being under his protection, there is nothing in the dark to hurt them. What is to be known more of God and good spirits, is to be deferr'd till the time we shall hereafter mention; and of evil spirits, 'twill be well if you can keep him from wrong fancies about them till he is ripe for that sort of knowledge.

§ 139. Having laid the foundations of virtue in a true notion of a God, such as the creed wisely teaches, as far as his age is capable, and by accustoming him to pray to Him; the next thing to be taken care of is to keep him exactly to speaking of *truth,* and by all the ways imaginable inclining him to be *good-natur'd.* Let him know that twenty faults are sooner to be forgiven than the *straining of truth* to cover any one *by an excuse.* And to teach him betimes to love and be *good-natur'd* to others, is to lay early the true foundation of an honest man; all injustice generally springing from too great love of ourselves and too little of others.

This is all I shall say of this matter in general, and is enough for laying the first foundations of virtue in a child: as he grows up, the tendency of his natural inclination must be observed; which, as it inclines him more than is convenient on one or t'other side from the right path of virtue, ought to have proper remedies applied. For few of *Adam's* children are so happy, as not to be born with some byass in their natural temper, which it is the business of education either to take off, or counterbalance. But to enter into particulars of this, would be beyond the design of this short treatise of education. I intend not a discourse of all the virtues and vices, how each virtue is to be attained, and every particular vice by its peculiar remedies cured: though I have mentioned some of the most ordinary faults, and the ways to be used in correcting them.

§ 140. *Wisdom* I take in the popular acceptation, for a man's managing his business ably and with foresight in this world. This is the product of a good natural temper, application of mind, and experience together, and so above the reach of children. The greatest thing that in them can be done towards it, is to hinder them, as much as may be, from being *cunning;* which, being the ape of *wisdom,* is the most distant from it that can be: and as an ape for the likeness it has to a man, wanting what really should make him so, is by so much the uglier; *cunning* is only the want of understanding, which because it cannot compass its ends by direct ways, would do it by a trick and circumvention; and the mischief of it is, a *cunning* trick helps but once, but hinders ever after. No cover was ever made either so big or so fine as to hide it self: no body was ever so *cunning* as to conceal their being so: and when they are once discovered, every body is shy, every body distrustful of *crafty* men; and all the world forwardly join to oppose and defeat them; whilst the open, fair, *wise* man has every body to make way for him, and goes directly to his business. To accustom a child to have true notions of things, and not to be satisfied till he has them; to raise his mind to great and worthy thoughts, and to keep him at a distance from falsehood and cunning, which has always a broad mixture of falsehood in it; is the fittest preparation of a child for *wisdom.* The rest, which is to be learn'd from time, experience, and observation, and an acquaintance with men, their tempers and designs, is not to be expected in the ignorance and inadvertency of childhood, or the inconsiderate heat and unweariness of youth: all that can be done towards it, during this unripe age, is, as I have said, to accustom them to truth and sincerity; to a submisson to reason; and as much as may be, to reflection on their own actions.

§ 141. The next good quality belonging to a gentleman,

is *good breeding.* There are two sorts of *ill breeding:* the one a *sheepish bashfulness,* and the other a *mis-becoming negligence and disrespect* in our carriage; both which are avoided by duly observing this one rule, *not to think meanly of ourselves, and not to think meanly of others.*

§ 142. The first part of this rule must not be understood in opposition to humility, but to assurance. We ought not to think so well of our selves, as to stand upon our own value; and assume to our selves a preference before others, because of any advantage we may imagine we have over them; but modestly to take what is offered, when it is our due. But yet we ought to think so well of our selves, as to perform those actions which are incumbent on, and expected of us, without discomposure or disorder, in whose presence soever we are; keeping that respect and distance which is due to every one's rank and quality. There is often in people, especially children, a clownish shame-facedness before strangers or those above them: they are confounded in their thoughts, words, and looks; and so lose themselves in that confusion as not to be able to do any thing, or at least not to do it with that freedom and gracefulness which pleases, and makes them be acceptable. The only cure for this, as for any other miscarriage, is by use to introduce the contrary habit. But since we cannot accustom ourselves to converse with strangers and persons of quality without being in their company, nothing can cure this part of *ill-breeding* but change and variety of company, and that of persons above us.

§ 143. As the before-mentioned consists in too great a concern how to behave ourselves towards others; so the other part of *ill-breeding* lies in the appearance of too *little care* of pleasing or *shewing respect* to those we have to do with. To avoid this these two things are requisite: first, a disposition of the mind not to offend others; and secondly, the most acceptable and agreeble way of expressing that disposition. From the one men are called *civil;* from the other *well-fashion'd.* The latter of these is that decency and gracefulness of looks, voice, words, motions, gestures, and of all the whole outward demeanour, which takes in company, and makes those with whom we may converse, easy and well pleased. This is, as it were, the language whereby that internal civility of the mind is expressed; which, as other languages are, being very much governed by the fashion and custom of every country, must, in the rules and practice of it, be learn'd chiefly from observation, and the carriage of those who are allow'd to be exactly *well-bred.* The other part, which lies deeper than the outside, is that general good-will and regard for all people, which makes any one have a care not to shew in his carriage any contempt, disrespect, or neglect of them; but to express, according to the fashion and way of that country, a respect and value for them according to their rank and condition. It is a disposition of the mind that shews it self in the carriage, whereby a man avoids making any one uneasy in conversation.

I shall take notice of four qualities, that are most directly opposite to this first and most taking of all the social virtues. And from some one of these four it is, that incivility commonly has its rise. I shall set them down, that children may be preserv'd or recover'd from their ill influence.

1. The first is, a natural *roughness,* which makes a man uncomplaisant to others, so that he has no deference for their inclinations, tempers, or conditions. 'Tis the sure badge of a clown, not to mind what pleases or displeases those he is with; and yet one may often find a man in fashionable clothes give an unbounded swing to his own humour, and suffer it to justle or over-run any one that stands in its way, with a perfect indifference how they take it. This is a brutality that every one sees and abhors, and no body can be easy with: and therefore this finds no place in any one who would be thought to have the least tincture of *good-breeding.* For the very end and business of *good-breeding* is to supple the natural stiffness, and so soften men's tempers, that they may bend to a compliance, and accommodate themselves to those they have to do with.

2. *Contempt,* or want of due respect, discovered either in looks, words, or gesture: this, from whomsoever it comes, brings always uneasiness with it. For no body can contentedly bear being slighted.

(5) HC XXXVII

3. *Censoriousness,* and finding fault with others, has a direct opposition to *civility.* Men, whatever they are or are not guilty of, would not have their faults display'd and set in open view and broad day-light, before their own or other people's eyes. Blemishes affixed to any one always carry shame with them: and the discovery, or even bare imputation of any defect is not borne without some uneasiness. *Raillery* is the most refined way of exposing the faults of others: but, because it is usually done with wit and good language, and gives entertainment to the company, people are led into a mistake, that where it keeps within fair bounds there is no incivility in it. And so the pleasantry of this sort of conversation often introduces it amongst people of the better rank; and such talkers are favourably heard and generally applauded by the laughter of the bystanders on their side. But they ought to consider, that the entertainment of the rest of the company is at the cost of that one who is set out in their burlesque colours, who therefore is not without uneasiness, unless the subject for which he is rallied be really in itself matter of commendation. For then the pleasant images and representations which make the *raillery* carrying praise as well as sport with them, the rallied person also finds his account, and takes part in the diversion. But because the right management of so nice and ticklish a business, wherein a little slip may spoil all, is not every body's talent, I think those who would secure themselves from provoking others, especially all young people, should carefully abstain from *raillery,* which by a small mistake or any wrong turn, may leave upon the mind of those who are made uneasy by it, the lasting memory of having been piquantly, tho' wittily, taunted for some thing censurable in them.

Besides raillery, *contradiction* is a sort of censoriousness wherein ill-breeding often shews it self. Complaisance does not require that we should always admit all the reasonings or relations that the company is entertain'd with, no, nor silently to let pass all that is vented in our hearing. The opposing the opinions, and rectifying the mistakes of others, is what truth and charity sometimes require of us, and civility does not oppose, if it be done with due caution and care of circumstances. But there are some people, that one may observe, possessed as it were with the spirit of contradiction, that steadily, and without regard to right or wrong, oppose some one, or, perhaps, every one of the company, whatever they say. This is so visible and outrageous a way of *censuring,* that no body can avoid thinking himself injur'd by it. All opposition to what another man has said, is so apt to be suspected of *censoriousness,* and is so seldom received without some sort of humiliation, that it ought to be made in the gentlest manner, and softest words can be found, and such as with the whole deportment may express no forwardness to contradict. All marks of respect and good will ought to accompany it, that whilst we gain the argument, we may not lose the esteem of those that hear us.

4. *Captiousness* is another fault opposite to *civility;* not only because it often produces misbecoming and provoking expressions and carriage; but because it is a tacit accusation and reproach of some incivility taken notice of in those whom we are angry with. Such a suspicion or intimation cannot be borne by any one without uneasiness. Besides, one angry body discomposes the whole company, and the harmony ceases upon any such jarring.

The happiness that all men so steadily pursue consisting in pleasure, it is easy to see why the *civil* are more acceptable than the useful. The ability, sincerity, and good intention of a man of weight and worth, or a real friend, seldom atones for the uneasiness that is produced by his grave and solid representations. Power and riches, nay virtue itself, are valued only as conducing to our happiness. And therefore he recommends himself ill to another as aiming at his happiness, who, in the services he does him, makes him uneasy in the manner of doing them. He that knows how to make those he converses with easy, without debasing himself to low and servile flattery, has found the true art of living in the world, and being both welcome and valued every where. *Civility* therefore is what in the first place should with great care be made habitual to children and young people.

§ 144. There is another fault in good manners, and that

is *excess of ceremony,* and an obstinate persisting to force
upon another what is not his due, and what he cannot take
without folly or shame. This seems rather a design to
expose than oblige: or at least looks like a contest for
mastery, and at best is but troublesome, and so can be no
part of *good-breeding,* which has no other use or end but
to make people easy and satisfied in their conversation with
us. This is a fault few young people are apt to fall into; but
yet if they are ever guilty of it, or are suspected to incline
that way, they should be told of it, and warned of this *mistaken civility.* The thing they should endeavour and aim at
in conversation, should be to shew respect, esteem, and good-
will, by paying to every one that common ceremony and
regard which is in civility due to them. To do this without
a suspicion of flattery, dissimulation, or meanness, is a great
skill, which good sense, reason, and good company can
only teach; but is of so much use in civil life that it is well
worth the studying.

§ 145. Though the managing ourselves well in this part
of our behaviour has the name of *good-breeding,* as if
peculiarly the effect of education; yet, as I have said,
young children should not be much perplexed about it;
I mean, about putting off their hats, and making legs
modishly. Teach them humility, and to be good-natur'd,
if you can, and this sort of manners will not be wanting;
*civility* being in truth nothing but a care not to shew any
slighting or contempt of any one in conversation. What
are the most allow'd and esteem'd ways of expressing this,
we have above observ'd. It is as peculiar and different,
in several countries of the world, as their languages; and
therefore, if it be rightly considered, rules and discourses
made to children about it, are as useless and impertinent,
as it would be now and then to give a rule or two of
the *Spanish* tongue to one that converses only with *Englishmen.* Be as busy as you please with discourses of
*civility* to your son, such as is his company, such will be
his manners. A plough-man of your neighbourhood that
has never been out of his parish, read what lectures you
please to him, will be as soon in his language as his carriage a courtier; that is, in neither will be more polite

than those he uses to converse with: and therefore, of this no other care can be taken till he be of an age to have a tutor put to him, who must not fail to be a well-bred man. And, in good earnest, if I were to speak my mind freely, so children do nothing out of obstinacy, pride, and ill-nature, 'tis no great matter how they put off their hats or make legs. If you can teach them to love and respect other people, they will, as their age requires it, find ways to express it acceptably to every one, according to the fashions they have been used to: and as to their motions and carriage of their bodies, a dancing-master, as has been said, when it is fit, will teach them what is most becoming. In the mean time, when they are young, people expect not that children should be over-mindful of these ceremonies; carelessness is allow'd to that age, and becomes them as well as compliments do grown people: or, at least, if some very nice people will think it a fault, I am sure it is a fault that should be over-look'd, and left to time, a tutor, and conversation to cure. And therefore I think it not worth your while to have your son (as I often see children are) molested or chid about it: but where there is *pride* or *ill-nature* appearing in his carriage, there he must be persuaded or shamed out of it.

Though children, when little, should not be much perplexed with rules and ceremonious parts of *breeding,* yet there is a sort of unmannerliness very apt to grow up with young people, if not early restrained, and that is, a forwardness to *interrupt* others that are speaking; and to stop them with some *contradiction.* Whether the custom of disputing, and the reputation of parts and learning usually given to it as if it were the only standard and evidence of knowledge, make young men so forward to watch occasions to correct others in their discourse, and not to slip any opportunity of shewing their talents: so it is, that I have found scholars most blamed in this point. There cannot be a greater rudeness, than to *interrupt* another in the current of his discourse; for if there be not impertinent folly in answering a man before we know what he will say, yet it is a plain declaration, that we are weary to hear him talk any longer, and have a dis-esteem of what he says; which we judging not fit to entertain the company, desire them to give audience to us, who have something to produce worth their attention. This shews a very great disrespect, and cannot but be offensive: and yet this is what almost all interruption constantly carries with it. To which, if there be added, as is usual, a *correcting* of any mistake, or a *contradiction* of what has been said, it is a mark of yet greater pride and self-conceitedness, when we thus intrude our selves for teachers, and take upon us either to set another right in his story, or shew the mistakes of his judgment.

I do not say this, that I think there should be no difference of opinions in conversation, nor opposition in men's discourses: this would be to take away the greatest advantage of society, and the improvements are to be made by ingenious company; where the light is to be got from the opposite arguings of men of parts, shewing the different sides of things and their various aspects and probabilities, would be quite lost, if every one were obliged to assent to, and say after the first speaker. 'Tis not the owning one's dissent from another, that I speak against, but the manner of doing it. Young men should be taught not to be forward to *interpose* their opinions, unless asked, or when others have done, and are silent; and then only by way of enquiry, not instruction. The positive asserting, and the magisterial air should be avoided; and when a general pause of the whole company affords an opportunity, they may modestly put in their question as learners.

This becoming decency will not cloud their parts, nor weaken the strength of their reason; but bespeak the more favourable attention, and give what they say the greater advantage. An ill argument, or ordinary observation, thus introduc'd, with some civil preface of deference and respect to the opinions of others, will procure them more credit and esteem than the sharpest wit, or profoundest science, with a rough, insolent, or noisy management, which always shocks the hearers, leaves an ill opinion of the man, though he get the better of it in the argument.

This therefore should be carefully watched in young people, stopp'd in the beginning, and the contrary habit introduced in all their conversation. And the rather, because forwardness to talk, frequent *interruptions* in arguing, and loud *wrangling,* are too often observable amongst grown people, even of rank, amongst us. The *Indians,* whom we call barbarous, observe much more decency and civility in their discourses and conversation, giving one another a fair silent hearing till they have quite done; and then answering them calmly, and without noise or passion. And if it be not so in this civiliz'd part of the world, we must impute it to a neglect in education, which has not yet reform'd this antient piece of barbarity amongst us. Was it not, think you, an entertaining spectacle, to see two ladies of quality accidentally seated on the opposite sides of a room, set round with company, fall into a dispute, and grow so eager in it, that in the heat of the controversy, edging by degrees their chairs forwards, they were in a little time got up close to one another in the middle of the room; where they for a good while managed the dispute as fiercely as two game-cocks in the pit, without minding or taking any notice of the circle, which could not all the while forbear smiling? This I was told by a person of quality, who was present at the combat, and did not omit to reflect upon the indecencies that warmth in *dispute* often runs people into; which, since custom makes too frequent, education should take the more care of. There is no body but condemns this in others, though they overlook it in themselves; and many who are sensible of it in themselves, and resolve against it, cannot yet get rid of an ill custom, which neglect in their education has suffer'd to settle into an habit.

§ 146. What has been above said concerning *company,* would perhaps, if it were well reflected on, give us a larger prospect, and let us see how much farther its influence reaches. 'Tis not the modes of civility alone, that are imprinted by *conversation:* the tincture of company sinks deeper than the out-side; and possibly, if a true estimate were made of the morality and religions of the world, we should find that the far greater part of mankind received even those opinions, and ceremonies they would die for, rather from the fashions of their countries, and the constant practice of those about them, than from any conviction of their reasons. I mention this only to let you see of what moment I think *company* is to your son in all the parts of his life, and therefore how much that one part is to be weighed and provided for; it being of greater force to work upon him, than all you can do besides.

§ 147. You will wonder, perhaps, that I put *learning* last, especially if I tell you I think it the least part. This may seem strange in the mouth of a bookish man; and this making usually the chief, if not only bustle and stir about children, this being almost that alone which is thought on, when people talk of education, makes it the greater paradox. When I consider, what ado is made about a little *Latin* and *Greek,* how many years are spent in it, and what a noise and business it makes to no purpose, I can hardly forbear thinking that the parents of children still live in fear of the school-master's rod, which they look on as the only instrument of education; as a language or two to be its whole business. How else is it possible that a child should be chain'd to the oar seven, eight, or ten of the best years of his life, to get a language or two, which, I think, might be had at a great deal cheaper rate of pains and time, and be learn'd almost in playing?

Forgive me therefore if I say, I cannot with patience think, that a young gentleman should be put into the herd, and be driven with a whip and scourge, as if he were to run the gantlet through the several classes, *ad capiendum ingenii cultum.* What then? say you, would you not have him write and read? Shall he be more ignorant than the clerk of our parish, who takes *Hopkins* and *Sternhold* for the best poets in the world, whom yet he makes worse than they are by his ill reading? Not so, not so fast, I beseech you. Reading and writing and *learning* I allow to be necessary, but yet not the chief business. I imagine you would think him a very foolish fellow, that should not value a virtuous or a wise man infinitely before a great scholar. Not but that I think *learning* a great help to both in well-dispos'd minds; but yet it must be confess'd also, that in others not so dispos'd, it helps them only to be the more foolish, or worse men. I say this, that when you consider the breeding of your son, and are looking out for a school-master or a tutor, you would not have (as is usual) Latin and *logick* only in your thoughts. *Learning* must be had, but in the second place, as subservient only to greater qualities. Seek out somebody that may know how discreetly to frame his manners: place him in hands where you may, as much as possible, secure his innocence, cherish, and nurse up the good, and gently correct and weed out any bad inclinations, and settle in him good habits. This is the main point, and this being provided for, *learning* may be had into the bargain, and that, as I think, at a very easy rate, by methods that may be thought on.

§ 148. When he can talk, 'tis time he should begin to *learn to read*. But as to this, give me leave here to inculcate again, what is very apt to be forgotten, *viz.* That great care is to be taken, that it be never made as a business to him, nor he look on it as a task. We naturally, as I said, even from our cradles, love liberty, and have therefore an aversion to many things for no other reason but because they are enjoin'd us. I have always had a fancy that *learning* might be made a play and recreation to children; and that they might be brought to desire to be taught, if it were proposed to them as a thing of honour, credit, delight, and recreation, or as a reward for doing something else; and if they were never chid or corrected for the neglect of it. That which confirms me in this opinion is, that amongst the *Portuguese,* 'tis so much a fashion and emulation amongst their children, to *learn to read* and write, that they cannot hinder them from it: they will learn it one from another, and are as intent on it, as if it were forbidden them. I remember that being at a friend's house, whose younger son, a child in coats, was not easily *brought* to his book (being taught *to read* at home by his mother) I advised to try another way, than requiring it of him as his duty; we therefore, in a discourse on purpose amongst our selves, in his hearing, but without taking any notice of him, declared, that it was the privilege and advantage of heirs and elder brothers, to be scholars; that this made them fine gentlemen, and beloved by every body: **and that for younger brothers, 'twas a favour to admit**

them to breeding; to be taught to *read* and write, was
more than came to their share; they might be ignorant
bumpkins and clowns, if they pleased. This so wrought
upon the child, that afterwards he desired to be taught;
would come himself to his mother to *learn,* and would not
let his maid be quiet till she heard him his lesson. I doubt
not but some way like this might be taken with other children; and when their tempers are found, some thoughts
be instill'd into them, that might set them upon desiring of
*learning,* themselves, and make them seek it as another
sort of play or recreation. But then, as I said before, it
must never be imposed as a task, nor made a trouble to
them. There may be dice and play-things, with the letters
on them to teach children the *alphabet* by playing; and
twenty other ways may be found, suitable to their particular
tempers, to make this kind of *learning a sport* to them.

§ 149. Thus children may be cozen'd into a knowledge
of the letters; be *taught to read,* without perceiving it to be
any thing but a sport, and play themselves into that which
others are whipp'd for. Children should not have any thing
like work, or serious, laid on them; neither their minds,
nor bodies will bear it. It injures their healths; and their
being forced and tied down to their books in an age at
enmity with all such restraint, has, I doubt not, been the
reason, why a great many have hated books and learning
all their lives after. 'Tis like a surfeit, that leaves an
aversion behind not to be removed.

§ 150. I have therefore thought, that if *play-things* were
fitted to this purpose, as they are usually to none, con-
trivances might be made *to teach children to read,* whilst
they thought they were only playing. For example, what if
an *ivory-ball* were made like that of the royal-oak lottery,
with thirty two sides, or one rather of twenty four or twenty
five sides; and upon several of those sides pasted on an A,
upon several others B, on others C, and on others D? I
would have you begin with but these four letters, or perhaps only two at first; and when he is perfect in them, then
add another; and so on till each side having one letter,
there be on it the whole alphabet. This I would have
others play with before him, it being as good a sort of

play to lay a stake who shall first throw an A or B, as who upon dice shall throw six or seven. This being a play amongst you, tempt him not to it, lest you make it business; for I would not have him understand 'tis any thing but a play of older people, and I doubt not but he will take to it of himself. And that he may have the more reason to think it is a play, that he is sometimes in favour admitted to, when the play is done the ball should be laid up safe out of his reach, that so it may not, by his having it in his keeping at any time, grow stale to him.

§ 151. To keep up his eagerness to it, let him think it a game belonging to those above him: and when, by this means, he knows the letters, by changing them into syllables, he may *learn to read,* without knowing how he did so, and never have any chiding or trouble about it, nor fall out with books because of the hard usage and vexation they have caus'd him. Children, if you observe them, take abundance of pains to learn several games, which, if they should be enjoined them, they would abhor as a task and business. I know a person of great quality (more yet to be honoured for his learning and virtue than for his rank and high place) who by pasting on the six vowels (for in our language Y is one) on the six sides of a die, and the remaining eighteen consonants on the sides of three other dice, has made this a play for his children, that he shall win who, at one cast, throws most words on these four dice; whereby his eldest son, yet in coats, has *play'd* himself *into spelling,* with great eagerness, and without once having been chid for it or forced to it.

§ 152. I have seen little girls exercise whole hours together and take abundance of pains to be expert at *dibstones* as they call it. Whilst I have been looking on, I have thought it wanted only some good contrivance to make them employ all that industry about something that might be more useful to them; and methinks 'tis only the fault and negligence of elder people that it is not so. Children are much less apt to be idle than men; and men are to be blamed if some part of that busy humour be not turned to useful things; which might be made usually as delightful to them as those they are employed in, if men would be but half so forward to lead the way, as these little apes would be to follow. I imagine some wise *Portuguese* heretofore began this fashion amongst the children of his country, where I have been told, as I said, it is impossible to hinder the children from *learning to read and write:* and in some parts of *France* they teach one another to sing and dance from the cradle.

§ 153. The *letters* pasted upon the sides of the dice, or polygon, were best to be of the size of those of the folio Bible, to begin with, and none of them capital letters; when once he can read what is printed in such letters, he will not long be ignorant of the great ones: and in the beginning he should not be perplexed with variety. With this die also, you might have a play just like the royal oak, which would be another variety, and play for cherries or apples, &c.

§ 154. Besides these, twenty other plays might be invented depending on *letters,* which those who like this way, may easily contrive and get made to this use if they will. But the four dice above-mention'd I think so easy and useful, that it will be hard to find any better, and there will be scarce need of any other.

§ 155. Thus much for *learning to read,* which let him never be driven to, nor chid for; cheat him into it if you can, but make it not a business for him. 'Tis better it be a year later *before he can read,* than that he should this way get an aversion to learning. If you have any contest with him, let it be in matters of moment, of truth, and good nature; but lay no task on him about A B C. Use your skill to make his will supple and pliant to reason: teach him to love credit and commendation; to abhor being thought ill or meanly of, especially by you and his mother, and then the rest will come all easily. But I think if you will do that, you must not shackle and tie him up with rules about indifferent matters, nor rebuke him for every little fault, or perhaps some that to others would seem great ones; but of this I have said enough already.

§ 156. When by these gentle ways he begins to *read,* some easy pleasant book, suited to his capacity, should be put into his hands, wherein the entertainment that he finds might draw him on, and reward his pains in reading, and yet not such as should fill his head with perfectly useless trumpery, or lay the principles of vice and folly. To this purpose, I think *Æsop's Fables* the best, which being stories apt to delight and entertain a child, may yet afford useful reflections to a grown man; and if his memory retain them all his life after, he will not repent to find them there, amongst his manly thoughts and serious business. If his *Æsop* has *pictures* in it, it will entertain him much the better, and encourage him to read, when it carries the increase of knowledge with it: for such visible objects children hear talked of in vain and without any satisfaction whilst they have no ideas of them; those ideas being not to be had from sounds, but from the things themselves or their pictures. And therefore I think as soon as he begins to spell, as many pictures of animals should be got him as can be found, with the printed names to them, which at the same time will invite him to read, and afford him matter of enquiry and knowledge. *Reynard the Fox* is another book I think may be made use of to the same purpose. And if those about him will talk to him often about the stories he has read, and hear him tell them, it will, besides other advantages, add encouragement and delight to his *reading,* when he finds there is some use and pleasure in it. These baits seem wholly neglected in the ordinary method; and 'tis usually long before learners find any use or pleasure in reading, which may tempt them to it, and so take books only for fashionable amusements, or impertinent troubles, good for nothing.

§ 157. The Lord's Prayer, the Creeds, and Ten Commandments, 'tis necessary he should learn perfectly by heart; but, I think, not by reading them himself in his primer, but by somebody's repeating them to him, even before he can read. But learning by heart, and *learning to read,* should not I think be mix'd, and so one made to clog the other. But his *learning to read* should be made as little trouble or business to him as might be.

What other books there are in *English* of the kind of those above-mentioned, fit to engage the liking of children, and tempt them to *read,* I do not know: but am apt to think, that children being generally delivered over to the method of schools, where the fear of the rod is to inforce, and not any pleasure of the employment to invite them to learn, this sort of useful books, amongst the number of silly ones that are of all sorts, have yet had the fate to be neglected; and nothing that I know has been considered of this kind out of the ordinary road of the horn-book, primer, psalter, Testament, and Bible.

§ 158. As for the *Bible,* which children are usually employ'd in to exercise and improve their talent *in reading,* I think the promiscuous reading of it through by chapters as they lie in order, is so far from being of any advantage to children, either for the perfecting their *reading,* or principling their religion, that perhaps a worse could not be found. For what pleasure or encouragement can it be to a child to exercise himself in reading those parts of a book where he understands nothing? And how little are the law of *Moses,* the song of *Solomon,* the prophecies in the Old, and the Epistles and *Apocalypse* in the New Testament, suited to a child's capacity? And though the history of the Evangelists and the *Acts* have something easier, yet, taken altogether, it is very disproportional to the understanding of childhood. I grant that the principles of religion are to be drawn from thence, and in the words of the scripture; yet none should be propos'd to a child, but such as are suited to a child's capacity and notions. But 'tis far from this to read through *the whole Bible,* and that for reading's sake. And what an odd jumble of thoughts must a child have in his head, if he have any at all, such as he should have concerning religion, who in his tender age reads all the parts of the *Bible* indifferently as the word of God without any other distinction! I am apt to think, that this in some men has been the very reason why they never had clear and distinct thougths of it all their lifetime.

§ 159. And now I am by chance fallen on this subject, give me leave to say, that there are some parts of the *Scripture* which may be proper to be put into the hands of a child to engage him to read; such as are the story of *Joseph* and his brethren, of *David* and *Goliath,* of *David* and

*Jonathan,* &c. and others that he should be made to read for
his instruction, as that, *What you would have others do unto
you, do you the same unto them;* and such other easy and plain
moral rules, which being fitly chosen, might often be made
use of, both for reading and instruction together; and so
often read till they are throughly fixed in the memory; and
then afterwards, as he grows ripe for them, may in their
turns on fit occasions be inculcated as the standing and
sacred rules of his life and actions. But the reading of the
whole Scripture indifferently, is what I think very inconvenient for children, till after having been made acquainted
with the plainest fundamental parts of it, they have got some
kind of general view of what they ought principally to believe and practise; which yet, I think, they ought to receive
in the very words of the scripture, and not in such as men
prepossess'd by systems and analogies are apt in this case
to make use of and force upon them. Dr. *Worthington,* to
avoid this, has made a catechism, which has all its answers
in the precise words of the Scripture; a thing of good example, and such a sound form of words as no Christian can
except against as not fit for his child to learn. Of this, as
soon as he can say the Lord's Prayer, Creed, the Ten Commandments, by heart, it may be fit for him to learn a question every day, or every week, as his understanding is able
to receive and his memory to retain them. And when he
has this catechism perfectly by heart, so as readily and
roundly to answer to any question in the whole book, it may
be convenient to lodge in his mind the remaining moral rules
scatter'd up and down in the Bible, as the best *exercise of
his memory,* and that which may be always a rule to him,
ready at hand, in the whole conduct of his life.

§ 160. When he can read *English* well, it will be seasonable to enter him in *writing:* and here the first thing should
be taught him is to *hold his pen right;* and this he should
be perfect in before he should be suffered to put it to paper:
For not only children but any body else that would do any
thing well, should never be put upon too much of it at once,
or be set to perfect themselves in two parts of an action at
the same time, if they can possibly be separated. I think
the *Italian* way of holding the pen between the thumb and

the fore-finger alone, may be best; but in this you may consult some good writing-master, or any other person who writes well and quick. When he has learn'd to hold his pen right, in the next place he should learn how to *lay his paper, and place his arm and body to it.* These practices being got over, the way to teach him to write without much trouble, is to get a plate graved with the characters of such a hand as you like best: but you must remember to have them a pretty deal bigger than he should ordinarily write; for every one naturally comes by degrees to write a less hand than he at first was taught, but never a bigger. Such a plate being graved, let several sheets of good writing-paper be printed off with red ink, which he has nothing to do but go over with a good pen fill'd with black ink, which will quickly bring his hand to the formation of those characters, being at first shewed where to begin, and how to form every letter. And when he can do that well, he must then exercise on fair paper; and so may easily be brought *to write* the hand you desire.

§ 161. When he can write well and quick, I think it may be convenient not only to continue the exercise of his hand in writing, but also to improve the use of it farther in *drawing;* a thing very useful to a gentleman in several occasions; but especially if he travel, as that which helps a man often to express, in a few lines well put together, what a whole sheet of paper in writing would not be able to represent and make intelligible. How many buildings may a man see, how many machines and habits meet with, the ideas whereof would be easily retain'd and communicated by a little skill in *drawing;* which being committed to words, are in danger to be lost, or at best but ill retained in the most exact descriptions? I do not mean that I would have your son a *perfect painter;* to be that to any tolerable degree, will require more time than a young gentleman can spare from his other improvements of greater moment. But so much insight into *perspective* and skill in *drawing,* as will enable him to represent tolerably on paper any thing he sees, except faces, may, I think, be got in a little time, especially if he have a genius to it; but where that is wanting, unless it be in the things absolutely necessary, it is better to let him

pass them by quietly, than to vex him about them to no purpose: and therefore in this, as in all other things not absolutely necessary, the rule holds, *nil invita Minerva.*

¶ 1. *Short-hand,* an art, as I have been told, known only
in *England,* may perhaps be thought worth the learning,
both for dispatch in what men write for their own memory,
and concealment of what they would not have lie open to
every eye. For he that has once learn'd any sort of character, may easily vary it to his own private use or fancy,
and with more contraction suit it to the business he would
employ it in. Mr. *Rich's,* the best contriv'd of any I have
seen, may, as I think, by one who knows and considers
grammar well, be made much easier and shorter. But for
the learning this compendious way of writing, there will
be no need hastily to look out a master; it will be early
enough when any convenient opportunity offers itself at
any time, after his hand is well settled in fair and quick
writing. For boys have but little use of *short-hand,* and
should by no means practise it till they write perfectly well,
and have throughly fixed the habit of doing so.

§ 162. As soon as he can speak *English,* 'tis time for him
to learn some other language. This no body doubts of,
when *French* is propos'd. And the reason is, because people
are accustomed to the right way of teaching that language,
which is by talking it into children in constant conversation, and not by grammatical rules. The *Latin* tongue would
easily be taught the same way, if his tutor, being constantly
with him, would talk nothing else to him; and make him
answer still in the same language. But because *French* is a
living language, and to be used more in speaking, that
should be first learned, that the yet pliant organs of speech
might be accustomed to a due formation of those sounds, and
he get the habit of pronouncing *French* well, which is the
harder to be done the longer it is delay'd.

§ 163. When he can speak and read *French* well, which
in this method is usually in a year or two, he should proceed to *Latin,* which 'tis a wonder parents, when they have
had the experiment in *French,* should not think ought to
be learned the same way, by talking and reading. Only care
is to be taken whilst he is learning these foreign languages,

by speaking and reading nothing else with his tutor, that he
do not forget to read *English,* which may be preserved by
his mother or some body else hearing him read some chosen
parts of the scripture or other *English* book every day.

§ 164. *Latin* I look upon as absolutely necessary to a
gentleman; and indeed custom, which prevails over every
thing, has made it so much a part of education, that even
those children are whipp'd to it, and made spend many
hours of their precious time uneasily in *Latin,* who after
they are once gone from school, are never to have more to
do with it as long as they live. Can there be any thing
more ridiculous, than that a father should waste his own
money and his son's time in setting him to learn the *Roman
language,* when at the same time he designs him for a trade,
wherein he having no use of *Latin,* fails not to forget that
little which he brought from school, and which 'tis ten to
one he abhors for the ill usage it procured him? Could it be
believed, unless we had every where amongst us examples
of it, that a child should be forced to learn the rudiments
of a language which he is never to use in the course of
life that he is designed to, and neglect all the while the
writing a good hand and casting accounts, which are of
great advantage in all conditions of life, and to most trades
indispensably necessary? But though these qualifications,
requisite to trade and commerce and the business of the
world, are seldom or never to be had at grammar-schools,
yet thither not only gentlemen send their younger sons,
intended for trades, but even tradesmen and farmers fail
not to send their children, though they have neither intention nor ability to make them scholars. If you ask them
why they do this, they think it as strange a question as if
you should ask them, why they go to church. Custom
serves for reason, and has, to those who take it for reason,
so consecrated this method, that it is almost religiously observed by them, and they stick to it, as if their children had
scarce an orthodox education unless they learned *Lilly's*
grammar.

§ 165. But how necessary soever *Latin* be to some, and
is thought to be to others to whom it is of no manner
of use and service; yet the ordinary way of learning it in

a grammar-school is that which having had thoughts about I cannot be forward to encourage. The reasons against it are so evident and cogent, that they have prevailed with some intelligent persons to quit the ordinary road, not without success, though the method made use of was not exactly what I imagine the easiest, and in short is this. To trouble the child with no *grammar* at all, but to have *Latin,* as *English* has been, without the perplexity of rules, talked into him; for if you will consider it, *Latin* is no more unknown to a child, when he comes into the world, than *English:* and yet he learns *English* without master, rule, or grammar; and so might he *Latin* too, as *Tully* did, if he had some body always to talk to him in this language. And when we so often see a *French* woman teach an *English* girl to speak and read *French* perfectly in a year or two, without any rule of grammar, or any thing else but prattling to her, I cannot but wonder how gentlemen have overseen this way for their sons, and thought them more dull or incapable than their daughters.

§ 166. If therefore a man could be got, who himself speaking good *Latin,* would always be about your son, talk constantly to him, and suffer him to speak or read nothing else, this would be the true and genuine way, and that which I would propose, not only as the easiest and best, wherein a child might, without pains or chiding, get a language, which others are wont to be whipt for at school six or seven years together: but also as that, wherein at the same time he might have his mind and manners formed, and he be instructed to boot in several sciences, such as are a good part of *geography, astronomy, chronology, anatomy,* besides some parts of *history,* and all other parts of knowledge of things that fall under the senses and require little more than memory. For there, if we would take the true way, our knowledge should begin, and in those things be laid the foundation; and not in the abstract notions of *logick* and *metaphysicks,* which are fitter to amuse than inform the understanding in its first setting out towards knowledge. When young men have had their heads employ'd a while in those abstract speculations without finding the success and improvement, or that use of them, which

they expected, they are apt to have mean thoughts either of
learning or themselves; they are tempted to quit their
studies, and throw away their books as containing nothing
but hard words and empty sounds; or else, to conclude, that
if there be any real knowledge in them, they themselves
have not understandings capable of it. That this is so, perhaps I could assure you upon my own experience. Amongst
other things to be learned by a young gentleman in this
method, whilst others of his age are wholly taken up with
*Latin* and languages, I may also set down *geometry* for one;
having known a young gentleman, bred something after
this way, able to demonstrate several propositions in *Euclid*
before he was thirteen.

§ 167. But if such a man cannot be got, who speaks good
*Latin,* and being able to instruct your son in all these parts
of knowledge, will undertake it by this method; the next
best is to have him taught as near this way as may be,
which is by taking some easy and pleasant book, such as
*Æsop's Fables,* and writing the *English* translation (made as
literal as it can be) in one line, and the *Latin* words which
answer each of them, just over it in another. These let him
read every day over and over again, till he perfectly understands the *Latin;* and then go on to another fable, till he
be also perfect in that, not omitting what he is already
perfect in, but sometimes reviewing that, to keep it in his
memory. And when he comes to write, let these be set
him for copies, which with the exercise of his hand will
also advance him to *Latin.* This being a more imperfect
way than by talking *Latin* unto him; the formation of the
verbs first, and afterwards the declensions of the nouns and
pronouns perfectly learned by heart, may facilitate his
acquaintance with the genius and manner of the *Latin
tongue,* which varies the signification of verbs and nouns,
not as the modern languages do by particles prefix'd, but
by changing the last syllables. More than this of grammar,
I think he need not have, till he can read himself *Sanctii
Minerva,* with *Scioppius* and *Perizonius's* notes.

In teaching of children, this too, I think, is to be observed, that in most cases where they stick, they are not to
be farther puzzled by putting them upon finding it out

themselves; as by asking such questions as these, (*viz.*) which is the nominative case, in the sentence they are to construe; or demanding what *aufero* signifies, to lead them to the knowledge what *abstlere* signifies, *&c.,* when they cannot readily tell. This wastes time only in disturbing them; for whilst they are learning, and apply themselves with attention, they are to be kept in good humour, and every thing made easy to them, and as pleasant as possible. Therefore, wherever they are at a stand, and are willing to go forwards, help them presently over the difficulty, without any rebuke or chiding, remembering, that where harsher ways are taken, they are the effect only of pride and peevishness in the teacher, who expects children should instantly be masters of as much as he knows; whereas he should rather consider, that his business is to settle in them habits, not angrily to inculcate rules, which serve for little in the conduct of our lives; at least are of no use to children, who forget them as soon as given. In sciences where their reason is to be exercised, I will not deny but this method may sometimes be varied, and difficulties proposed on purpose to excite industry, and accustom the mind to employ its own strength and sagacity in reasoning. But yet, I guess, this is not to be done to children, whilst very young, nor at their entrance upon any sort of knowledge: then every thing of itself is difficult, and the great use and skill of a teacher is to make all as easy as he can: but particularly in learning of languages there is least occasion for posing of children. For languages being to be learned by rote, custom and memory, are then spoken in greatest perfection, when all rules of grammar are utterly forgotten. I grant the grammar of a language is sometimes very carefully to be studied, but it is not to be studied but by a grown man, when he applies himself to the understanding of any language critically, which is seldom the business of any but professed scholars. This I think will be agreed to, that if a gentleman be to study any language, it ought to be that of his own country, that he may understand the language which he has constant use of, with the utmost accuracy.

There is yet a further reason, why masters and teachers

should raise no difficulties to their scholars; but on the contrary should smooth their way, and readily help them forwards, where they find them stop. Children's minds are narrow and weak, and usually susceptible but of one thought at once. Whatever is in a child's head, fills it for the time, especially if set on with any passion. It should therefore be the skill and art of the teacher to clear their heads of all other thoughts whilst they are learning of any thing, the better to make room for what he would instill into them, that it may be received with attention and application, without which it leaves no impression. The natural temper of children disposes their minds to wander. Novelty alone takes them; whatever that presents, they are presently eager to have a taste of, and are as soon satiated with it. They quickly grow weary of the same thing, and so have almost their whole delight in change and variety. It is a contradiction to the natural state of childhood for them to fix their fleeting thoughts. Whether this be owing to the temper of their brains, or the quickness or instability of their animal spirits, over which the mind has not yet got a full command; this is visible, that it is a pain to children to keep their thoughts steady to any thing. A lasting continued attention is one of the hardest tasks can be imposed on them; and therefore, he that requires their application, should endeavour to make what he proposes as grateful and agreeable as possible; at least he ought to take care not to join any displeasing or frightful idea with it. If they come not to their books with some kind of liking and relish, 'tis no wonder their thoughts should be perpetually shifting from what disgusts them; and seek better entertainment in more pleasing objects, after which they will unavoidably be gadding.

'Tis, I know, the usual method of tutors, to endeavour to procure attention in their scholars, and to fix their minds to the business in hand, by rebukes and corrections, if they find them ever so little wandering. But such treatment is sure to produce the quite contrary effect. Passionate words or blows from the tutor fill the child's mind with terror and affrightment, which immediately takes it wholly up, and leaves no room for other impressions. I believe there is no body that reads this, but may recollect what disorder hasty or imperious words from his parents or teachers have caused in his thoughts; how for the time it has turned his brains, so that he scarce knew what was said by or to him. He presently lost the sight of what he was upon, his mind was filled with disorder and confusion, and in that state was no longer capable of attention to any thing else.

'Tis true, parents and governors ought to settle and establish their authority by an awe over the minds of those under their tuition; and to rule them by that: but when they have got an ascendant over them, they should use it with great moderation, and not make themselves such scarecrows that their scholars should always tremble in their sight. Such an austerity may make their government easy to themselves, but of very little use to their pupils. 'Tis impossible children should learn any thing whilst their thoughts are possessed and disturbed with any passion, especially fear, which makes the strongest impression on their yet tender and weak spirits. Keep the mind in an easy calm temper, when you would have it receive your instructions or any increase of knowledge. 'Tis as impossible to draw fair and regular characters on a trembling mind as on a shaking paper.

The great skill of a teacher is to get and keep the attention of his scholar; whilst he has that, he is sure to advance as fast as the learner's abilities will carry him; and without that, all his bustle and pother will be to little or no purpose. To attain this, he should make the child comprehend (as much as may be) the usefulness of what he teaches him, and let him see, by what he has learnt, that he can do something which he could not do before; something, which gives him some power and real advantage above others who are ignorant of it. To this he should add sweetness in all his instructions, and by a certain tenderness in his whole carriage, make the child sensible that he loves him and designs nothing but his good, the only way to beget love in the child, which will make him hearken to his lessons, and relish what he teaches him.

Nothing but obstinacy should meet with any imperiousness or rough usage. All other faults should be corrected with a gentle hand; and kind engaging words will work better and more effectually upon a willing mind, and even prevent a good deal of that perverseness which rough and imperious usage often produces in well disposed and generous minds. 'Tis true, obstinacy and wilful neglects must be mastered, even though it cost blows to do it: but I am apt to think perverseness in the pupils is often the effect of frowardness in the *tutor;* and that most children would seldom have deserved blows, if needless and misapplied roughness had not taught them ill-nature, and given them an aversion for their teacher and all that comes from him.

Inadvertency, forgetfulness, unsteadiness, and wandering of thought, are the natural faults of childhood; and therefore, where they are not observed to be wilful, are to be mention'd softly, and gain'd upon by time. If every slip of this kind produces anger and rating, the occasions of rebuke and corrections will return so often, that the tutor will be a constant terror and uneasiness to his pupils. Which one thing is enough to hinder their profiting by his lessons, and to defeat all his methods of instruction.

Let the awe he has got upon their minds be so tempered with the constant marks of tenderness and good will, that affection may spur them to their duty, and make them find a pleasure in complying with his dictates. This will bring them with satisfaction to their tutor; make them hearken to him, as to one who is their friend, that cherishes them, and takes pains for their good: this will keep their thoughts easy and free whilst they are with him, the only temper wherein the mind is capable of receiving new informations, and of admitting into itself those impressions, which, if not taken and retain'd, all that they and their teachers do together is lost labour; there is much uneasiness and little learning.

§ 168. When by this way of interlining *Latin* and *English* one with another, he has got a moderate knowledge of the *Latin tongue,* he may then be advanced a little farther to the reading of some other easy *Latin*-book, such as *Justin* or *Eutropius;* and to make the reading and understanding of it the less tedious and difficult to him, let him help himself if he pleases with the *English* translation. Nor let the objection that he will then know it only by rote, fright any one. This, when well consider'd, is not of any moment against, but plainly for this way of learning a language. For languages are only to be learned by rote; and a man who does not speak *English* or *Latin* perfectly by rote, so that having thought of the thing he would speak of, his tongue of course, without thought of rule or grammar, falls into the proper expression and idiom of that language, does not speak it well, nor is master of it. And I would fain have any one name to me that tongue, that any one can learn, or speak as he should do, by the rules of grammar. Languages were made not by rules or art, but by accident, and the common use of the people. And he that will speak them well, has no other rule but that; nor any thing to trust to, but his memory, and the habit of speaking after the fashion learned from those, that are allowed to speak properly, which in other words is only to speak by rote.

It will possibly be asked here, is *grammar* then of no use? and have those who have taken so much pains in reducing several languages to rules and observations; who have writ so much about *declensions* and *conjugations,* about *concords* and *syntaxis,* lost their labour, and been learned to no purpose? I say not so; *grammar* has its place too. But this I think I may say, there is more stir a great deal made with it than there needs, and those are tormented about it, to whom it does not at all belong; I mean children, at the age wherein they are usually perplexed with it in grammar-schools.

There is nothing more evident, than that languages learnt by rote serve well enough for the common affairs of life and ordinary commerce. Nay, persons of quality of the softer sex, and such of them as have spent their time in well-bred company, shew us, that this plain natural way, without the least study or knowledge of *grammar,* can carry them to a great degree of elegancy and politeness in their language: and there are ladies who, without knowing what *tenses* and *participles, adverbs* and *prepositions* are, speak as properly and as correctly (they might take it for an ill compliment if I said as any country school-master) as most gen-

tlemen who have been bred up in the ordinary methods
of grammar-schools. Grammar therefore we see may be
spared in some cases. The question then will be, to whom
should it be taught, and when? To this I answer:

1. Men learn languages for the ordinary intercourse of
society and communication of thoughts in common life,
without any farther design in the use of them. And for
this purpose, the original way of learning a language by
conversation not only serves well enough, but is to be preferred as the most expedite, proper and natural. Therefore,
to this use of language one may answer, that grammar is
not necessary. This so many of my readers must be forced
to allow, as understand what I here say, and who conversing with others, understand them without having ever
been taught the grammar of the *English* tongue. Which
I suppose is the case of incomparably the greatest part of
*English* men, of whom I have never yet known any one
who learned his mother-tongue by rules.

2. Others there are, the greatest part of whose business
in this world is to be done with their tongues and with
their pens; and to these it is convenient, if not necessary,
that they should speak properly and correctly, whereby they
may let their thoughts into other men's minds the more
easily, and with the greater impression. Upon this account
it is, that any sort of speaking, so as will make him be
understood, is not thought enough for a gentleman. He
ought to study grammar amongst the other helps of speaking
well, but it must be the grammar of his own tongue, of the
language he uses, that he may understand his own country
speech nicely, and speak it properly, without shocking the
ears of those it is addressed to, with solecisms and offensive irregularities. And to this purpose grammar is necessary; but it is the grammar only of their own proper
tongues, and to those only who would take pains in cultivating their language, and in perfecting their stiles.
Whether all gentlemen should not do this, I leave to be
considered, since the want of propriety and grammatical
exactness is thought very misbecoming one of that rank,
and usually draws on one guilty of such faults the censure
of having had a lower breeding and worse company than

suits with his quality. If this be so, (as I suppose it is) it
will be matter of wonder why young gentlemen are forced
to learn the grammars of foreign and dead languages, and
are never once told of the grammar of their own tongues:
they do not so much as know there is any such thing, much
less is it made their business to be instructed in it. Nor is
their own language ever proposed to them as worthy their
care and cultivating, though they have daily use of it, and are
not seldom, in the future course of their lives, judg'd of by
their handsome or awkward way of expressing themselves
in it. Whereas the languages whose grammars they have
been so much employed in, are such as probably they shall
scarce ever speak or write; or if, upon occasion, this should
happen, they should be excused for the mistakes and faults
they make in it. Would not a *Chinese* who took notice
of this way of breeding, be apt to imagine that all our
young gentlemen were designed to be teachers and professors of the dead languages of foreign countries, and not
to be men of business in their own?

3. There is a third sort of men, who apply themselves
to two or three foreign, dead, and (which amongst us are
called the) learned languages, make them their study, and
pique themselves upon their skill in them. No doubt, those
who propose to themselves the learning of any language
with this view, and would be critically exact in it, ought
carefully to study the grammar of it. I would not be mistaken here, as if this were to undervalue *Greek* and *Latin*.
I grant these are languages of great use and excellency,
and a man can have no place among the learned in this part
of the world, who is a stranger to them. But the knowledge
a gentleman would ordinarily draw for his use out of the
*Roman* and *Greek* writers, I think he may attain without
studying the grammars of those tongues, and by bare reading, may come to understand them sufficiently for all his
purposes. How much farther he shall at any time be concerned to look into the grammar and critical niceties of
either of these tongues, he himself will be able to determine when he comes to propose to himself the study of any
thing that shall require it. Which brings me to the other
part of the enquiry, *viz.*

### *When Grammar should be taught?*

To which, upon the premised grounds, the answer is obvious, *viz.*

That if grammar ought to be taught at any time, it must be to one that can speak the language already; how else can he be taught the grammar of it? This at least is evident from the practice of the wise and learned nations amongst the antients. They made it a part of education to cultivate their own, not foreign tongues. The *Greeks* counted all other nations barbarous, and had a contempt for their languages. And tho' the *Greek* learning grew in credit amongst the *Romans,* towards the end of their commonwealth, yet it was the *Roman* tongue that was made the study of their youth: their own language they were to make use of, and therefore it was their own language they were instructed and exercised in.

But, more particularly to determine the proper season for grammar, I do not see how it can reasonably be made any one's study, but as an introduction to rhetorick; when it is thought time to put any one upon the care of polishing his tongue, and of speaking better than the illiterate, then is the time for him to be instructed in the rules of grammar, and not before. For grammar being to teach men not to speak, but to speak correctly and according to the exact rules of the tongue, which is one part of elegancy, there is little use of the one to him that has no need of the other; where rhetorick is not necessary, grammar may be spared. I know not why any one should waste his time, and beat his head about the *Latin* grammar, who does not intend to be a critick, or make speeches and write dispatches in it. When any one finds in himself a necessity or disposition to study any foreign language to the bottom, and to be nicely exact in the knowledge of it, it will be time enough to take a grammatical survey of it. If his use of it be only to understand some books writ in it, without a critical knowledge of the tongue itself, reading alone, as I have said, will attain this end, without charging the mind with the multiplied rules and intricacies of grammar.

§ 169. For the exercise of his writing, let him sometimes

translate *Latin* into *English:* but the learning of *Latin* being nothing but the learning of words, a very unpleasant business both to young and old, join as much other real knowledge with it as you can, beginning still with that which lies most obvious to the senses; such as is the knowledge of *minerals, plants* and *animals,* and particularly timber and fruit-trees, their parts, and ways of propagation, wherein a great deal may be taught a child which will not be useless to the man: but more especially *geography, astronomy,* and *anatomy.* But whatever you are teaching him, have a care still that you do not clog him with too much at once; or make any thing his business but downright virtue, or reprove him for any thing but vice, or some apparent tendency to it.

§ 170. But if after all his fate be to go to school to get the *Latin* tongue, 'twill be in vain to talk to you concerning the method I think best to be observ'd in schools; you must submit to that you find there, not expect to have it changed for your son; but yet by all means obtain, if you can, that he be not employed in making *Latin themes* and *declamations,* and least of all, *verses* of any kind. You may insist on it, if it will do any good, that you have no design to make him either a *Latin* orator or poet, but barely would have him understand perfectly a *Latin* author; and that you observe, those who teach any of the modern languages, and that with success, never amuse their scholars to make speeches or verses either in *French* or *Italian,* their business being language barely, and not invention.

§ 171. But to tell you a little more fully why I would not have him exercised in making of *themes* and *verses.* 1. As to *themes,* they have, I confess, the pretence of something useful, which is to teach people to speak handsomely and well on any subject; which, if it could be attained this way, I own would be a great advantage, there being nothing more becoming a gentleman, nor more useful in all the occurrences of life, than to be able, on any occasion, to speak well and to the purpose. But this I say, that the making of *themes,* as is usual at schools, helps not one jot towards it: for do but consider what it is, in making a *theme,* that a young lad is employed about; it is to make

a speech on some *Latin* saying; as *Omnia vincit amor;* or
*Non licet in Bello bis peccare, &c.* And here the poor lad,
who wants knowledge of those things he is to speak of,
which is to be had only from time and observation, must
set his invention on the rack, to say something where he
knows nothing; which is a sort of *Egyptian* tyranny, to bid
them make bricks who have not yet any of the materials.
And therefore it is usual in such cases for the poor children
to go to those of higher forms with this petition, *Pray give
me a little sense;* which, whether it be more reasonable or
more ridiculous, it is not easy to determine. Before a man
can be in any capacity to speak on any subject, 'tis necessary
he be acquainted with it; or else it is as foolish to set him
to discourse of it, as to set a blind man to talk of colours,
or a deaf man of musick. And would you not think him a
little crack'd, who would require another to make an argument on a moot point, who understands nothing of our
laws? And what, I pray, do school-boys understand concerning those matters which are used to be proposed to them
in their *themes* as subjects to discourse on, to whet and
exercise their fancies?

§ 172. In the next place, consider the language that
their *themes* are made in: 'tis *Latin,* a language foreign
in their country, and long since dead every where: a
language which your son, 'tis a thousand to one, shall never
have an occasion once to make a speech in as long as
he lives after he comes to be a man; and a language
wherein the manner of expressing one's self is so far different from ours, that to be perfect in that would very little
improve the purity and facility of his *English* stile. Besides
that, there is now so little room or use for set speeches
in our own language in any part of our *English* business,
that I can see no pretence for this sort of exercise in our
schools, unless it can be supposed, that the making of set
*Latin* speeches should be the way to teach men to speak
well in *English extempore.* The way to that, I should think
rather to be this: that there should be propos'd to young
gentlemen rational and useful questions, suited to their age
and capacities, and on subjects not wholly unknown to
them nor out of their way: such as these, when they are

ripe for exercises of this nature, they should *extempore,*
or after a little meditation upon the spot, speak to, without
penning of any thing: for I ask, if we will examine the
effects of this way of learning to speak well, who speak
best in any business, when occasion calls them to it upon
any debate, either those who have accustomed themselves to
compose and write down beforehand what they would say;
or those, who thinking only of the matter, to understand
that as well as they can, use themselves only to speak
*extempore?* And he that shall judge by this, will be little apt
to think, that the accustoming him to studied speeches and
set compositions, is the way to fit a young gentleman for
business.

§ 173. But perhaps we shall be told, 'tis to improve and
perfect them in the *Latin* tongue. 'Tis true, that is their
proper business at school; but the making of *themes* is not
the way to it: that perplexes their brains about invention
of things to be said, not about the signification of words to
be learn'd; and when they are making a *theme,* 'tis thoughts
they search and sweat for, and not language. But the learning and mastery of a tongue being uneasy and unpleasant
enough in itself, should not be cumbred with any other
difficulties, as is done in this way of proceeding. In fine,
if boys' invention be to be quicken'd by such exercise, let
them make *themes* in *English,* where they have facility and
a command of words, and will better see what kind of
thoughts they have, when put into their own language. And
if the *Latin* tongue be to be learned, let it be done the
easiest way, without toiling and disgusting the mind by so
uneasy an employment as that of making speeches joined
to it.

§ 174. If these may be any reasons against children's
making *Latin* themes at school, I have much more to say,
and of more weight, against their making *verses;* verses
of any sort: for if he has no *genius* to *poetry,* 'tis the most
unreasonable thing in the world to torment a child and
waste his time about that which can never succeed; and
if he have a poetick vein, 'tis to me the strangest thing
in the world that the father should desire or suffer it
to be cherished or improved. Methinks the parents should

labour to have it stifled and suppressed as much as may be; and I know not what reason a father can have to wish his son a poet, who does not desire to have him bid defiance to all other callings and business; which is not yet the worst of the case; for if he proves a successful rhymer, and gets once the reputation of a wit, I desire it may be considered what company and places he is like to spend his time in, nay, and estate too: for it is very seldom seen, that any one discovers mines of gold or silver in *Parnassus.* 'Tis a pleasant air, but a barren soil; and there are very few instances of those who have added to their patrimony by any thing they have reaped from thence. Poetry and gaming, which usually go together, are alike in this too, that they seldom bring any advantage but to those who have nothing else to live on. Men of estates almost constantly go away losers; and 'tis well if they escape at a cheaper rate than their whole estates, or the greatest part of them. If therefore you would not have your son the fiddle to every jovial company, without whom the sparks could not relish their wine nor know how to pass an afternoon idly; if you would not have him to waste his time and estate to divert others, and contemn the dirty acres left him by his ancestors, I do not think you will much care he should be a *poet,* or that his school-master should enter him in versifying. But yet, if any one will think poetry a desirable quality in his son, and that the study of it would raise his fancy and parts, he must needs yet confess, that to that end reading the excellent *Greek* and *Roman* poets is of more use than making bad verses of his own, in a language that is not his own. And he whose design it is to excel in *English* poetry, would not, I guess, think the way to it were to make his first essays in *Latin* verses.

§ 175. Another thing very ordinary in the vulgar method of grammar-schools there is, of which I see no use at all, unless it be to baulk young lads in the way to learning languages, which, in my opinion, should be made as easy and pleasant as may be; and that which was painful in it, as much as possible quite removed. That which I mean, and here complain of, is, their being forced to learn by heart, great parcels of the authors which are taught them; wherein I can discover no advantage at all, especially to the business they are upon. Languages are to be learned only by reading and talking, and not by scraps of authors got by heart; which when a man's head is stuffed with, he has got the just furniture of a pedant, and 'tis the ready way to make him one; than which there is nothing less becoming a gentleman. For what can be more ridiculous, than to mix the rich and handsome thoughts and sayings of others with a deal of poor stuff of his own; which is thereby the more exposed, and has no other grace in it, nor will otherwise recommend the speaker, than a thread-bare russet coat would, that was set off with large patches of scarlet and glittering brocade. Indeed, where a passage comes in the way, whose matter is worth remembrance, and the expression of it very close and excellent, (as there are many such in the antient authors) it may not be amiss to lodge it in the mind of young scholars, and with such admirable strokes of those great masters sometimes exercise the memories of school-boys. But their learning of their lessons by heart, as they happen to fall out in their books, without choice or distinction, I know not what it serves for, but to misspend their time and pains, and give them a disgust and aversion to their books, wherein they find nothing but useless trouble.

§ 176. I hear it is said, that children should be employ'd in getting things by heart, to exercise and improve their memories. I could wish this were said with as much authority of reason, as it is with forwardness of assurance, and that this practice were established upon good observation more than old custom: for it is evident, that strength of memory is owing to an happy constitution, and not to any habitual improvement got by exercise. 'Tis true, what the mind is intent upon, and, for fear of letting it slip, often imprints afresh on itself by frequent reflection, that it is apt to retain, but still according to its own natural strength of retention. An impression made on bees-wax or lead, will not last so long as on brass or steel. Indeed, if it be renew'd often, it may last the longer; but every new reflecting on it is a new impression; and 'tis from thence one is to reckon, if one would know how long the mind retains it. But the learning pages of *Latin* by heart, no more fits the memory for retention of any thing else, than the graving of one sentence in lead makes it the more capable of retaining firmly any other characters. If such a sort of exercise of the memory were able to give it strength, and improve our parts, players of all other people must needs have the best memories and be the best company. But whether the scraps they have got into their heads this way, make them remember other things the better; and whether their parts be improved proportionably to the pains they have taken in getting by heart others' sayings, experience will shew. Memory is so necessary to all parts and conditions of life, and so little is to be done without it, that we are not to fear it should grow dull and useless for want of exercise, if exercise would make it grow stronger. But I fear this faculty of the mind is not capable of much help and amendment in general by any exercise or endeavour of ours, at least not by that used upon this pretence in grammar-schools. And if *Xerxes* was able to call every common soldier by name in his army that consisted of no less than an hundred thousand men, I think it may be guessed, he got not this wonderful ability by learning his lessons by heart when he was a boy. This method of exercising and improving the memory by toilsome repetitions without book of what they read, is, I think, little used in the education of princes, which if it had that advantage is talked of, should be as little neglected in them as in the meanest school-boys: princes having as much need of good memories as any men living, and have generally an equal share in this faculty with other men; though it has never been taken care of this way. What the mind is intent upon and careful of, that it remembers best, and for the reason above-mentioned: to which, if method and order be joined, all is done, I think, that can be, for the help of a weak memory; and he that will take any other way to do it, especially that of charging it with a train of other peoples' words, which he that learns cares not for, will, I guess, scarce find the profit answer half the time and pains employ'd in it.

I do not mean hereby, that there should be no exercise given to children's memories. I think their memories should be employ'd, but not in learning by rote whole pages out of books, which, the lesson being once said, and that task over, are delivered up again to oblivion and neglected for ever. This mends neither the memory nor the mind. What they should learn by heart out of authors, I have above mentioned: and such wise and useful sentences being once given in charge to their memories, they should never be suffer'd to forget again, but be often called to account for them: whereby, besides the use those sayings may be to them in their future life, as so many good rules and observations, they will be taught to reflect often, and bethink themselves what they have to remember, which is the only way to make the memory quick and useful. The custom of frequent reflection will keep their minds from running adrift, and call their thoughts home from useless unattentive roving: and therefore I think it may do well, to give them something every day to remember, but something still, that is in itself worth the remembring, and what you would never have out of mind, whenever you call, or they themselves search for it. This will oblige them often to turn their thoughts inwards, than which you cannot wish them a better intellectual habit.

§ 177. But under whose care soever a child is put to be taught during the tender and flexible years of his life, this is certain, it should be one who thinks *Latin* and *language* the least part of education; one who knowing how much virtue and a well-temper'd soul is to be preferred to any sort of *learning* or *language,* makes it his chief business to form the mind of his scholars, and give that a right disposition; which if once got, though all the rest should be neglected, would in due time produce all the rest; and which, if it be not got and settled so as to keep out ill and vicious habits, *languages* and *sciences* and all the other accomplishments of education, will be to no purpose but to make the worse or more dangerous man. And indeed whatever stir there is made about getting of *Latin* as the great and difficult business, his mother may teach it him herself, if she will but spend two or three hours in a day with him, and make him read the Evangelists in *Latin* to her: for she need but buy a *Latin* Testament, and having got some body to mark the last syllable but one where it is long in words above two syllables, (which is enough to regulate her pronunciation, and accenting the words) read daily in the *Gospels,* and then let her avoid understanding them in *Latin* if she can. And when she understands the Evangelists in *Latin,* let her, in the same manner, read *Æsop's* Fables, and so proceed on to *Eutropius, Justin,* and other such books. I do not mention this, as an imagination of what I fancy may do, but as of a thing I have known done, and the *Latin* tongue with ease got this way.

But, to return to what I was saying: he that takes on him the charge of bringing up young men, especially young gentlemen, should have something more in him than *Latin,* more than even a knowledge in the liberal sciences: he should be a person of eminent virtue and prudence, and with good sense, have good humour, and the skill to carry himself with gravity, ease and kindness, in a constant conversation with his pupils. But of this I have spoken at large in another place.

§ 178. At the same time that he is learning *French* and *Latin,* a child, as has been said, may also be enter'd in *Arithmetick, Geography, Chronology, History* and *Geometry* too. For if these be taught him in *French* or *Latin,* when he begins once to understand either of these tongues, he will get a knowledge in these sciences, and the language to boot.

*Geography* I think should be begun with: for the learning of the figure of the *globe,* the situation and boundaries of the four parts of the world, and that of particular kingdoms and countries, being only an exercise of the eyes and memory, a child with pleasure will learn and retain them. And this is so certain, that I now live in the house with a child whom his mother has so well instructed this way in *geography,* that he knew the limits of the four parts of the world, could readily point, being ask'd, to any country upon the globe, or any county in the map of *England;* knew all the great rivers, promontories, straits and bays in the world, and could find the longitude and latitude of any place, before he was six years old. These

things, that he will thus learn by sight, and have by rote
in his memory, are not all, I confess, that he is to learn
upon the *globes*. But yet it is a good step and preparation to it, and will make the remainder much easier, when
his judgment is grown ripe enough for it: besides that,
it gets so much time now; and by the pleasure of knowing things, leads him on insensibly to the gaining of languages.

§ 179. When he has the natural parts of the globe well
fix'd in his memory, it may then be time to begin *arithmetick*.
By the natural parts of the globe, I mean the several positions of the parts of the earth and sea, under different
names and distinctions of countries, not coming yet to
those artificial and imaginary lines which have been invented, and are only suppos'd for the better improvement
of that science.

§ 180. *Arithmetick* is the easiest, and consequently the
first sort of abstract reasoning, which the mind commonly
bears or accustoms itself to: and is of so general use in
all parts of life and business, that scarce any thing is to
be done without it. This is certain, a man cannot have
too much of it, nor too perfectly: he should therefore
begin to be exercis'd in *counting,* as soon, and as far, as he
is capable of it; and do something in it every day, till he
is master of the art of *numbers.* When he understands
*addition* and *subtraction,* he then may be advanced farther
in *geography,* after he is acquainted with the *poles, zones,
parallel circles,* and *meridians,* be taught *longitude* and
*latitude,* and by them be made to understand the use of
maps, and by the numbers placed on their sides, to know
the respective situation of countries, and how to find them
out on the terrestrial globe. Which when he can readily
do, he may then be entered in the celestial; and there
going over all the circles again, with a more particular
observation of the Ecliptick, or Zodiack, to fix them all
very clearly and distinctly in his mind, he may be taught
the figure and position of the several constellations, which
may be shewed him first upon the globe, and then in the
heavens.

When that is done, and he knows pretty well the constellations of this our hemisphere, it may be time to give him some notions of this our planetary world; and to that purpose, it may not be amiss to make him a draught of the *Copernican* system, and therein explain to him the situation of the planets, their respective distances from the sun, the centre of their revolutions. This will prepare him to understand the motion and theory of the planets, the most easy and natural way. For since astronomers no longer doubt of the motion of the planets about the sun, it is fit he should proceed upon that hypothesis, which is not only the simplest and least perplexed for a learner, but also the likeliest to be true in itself. But in this, as in all other parts of instruction, great care must be taken with children, to begin with that which is plain and simple, and to teach them as little as can be at once, and settle that well in their heads before you proceed to the next, or any thing new in that science. Give them first one simple idea, and see that they take it right, and perfectly comprehend it before you go any farther, and then add some other simple idea which lies next in your way to what you aim at; and so proceeding by gentle and insensible steps, children without confusion and amazement will have their understandings opened and their thoughts extended farther than could have been expected. And when any one has learn'd any thing himself, there is no such way to fix it in his memory, and to encourage him to go on, as to set him to teach it others.

§ 181. When he has once got such an acquaintance with the globes, as is above mentioned, he may be fit to be tried in a little *geometry;* wherein I think the six first books of *Euclid* enough for him to be taught. For I am in some doubt, whether more to a man of business be necessary or useful. At least, if he have a genius and inclination to it, being enter'd so far by his tutor, he will be able to go on of himself without a teacher.

The *globes* therefore must be studied, and that diligently; and I think may be begun betimes, if the tutor will be but careful to distinguish what the child is capable of knowing, and what not; for which this may be a rule that perhaps will go a pretty way, *viz.* that children may be taught any thing that falls under their senses, especially their sight, as far as their memories only are exercised: and thus a child very young may learn, which is the *Æquator,* which the *Meridian,* &c. which *Europe,* and which *England,* upon the globes, as soon almost as he knows the rooms of the house he lives in, if care be taken not to teach him too much at once, nor to set him upon a new part, till that which he is upon be perfectly learned and fixed in his memory.

§ 182. With geography, *chronology* ought to go hand in hand. I mean the general part of it, so that he may have in his mind a view of the whole current of time, and the several considerable *epochs* that are made use of in history. Without these two, history, which is the great mistress of prudence and civil knowledge, and ought to be the proper study of a gentleman, or man of business in the world; without geography and *chronology,* I say, history will be very ill retain'd, and very little useful; but be only a jumble of matters of fact, confusedly heaped together without order or instruction. 'Tis by these two that the actions of mankind are ranked into their proper places of time and countries, under which circumstances they are not only much easier kept in the memory, but in that natural order, are only capable to afford those observations which make a man the better and the abler for reading them.

§ 183. When I speak of *chronology* as a science he should be perfect in, I do not mean the little controversies that are in it. These are endless, and most of them of so little importance to a gentleman, as not to deserve to be enquir'd into, were they capable of an easy decision. And therefore all that learned noise and dust of the chronologist is wholly to be avoided. The most useful book I have seen in that part of learning, is a small treatise of *Strauchius,* which is printed in twelves, under the title of *Breviarium Chronologicum,* out of which may be selected all that is necessary to be taught a young gentleman concerning *chronology;* for all that is in that treatise a learner need not be cumbred with. He has in him the most remarkable or useful *epochs* reduced all to that of the *Julian*

*Period,* which is the easiest and plainest and surest method that can be made use of in *chronology.* To this treatise of *Strauchius, Helvicus's* tables may be added, as a book to be turned to on all occasions.

§ 184. As nothing teaches, so nothing delights more than history. The first of these recommends it to the study of grown men, the latter makes me think it the fittest for a young lad, who as soon as he is instructed in chronology, and acquainted with the several *epochs* in use in this part of the world, and can reduce them to the *Julian Period,* should then have some *Latin history* put into his hand. The choice should be directed by the easiness of the stile; for whereever he begins, chronology will keep it from confusion; and the pleasantness of the subject inviting him to read, the language will insensibly be got without that terrible vexation and uneasiness which children suffer where they are put into books beyond their capacity; such as are the *Roman* orators and poets, only to learn the *Roman* language. When he has by reading master'd the easier, such perhaps as *Justin, Eutropius, Quintius Curtius, &c.* the next degree to these will give him no great trouble: and thus by a gradual progress from the plainest and easiest *historians,* he may at last come to read the most difficult and sublime of the *Latin* authors, such as are *Tully, Virgil,* and *Horace.*

§ 185. The knowledge of *virtue,* all along from the beginning, in all the instances he is capable of, being taught him more by practice than rules; and the love of reputation, instead of satisfying his appetite, being made habitual in him, I know not whether he should read any other discourses of morality but what he finds in the Bible; or have any system of *ethicks* put into his hand till he can read *Tully's Offices* not as a school-boy to learn *Latin,* but as one that would be informed in the principles and precepts of virtue for the conduct of his life.

§ 186. When he has pretty well digested *Tully's Offices,* and added to it, *Puffendorf de Officio Hominis & Civis,* it may be seasonable to set him upon *Grotius de Jure Belli & Pacis,* or, which perhaps is the better of the two, *Puffendorf de Jure naturali & Gentium;* wherein he will be instructed in the natural rights of men, and the original and foundations of society, and the duties resulting from thence. This *general part of civil-law* and history, are studies which a gentleman should not barely touch at, but constantly dwell upon, and never have done with. A virtuous and well-behaved young man, that is well-versed in the *general part of the civil-law* (which concerns not the chicane of private cases, but the affairs and intercourse of civilized nations in general, grounded upon principles of reason) understands *Latin* well, and can write a good hand, one may turn loose into the world with great assurance that he will find employment and esteem every where.

§ 187. It would be strange to suppose an *English* gentleman should be ignorant of the *law* of his country. This, whatever station he is in, is so requisite, that from a Justice of the Peace to a Minister of State I know no place he can well fill without it. I do not mean the chicane or wrangling and captious part of the law: a gentleman, whose business is to seek the true measures of right and wrong, and not the arts how to avoid doing the one, and secure himself in doing the other, ought to be as far from such a study of the *law,* as he is concerned diligently to apply himself to that wherein he may be serviceable to his country. And to that purpose, I think the right way for a gentleman to study *our law,* which he does not design for his calling, is to take a view of our *English* constitution and government in the antient books of the *common-law,* and some more modern writers, who out of them have given an account of this government. And having got a true idea of that, then to read our history, and with it join in every king's reign the *laws* then made. This will give an insight into the reason of our *statutes,* and shew the true ground upon which they came to be made, and what weight they ought to have.

§ 188. *Rhetorick* and *logick* being the arts that in the ordinary method usually follow immediately after grammar, it may perhaps be wondered that I have said so little of them. The reason is, because of the little advantage young people receive by them: for I have seldom or never observed any one to get the skill of reasoning well, or speaking handsomely, by studying those rules which pretend to reach it: and therefore I would have a young gentleman take a view of them in the shortest systems could be found, without dwelling long on the contemplation and study of those formalities. Right reasoning is founded on something else than the *predicaments* and *predicables,* and does not consist in talking in *mode* and *figure* it self. But 'tis beside my present business to enlarge upon this speculation. To come therefore to what we have in hand; if you would have your son *reason well,* let him read *Chillingworth;* and if you would have him speak well, let him be conversant in *Tully,* to give him the true *idea* of *eloquence;* and let him read those things that are well writ in *English,* to perfect his style in the purity of our language.

§ 189. If the use and end of right reasoning be to have right notions and a right judgment of things, to distinguish betwixt truth and falsehood, right and wrong, and to act accordingly; be sure not to let your son be bred up in the art and formality of disputing, either practising it himself, or admiring it in others; unless instead of an able man, you desire to have him an insignificant wrangler, opiniator in discourse, and priding himself in contradicting others; or, which is worse, questioning every thing, and thinking there is no such thing as truth to be sought, but only victory, in disputing. There cannot be any thing so disingenuous, so misbecoming a gentleman or any one who pretends to be a rational creature, as not to yield to plain reason and the conviction of clear arguments. Is there any thing more consistent with civil conversation, and the end of all debate, than not to take an answer, though never so full and satisfactory, but still to go on with the dispute as long as equivocal sounds can furnish (a *medius terminus*) a term to wrangle with on the one side, or a distinction on the other; whether pertinent or impertinent, sense or nonsense, agreeing with or contrary to what he had said before, it matters not. For this, in short, is the way and perfection of logical disputes, that the opponent never takes any answer, nor the respondent ever yields to any argument. This neither of them must do, whatever becomes of truth or knowledge, unless he will pass for a poor baffled wretch, and lie under the disgrace of not being able to maintain whatever he has once affirm'd, which is the great aim and glory in disputing. Truth is to be found and supported by a mature and due consideration of things themselves, and not by artificial terms and ways of arguing: these lead not men so much into the discovery of truth, as into a captious and fallacious use of doubtful words, which is the most useless and most offensive way of talking, and such as least suits a gentleman or a lover of truth of any thing in the world.

There can scarce be a greater defect in a gentleman than not to express himself well either in writing or speaking. But yet I think I may ask my reader, whether he doth not know a great many, who live upon their estates, and so with the name should have the qualities of gentlemen, who cannot so much as tell a story as they should, much less speak clearly and persuasively in any business. This I think not to be so much their fault, as the fault of their education; for I must, without partiality, do my countrymen this right, that where they apply themselves, I see none of their neighbours outgo them. They have been taught *rhetorick,* but yet never taught how to express themselves handsomely with their tongues or pens in the language they are always to use; as if the names of the figures that embellish'd the discourses of those who understood the art of speaking, were the very art and skill of speaking well. This, as all other things of practice, is to be learn'd not by a few or a great many rules given, but by exercise and application according to good rules, or rather patterns, till habits are got, and a facility of doing it well.

Agreeable hereunto, perhaps it might not be amiss to make children, as soon as they are capable of it, often to tell a story of any thing they know; and to correct at first the most remarkable fault they are guilty of in their way of putting it together. When that fault is cured, then to shew them the next, and so on, till one after another, all, at least the gross ones, are mended. When they can tell tales pretty well, then it may be the time to make them write them. The Fables of *Æsop,* the only book almost that I know fit for children, may afford them matter for this exercise of writing *English,* as well as for reading and translating, to enter them in the *Latin* tongue. When they have got past the faults of grammar, and can join in a continued coherent discourse the several parts of a story, without bald and unhandsome forms of transition (as is usual) often repeated, he that desires to perfect them yet farther in this, which is the first step to speaking well and needs no invention, may have recourse to *Tully,* and by putting in practice those rules which that master of eloquence gives in his first book *de inventione,* § 20, make them know wherein the skill and graces of an handsome narrative, according to the several subjects and designs of it, lie. Of each of which rules fit examples may be found out, and therein they may be shewn how others have practised them. The antient classick authors afford plenty of such examples, which they should be made not only to translate, but have set before them as patterns for their daily imitation.

When they understand how to write *English* with due connexion, propriety, and order, and are pretty well masters of a tolerable narrative style, they may be advanced to writing of letters; wherein they should not be put upon any strains of wit or compliment, but taught to express their own plain easy sense, without any incoherence, confusion or roughness. And when they are perfect in this, they may, to raise their thoughts, have set before them the examples of *Voitures,* for the entertainment of their friends at a distance, with letters of compliment, mirth, raillery or diversion; and *Tully's Epistles,* as the best pattern whether for business or conversation. The writing of letters has so much to do in all the occurrences of human life, that no gentleman can avoid shewing himself in this kind of writing. Occasions will daily force him to make this use of his pen, which, besides the consequences that, in his affairs, his well or ill managing of it often draws after it, always lays him open to a severer examination of his breeding, sense, and abilities, than oral discourses; whose transient faults dying for the most part with the sound that gives them life, and so not subject to a strict review, more easily escape observation and censure.

Had the methods of education been directed to their right end, one would have thought this so necessary a part could not have been neglected whilst themes and verses in *Latin,* of no use at all, were so constantly every where pressed, to the racking of children's inventions beyond their strength and hindering their chearful progress in learning the tongues by unnatural difficulties. But custom has so ordain'd it, and who dares disobey? And would it not be very unreasonable to require of a learned country school-master (who has all the tropes and figures in *Farnaby's Rhetorick* at his fingers' ends) to teach his scholar to express himself handsomely in *English,* when it appears to be so little his business or thought, that the boy's mother (despised, 'tis like, as illiterate for not having read a system of *logick* and *rhetorick*) outdoes him in it?

To write and speak correctly gives a grace and gains a favourable attention to what one has to say: and since 'tis *English* that an *English* gentleman will have constant use of, that is the language he should chiefly cultivate, and wherein most care should be taken to polish and perfect his style. To speak or write better *Latin* than *English,* may make a man be talk'd of, but he would find it more to his purpose to express himself well in his own tongue, that he uses every moment, than to have the vain commendation of others for a very insignificant quality. This I find universally neglected, and no care taken any where to improve young men in their own language, that they may thoroughly understand and be masters of it. If any one among us have a facility or purity more than ordinary in his mother tongue, it is owing to chance, or his genius, or any thing rather than to his education or any care of his teacher. To mind what *English* his pupil speaks or writes, is below the dignity of one bred up amongst *Greek* and *Latin,* though he have but little of them himself. These are the learned languages fit only for learned men to meddle with and teach; *English* is the language of the illiterate vulgar: tho' yet we see the polity of some of our neighbours hath not thought it beneath the publick care to promote and reward the im-

provement of their own language. Polishing and enriching
their tongue is no small business amongst them; it hath col-
leges and stipends appointed it, and there is raised amongst
them a great ambition and emulation of writing correctly:
and we see what they are come to by it, and how far they
have spread one of the worst languages possibly in this part
of the world, if we look upon it as it was in some few reigns
backwards, whatever it be now. The great men among the
*Romans* were daily exercising themselves in their own language; and we find yet upon record the names of orators,
who taught some of their emperors *Latin,* though it were
their mother tongue.

'Tis plain the *Greeks* were yet more nice in theirs. All
other speech was barbarous to them but their own, and no
foreign language appears to have been studied or valued
amongst that learned and acute people; tho' it be past doubt
that they borrowed their learning and philosophy from
abroad.

I am not here speaking against *Greek* and *Latin;* I think
they ought to be studied, and the *Latin* at least understood
well by every gentleman. But whatever foreign languages
a young man meddles with (and the more he knows the
better) that which he should critically study, and labour
to get a facility, clearness and elegancy to express himself
in, should be his own; and to this purpose he should daily
be exercised in it.

§ 190. *Natural philosophy,* as a speculative science, I
imagine we have none, and perhaps I may think I have reason to say we never shall be able to make a science of it.
The works of nature are contrived by a wisdom, and operate
by ways too far surpassing our faculties to discover or
capacities to conceive, for us ever to be able to reduce them
into a science. *Natural philosophy* being the knowledge of
the principles, properties and operations of things as they are
in themselves, I imagine there are two parts of it, one comprehending *spirits,* with their nature and qualities, and the
other *bodies.* The first of these is usually referred to *metaphysicks:* but under what title soever the consideration of
*spirits* comes, I think it ought to go before the study of matter and body, not as a science that can be methodized into

a system, and treated of upon principles of knowledge; but as an enlargement of our minds towards a truer and fuller comprehension of the intellectual world to which we are led both by reason and revelation. And since the clearest and largest discoveries we have of other *spirits,* besides God and our own souls, is imparted to us from heaven by revelation, I think the information that at least young people should have of them, should be taken from that revelation. To this purpose, I conclude, it would be well, if there were made a good history of the Bible, for young people to read; wherein if every thing that is fit to be put into it, were laid down in its due order of time, and several things omitted which are suited only to riper age, that confusion which is usually produced by promiscuous reading of the Scripture, as it lies now bound up in our Bibles, would be avoided. And also this other good obtained, that by reading of it constantly, there would be instilled into the minds of children a notion and belief of *spirits,* they having so much to do in all the transactions of that history, which will be a good preparation to the study of *bodies.* For without the notion and allowance of *spirit,* our philosophy will be lame and defective in one main part of it, when it leaves out the contemplation of the most excellent and powerful part of the creation.

§ 191. Of this *History of the Bible,* I think too it would be well if there were a short and plain epitome made, containing the chief and most material heads, for children to be conversant in as soon as they can read. This, though it will lead them early into some notion of *spirits,* yet it is not contrary to what I said above, that I would not have children troubled, whilst young, with notions of *spirits;* whereby my meaning was, that I think it inconvenient that their yet tender minds should receive early impressions of *goblins, spectres,* and *apparitions,* wherewith their maids and those about them are apt to fright them into a compliance with their orders, which often proves a great inconvenience to them all their lives after, by subjecting their minds to frights, fearful apprehensions, weakness and superstition; which when coming abroad into the world and conversation they grow weary and ashamed of, it not seldom happens, that to make, as they think, a thorough cure, and ease themselves of a load which has sat so heavy on them, they throw away the thoughts of all *spirits* together, and so run into the other, but worse, extream.

§ 192. The reason why I would have this premised to the *study of bodies,* and the Doctrine of the Scriptures well imbibed before young men be entered in *natural philosophy,* is, because matter, being a thing that all our senses are constantly conversant with, it is so apt to possess the mind, and exclude all other beings but matter, that prejudice, grounded on such principles, often leaves no room for the admittance of spirits, or the allowing any such things as *immaterial beings in rerum natura;* when yet it is evident that by mere matter and motion none of the great phænomena of nature can be resolved, to instance but in that common one of gravity, which I think impossible to be explained by any natural operation of matter, or any other law of motion, but the positive will of a superior being so ordering it. And therefore since the deluge cannot be well explained without admitting something out of the ordinary course of nature, I propose it to be considered whether God's altering the centre of gravity in the earth for a time (a thing as intelligible as gravity it self, which perhaps a little variation of causes unknown to us would produce) will not more easily account for *Noah's* flood than any hypothesis yet made use of to solve it. I hear the great objection to this, is, that it would produce but a partial deluge. But the alteration of the centre of gravity once allowed, 'tis no hard matter to conceive that the divine power might make the centre of gravity, plac'd at a due distance from the centre of the earth, move round it in a convenient space of time, whereby the flood would become universal, and, as I think, answer all the phænomena of the deluge as delivered by *Moses,* at an easier rate than those many hard suppositions that are made use of to explain it. But this is not a place for that argument, which is here only mentioned by the bye, to shew the necessity of having recourse to something beyond bare matter and its motion in the explication of nature; to which the notions of spirits and their power, as delivered in the Bible, where so much is attributed to their operation, may be a fit preparative, reserving to a fitter opportunity a fuller explication of this hypothesis, and the application of it to all the parts of the deluge, and any difficulties can be supposed in the history of the flood, as recorded in the scripture.

§ 193. But to return to the study of *natural philosophy*. Tho' the world be full of systems of it, yet I cannot say, I know any one which can be taught a young man as a science wherein he may be sure to find truth and certainty, which is what all sciences give an expectation of. I do not hence conclude, that none of them are to be read. It is necessary for a gentleman in this learned age to look into some of them to fit himself for conversation: but whether that of *Des Cartes* be put into his hands, as that which is most in fashion, or it be thought fit to give him a short view of that and several others also, I think the systems of *natural philosophy* that have obtained in this part of the world, are to be read more to know the *hypotheses,* and to understand the terms and ways of talking of the several sects, than with hopes to gain thereby a comprehensive, scientifical and satisfactory knowledge of the works of nature. Only this may be said, that the modern *Corpuscularians* talk in most things more intelligibly than the *Peripateticks,* who possessed the schools immediately before them. He that would look further back, and acquaint himself with the several opinions of the antients, may consult Dr. *Cudworth's Intellectual System,* wherein that very learned author hath with such accurateness and judgment collected and explained the opinions of the *Greek* philosophers, that what principles they built on, and what were the chief *hypotheses* that divided them, is better to be seen in him than any where else that I know. But I would not deter any one from the study of nature because all the knowledge we have or possibly can have of it cannot be brought into a science. There are very many things in it that are convenient and necessary to be known to a gentleman; and a great many other that will abundantly reward the pains of the curious with delight and advantage. But these, I think, are rather to be found amongst such writers as have employed themselves in making rational experiments and observations than in starting barely speculative systems. Such writings therefore, as many of Mr. *Boyle's* are, with others that have writ of *hus-*

*bandry, planting, gardening,* and the like, may be fit for a gentleman, when he has a little acquainted himself with some of the systems of the *natural philosophy* in fashion.

§ 194. Though the systems of *physicks* that I have met with, afford little encouragement to look for certainty or science in any treatise which shall pretend to give us a body of *natural philosophy* from the first principles of bodies in general, yet the incomparable Mr. *Newton* has shewn, how far mathematicks applied to some parts of nature may, upon principles that matter of fact justify, carry us in the knowledge of some, as I may so call them, particular provinces of the incomprehensible universe. And if others could give us so good and clear an account of other parts of *nature,* as he has of this our planetary world, and the most considerable phænomena observable in it, in his admirable book, *Philosophiæ naturalis Principia Mathematica,* we might in time hope to be furnished with more true and certain knowledge in several parts of this stupendous machine, than hitherto we could have expected. And though there are very few that have mathematicks enough to understand his demonstrations, yet the most accurate mathematicians who have examin'd them allowing them to be such, his book will deserve to be read, and give no small light and pleasure to those, who, willing to understand the motions, properties, and operations of the great masses of matter, in this our solar system, will but carefully mind his conclusions, which may be depended on as propositions well proved.

§ 195. This is, in short, what I have thought concerning a young gentleman's studies; wherein it will possibly be wonder'd that I should omit *Greek,* since amongst the *Grecians* is to be found the original as it were, and foundation of all that learning which we have in this part of the world. I grant it so; and will add, that no man can pass for a scholar that is ignorant of the *Greek* tongue. But I am not here considering the education of a profess'd scholar, but of a gentleman, to whom *Latin* and *French,* as the world now goes, is by every one acknowledg'd to be necessary. When he comes to be a man, if he has a mind to carry his studies farther, and look into the *Greek* learning, he will then easily get that tongue himself: and if he has not that inclination, his learning of it under a tutor will be but lost labour, and much of his time and pains spent in that which will be neglected and thrown away as soon as he is at liberty. For how many are there of an hundred, even amongst scholars themselves, who retain the *Greek* they carried from school; or ever improve it to a familiar reading and perfect understanding of *Greek* authors?

To conclude this part, which concerns a young gentleman's studies, his tutor should remember, that his business is not so much to teach him all that is knowable, as to raise in him a love and esteem of knowledge; and to put him in the right way of knowing and improving himself when he has a mind to it.

The thoughts of a judicious author on the subject of languages, I shall here give the reader, as near as I can, in his own way of expressing them: he says, "One can scarce burden children too much with the knowledge of languages. They are useful to men of all conditions, and they equally open them the entrance, either to the most profound, or the more easy and entertaining parts of learning. If this irksome study be put off to a little more advanced age, young men either have not resolution enough to apply it out of choice or steadiness to carry it on. And if any one has the gift of perseverance, it is not without the inconvenience of spending that time upon languages, which is destined to other uses: and he confines to the study of words that age of his life that is above it, and requires things; at least it is the losing the best and beautifullest season of one's life. This large foundation of languages cannot be well laid but when every thing makes an easy and deep impression on the mind; when the memory is fresh, ready, and tenacious; when the head and heart are as yet free from cares, passions, and designs; and those on whom the child depends have authority enough to keep him close to a long continued application. I am persuaded that the small number of truly learned, and the multitude of superficial pretenders, is owing to the neglect of this."

I think every body will agree with this observing gentleman, that languages are the proper study of our first years.

But 'tis to be consider'd by the parents and tutors, what tongues 'tis fit the child should learn. For it must be confessed, that it is fruitless pains and loss of time, to learn a language which in the course of life that he is designed to, he is never like to make use of, or which one may guess by his temper he will wholly neglect and lose again, as soon as an approach to manhood, setting him free from a governor, shall put him into the hands of his own inclination, which is not likely to allot any of his time to the cultivating the learned tongues, or dispose him to mind any other language but what daily use or some particular necessity shall force upon him.

But yet for the sake of those who are designed to be scholars, I will add what the same author subjoins to make good his foregoing remark. It will deserve to be considered by all who desire to be truly learned, and therefore may be a fit rule for tutors to inculcate and leave with their pupils to guide their future studies.

"The study, *says he,* of the original text can never be sufficiently recommended. 'Tis the shortest, surest, and most agreeable way to all sorts of learning. Draw from the spring-head, and take not things at second hand. Let the writings of the great masters be never laid aside, dwell upon them, settle them in your mind, and cite them upon occasion; make it your business throughly to understand them in their full extent and all their circumstances: acquaint yourself fully with the principles of original authors; bring them to a consistency, and then do you yourself make your deductions. In this state were the first commentators, and do not you rest till you bring yourself to the same. Content not yourself with those borrowed lights, nor guide yourself by their views but where your own fails you and leaves you in the dark. Their explications are not your's, and will give you the slip. On the contrary, your own observations are the product of your own mind, where they will abide and be ready at hand upon all occasions in converse, consultation, and dispute. Lose not the pleasure it is to see that you are not stopp'd in your reading but by difficulties that are invincible; where the commentators and scholiasts themselves are at a stand and have nothing to say. Those copious expositors of other places, who with a vain and pompous overflow of learning poured out on passages plain and easy in themselves, are very free of their words and pains, where there is no need. Convince yourself fully by this ordering your studies, that 'tis nothing but men's laziness which hath encouraged pedantry to cram rather than enrich libraries, and to bury good authors under heaps of notes and commentaries, and you will perceive that sloth herein hath acted against itself and its own interest by multiplying reading and enquiries, and encreasing the pains it endeavoured to avoid."

This, tho' it may seem to concern none but direct scholars, is of so great moment for the right ordering of their education and studies, that I hope I shall not be blamed for inserting of it here; especially if it be considered, that it may be of use to gentlemen too, when at any time they have a mind to go deeper than the surface, and get to themselves a solid, satisfactory, and masterly insight in any part of learning.

Order and constancy are said to make the great difference between one man and another: this I am sure, nothing so much clears a learner's way, helps him so much on in it, and makes him go so easy and so far in any enquiry, as a good *method*. His governor should take pains to make him sensible of this, accustom him to order, and teach him *method* in all the applications of his thoughts; shew him wherein it lies, and the advantages of it; acquaint him with the several sorts of it, either from general to particulars, or from particulars to what is more general; exercise him in both of them, and make him see in what cases each different *method* is most proper, and to what ends it best serves.

In history the order of time should govern, in philosophical enquiries that of nature, which in all progression is to go from the place one is then in, to that which joins and lies next to it; and so it is in the mind, from the knowledge it stands possessed of already, to that which lies next, and is coherent to it, and so on to what it aims at, by the simplest and most uncompounded parts it can divide the matter into. To this purpose, it will be of great use to his pupil to accustom him to distinguish well, that is, to have distinct notions, whereever the mind can find any real difference; but as carefully to avoid distinctions in terms, where he has not distinct and different clear ideas.

§ 196. Besides what is to be had from study and books, there are other *accomplishments* necessary for a gentleman, to be got by exercise, and to which time is to be allowed, and for which masters must be had.

*Dancing* being that which gives *graceful motions* all the life, and above all things manliness, and a becoming confidence to young children, I think it cannot be learned too early, after they are once of an age and strength capable of it. But you must be sure to have a good master, that knows, and can teach, what is graceful and becoming, and what gives a freedom and easiness to all the motions of the body. One that teaches not this, is worse than none at all: natural unfashionableness being much better than apish affected postures; and I think it much more passable, to put off the hat and make a leg like an honest country gentleman than like an ill-fashioned dancing-master. For as for the jigging part, and the figures of dances, I count that little or nothing, farther than as it tends to perfect *graceful carriage*.

§ 197. *Musick* is thought to have some affinity with dancing, and a good hand upon some instruments is by many people mightily valued. But it wastes so much of a young man's time to gain but a moderate skill in it; and engages often in such odd company, that many think it much better spared: and I have amongst men of parts and business so seldom heard any one commended or esteemed for having an excellency in *musick,* that amongst all those things that ever came into the list of accomplishments, I think I may give it the last place. Our short lives will not serve us for the attainment of all things; nor can our minds be always intent on something to be learned. The weakness of our constitutions both of mind and body, requires that we should be often unbent: and he that will make a good use of any part of his life, must allow a large portion of it to recreation. At least, this must not be denied to young people; unless whilst you with too much haste make them old, you have the displeasure to set them in their graves or a second childhood sooner than you could wish. And therefore, I think, that the time and pains allotted to serious improvements, should be employed about things of most use and consequence, and that too in the methods the most easy and short that could be at any rate obtained: and perhaps, as I have above said, it would be none of the least secrets of education, to make the exercises of the body and the mind the *recreation* one to another. I doubt not but that something might be done in it, by a prudent man, that would well consider the temper and inclination of his pupil. For he that is wearied either with study or dancing does not desire presently to go to sleep, but to do something else which may divert and delight him. But this must be always remembered, that nothing can come into the account of *recreation*, that is not done with delight.

§ 198. *Fencing* and *riding the great horse,* are looked upon so necessary parts of breeding, that it would be thought a great *omission* to neglect them; the latter of the two being for the most part to be learned only in great towns, is one of the best exercises for health, which is to be had in those places of ease and luxury: and upon that account makes a fit part of a young gentleman's employment during his abode there. And as far as it conduces to give a man a firm and graceful seat on horseback, and to make him able to teach his horse to stop and turn quick, and to rest on his hanches, is of use to a gentleman both in peace and war. But whether it be of moment enough to be made a business of, and deserve to take up more of his time than should barely for his health be employed at due intervals in some such vigorous exercise, I shall leave to the discretion of parents and tutors; who will do well to remember, in all the parts of education, that most time and application is to be bestowed on that which is like to be of greatest consequence and frequentest use in the ordinary course and occurrences of that life the young man is designed for.

§ 199. As for *fencing,* it seems to me a good exercise for health, but dangerous to the life; the confidence of their skill being apt to engage in quarrels those that think they have learned to use their swords. This presumption makes them often more touchy than needs on point of honour and slight or no provocations. Young men, in their warm blood, are forward to think they have in vain learned to fence, if they never shew their skill and courage in a duel; and they seem to have reason. But how many sad tragedies that reason has been the occasion of, the tears of many a mother can witness. A man that cannot *fence,* will be more careful to keep out of bullies' and gamesters' company, and will not be half so apt to stand upon punctilios, nor to give affronts, or fiercely justify them when given, which is that which usually makes the quarrel. And when a man is in the field, a moderate skill in fencing rather exposes him to the sword of his enemy than secures him from it. And certainly a man of courage who cannot fence at all and therefore will put all upon one thrust and not stand parrying, has the odds against a moderate fencer, especially if he has skill in wrestling. And therefore, if any provision be to be made against such accidents, and a man be to prepare his son for duels, I had much rather mine should be a good *wrestler* than an ordinary fencer, which is the most a gentleman can attain to in it, unless he will be constantly in the fencing-school and every day exercising. But since fencing and riding the great horse are so generally looked upon as necessary qualifications in the breeding of a gentleman, it will be hard wholly to deny any one of that rank these marks of distinction. I shall leave it therefore to the father to consider, how far the temper of his son and the station he is like to be in, will allow or encourage him to comply with fashions which, having very little to do with civil life, were yet formerly unknown to the most warlike nations, and seem to have added little of force or courage to those who have received them; unless we will think martial skill or prowess have been improved by duelling, with which fencing came into, and with which I presume it will go out of the world.

§ 200. These are my present thoughts concerning *learning* and *accomplishments.* The great business of all is virtue and *wisdom*:

> *Nullum numen abest si sit Prudentia.*

Teach him to get a mastery over his inclinations, and *submit his appetite to reason.* This being obtained, and by

constant practice settled into habit, the hardest part of
the task is over. To bring a young man to this, I know
nothing which so much contributes as the love of praise
and commendation, which should therefore be instilled
into him by all arts imaginable. Make his mind as sensible
of credit and shame as may be; and when you have done
that, you have put a principle into him, which will influence
his actions when you are not by, to which the fear of
a little smart of a rod is not comparable, and which will
be the proper stock whereon afterwards to graff the true
principles of morality and religion.

§ 201. I have one thing more to add, which as soon
as I mention I shall run the danger of being suspected to
have forgot what I am about, and what I have above written
concerning education all tending towards a gentleman's calling, with which a trade seems wholly inconsistent. And
yet I cannot forbear to say, I would have him *learn a
trade, a manual trade;* nay two or three, but one more
particularly.

§ 202. The busy inclination of children being always
to be directed to something that may be useful to them,
the advantages proposed from what they are set about
may be considered of two kinds: 1. Where the skill itself
that is got by exercise is worth the having. Thus skill
not only in languages and learned sciences, but in painting,
turning, gardening, tempering and working in iron, and
all other useful arts is worth the having. 2. Where the
exercise itself, without any consideration, is necessary or
useful for health. Knowledge in some things is so necessary to be got by children whilst they are young, that some
part of their time is to be allotted to their improvement
in them, though those employments contribute nothing
at all to their health. Such are reading and writing and
all other sedentary studies for the cultivating of the mind,
which unavoidably take up a great part of a gentleman's
time, quite from their cradles. *Other manual arts,* which
are both got and exercised by labour, do many of them
by that exercise not only increase our dexterity and skill,
but contribute to our health too, especially such as employ
us in the open air. In these, then, health and improve-

ment may be join'd together; and of these should some
fit ones be chosen, to be made the recreations of one
whose chief business is with books and study. In this
choice the age and inclination of the person is to be considered, and constraint always to be avoided in bringing
him to it. For command and force may often create,
but can never cure, an aversion: and whatever any one
is brought to by compulsion, he will leave as soon as he
can, and be little profited and less recreated by, whilst he
is at it.

§ 203. That which of all others would please me best,
would be a *painter,* were there not an argument or two
against it not easy to be answered. First, ill painting
is one of the worst things in the world; and to attain a tolerable degree of skill in it, requires too much of a man's time.
If he has a natural inclination to it, it will endanger
the neglect of all other more useful studies to give way to
that; and if he have no inclination to it, all the time, pains
and money shall be employed in it, will be thrown away
to no purpose. Another reason why I am not for painting
in a gentleman, is, because it is a sedentary recreation,
which more employs the mind than the body. A gentleman's
more serious employment I look on to be study; and when
that demands relaxation and refreshment, it should be in
some exercise of the body, which unbends the thought, and
confirms the health and strength. For these two reasons I
am not for *painting.*

§ 204. In the next place, for a country gentleman I
should propose one, or rather both these, *viz. Gardening* or
*husbandry* in general, and working in wood, as a *carpenter,
joiner,* or *turner,* these being fit and healthy recreations for
a man of study or business. For since the mind endures
not to be constantly employed in the same thing or way,
and sedentary or studious men should have some exercise, that at the same time might divert their minds and
employ their bodies, I know none that could do it better
for a country gentleman than these two; the one of them
affording him exercise when the weather or season keeps
him from the other. Besides that, by being skill'd in
the one of them, he will be able to govern and teach his

gardener; by the other, contrive and make a great many things both of delight and use: though these I propose not as the chief end of his labour, but as temptations to it; diversion from his other more serious thoughts and employments by useful and healthy manual exercise being what I chiefly aim at in it.

§ 205. The great men among the ancients understood very well how to reconcile manual labour with affairs of state, and thought it no lessening to their dignity to make the one the recreation to the other. That indeed which seems most generally to have employed and diverted their spare hours, was agriculture. *Gideon* among the *Jews* was taken from threshing, as well as *Cincinnatus* amongst the *Romans* from the plough, to command the armies of their countries against their enemies; and 'tis plain their dexterous handling of the flayl or the plough, and being good workmen with these tools, did not hinder their skill in arms, nor make them less able in the arts of war or government. They were great captains and statesmen as well as husbandmen. *Cato Major,* who had with great reputation born all the great offices of the commonwealth, has left us an evidence under his own hand, how much he was versed in country affairs; and, as I remember, *Cyrus* thought *gardening* so little beneath the dignity and grandeur of a throne, that he shew'd *Xenophon* a large field of fruit-trees all of his own planting. The records of antiquity, both among *Jews* and *Gentiles,* are full of instances of this kind, if it were necessary to recommend useful recreations by examples.

§ 206. Nor let it be thought that I mistake, when I call these or the like exercises of manual arts, *diversions* or *recreations:* for *recreation* is not being idle (as every one may observe) but easing the wearied part by change of business: and he that thinks *diversion* may not lie in hard and painful labour, forgets the early rising, hard riding, heat, cold and hunger of huntsmen, which is yet known to be the constant recreation of men of the greatest condition. *Delving, planting inoculating,* or any the like profitable employments, would be no less a *diversion* than any of the idle sports in fashion, if men could but

be brought to delight in them, which custom and skill in a
trade will quickly bring any one to do. And I doubt
not but there are to be found those, who being frequently
called to cards or any other play by those they could not
refuse, have been more tired with these *recreations* than
with any the most serious employment of life, though
the play has been such as they have naturally had no
aversion to, and with which they could willingly sometimes divert themselves.

§ 207. Play, wherein persons of condition, especially
ladies, waste so much of their time, is a plain instance to
me that men cannot be perfectly idle; they must be doing
something; for how else could they sit so many hours
toiling at that which generally gives more vexation than
delight to people whilst they are actually engag'd in it?
'Tis certain, gaming leaves no satisfaction behind it to
those who reflect when it is over, and it no way profits
either body or mind: as to their estates, if it strike so
deep as to concern them, it is a *trade* then, and not a
*recreation,* wherein few that have any thing else to live
on thrive: and at best, a thriving gamester has but a
poor trade on't, who fills his pockets at the price of his
reputation.

Recreation belongs not to people who are strangers to
business, and are not wasted and wearied with the employment of their calling. The skill should be, so to order
their time of recreation, that it may relax and refresh the
part that has been exercised and is tired, and yet do something which besides the present delight and ease, may
produce what will afterwards be profitable. It has been
nothing but the vanity and pride of greatness and riches,
that has brought unprofitable and dangerous *pastimes* (as
they are called) into fashion, and persuaded people into
a belief, that the learning or putting their hands to any
thing that was useful, could not be a *diversion* fit for a
gentleman. This has been that which has given *cards,
dice* and *drinking* so much credit in the world: and
a great many throw away their spare hours in them.
through the prevalency of custom, and want of some
better employment to fill up the vacancy of leisure, more

than from any real delight is to be found in them. They cannot bear the dead weight of unemployed time lying upon their hands, nor the uneasiness it is to do nothing at all: and having never learned any laudable manual art wherewith to divert themselves, they have recourse to those foolish or ill ways in use, to help off their time, which a rational man, till corrupted by custom, could find very little pleasure in.

§ 208. I say not this, that I would never have a young gentleman accommodate himself to the innocent *diversions* in fashion amongst those of his age and condition. I am so far from having him austere and morose to that degree, that I would persuade him to more than ordinary complaisance for all the gaieties and *diversions* of those he converses with, and be averse or testy in nothing they should desire of him, that might become a gentleman and an honest man. Though as to *cards* and *dice,* I think the safest and best way is never to learn any play upon them, and so to be incapacitated for those dangerous temptations and incroaching wasters of useful time. But allowance being made for *idle and jovial conversation* and all fashionable becoming recreations; I say, a young man will have time enough from his serious and main business, to learn almost any *trade*. 'Tis want of application, and not of leisure, that men are not skilful in more arts than one; and an hour in a day, constantly employed in such a way of *diversion,* will carry a man in a short time a great deal farther than he can imagine: which, if it were of no other use but to drive the common, vicious, useless, and dangerous pastimes out of fashion, and to shew there was no need of them, would deserve to be encouraged. If men from their youth were weaned from that sauntring humour wherein some out of custom let a good part of their lives run uselessly away, without either business or recreation, they would find time enough to acquire *dexterity and skill in hundreds of things,* which, though remote from their proper callings, would not at all interfere with them. And therefore, I think, for this, as well as other reasons beforementioned, a lazy, listless humour that idly dreams away the days, is of all others the least to be indulged or permitted in young people. It is the proper state of one sick and out of order in his health, and is tolerable in no body else of what age or condition soever.

§ 209. To the arts above-mentioned may be added *perfuming, varnishing, graving,* and several sorts of working in *iron, brass,* and *silver;* and if, as it happens to most young gentlemen, that a considerable part of his time be spent in a great town, he may learn to cut, polish, and set *precious stones,* or employ himself in grinding and polishing *optical glasses.* Amongst the great variety there is of ingenious *manual arts,* 'twill be impossible that no one should be found t ˶ please and delight him, unless he be either idle or debauched, which is not to be supposed in a right way of education. And since he cannot be always employ'd in study, reading, and conversation, there will be many an hour, besides what his exercises will take up, which, if not spent this way, will be spent worse. For I conclude, a young man will seldom desire to sit perfectly still and idle; or, if he does, 'tis a fault that ought to be mended.

§ 210. But if his mistaken parents, frighted with the disgraceful names of *mechanick* and *trade,* shall have an aversion to any thing of this kind in their children; yet there is one thing relating to trade, which, when they consider, they will think absolutely necessary for their sons to learn.

*Merchants' accompts,* tho' a science not likely to help a gentleman to get an estate, yet possibly there is not any thing of more use and efficacy, to make him preserve the estate he has. 'Tis seldom observed, that he keeps an accompt of his income and expences, and thereby has constantly under view the course of his domestick affairs, lets them run to ruin: and I doubt not but many a man gets behind-hand before he is aware, or runs farther on when he is once in, for want of this care, or the skill to do it. I would therefore advise all gentlemen to learn perfectly *merchants' accompts,* and not to think it is a skill that belongs not to them, because it has received its name from, and has been chiefly practised by men of traffick.

§ 211. When my young master has once got the skill of *keeping accounts* (which is a business of reason more than arithmetick) perhaps it will not be amiss that his father from thenceforth require him to do it in all his concernments. Not that I would have him set down every pint of wine or play that costs him money; the general name of expences will serve for such things well enough: nor would I have his father look so narrowly into these accompts, as to take occasion from thence to criticise on his expences; he must remember that he himself was once a young man, and not forget the thoughts he had then, nor the right his son has to have the same, and to have allowance made for them. If therefore I would have the young gentleman oblig'd to keep an account, it is not at all to have that way a check upon his expences (for what the father allows him, he ought to let him be fully master of) but only, that he might be brought early into the custom of doing it, and that it might be made familiar and habitual to him betimes, which will be so useful and necessary to be constantly practised the whole course of his life. A noble *Venetian*, whose son wallowed in the plenty of his father's riches, finding his son's expences grow very high and extravagant, ordered his cashier to let him have for the future no more money than what he should count when he received it. This one would think no great restraint to a young gentleman's expences; who could freely have as much money as he would tell. But yet this, to one that was used to nothing but the pursuit of his pleasures, prov'd a very great trouble, which at last ended in this sober and advantageous reflection: if it be so much pains to me barely to count the money I would spend, what labour and pains did it cost my ancestors, not only to count, but get it? This rational thought, suggested by this little pains impos'd upon him, wrought so effectually upon his mind, that it made him take up, and from that time forwards prove a good husband. This, at least, every body must allow, that nothing is likelier to keep a man within compass than the having constantly before his eyes the state of his affairs in a regular course of *accompt*.

§ 212. The last part usually in education is *travel*, which is commonly thought to finish the work, and complete the gentleman. I confess *travel* into foreign countries has great advantages, but the time usually chosen to send young men abroad, is, I think, of all other, that which renders their least capable of reaping those *advantages.* Those which are propos'd, as to the main of them, may be reduced to these two: first, language, secondly, an improvement in wisdom and prudence, by seeing men, and conversing with people of tempers, customs and ways of living, different from one another, and especially from those of his parish and neighbourhood. But from sixteen to one and twenty, which is the ordinary *time of travel,* men are, of all their lives, the least suited to these improvements. The first season to get foreign languages, and form the tongue to their true accents, I should think, should be from seven to fourteen or sixteen, and then too a tutor with them is useful and necessary, who may with those languages teach them other things. But to put them out of their parents' view at a great distance under a governor, when they think themselves to be too much men to be governed by others, and yet have not prudence and experience enough to govern themselves, what is it, but to expose them to all the greatest dangers of their whole life, when they have the least fence and guard against them? 'Till that boiling boisterous part of life comes in, it may be hoped the tutor may have some authority: neither the stubbornness of age, nor the temptation or examples of others, can take him from his tutor's conduct till fifteen or sixteen: but then, when he begins to comfort himself with men, and thinks himself one; when he comes to relish and pride himself in manly vices, and thinks it a shame to be any longer under the controul and conduct of another, what can be hoped from even the most careful and discreet governor, when neither he has power to compel, nor his pupil a disposition to be persuaded; but on the contrary, has the advice of warm blood and prevailing fashion, to hearken to the temptations of his companions, just as wise as himself, rather than to the persuasions of his tutor, who is now looked on as an enemy to his freedom? And when is a man so like to miscarry, as when at the same time he is both raw and unruly? This is the season of all his life that most requires the eye and authority of his parents and friends to govern it. The flexibleness of the former part of a man's

age, not yet grown up to be headstrong, makes it more
governable and safe; and in the after-part, reason and
foresight begin a little to take place, and mind a man of
his safety and improvement. The time therefore I should
think the fittest for a young gentleman to be *sent abroad*,
would be, either when he is younger, under a tutor, whom
he might be the better for; or when he is some years older,
without a governor; when he is of age to govern himself,
and make observations of what he finds in other countries
worthy his notice, and that might be of use to him after
his return; and when too, being throughly acquainted
with the laws and fashions, the natural and moral advantages and defects of his own country, he has something to
exchange with those abroad, from whose conversation he
hoped to reap any knowledge.

§ 213. [Wanting].

§ 214. The ordering of travel otherwise, is that, I imagine, which makes so many young gentlemen come back
so little improved by it. And if they do bring home with
them any knowledge of the places and people they have
seen, it is often an admiration of the worst and vainest
practices they met with abroad; retaining a relish and
memory of those things wherein their liberty took its first
swing, rather than of what should make them better and
wiser after their return. And indeed how can it be otherwise, going abroad at the age they do under the care of another, who is to provide their necessaries, and make their observations for them? Thus under the shelter and pretence of
a governor, thinking themselves excused from standing upon
their own legs or being accountable for their own conduct,
they very seldom trouble themselves with enquiries or making useful observations of their own. Their thoughts run
after play and pleasure, wherein they take it as a lessening
to be controll'd; but seldom trouble themselves to examine
the designs, observe the address, and consider the arts,
tempers, and inclinations of men they meet with; that so they
may know how to comport themselves towards them. Here
he that travels with them is to screen them; get them out
when they have run themselves into the briars; and in all
their miscarriages be answerable for them.

(7) HC XXXVII

§ 215. I confess, the knowledge of men is so great a skill, that it is not to be expected a young man should presently be perfect in it. But yet his *going abroad* is to little purpose, if *travel* does not sometimes open his eyes, make him cautious and wary, and accustom him to look beyond the outside, and, under the inoffensive guard of a civil and obliging carriage, keep himself free and safe in his conversation with strangers and all sorts of people without forfeiting their good opinion. He that is sent out to *travel* at the age, and with the thoughts of a man designing to improve himself, may get into the conversation and acquaintance of persons of condition where he comes; which, tho' a thing of most advantage to a gentleman that travels, yet I ask, amongst our young men that go abroad under tutors, what one is there of an hundred, that ever visits any person of quality? Much less makes an acquaintance with such, from whose conversation he may learn what is good breeding in that country, and what is worth observation in it; tho' from such persons it is, one may learn more in one day, than in a year's rambling from one inn to another. Nor indeed, is it to be wondered; for men of worth and parts will not easily admit the familiarity of boys who yet need the care of a tutor; tho' a young gentleman and stranger, appearing like a man, and shewing a desire to inform himself in the customs, manners, laws, and government of the country he is in, will find welcome assistance and entertainment amongst the best and most knowing persons every where, who will be ready to receive, encourage and countenance, an ingenuous and inquisitive foreigner.

§ 216. This, how true soever it be, will not I fear alter the custom, which has cast the time of travel upon the worst part of a man's life; but for reasons not taken from their improvement. The young lad must not be ventured abroad at eight or ten, for fear of what may happen to the tender child, tho' he then runs ten times less risque than at sixteen or eighteen. Nor must he stay at home till that dangerous, heady age be over, because he must be back again by one and twenty, to marry and propagate. The father cannot stay any longer for the portion, nor the mother for a new set of babies to play with; and so my young master, whatever comes on it, must have a wife look'd out for him by that time he is of age; tho' it would be no prejudice to his strength, his parts, or his issue, if it were respited for some time, and he had leave to get, in years and knowledge, the start a little of his children, who are often found to tread too near upon the heels of their fathers, to the no great satisfaction either of son or father. But the young gentleman being got within view of matrimony, 'tis time to leave him to his mistress.

§ 217. Tho' I am now come to a conclusion of what obvious remarks have suggested to me concerning education, I would not have it thought that I look on it as a just treatise on this subject. There are a thousand other things that may need consideration; especially if one should take in the various tempers, different inclinations, and particular defaults, that are to be found in children, and prescribe proper remedies. The variety is so great that it would require a volume; nor would that reach it. Each man's mind has some peculiarity, as well as his face, that distinguishes him from all others; and there are possibly scarce two children who can be conducted by exactly the same method. Besides that, I think a prince, a nobleman, and an ordinary gentleman's son, should have different ways of breeding. But having had here only some general views in reference to the main end and aims in education, and those designed for a gentleman's son, whom, being then very little, I considered only as white paper, or wax, to be moulded and fashioned as one pleases; I have touched little more than those heads which I judged necessary for the breeding of a young gentleman of his condition in general; and have now published these my occasional thoughts with this hope, that tho' this be far from being a complete treatise on this subject, or such as that every one may find what will just fit his child in it, yet it may give some small light to those, whose concern for their dear little ones makes them so irregularly bold, that they dare venture to consult their own reason in the education of their children, rather than wholly to rely upon old custom.

# THREE DIALOGUES BETWEEN HYLAS AND PHILONOUS, ETC.

BY

GEORGE BERKELEY

# INTRODUCTORY NOTE

GEORGE BERKELEY, *Bishop of Cloyne, was born in the County of Kilkenny, Ireland, March 12, 1685. He was educated at Trinity College, Dublin, where he became acquainted with the writings of Locke, and grew enthusiastically interested in the "new philosophy," as it was called, in contrast to the scholasticism which Trinity College had not yet officially discarded. When he was only twenty-four he published his "Essay Towards a New Theory of Vision," and in the next year his "Treatise Concerning the Principles of Human Knowledge"; but being disappointed in the comparative neglect of his new ideas by the philosophers of the day, he proceeded to discuss both objections and answers in the "Dialogues Between Hylas and Philonous," published in 1713, and here reprinted.*

*Meantime, Berkeley had been appointed to various college offices; and in 1713 he crossed to England and gained access to the circles of Addison and Pope. Through Swift's influence he went to Italy as chaplain to Lord Peterborough; and after several years, spent partly in London and partly on the Continent, he returned to Ireland in 1721 as chaplain to the Lord Lieutenant, became Dean of Derry, and inherited property.*

*Berkeley had now become possessed with the idea of a great future for Christianity in America, planned a college in Bermuda, and, while the grants of money which he hoped for were in suspense, he crossed the Atlantic and spent the years 1728-31 in Rhode Island. Becoming hopeless of ever getting the required endowment for his college, he returned to England, published "Alciphron," which he had written on his American farm, and retired to the Bishopric of Cloyne, where he lived almost to the end of his life, practising benevolence in his diocese and publishing the virtues of tar-water, a panacea in which he believed with characteristic enthusiasm. He died at Oxford, January 14, 1753.*

*The following Dialogues are the best defense of Berkeley's main doctrines, and are regarded by Leslie Stephen as "the finest specimen in our language of the conduct of argument by dialogue." His chief editor, Fraser, calls them "the gem of British metaphysical literature."*

# THREE DIALOGUES

BETWEEN

# HYLAS AND PHILONOUS

THE DESIGN OF WHICH IS PLAINLY TO DEMONSTRATE
THE REALITY AND PERFECTION OF

## HUMAN KNOWLEDGE

THE INCORPOREAL NATURE OF THE

## SOUL

AND THE IMMEDIATE PROVIDENCE OF A

## DEITY

IN OPPOSITION TO

## SCEPTICS AND ATHEISTS

ALSO TO OPEN A METHOD FOR RENDERING THE SCIENCES MORE
EASY, USEFUL, AND COMPENDIOUS

*First published in* 1713

# THREE DIALOGUES

BETWEEN

## HYLAS AND PHILONOUS, IN OPPOSITION
## TO SCEPTICS AND ATHEISTS

## THE FIRST DIALOGUE

**P**HILONOUS. Good morrow, Hylas: I did not expect to find you abroad so early.

HYLAS. It is indeed something unusual; but my thoughts were so taken up with a subject I was discoursing of last night, that finding I could not sleep, I resolved to rise and take a turn in the garden.

PHIL. It happened well, to let you see what innocent and agreeable pleasures you lose every morning. Can there be a pleasanter time of the day, or a more delightful season of the year? That purple sky, those wild but sweet notes of birds, the fragrant bloom upon the trees and flowers, the gentle influence of the rising sun, these and a thousand nameless beauties of nature inspire the soul with secret transports; its faculties too being at this time fresh and lively, are fit for those meditations, which the solitude of a garden and tranquillity of the morning naturally dispose us to. But I am afraid I interrupt your thoughts: for you seemed very intent on something.

HYL. It is true, I was, and shall be obliged to you if you will permit me to go on in the same vein; not that I would by any means deprive myself of your company, for my thoughts always flow more easily in conversation with a friend, than when I am alone: but my request is, that you would suffer me to impart my reflexions to you.

PHIL. With all my heart, it is what I should have requested myself if you had not prevented me.

HYL. I was considering the odd fate of those men who have in all ages, through an affectation of being distinguished from the vulgar, or some unaccountable turn of thought, pretended either to believe nothing at all, or to believe the most extravagant things in the world. This however might be borne, if their paradoxes and scepticism did not draw after them some consequences of general disadvantage to mankind. But the mischief lieth here; that when men of less leisure see them who are supposed to have spent their whole time in the pursuits of knowledge professing an entire ignorance of all things, or advancing such notions as are repugnant to plain and commonly received principles, they will be tempted to entertain suspicions concerning the most important truths, which they had hitherto held sacred and unquestionable.

PHIL. I entirely agree with you, as to the ill tendency of the affected doubts of some philosophers, and fantastical conceits of others. I am even so far gone of late in this way of thinking, that I have quitted several of the sublime notions I had got in their schools for vulgar opinions. And I give it you on my word; since this revolt from metaphysical notions to the plain dictates of nature and common sense, I find my understanding strangely enlightened, so that I can now easily comprehend a great many things which before were all mystery and riddle.

HYL. I am glad to find there was nothing in the accounts I heard of you.

PHIL. Pray, what were those?

HYL. You were represented, in last night's conversation, as one who maintained the most extravagant opinion that ever entered into the mind of man, to wit, that there is no such thing as *material substance* in the world.

PHIL. That there is no such thing as what *philosophers* call *material substance,* I am seriously persuaded: but, if I were made to see anything absurd or sceptical in this, I should then have the same reason to renounce this that I imagine I have now to reject the contrary opinion.

HYL. What! can anything be more fantastical, more repugnant to Common Sense, or a more manifest piece of Scepticism, than to believe there is no such thing as *matter?*

PHIL. Softly, good Hylas. What if it should prove that you, who hold there is, are, by virtue of that opinion, a greater sceptic, and maintain more paradoxes and repugnances to Common Sense, than I who believe no such thing?

HYL. You may as soon persuade me, the part is greater than the whole, as that, in order to avoid absurdity and Scepticism, I should ever be obliged to give up my opinion in this point.

PHIL. Well then, are you content to admit that opinion for true, which upon examination shall appear most agreeable to Common Sense, and remote from Scepticism?

HYL. With all my heart. Since you are for raising disputes about the plainest things in nature, I am content for once to hear what you have to say.

PHIL. Pray, Hylas, what do you mean by a *sceptic?*

HYL. I mean what all men mean—one that doubts of everything.

PHIL. He then who entertains no doubts concerning some particular point, with regard to that point cannot be thought a sceptic.

HYL. I agree with you.

PHIL. Whether doth doubting consist in embracing the affirmative or negative side of a question?

HYL. In neither; for whoever understands English cannot but know that *doubting* signifies a suspense between both.

PHIL. He then that denies any point, can no more be said to doubt of it, than he who affirmeth it with the same degree of assurance.

HYL. True.

PHIL. And, consequently, for such his denial is no more to be esteemed a sceptic than the other.

HYL. I acknowledge it.

PHIL. How cometh it to pass then, Hylas, that you pronounce me a *sceptic,* because I deny what you affirm, to wit, the existence of Matter? Since, for aught you can tell, I am as peremptory in my denial, as you in your affirmation.

HYL. Hold, Philonous, I have been a little out in my

definition; but every false step a man makes in discourse is not to be insisted on. I said indeed that a *sceptic* was one who doubted of everything; but I should have added, or who denies the reality and truth of things.

Phil. What things? Do you mean the principles and theorems of sciences? But these you know are universal intellectual notions, and consequently independent of Matter. The denial therefore of this doth not imply the denying them.

Hyl. I grant it. But are there no other things? What think you of distrusting the senses, of denying the real existence of sensible things, or pretending to know nothing of them. Is not this sufficient to denominate a man a *sceptic?*

Phil. Shall we therefore examine which of us it is that denies the reality of sensible things, or professes the greatest ignorance of them; since, if I take you rightly, he is to be esteemed the greatest *sceptic?*

Hyl. That is what I desire.

Phil. What mean you by Sensible Things?

Hyl. Those things which are perceived by the senses. Can you imagine that I mean anything else?

Phil. Pardon me, Hylas, if I am desirous clearly to apprehend your notions, since this may much shorten our inquiry. Suffer me then to ask you this farther question. Are those things only perceived by the senses which are perceived immediately? Or, may those things properly be said to be *sensible* which are perceived mediately, or not without the intervention of others?

Hyl. I do not sufficiently understand you.

Phil. In reading a book, what I immediately perceive are the letters; but mediately, or by means of these, are suggested to my mind the notions of God, virtue, truth, &c. Now, that the letters are truly sensible things, or perceived by sense, there is no doubt: but I would know whether you take the things suggested by them to be so too.

Hyl. No, certainly: it were absurd to think *God* or *virtue* sensible things; though they may be signified and suggested to the mind by sensible marks, with which they have an arbitrary connexion.

PHIL. It seems then, that by *sensible things* you mean those only which can be perceived *immediately* by sense?

HYL. Right.

PHIL. Doth it not follow from this, that though I see one part of the sky red, and another blue, and that my reason doth thence evidently conclude there must be some cause of that diversity of colours, yet that cause cannot be said to be a sensible thing, or perceived by the sense of seeing?

HYL. It doth.

PHIL. In like manner, though I hear variety of sounds, yet I cannot be said to hear the causes of those sounds?

HYL. You cannot.

PHIL. And when by my touch I perceive a thing to be hot and heavy, I cannot say, with any truth or propriety, that I feel the cause of its heat or weight?

HYL. To prevent any more questions of this kind, I tell you once for all, that by *sensible things* I mean those only which are perceived by sense; and that in truth the senses perceive nothing which they do not perceive *immediately:* for they make no inferences. The deducing therefore of causes or occasions from effects and appearances, which alone are perceived by sense, entirely relates to reason.

PHIL. This point then is agreed between us—That *sensible things are those only which are immediately perceived by sense.* You will farther inform me, whether we immediately perceive by sight anything beside light, and colours, and figures; or by hearing, anything but sounds; by the palate, anything beside tastes; by the smell, beside odours; or by the touch, more than tangible qualities.

HYL. We do not.

PHIL. It seems, therefore, that if you take away all sensible qualities, there remains nothing sensible?

HYL. I grant it.

PHIL. Sensible things therefore are nothing else but so many sensible qualities, or combinations of sensible qualities?

HYL. Nothing else.

PHIL. *Heat* then is a sensible thing?

HYL. Certainly.

PHIL. Doth the *reality* of sensible things consist in being perceived? or, is it something distinct from their being perceived, and that bears no relation to the mind?

HYL. To *exist* is one thing, and to be *perceived* is another.

PHIL. I speak with regard to sensible things only. And of these I ask, whether by their real existence you mean a subsistence exterior to the mind, and distinct from their being perceived?

HYL. I mean a real absolute being, distinct from, and without any relation to, their being perceived.

PHIL. Heat therefore, if it be allowed a real being, must exist without the mind?

HYL. It must.

PHIL. Tell me, Hylas, is this real existence equally compatible to all degrees of heat, which we perceive; or is there any reason why we should attribute it to some, and deny it to others? And if there be, pray let me know that reason.

HYL. Whatever degree of heat we perceive by sense, we may be sure the same exists in the object that occasions it.

PHIL. What! the greatest as well as the least?

HYL. I tell you, the reason is plainly the same in respect of both. They are both perceived by sense; nay, the greater degree of heat is more sensibly perceived; and consequently, if there is any difference, we are more certain of its real existence than we can be of the reality of a lesser degree.

PHIL. But is not the most vehement and intense degree of heat a very great pain?

HYL. No one can deny it.

PHIL. And is any unperceiving thing capable of pain or pleasure?

HYL. No, certainly.

PHIL. Is your material substance a senseless being, or a being endowed with sense and perception?

HYL. It is senseless without doubt.

PHIL. It cannot therefore be the subject of pain?

HYL. By no means.

PHIL. Nor consequently of the greatest heat perceived by sense, since you acknowledge this to be no small pain?

HYL. I grant it.

PHIL. What shall we say then of your external object; is it a material Substance, or no?

HYL. It is a material substance with the sensible qualities inhering in it.

PHIL. How then can a great heat exist in it, since you own it cannot in a material substance? I desire you would clear this point.

HYL. Hold, Philonous, I fear I was out in yielding intense heat to be a pain. It should seem rather, that pain is something distinct from heat, and the consequence or effect of it.

PHIL. Upon putting your hand near the fire, do you perceive one simple uniform sensation, or two distinct sensations?

HYL. But one simple sensation.

PHIL. Is not the heat immediately perceived?

HYL. It is.

PHIL. And the pain?

HYL. True.

PHIL. Seeing therefore they are both immediately perceived at the same time, and the fire affects you only with one simple or uncompounded idea, it follows that this same simple idea is both the intense heat immediately perceived, and the pain; and, consequently, that the intense heat immediately perceived is nothing distinct from a particular sort of pain.

HYL. It seems so.

PHIL. Again, try in your thoughts, Hylas, if you can conceive a vehement sensation to be without pain or pleasure.

HYL. I cannot.

PHIL. Or can you frame to yourself an idea of sensible pain or pleasure in general, abstracted from every particular idea of heat, cold, tastes, smells? &c.

HYL.—I do not find that I can.

PHIL. Doth it not therefore follow, that sensible pain is nothing distinct from those sensations or ideas, in an intense degree?

HYL. It is undeniable; and, to speak the truth, I begin to suspect a very great heat cannot exist but in a mind perceiving it.

PHIL. What! are you then in that sceptical state of suspense, between affirming and denying?

HYL. I think I may be positive in the point. A very violent and painful heat cannot exist without the mind.

PHIL. It hath not therefore, according to you, any *real* being?

HYL. I own it.

PHIL. Is it therefore certain, that there is no body in nature really hot?

HYL. I have not denied there is any real heat in bodies. I only say, there is no such thing as an intense real heat.

PHIL. But, did you not say before that all degrees of heat were equally real; or, if there was any difference, that the greater were more undoubtedly real than the lesser?

HYL. True: but it was because I did not then consider the ground there is for distinguishing between them, which I now plainly see. And it is this: because intense heat is nothing else but a particular kind of painful sensation; and pain cannot exist but in a perceiving being; it follows that no intense heat can really exist in an unperceiving corporeal substance. But this is no reason why we should deny heat in an inferior degree to exist in such a substance.

PHIL. But how shall we be able to discern those degrees of heat which exist only in the mind from those which exist without it?

HYL. That is no difficult matter. You know the least pain cannot exist unperceived; whatever, therefore, degree of heat is a pain exists only in the mind. But, as for all other degrees of heat, nothing obliges us to think the same of them.

PHIL. I think you granted before that no unperceiving being was capable of pleasure, any more than of pain.

HYL. I did.

PHIL. And is not warmth, or a more gentle degree of heat than what causes uneasiness, a pleasure?

HYL. What then?

PHIL. Consequently, it cannot exist without the mind in an unperceiving substance, or body.

HYL. So it seems.

PHIL. Since, therefore, as well those degrees of heat that

are not painful, as those that are, can exist only in a thinking substance; may we not conclude that external bodies are absolutely incapable of any degree of heat whatsoever?

HYL. On second thoughts, I do not think it so evident that warmth is a pleasure as that a great degree of heat is a pain.

PHIL. I do not pretend that warmth is as great a pleasure as heat is a pain. But, if you grant it to be even a small pleasure, it serves to make good my conclusion.

HYL. I could rather call it an *indolence*. It seems to be nothing more than a privation of both pain and pleasure. And that such a quality or state as this may agree to an unthinking substance, I hope you will not deny.

PHIL. If you are resolved to maintain that warmth, or a gentle degree of heat, is no pleasure, I know not how to convince you otherwise than by appealing to your own sense. But what think you of cold?

HYL. The same that I do of heat. An intense degree of cold is a pain; for to feel a very great cold, is to perceive a great uneasiness: it cannot therefore exist without the mind; but a lesser degree of cold may, as well as a lesser degree of heat.

PHIL. Those bodies, therefore, upon whose application to our own, we perceive a moderate degree of heat, must be concluded to have a moderate degree of heat or warmth in them; and those, upon whose application we feel a like degree of cold, must be thought to have cold in them.

HYL. They must.

PHIL. Can any doctrine be true that necessarily leads a man into an absurdity?

HYL. Without doubt it cannot.

PHIL. Is it not an absurdity to think that the same thing should be at the same time both cold and warm?

HYL. It is.

PHIL. Suppose now one of your hands hot, and the other cold, and that they are both at once put into the same vessel of water, in an intermediate state; will not the water seem cold to one hand, and warm to the other?

HYL. It will.

PHIL. Ought we not therefore, by your principles, to conclude it is really both cold and warm at the same time, that is, according to your own concession, to believe an absurdity?

HYL. I confess it seems so.

PHIL. Consequently, the principles themselves are false, since you have granted that no true principle leads to an absurdity.

HYL. But, after all, can anything be more absurd than to say, *there is no heat in the fire?*

PHIL. To make the point still clearer; tell me whether, in two cases exactly alike, we ought not to make the same judgment?

HYL. We ought.

PHIL. When a pin pricks your finger, doth it not rend and divide the fibres of your flesh?

HYL. It doth.

PHIL. And when a coal burns your finger, doth it any more?

HYL. It doth not.

PHIL. Since, therefore, you neither judge the sensation itself occasioned by the pin, nor anything like it to be in the pin; you should not, conformably to what you have now granted, judge the sensation occasioned by the fire, or anything like it, to be in the fire.

HYL. Well, since it must be so, I am content to yield this point, and acknowledge that heat and cold are only sensations existing in our minds. But there still remain qualities enough to secure the reality of external things.

PHIL. But what will you say, Hylas, if it shall appear that the case is the same with regard to all other sensible qualities, and that they can no more be supposed to exist without the mind, than heat and cold?

HYL. Then indeed you will have done something to the purpose; but that is what I despair of seeing proved.

PHIL. Let us examine them in order. What think you of *tastes*—do they exist without the mind, or no?

HYL. Can any man in his senses doubt whether sugar is sweet, or wormwood bitter?

PHIL. Inform me, Hylas. Is a sweet taste a particular kind of pleasure or pleasant sensation, or is it not?

HYL. It is.

PHIL. And is not bitterness some kind of uneasiness or pain?

HYL. I grant it.

PHIL. If therefore sugar and wormwood are unthinking corporeal substances existing without the mind, how can sweetness and bitterness, that is, pleasure and pain, agree to them?

HYL. Hold, Philonous, I now see what it was deluded me all this time. You asked whether heat and cold, sweetness and bitterness, were not particular sorts of pleasure and pain; to which I answered simply, that they were. Whereas I should have thus distinguished:—those qualities, as perceived by us, are pleasures or pains; but not as existing in the external objects. We must not therefore conclude absolutely, that there is no heat in the fire, or sweetness in the sugar, but only that heat or sweetness, as perceived by us, are not in the fire or sugar. What say you to this?

PHIL. I say it is nothing to the purpose. Our discourse proceeded altogether concerning sensible things, which you defined to be, *the things we immediately perceive by our senses.* Whatever other qualities, therefore, you speak of as distinct from these, I know nothing of them, neither do they at all belong to the point in dispute. You may, indeed, pretend to have discovered certain qualities which you do not perceive, and assert those insensible qualities exist in fire and sugar. But what use can be made of this to your present purpose, I am at a loss to conceive. Tell me then once more, do you acknowledge that heat and cold, sweetness and bitterness (meaning those qualities which are perceived by the senses), do not exist without the mind?

HYL. I see it is to no purpose to hold out, so I give up the cause as to those mentioned qualities. Though I profess it sounds oddly, to say that sugar is not sweet.

PHIL. But, for your farther satisfaction, take this along with you: that which at other times seems sweet, shall, to a distempered palate, appear bitter. And, nothing can be plainer than that divers persons perceive different tastes in the same food; since that which one man delights in, another abhors. And how could this be, if the taste was something really inherent in the food?

HYL. I acknowledge I know not how.

PHIL. In the next place, *odours* are to be considered. And, with regard to these, I would fain know whether what hath been said of tastes doth not exactly agree to them? Are they not so many pleasing or displeasing sensations?

HYL. They are.

PHIL. Can you then conceive it possible that they should exist in an unperceiving thing?

HYL. I cannot.

PHIL. Or, can you imagine that filth and ordure affect those brute animals that feed on them out of choice, with the same smells which we perceive in them?

HYL. By no means.

PHIL. May we not therefore conclude of smells, as of the other forementioned qualities, that they cannot exist in any but a perceiving substance or mind?

HYL. I think so.

PHIL. Then as to *sounds,* what must we think of them: are they accidents really inherent in external bodies, or not?

HYL. That they inhere not in the sonorous bodies is plain from hence: because a bell struck in the exhausted receiver of an air-pump sends forth no sound. The air, therefore, must be thought the subject of sound.

PHIL. What reason is there for that, Hylas?

HYL. Because, when any motion is raised in the air, we perceive a sound greater or lesser, according to the air's motion; but without some motion in the air, we never hear any sound at all.

PHIL. And granting that we never hear a sound but when some motion is produced in the air, yet I do not see how you can infer from thence, that the sound itself is in the air.

HYL. It is this very motion in the external air that produces in the mind the sensation of *sound.* For, striking on the drum of the ear, it causeth a vibration, which by the auditory nerves being communicated to the brain, the soul is thereupon affected with the sensation called *sound*.

PHIL. What! is sound then a sensation?

HYL. I tell you, as perceived by us, it is a particular sensation in the mind.

PHIL. And can any sensation exist without the mind?

HYL. No, certainly.

PHIL. How then can sound, being a sensation, exist in the air, if by the *air* you mean a senseless substance existing without the mind?

HYL. You must distinguish, Philonous, between sound as it is perceived by us, and as it is in itself; or (which is the same thing) between the sound we immediately perceive, and that which exists without us. The former, indeed, is a particular kind of sensation, but the latter is merely a vibrative or undulatory motion in the air.

PHIL. I thought I had already obviated that distinction, by the answer I gave when you were applying it in a like case before. But, to say no more of that, are you sure then that sound is really nothing but motion?

HYL. I am.

PHIL. Whatever therefore agrees to real sound, may with truth be attributed to motion?

HYL. It may.

PHIL. It is then good sense to speak of *motion* as of a thing that is *loud, sweet, acute, or grave.*

HYL. I see you are resolved not to understand me. Is it not evident those accidents or modes belong only to sensible sound, or *sound* in the common acceptation of the word, but not to *sound* in the real and philosophic sense; which, as I just now told you, is nothing but a certain motion of the air?

PHIL. It seems then there are two sorts of sound—the one vulgar, or that which is heard, the other philosophical and real?

HYL. Even so.

PHIL. And the latter consists in motion?

HYL. I told you so before.

PHIL. Tell me, Hylas, to which of the senses, think you, the idea of motion belongs? to the hearing?

HYL. No, certainly; but to the sight and touch.

PHIL. It should follow then, that, according to you, real sounds may possibly be *seen* or *felt,* but never *heard.*

HYL. Look you, Philonous, you may, if you please, make a jest of my opinion, but that will not alter the truth of things. I own, indeed, the inferences you draw me into sound something oddly; but common language, you know, is framed by, and for the use of the vulgar: we must not therefore wonder if expressions adapted to exact philosophic notions seem uncouth and out of the way.

PHIL. Is it come to that? I assure you, I imagine myself to have gained no small point, since you make so light of departing from common phrases and opinions; it being a main part of our inquiry, to examine whose notions are widest of the common road, and most repugnant to the general sense of the world. But, can you think it no more than a philosophical paradox, to say that *real sounds are never heard,* and that the idea of them is obtained by some other sense? And is there nothing in this contrary to nature and the truth of things?

HYL. To deal ingenuously, I do not like it. And, after the concessions already made, I had as well grant that sounds too have no real being without the mind.

PHIL. And I hope you will make no difficulty to acknowledge the same of *colours.*

HYL. Pardon me: the case of colours is very different. Can anything be plainer than that we see them on the objects?

PHIL. The objects you speak of are, I suppose, corporeal Substances existing without the mind?

HYL. They are.

PHIL. And have true and real colours inhering in them?

HYL. Each visible object hath that colour which we see in it.

PHIL. How! is there anything visible but what we perceive by sight?

HYL. There is not.

PHIL. And, do we perceive anything by sense which we do not perceive immediately?

HYL. How often must I be obliged to repeat the same thing? I tell you, we do not.

PHIL. Have patience, good Hylas; and tell me once more, whether there is anything immediately perceived by the senses, except sensible qualities. I know you asserted there was not; but I would now be informed, whether you still persist in the same opinion.

HYL. I do.

PHIL. Pray, is your corporeal substance either a sensible quality, or made up of sensible qualities?

HYL. What a question that is! who ever thought it was?

PHIL. My reason for asking was, because in saying, *each visible object hath that colour which we see in it,* you make visible objects to be corporeal substances; which implies either that corporeal substances are sensible qualities, or else that there is something besides sensible qualities perceived by sight: but, as this point was formerly agreed between us, and is still maintained by you, it is a clear consequence, that your *corporeal substance* is nothing distinct from *sensible qualities.*

HYL. You may draw as many absurd consequences as you please, and endeavour to perplex the plainest things; but you shall never persuade me out of my senses. I clearly understand my own meaning.

PHIL. I wish you would make me understand it too. But, since you are unwilling to have your notion of corporeal substance examined, I shall urge that point no farther. Only be pleased to let me know, whether the same colours which we see exist in external bodies, or some other.

HYL. The very same.

PHIL. What! are then the beautiful red and purple we see on yonder clouds really in them? Or do you imagine they have in themselves any other form than that of a dark mist or vapour?

HYL. I must own, Philonous, those colours are not really in the clouds as they seem to be at this distance. They are only apparent colours.

PHIL. *Apparent* call you them? how shall we distinguish these apparent colours from real?

HYL. Very easily. Those are to be thought apparent

which, appearing only at a distance, vanish upon a nearer approach.

PHIL. And those, I suppose, are to be thought real which are discovered by the most near and exact survey.

HYL. Right.

PHIL. Is the nearest and exactest survey made by the help of a microscope, or by the naked eye?

HYL. By a microscope, doubtless.

PHIL. But a microscope often discovers colours in an object different from those perceived by the unassisted sight. And, in case we had microscopes magnifying to any assigned degree, it is certain that no object whatsoever, viewed through them, would appear in the same colour which it exhibits to the naked eye.

HYL. And what will you conclude from all this? You cannot argue that there are really and naturally no colours on objects: because by artificial managements they may be altered, or made to vanish.

PHIL. I think it may evidently be concluded from your own concessions, that all the colours we see with our naked eyes are only apparent as those on the clouds, since they vanish upon a more close and accurate inspection which is afforded us by a microscope. Then, as to what you say by way of prevention: I ask you whether the real and natural state of an object is better discovered by a very sharp and piercing sight, or by one which is less sharp?

HYL. By the former without doubt.

PHIL. Is it not plain from *Dioptrics* that microscopes make the sight more penetrating, and represent objects as they would appear to the eye in case it were naturally endowed with a most exquisite sharpness?

HYL. It is.

PHIL. Consequently the microscopical representation is to be thought that which best sets forth the real nature of the thing, or what it is in itself. The colours, therefore, by it perceived are more genuine and real than those perceived otherwise.

HYL. I confess there is something in what you say.

PHIL. Besides, it is not only possible but manifest, that there actually are animals whose eyes are by nature framed to perceive those things which by reason of their minuteness escape our sight. What think you of those inconceivably small animals perceived by glasses? must we suppose they are all stark blind? Or, in case they see, can it be imagined their sight hath not the same use in preserving their bodies from injuries, which appears in that of all other animals? And if it hath, is it not evident they must see particles less than their own bodies; which will present them with a far different view in each object from that which strikes our senses? Even our own eyes do not always represent objects to us after the same manner. In the jaundice every one knows that all things seem yellow. Is it not therefore highly probable those animals in whose eyes we discern a very different texture from that of ours, and whose bodies abound with different humours, do not see the same colours in every object that we do? From all which, should it not seem to follow that all colours are equally apparent, and that none of those which we perceive are really inherent in any outward object?

HYL. It should.

PHIL. The point will be past all doubt, if you consider that, in case colours were real properties or affections inherent in external bodies, they could admit of no alteration without some change wrought in the very bodies themselves: but, is it not evident from what hath been said that, upon the use of microscopes, upon a change happening in the humours of the eye, or a variation of distance, without any manner of real alteration in the thing itself, the colours of any object are either changed, or totally disappear? Nay, all other circumstances remaining the same, change but the situation of some objects, and they shall present different colours to the eye. The same thing happens upon viewing an object in various degrees of light. And what is more known than that the same bodies appear differently coloured by candle-light from what they do in the open day? Add to these the experiment of a prism which, separating the heterogeneous rays of light, alters the colour of any object, and will cause the whitest to appear of a deep blue or red to the naked eye. And now tell me whether you are still of opinion that every body hath its true real colour inhering in it; and, if you think it hath, I would fain know farther from you, what certain distance and position of the object, what peculiar texture and formation of the eye, what degree or kind of light is necessary for ascertaining that true colour, and distinguishing it from apparent ones.

HYL. I own myself entirely satisfied, that they are all equally apparent, and that there is no such thing as colour really inhering in external bodies, but that it is altogether in the light. And what confirms me in this opinion is, that in proportion to the light colours are still more or less vivid; and if there be no light, then are there no colours perceived. Besides, allowing there are colours on external objects, yet, how is it possible for us to perceive them? For no external body affects the mind, unless it acts first on our organs of sense. But the only action of bodies is motion; and motion cannot be communicated otherwise than by impulse. A distant object therefore cannot act on the eye; nor consequently make itself or its properties perceivable to the soul. Whence it plainly follows that it is immediately some contiguous substance, which, operating on the eye, occasions a perception of colours: and such is light.

PHIL. How! is light then a substance?

HYL. I tell you, Philonous, external light is nothing but a thin fluid substance, whose minute particles being agitated with a brisk motion, and in various manners reflected from the different surfaces of outward objects to the eyes, communicate different motions to the optic nerves; which, being propagated to the brain, cause therein various impressions; and these are attended with the sensations of red, blue, yellow, &c.

PHIL. It seems then the light doth no more than shake the optic nerves.

HYL. Nothing else.

PHIL. And consequent to each particular motion of the nerves, the mind is affected with a sensation, which is some particular colour.

HYL. Right.

PHIL. And these sensations have no existence without the mind.

HYL. They have not.

PHIL. How then do you affirm that colours are in the light; since by *light* you understand a corporeal substance external to the mind?

HYL. Light and colours, as immediately perceived by us, I grant cannot exist without the mind. But in themselves they are only the motions and configurations of certain insensible particles of matter.

PHIL. Colours then, in the vulgar sense, or taken for the immediate objects of sight, cannot agree to any but a perceiving substance.

HYL. That is what I say.

PHIL. Well then, since you give up the point as to those sensible qualities which are alone thought colours by all mankind beside, you may hold what you please with regard to those invisible ones of the philosophers. It is not my business to dispute about *them;* only I would advise you to bethink yourself, whether, considering the inquiry we are upon, it be prudent for you to affirm—*the red and blue which we see are not real colours, but certain unknown motions and figures which no man ever did or can see are truly so.* Are not these shocking notions, and are not they subject to as many ridiculous inferences, as those you were obliged to renounce before in the case of sounds?

HYL. I frankly own, Philonous, that it is in vain to stand out any longer. Colours, sounds, tastes, in a word all those termed *secondary qualities,* have certainly no existence without the mind. But by this acknowledgment I must not be supposed to derogate anything from the reality of Matter, or external objects; seeing it is no more than several philosophers maintain, who nevertheless are the farthest imaginable from denying Matter. For the clearer understanding of this, you must know sensible qualities are by philosophers divided into *Primary* and *Secondary.* The former are Extension, Figure, Solidity, Gravity, Motion, and Rest; and these they hold exist really in bodies. The latter are those above enumerated; or, briefly, *all sensible qualities beside the Primary;* which they assert are only so many sensations or ideas existing nowhere but in the mind. But all this, I doubt not, you are apprised of. For my part,

I have been a long time sensible there was such an opinion current among philosophers, but was never thoroughly convinced of its truth until now.

PHIL. You are still then of opinion that *extension* and *figures* are inherent in external unthinking substances?

HYL. I am.

PHIL. But what if the same arguments which are brought against Secondary Qualities will hold good against these also?

HYL. Why then I shall be obliged to think, they too exist only in the mind.

PHIL. Is it your opinion the very figure and extension which you perceive by sense exist in the outward object or material substance?

HYL. It is.

PHIL. Have all other animals as good grounds to think the same of the figure and extension which they see and feel?

HYL. Without doubt, if they have any thought at all.

PHIL. Answer me, Hylas. Think you the senses were bestowed upon all animals for their preservation and well-being in life? or were they given to men alone for this end?

HYL. I make no question but they have the same use in all other animals.

PHIL. If so, is it not necessary they should be enabled by them to perceive their own limbs, and those bodies which are capable of harming them?

HYL. Certainly.

PHIL. A mite therefore must be supposed to see his own foot, and things equal or even less than it, as bodies of some considerable dimension; though at the same time they appear to you scarce discernible, or at best as so many visible points?

HYL. I cannot deny it.

PHIL. And to creatures less than the mite they will seem yet larger?

HYL. They will.

PHIL. Insomuch that what you can hardly discern will

to another extremely minute animal appear as some huge mountain?

HYL All this I grant.

PHIL. Can one and the same thing be at the same time in itself of different dimensions?

HYL. That were absurd to imagine.

PHIL. But, from what you have laid down it follows that both the extension by you perceived, and that perceived by the mite itself, as likewise all those perceived by lesser animals, are each of them the true extension of the mite's foot; that is to say, by your own principles you are led into an absurdity.

HYL. There seems to be some difficulty in the point.

PHIL. Again, have you not acknowledged that no real inherent property of any object can be changed without some change in the thing itself?

HYL. I have.

PHIL. But, as we approach to or recede from an object, the visible extension varies, being at one distance ten or a hundred times greater than another. Doth it not therefore follow from hence likewise that it is not really inherent in the object?

HYL. I own I am at a loss what to think.

PHIL Your judgment will soon be determined, if you will venture to think as freely concerning this quality as you have done concerning the rest. Was it not admitted as a good argument, that neither heat nor cold was in the water, because it seemed warm to one hand and cold to the other?

HYL. It was.

PHIL. Is it not the very same reasoning to conclude, there is no extension or figure in an object, because to one eye it shall seem little, smooth, and round, when at the same time it appears to the other, great, uneven, and regular?

HYL. The very same. But does this latter fact ever happen?

PHIL. You may at any time make the experiment, by looking with one eye bare, and with the other through a microscope.

HYL. I know not how to maintain it; and yet I am loath

to give up *extension,* I see so many odd consequences following upon such a concession.

PHIL. Odd, say you? After the concessions already made, I hope you will stick at nothing for its oddness. [[1]But, on the other hand, should it not seem very odd, if the general reasoning which includes all other sensible qualities did not also include extension? If it be allowed that no idea, nor anything like an idea, can exist in an unperceiving substance, then surely it follows that no figure, or mode of extension, which we can either perceive, or imagine, or have any idea of, can be really inherent in Matter; not to mention the peculiar difficulty there must be in conceiving• a material substance, prior to and distinct from extension to be the *substratum* of extension. Be the sensible quality what it will—figure, or sound, or colour, it seems alike impossible it should subsist in that which doth not perceive it.]

HYL. I give up the point for the present, reserving still a right to retract my opinion, in case I shall hereafter discover any false step in my progress to it.

PHIL. That is a right you cannot be denied. Figures and extension being despatched, we proceed next to *motion.* Can a real motion in any external body be at the same time very swift and very slow?

HYL. It cannot.

PHIL. Is not the motion of a body swift in a reciprocal proportion to the time it takes up in describing any given space? Thus a body that describes a mile in an hour moves three times faster than it would in case it described only a mile in three hours.

HYL. I agree with you.

PHIL. And is not time measured by the succession of ideas in our minds?

HYL. It is.

PHIL. And is it not possible ideas should succeed one another twice as fast in your mind as they do in mine, or in that of some spirit of another kind?

HYL. I own it.

---

[1] What follows, within brackets, is not contained in the first and second editions.

PHIL. Consequently the same body may to another seem to perform its motion over any space in half the time that it doth to you. And the same reasoning will hold as to any other proportion: that is to say, according to your principles (since the motions perceived are both really in the object) it is possible one and the same body shall be really moved the same way at once, both very swift and very slow. How is this consistent either with common sense, or with what you just now granted?

HYL. I have nothing to say to it.

PHIL. Then as for *solidity;* either you do not mean any sensible quality by that word, and so it is beside our inquiry: or if you do, it must be either hardness or resistance. But both the one and the other are plainly relative to our senses: it being evident that what seems hard to one animal may appear soft to another, who hath greater force and firmness of limbs. Nor is it less plain that the resistance I feel is not in the body.

HYL. I own the very *sensation* of resistance, which is all you immediately perceive, is not in the body; but the *cause* of that sensation is.

PHIL. But the causes of our sensations are not things immediately perceived, and therefore are not sensible. This point I thought had been already determined.

HYL. I own it was; but you will pardon me if I seem a little embarrassed: I know not how to quit my old notions.

PHIL. To help you out, do but consider that if *extension* be once acknowledged to have no existence without the mind, the same must necessarily be granted of motion, solidity, and gravity; since they all evidently suppose extension. It is therefore superfluous to inquire particularly concerning each of them. In denying extension, you have denied them all to have any real existence.

HYL. I wonder, Philonous, if what you say be true, why those philosophers who deny the Secondary Qualities any real existence should yet attribute it to the Primary. If there is no difference between them, how can this be accounted for?

PHIL. It is not my business to account for every opinion of the philosophers. But, among other reasons which may be assigned for this, it seems probable that pleasure and pain being rather annexed to the former than the latter may be one. Heat and cold, tastes and smells, have something more vividly pleasing or disagreeable than the ideas of extension, figure, and motion affect us with. And, it being too visibly absurd to hold that pain or pleasure can be in an unperceiving substance, men are more easily weaned from believing the external existence of the Secondary than the Primary Qualities. You will be satisfied there is something in this, if you recollect the difference you made between an intense and more moderate degree of heat; allowing the one a real existence, while you denied it to the other. But, after all, there is no rational ground for that distinction; for, surely an indifferent sensation is as truly *a sensation* as one more pleasing or painful; and consequently should not any more than they be supposed to exist in an unthinking subject.

HYL. It is just come into my head, Philonous, that I have somewhere heard of a distinction between absolute and sensible extension. Now, though it be acknowledged that *great* and *small,* consisting merely in the relation which other extended beings have to the parts of our own bodies, do not really inhere in the substances themselves; yet nothing obliges us to hold the same with regard to *absolute extension,* which is something abstracted from *great* and *small,* from this or that particular magnitude or figure. So likewise as to motion; *swift* and *slow* are altogether relative to the succession of ideas in our own minds. But, it doth not follow, because those modifications of motion exist not without the mind, that therefore absolute motion abstracted from them doth not.

PHIL. Pray what is it that distinguishes one motion, or one part of extension, from another? Is it not something sensible, as some degree of swiftness or slowness, some certain magnitude or figure peculiar to each?

HYL. I think so.

PHIL. These qualities, therefore, stripped of all sensible properties, are without all specific and numerical differences, as the schools call them.

HYL. They are.

PHIL. That is to say, they are extension in general, and motion in general.

HYL. Let it be so.

PHIL. But it is a universally received maxim that *Everything which exists is particular.* How then can motion in general, or extension in general, exist in any corporeal substance?

HYL. I will take time to solve your difficulty.

PHIL. But I think the point may be speedily decided. Without doubt you can tell whether you are able to frame this or that idea. Now I am content to put our dispute on this issue. If you can frame in your thoughts a distinct *abstract idea* of motion or extension, divested of all those sensible modes, as swift and slow, great and small, round and square, and the like, which are acknowledged to exist only in the mind, I will then yield the point you contend for. But if you cannot, it will be unreasonable on your side to insist any longer upon what you have no notion of.

HYL. To confess ingenuously, I cannot.

PHIL. Can you even separate the ideas of extension and motion from the ideas of all those qualities which they who make the distinction term *secondary?*

HYL. What! is it not an easy matter to consider extension and motion by themselves, abstracted from all other sensible qualities? Pray how do the mathematicians treat of them?

PHIL. I acknowledge, Hylas, it is not difficult to form general propositions and reasonings about those qualities, without mentioning any other; and, in this sense, to consider or treat of them abstractedly. But, how doth it follow that, because I can pronounce the word *motion* by itself, I can form the idea of it in my mind exclusive of body? or, because theorems may be made of extension and figures, without any mention of *great* or *small,* or any other sensible mode or quality, that therefore it is possible such an abstract idea of extension, without any particular size or figure, or sensible quality[2], should be distinctly formed, and apprehended by the mind? Mathematicians

---

[2] ' Size or figure, or sensible quality '—' size, colour, &c.,' in the first and second editions.

(8) HC XXXVII

treat of quantity, without regarding what other sensible qualities it is attended with, as being altogether indifferent to their demonstrations. But, when laying aside the words, they contemplate the bare ideas, I believe you will find, they are not the pure abstracted ideas of extension.

HYL. But what say you to *pure intellect?* May not abstracted ideas be framed by that faculty?

PHIL. Since I cannot frame abstract ideas at all, it is plain I cannot frame them by the help of *pure intellect;* whatsoever faculty you understand by those words. Besides, not to inquire into the nature of pure intellect and its spiritual objects, as *virtue, reason, God,* or the like, thus much seems manifest—that sensible things are only to be perceived by sense, or represented by the imagination. Figures, therefore, and extension, being originally perceived by sense, do not belong to pure intellect: but, for your farther satisfaction, try if you can frame the idea of any figure, abstracted from all particularities of size, or even from other sensible qualities.

HYL. Let me think a little—I do not find that I can.

PHIL. And can you think it possible that should really exist in nature which implies a repugnancy in its conception?

HYL. By no means.

PHIL. Since therefore it is impossible even for the mind to disunite the ideas of extension and motion from all other sensible qualities, doth it not follow, that where the one exist there necessarily the other exist likewise?

HYL. It should seem so.

PHIL. Consequently, the very same arguments which you admitted as conclusive against the Secondary Qualities are, without any farther application of force, against the Primary too. Besides, if you will trust your senses, is it not plain all sensible qualities coexist, or to them appear as being in the same place? Do they ever represent a motion, or figure, as being divested of all other visible and tangible qualities?

HYL. You need say no more on this head. I am free to own, if there be no secret error or oversight in our proceedings hitherto, that *all* sensible qualities are alike to be denied existence without the mind. But, my fear is that I have been too liberal in my former concessions, or overlooked some fallacy or other. In short, I did not take time to think.

PHIL. For that matter, Hylas, you may take what time you please in reviewing the progress of our inquiry. You are at liberty to recover any slips you might have made, or offer whatever you have omitted which makes for your first opinion.

HYL. One great oversight I take to be this—that I did not sufficiently distinguish the *object* from the *sensation*. Now, though this latter may not exist without the mind, yet it will not thence follow that the former cannot.

PHIL. What object do you mean? the object of the senses?

HYL. The same.

PHIL. It is then immediately perceived?

HYL. Right.

PHIL. Make me to understand the difference between what is immediately perceived and a sensation.

HYL. The sensation I take to be an act of the mind perceiving; besides which, there is something perceived; and this I call the *object*. For example, there is red and yellow on that tulip. But then the act of perceiving those colours is in me only, and not in the tulip.

PHIL. What tulip do you speak of? Is it that which you see?

HYL. The same.

PHIL. And what do you see beside colour, figure, and extension?

HYL. Nothing.

PHIL. What you would say then is that the red and yellow are coexistent with the extension; is it not?

HYL. That is not all; I would say they have a real existence without the mind, in some unthinking substance.

PHIL. That the colours are really in the tulip which I see is manifest. Neither can it be denied that this tulip may exist independent of your mind or mine; but, that any immediate object of the senses—that is, any idea, or combination of ideas—should exist in an unthinking substance, or exterior to *all* minds, is in itself an evident contradiction. Nor can I imagine how this follows from what you said just now, to wit, that the red and yellow were on the tulip *you saw,* since you do not pretend to *see* that unthinking substance.

HYL. You have an artful way, Philonous, of diverting our inquiry from the subject.

PHIL. I see you have no mind to be pressed that way. To return then to your distinction between *sensation* and *object;* if I take you right, you distinguish in every perception two things, the one an action of the mind, the other not.

HYL. True.

PHIL. And this action cannot exist in, or belong to, any unthinking thing; but, whatever beside is implied in a perception may?

HYL. That is my meaning.

PHIL. So that if there was a perception without any act of the mind, it were possible such a perception should exist in an unthinking substance?

HYL. I grant it. But it is impossible there should be such a perception.

PHIL. When is the mind said to be active?

HYL. When it produces, puts an end to, or changes, anything.

PHIL. Can the mind produce, discontinue, or change anything, but by an act of the will?

HYL. It cannot.

PHIL. The mind therefore is to be accounted *active* in its perceptions so far forth as *volition* is included in them?

HYL. It is.

PHIL. In plucking this flower I am active; because I do it by the motion of my hand, which was consequent upon my volition; so likewise in applying it to my nose. But is either of these smelling?

HYL. No.

PHIL. I act too in drawing the air through my nose; because my breathing so rather than otherwise is the effect of my volition. But neither can this be called *smelling:* for, if it were, I should smell every time I breathed in that manner?

HYL. True.

PHIL. Smelling then is somewhat consequent to all this?

HYL. It is.

PHIL. But I do not find my will concerned any farther. Whatever more there is—as that I perceive such a particular smell, or any smell at all—this is independent of my will, and therein I am altogether passive. Do you find it otherwise with you, Hylas?

HYL. No, the very same.

PHIL. Then, as to seeing, is it not in your power to open your eyes, or keep them shut; to turn them this or that way?

HYL. Without doubt.

PHIL. But, doth it in like manner depend on *your* will that in looking on this flower you perceive *white* rather than any other colour? Or, directing your open eyes towards yonder part of the heaven, can you avoid seeing the sun? Or is light or darkness the effect of your volition?

HYL. No, certainly.

PHIL. You are then in these respects altogether passive?

HYL. I am.

PHIL. Tell me now, whether *seeing* consists in perceiving light and colours, or in opening and turning the eyes?

HYL. Without doubt, in the former.

PHIL. Since therefore you are in the very perception of light and colours altogether passive, what is become of that action you were speaking of as an ingredient in every sensation? And, doth it not follow from your own concessions, that the perception of light and colours, including no action in it, may exist in an unperceiving substance? And is not this a plain contradiction?

HYL. I know not what to think of it.

PHIL. Besides, since you distinguish the *active* and *passive* in every perception, you must do it in that of pain. But how is it possible that pain, be it as little active as you please, should exist in an unperceiving substance? In short, do but consider the point, and then confess ingenuously, whether light and colours, tastes, sounds, &c. are not all equally passions or sensations in the soul. You may indeed call them *external objects,* and give them in words what subsistence you please. But, examine your own thoughts, and then tell me whether it be not as I say?

HYL. I acknowledge, Philonous, that, upon a fair observation of what passes in my mind, I can discover nothing else but that I am a thinking being, affected with variety of sensations; neither is it possible to conceive how a sensation should exist in an unperceiving substance.—But then, on the other hand, when I look on sensible things in a different view, considering them as so many modes and qualities, I find it necessary to suppose a *material substratum,* without which they cannot be conceived to exist.

PHIL. *Material substratum* call you it? Pray, by which of your senses came you acquainted with that being?

HYL. It is not itself sensible; its modes and qualities only being perceived by the senses.

PHIL. I presume then it was by reflexion and reason you obtained the idea of it?

HYL. I do not pretend to any proper positive *idea* of it. However, I conclude it exists, because qualities cannot be conceived to exist without a support.

PHIL. It seems then you have only a relative *notion* of it, or that you conceive it not otherwise than by conceiving the relation it bears to sensible qualities?

HYL. Right.

PHIL. Be pleased therefore to let me know wherein that relation consists.

HYL. Is it not sufficiently expressed in the term *substratum,* or *substance?*

PHIL. If so, the word *substratum* should import that it is spread under the sensible qualities or accidents?

HYL True.

PHIL. And consequently under extension?

HYL. I own it.

PHIL. It is therefore somewhat in its own nature entirely distinct from extension?

HYL. I tell you, extension is only a mode, and Matter is something that supports modes. And is it not evident the thing supported is different from the thing supporting?

PHIL. So that something distinct from, and exclusive of, extension is supposed to be the *substratum* of extension?

HYL. Just so.

PHIL. Answer me, Hylas. Can a thing be spread without extension? or is not the idea of extension necessarily included in *spreading?*

HYL. It is.

PHIL. Whatsoever therefore you suppose spread under anything must have in itself an extension distinct from the extension of that thing under which it is spread?

HYL. It must.

PHIL. Consequently, every corporeal substance, being the *substratum* of extension, must have in itself another extension, by which it is qualified to be a *substratum:* and so on to infinity. And I ask whether this be not absurd in itself, and repugnant to what you granted just now, to wit, that the *substratum* was something distinct from and exclusive of extension?

HYL. Aye but, Philonous, you take me wrong. I do not mean that Matter is *spread* in a gross literal sense under extension. The word *substratum* is used only to express in general the same thing with *substance.*

PHIL. Well then, let us examine the relation implied in the term *substance.* Is it not that it stands under accidents?

HYL. The very same.

PHIL. But, that one thing may stand under or support another, must it not be extended?

HYL. It must.

PHIL. Is not therefore this supposition liable to the same absurdity with the former?

HYL. You still take things in a strict literal sense. That is not fair, Philonous.

PHIL. I am not for imposing any sense on your words: you are at liberty to explain them as you please. Only, I beseech you, make me understand something by them. You tell me Matter supports or stands under accidents. How! is it as your legs support your body?

HYL. No; that is the literal sense.

PHIL. Pray let me know any sense, literal or not literal, that you understand it in.—How long must I wait for an answer, Hylas?

HYL. I declare I know not what to say. I once thought

I understood well enough what was meant by Matter's supporting accidents. But now, the more I think on it the less can I comprehend it: in short I find that I know nothing of it.

PHIL. It seems then you have no idea at all, neither relative nor positive, of Matter; you know neither what it is in itself, nor what relation it bears to accidents?

HYL. I acknowledge it.

PHIL. And yet you asserted that you could not conceive how qualities or accidents should really exist, without conceiving at the same time a material support of them?

HYL. I did.

PHIL. That is to say, when you conceive the *real* existence of qualities, you do withal conceive Something which you cannot conceive?

HYL. It was wrong, I own. But still I fear there is some fallacy or other. Pray what think you of this? It is just come into my head that the ground of all our mistake lies in your treating of each quality by itself. Now, I grant that each quality cannot singly subsist without the mind. Colour cannot without extension, neither can figure without some other sensible quality. But, as the several qualities united or blended together form entire sensible things, nothing hinders why such things may not be supposed to exist without the mind.

PHIL. Either, Hylas, you are jesting, or have a very bad memory. Though indeed we went through all the qualities by name one after another, yet my arguments or rather your concessions, nowhere tended to prove that the Secondary Qualities did not subsist each alone by itself; but, that they were not *at all* without the mind. Indeed, in treating of figure and motion we concluded they could not exist without the mind, because it was impossible even in thought to separate them from all secondary qualities, so as to conceive them existing by themselves. But then this was not the only argument made use of upon that occasion. But (to pass by all that hath been hitherto said, and reckon it for nothing, if you will have it so) I am content to put the whole upon this issue. If you can conceive it possible for any mixture or combination

of qualities, or any sensible object whatever, to exist
without the mind, then I will grant it actually to be so.

HYL. If it comes to that the point will soon be decided.
What more easy than to conceive a tree or house existing
by itself, independent of, and unperceived by, any mind
whatsoever? I do at this present time conceive them
existing after that manner.

PHIL. How say you, Hylas, can you see a thing which is
at the same time unseen?

HYL. No, that were a contradiction.

PHIL. Is it not as great a contradiction to talk of *conceiving* a thing which is *unconceived?*

HYL. It is.

PHIL. The tree or house therefore which you think of is
conceived by you?

HYL. How should it be otherwise?

PHIL. And what is conceived is surely in the mind?

HYL. Without question, that which is conceived is in the
mind.

PHIL. How then came you to say, you conceived a house
or tree existing independent and out of all minds whatsoever?

HYL. That was I own an oversight; but stay, let me
consider what led me into it.—It is a pleasant mistake
enough. As I was thinking of a tree in a solitary place,
where no one was present to see it, methought that was
to conceive a tree as existing unperceived or unthought
of; not considering that I myself conceived it all the
while. But now I plainly see that all I can do is to frame
ideas in my own mind. I may indeed conceive in my
own thoughts the idea of a tree, or a house, or a mountain, but that is all. And this is far from proving that
I can conceive them *existing out of the minds of all
Spirits.*

PHIL. You acknowledge then that you cannot possibly
conceive how any one corporeal sensible thing should exist
otherwise than in the mind?

HYL. I do.

PHIL. And yet you will earnestly contend for the truth
of that which you cannot so much as conceive?

Hyl. I profess I know not what to think; but still there are some scruples remain with me. Is it not certain I *see things at a distance?* Do we not perceive the stars and moon, for example, to be a great way off? Is not this, I say, manifest to the senses?

Phil. Do you not in a dream too perceive those or the like objects?

Hyl. I do.

Phil. And have they not then the same appearance of being distant?

Hyl. They have.

Phil. But you do not thence conclude the apparitions in a dream to be without the mind?

Hyl. By no means.

Phil. You ought not therefore to conclude that sensible objects are without the mind, from their appearance, or manner wherein they are perceived.

Hyl. I acknowledge it. But doth not my sense deceive me in those cases?

Phil. By no means. The idea or thing which you immediately perceive, neither sense nor reason informs you that *it* actually exists without the mind. By sense you only know that you are affected with such certain sensations of light and colours, &c. And these you will not say are without the mind.

Hyl. True: but, beside all that, do you not think the sight suggests something of *outness* or *distance?*

Phil. Upon approaching a distant object, do the visible size and figure change perpetually, or do they appear the same at all distances?

Hyl. They are in a continual change.

Phil. Sight therefore doth not suggest, or any way inform you, that the visible object you immediately perceive exists at a distance, or will be perceived when you advance farther onward; there being a continued series of visible objects succeeding each other during the whole time of your approach.

Hyl. It doth not; but still I know, upon seeing an object, what object I shall perceive after having passed over a certain distance: no matter whether it be exactly the same or no: there is still something of distance suggested in the case.

PHIL. Good Hylas, do but reflect a little on the point, and then tell me whether there be any more in it than this: from the ideas you actually perceive by sight, you have by experience learned to collect what other ideas you will (according to the standing order of nature) be affected with, after such a certain succession of time and motion.

HYL. Upon the whole, I take it to be nothing else.

PHIL. Now, is it not plain that if we suppose a man born blind was on a sudden made to see, he could at first have no experience of what may be *suggested* by sight?

HYL. It is.

PHIL. He would not then, according to you, have any notion of distance annexed to the things he saw; but would take them for a new set of sensations, existing only in his mind?

HYL. It is undeniable.

PHIL. But, to make it still more plain: is not *distance* a line turned endwise to the eye?

HYL. It is.

PHIL. And can a line so situated be perceived by sight?

HYL. It cannot.

PHIL. Doth it not therefore follow that distance is not properly and immediately perceived by sight?

HYL. It should seem so.

PHIL. Again, is it your opinion that colours are at a distance?

HYL. It must be acknowledged they are only in the mind.

PHIL. But do not colours appear to the eye as coexisting in the same place with extension and figures?

HYL. They do.

PHIL. How can you then conclude from sight that figures exist without, when you acknowledge colours do not; the sensible appearance being the very same with regard to both?

HYL. I know not what to answer.

PHIL. But, allowing that distance was truly and immediately perceived by the mind, yet it would not thence follow it existed out of the mind. For, whatever is immediately perceived is an idea: and can any idea exist out of the mind?

HYL. To suppose that were absurd: but, inform me, Philonous, can we perceive or know nothing beside our ideas?

PHIL. As for the rational deducing of causes from effects, that is beside our inquiry. And, by the senses you can best tell whether you perceive anything which is not immediately perceived. And I ask you, whether the things immediately perceived are other than your own sensations or ideas? You have indeed more than once, in the course of this conversation, declared yourself on those points; but you seem, by this last question, to have departed from what you then thought.

HYL. To speak the truth, Philonous, I think there are two kinds of objects:—the one perceived immediately, which are likewise called *ideas;* the other are real things or external objects, perceived by the mediation of ideas, which are their images and representations. Now, I own ideas do not exist without the mind; but the latter sort of objects do. I am sorry I did not think of this distinction sooner; it would probably have cut short your discourse.

PHIL. Are those external objects perceived by sense or by some other faculty?

HYL. They are perceived by sense.

PHIL. How! Is there any thing perceived by sense which is not immediately perceived?

HYL. Yes, Philonous, in some sort there is. For example, when I look on a picture or statue of Julius Cæsar, I may be said after a manner to perceive him (though not immediately) by my senses.

PHIL. It seems then you will have our ideas, which alone are immediately perceived, to be pictures of external things: and that these also are perceived by sense, inasmuch as they have a conformity or resemblance to our ideas?

HYL. That is my meaning.

PHIL. And, in the same way that Julius Cæsar, in himself invisible, is nevertheless perceived by sight; real things, in themselves imperceptible, are perceived by sense.

HYL. In the very same.

PHIL. Tell me, Hylas, when you behold the picture of Julius Cæsar, do you see with your eyes any more than some colours and figures, with a certain symmetry and composition of the whole?

HYL. Nothing else.

PHIL. And would not a man who had never known anything of Julius Cæsar see as much?

HYL. He would.

PHIL. Consequently he hath his sight, and the use of it, in as perfect a degree as you?

HYL. I agree with you.

PHIL. Whence comes it then that your thoughts are directed to the Roman emperor, and his are not? This cannot proceed from the sensations or ideas of sense by you then perceived; since you acknowledge you have no advantage over him in that respect. It should seem therefore to proceed from reason and memory: should it not?

HYL. It should.

PHIL. Consequently, it will not follow from that instance that anything is perceived by sense which is not immediately perceived. Though I grant we may, in one acceptation, be said to perceive sensible things mediately by sense: that is, when, from a frequently perceived connexion, the immediate perception of ideas by one sense *suggests* to the mind others, perhaps belonging to another sense, which are wont to be connected with them. For instance, when I hear a coach drive along the streets, immediately I perceive only the sound; but, from the experience I have had that such a sound is connected with a coach, I am said to hear the coach. It is nevertheless evident that, in truth and strictness, nothing can be *heard* but *sound;* and the coach is not then properly perceived by sense, but suggested from experience. So likewise when we are said to see a red-hot bar of iron; the solidity and heat of the iron are not the objects of sight, but suggested to the imagination by the colour and figure which are properly perceived by that sense. In short, those things alone are actually and strictly perceived by any sense, which would have been perceived in case that same sense had then been

first conferred on us. As for other things, it is plain they
are only suggested to the mind by experience, grounded on
former perceptions. But, to return to your comparison of
Cæsar's picture, it is plain, if you keep to that, you must
hold the real things, or archetypes of our ideas, are not perceived by sense, but by some internal faculty of the soul,
as reason or memory. I would therefore fain know what
arguments you can draw from reason for the existence of
what you call *real things* or *material objects*. Or, whether
you remember to have seen them formerly as they are in
themselves; or, if you have heard or read of any one that
did.

HYL. I see, Philonous, you are disposed to raillery; but
that will never convince me.

PHIL. My aim is only to learn from you the way to come
at the knowledge of *material beings*. Whatever we perceive is perceived immediately or mediately: by sense, or
by reason and reflexion. But, as you have excluded sense,
pray shew me what reason you have to believe their existence; or what *medium* you can possibly make use of to
prove it, either to mine or your own understanding.

HYL. To deal ingenuously, Philonous, now I consider
the point, I do not find I can give you any good reason
for it. But, thus much seems pretty plain, that it is at
least possible such things may really exist. And, as long
as there is no absurdity in supposing them, I am resolved
to believe as I did, till you bring good reasons to the
contrary.

PHIL. What! Is it come to this, that you only *believe*
the existence of material objects, and that your belief is
founded barely on the possibility of its being true? Then
you will have me bring reasons against it: though another
would think it reasonable the proof should lie on him who
holds the affirmative. And, after all, this very point which
you are now resolved to maintain, without any reason, is
in effect what you have more than once during this discourse seen good reason to give up. But, to pass over all
this; if I understand you rightly, you say our ideas do not
exist without the mind, but that they are copies, images,
or representations, of certain originals that do?

Hyl. You take me right.

Phil. They are then like external things?

Hyl. They are.

Phil. Have those things a stable and permanent nature, independent of our senses; or are they in a perpetual change, upon our producing any motions in our bodies— suspending, exerting, or altering, our faculties or organs of sense?

Hyl. Real things, it is plain, have a fixed and real nature, which remains the same notwithstanding any change in our senses, or in the posture and motion of our bodies; which indeed may affect the ideas in our minds, but it were absurd to think they had the same effect on things existing without the mind.

Phil. How then is it possible that things perpetually fleeting and variable as our ideas should be copies or images of anything fixed and constant? Or, in other words, since all sensible qualities, as size, figure, colour, &c., that is, our ideas, are continually changing, upon every altera- tion in the distance, medium, or instruments of sensation; how can any determinate material objects be properly rep- resented or painted forth by several distinct things, each of which is so different from and unlike the rest? Or, if you say it resembles some one only of our ideas, how shall we be able to distinguish the true copy from all the false ones?

Hyl. I profess, Philonous, I am at a loss. I know not what to say to this.

Phil. But neither is this all. Which are material objects in themselves—perceptible or imperceptible?

Hyl. Properly and immediately nothing can be per- ceived but ideas. All material things, therefore, are in themselves insensible, and to be perceived only by our ideas.

Phil. Ideas then are sensible, and their archetypes or originals insensible?

Hyl. Right.

Phil. But how can that which is sensible be *like* that which is insensible? Can a real thing, in itself *invisible,* be like a *colour;* or a real thing, which is not *audible,* be like a *sound?* In a word, can anything be like a sensation or idea, but another sensation or idea?

HYL. I must own, I think not.

PHIL. Is it possible there should be any doubt on the point? Do you not perfectly know your own ideas?

HYL. I know them perfectly; since what I do not perceive or know can be no part of my idea.

PHIL. Consider, therefore, and examine them, and then tell me if there be anything in them which can exist without the mind: or if you can conceive anything like them existing without the mind.

HYL. Upon inquiry, I find it is impossible for me to conceive or understand how anything but an idea can be like an idea. And it is most evident that *no idea can exist without the mind.* ·

PHIL. You are therefore, by your principles, forced to deny the *reality* of sensible things; since you made it to consist in an absolute existence exterior to the mind. That is to say, you are a downright sceptic. So I have gained my point, which was to shew your principles led to Scepticism.

HYL. For the present I am, if not entirely convinced, at least silenced.

PHIL. I would fain know what more you would require in order to a perfect conviction. Have you not had the liberty of explaining yourself all manner of ways? Were any little slips in discourse laid hold and insisted on? Or were you not allowed to retract or reinforce anything you had offered, as best served your purpose? Hath not everything you could say been heard and examined with all the fairness imaginable? In a word, have you not in every point been convinced out of your own mouth? And, if you can at present discover any flaw in any of your former concessions, or think of any remaining subterfuge, any new distinction, colour, or comment whatsoever, why do you not produce it?

HYL. A little patience, Philonous. I am at present so amazed to see myself ensnared, and as it were imprisoned in the labyrinths you have drawn me into, that on the sudden it cannot be expected I should find my way out.

You must give me time to look about me and recollect myself.

PHIL. Hark; is not this the college bell?

HYL. It rings for prayers.

PHIL. We will go in then, if you please, and meet here again to-morrow morning. In the meantime, you may employ your thoughts on this morning's discourse, and try if you can find any fallacy in it, or invent any new means to extricate yourself.

HYL. Agreed.

# THE SECOND DIALOGUE

HYLAS. I beg your pardon, Philonous, for not meeting you sooner. All this morning my head was so filled with our late conversation that I had not leisure to think of the time of the day, or indeed of anything else.

PHILONOUS. I am glad you were so intent upon it, in hopes if there were any mistakes in your concessions, or fallacies in my reasonings from them, you will now discover them to me.

HYL. I assure you I have done nothing ever since I saw you but search after mistakes and fallacies, and, with that view, have minutely examined the whole series of yesterday's discourse: but all in vain, for the notions it led me into, upon review, appear still more clear and evident; and, the more I consider them, the more irresistibly do they force my assent.

PHIL. And is not this, think you, a sign that they are genuine, that they proceed from nature, and are conformable to right reason? Truth and beauty are in this alike, that the strictest survey sets them both off to advantage; while the false lustre of error and disguise cannot endure being reviewed, or too nearly inspected.

HYL. I own there is a great deal in what you say. Nor can any one be more entirely satisfied of the truth of those odd consequences, so long as I have in view the reasonings that lead to them. But, when these are out of my thoughts, there seems, on the other hand, something so satisfactory, so natural and intelligible, in the modern way of explaining things that, I profess, I know not how to reject it.

PHIL. I know not what way you mean.

HYL. I mean the way of accounting for our sensations or ideas.

PHIL. How is that?

HYL. It is supposed the soul makes her residence in some part of the brain, from which the nerves take their rise, and are thence extended to all parts of the body; and that outward objects, by the different impressions they make on the organs of sense, communicate certain vibrative motions to the nerves; and these being filled with spirits propagate them to the brain or seat of the soul, which, according to the various impressions or traces thereby made in the brain, is variously affected with ideas.

PHIL. And call you this an explication of the manner whereby we are affected with ideas?

HYL. Why not, Philonous? Have you anything to object against it?

PHIL. I would first know whether I rightly understand your hypothesis. You make certain traces in the brain to be the causes or occasions of our ideas. Pray tell me whether by the *brain* you mean any sensible thing.

HYL. What else think you I could mean?

PHIL. Sensible things are all immediately perceivable; and those things which are immediately perceivable are ideas; and these exist only in the mind. Thus much you have, if I mistake not, long since agreed to.

HYL. I do not deny it.

PHIL. The brain therefore you speak of, being a sensible thing, exists only in the mind. Now, I would fain know whether you think it reasonable to suppose that one idea or thing existing in the mind occasions all other ideas. And, if you think so, pray how do you account for the origin of that primary idea or brain itself?

HYL. I do not explain the origin of our ideas by that brain which is perceivable to sense—this being itself only a combination of sensible ideas—but by another which I imagine.

PHIL. But are not things imagined as truly *in the mind* as things perceived?

HYL. I must confess they are.

PHIL. It comes, therefore, to the same thing; and you have been all this while accounting for ideas by certain motions or impressions of the brain; that is, by some alterations in an idea, whether sensible or imaginable it matters not.

HYL. I begin to suspect my hypothesis.

PHIL. Besides spirits, all that we know or conceive are our own ideas. When, therefore, you say all ideas are occasioned by impressions in the brain, do you conceive this brain or no? If you do, then you talk of ideas imprinted in an idea causing that same idea, which is absurd. If you do not conceive it, you talk unintelligibly, instead of forming a reasonable hypothesis.

HYL. I now clearly see it was a mere dream. There is nothing in it.

PHIL. You need not be much concerned at it; for after all, this way of explaining things, as you called it, could never have satisfied any reasonable man. What connexion is there between a motion in the nerves, and the sensations of sound or colour in the mind? Or how is it possible these should be the effect of that?

HYL. But I could never think it had so little in it as now it seems to have.

PHIL. Well then, are you at length satisfied that no sensible things have a real existence; and that you are in truth an arrant sceptic?

HYL. It is too plain to be denied.

PHIL. Look! are not the fields covered with a delightful verdure? Is there not something in the woods and groves, in the rivers and clear springs, that soothes, that delights, that transports the soul? At the prospect of the wide and deep ocean, or some huge mountain whose top is lost in the clouds, or of an old gloomy forest, are not our minds filled with a pleasing horror? Even in rocks and deserts is there not an agreeable wildness? How sincere a pleasure is it to behold the natural beauties of the earth! To preserve and renew our relish for them, is not the veil of night alternately drawn over her face, and doth she not change her dress with the seasons? How aptly are the elements disposed! What variety and use [¹ in the meanest productions of nature]! What delicacy, what beauty, what

¹ ' In stones and minerals '—in first and second editions.

contrivance, in animal and vegetable bodies! How exquisitely are all things suited, as well to their particular ends, as to constitute opposite parts of the whole! And, while they mutually aid and support, do they not also set off and illustrate each other? Raise now your thoughts from this ball of earth to all those glorious luminaries that adorn the high arch of heaven. The motion and situation of the planets, are they not admirable for use and order? Were those (miscalled *erratic*) globes once known to stray, in their repeated journeys through the pathless void? Do they not measure areas round the sun ever proportioned to the times? So fixed, so immutable are the laws by which the unseen Author of nature actuates the universe. How vivid and radiant is the lustre of the fixed stars! How magnificent and rich that negligent profusion with which they appear to be scattered throughout the whole azure vault! Yet, if you take the telescope, it brings into your sight a new host of stars that escape the naked eye. Here they seem contiguous and minute, but to a nearer view immense orbs of light at various distances, far sunk in the abyss of space. Now you must call imagination to your aid. The feeble narrow sense cannot descry innumerable worlds revolving round the central fires; and in those worlds the energy of an all-perfect Mind displayed in endless forms. But, neither sense nor imagination are big enough to comprehend the boundless extent, with all its glittering furniture. Though the labouring mind exert and strain each power to its utmost reach, there still stands out ungrasped a surplusage immeasurable. Yet all the vast bodies that compose this mighty frame, how distant and remote soever, are by some secret mechanism, some Divine art and force, linked in a mutual dependence and intercourse with each other; even with this earth, which was almost slipt from my thoughts and lost in the crowd of worlds. Is not the whole system immense, beautiful, glorious beyond expression and beyond thought! What treatment, then, do those philosophers deserve, who would deprive these noble and delightful scenes of all *reality?* How should those Principles be entertained that lead us to think all the visible beauty of the creation a false imaginary glare? To be plain, can you expect this Scepticism of yours will not be thought extravagantly absurd by all men of sense?

HYL. Other men may think as they please; but for your part you have nothing to reproach me with. My comfort is, you are as much a sceptic as I am.

PHIL. There, Hylas, I must beg leave to differ from you.

HYL. What! Have you all along agreed to the premises, and do you now deny the conclusion, and leave me to maintain those paradoxes by myself which you led me into? This surely is not fair.

PHIL. I deny that I agreed with you in those notions that led to Scepticism. You indeed said the *reality* of sensible things consisted in an *absolute existence out of the minds of spirits,* or distinct from their being perceived. And pursuant to this notion of reality, *you* are obliged to deny sensible things any real existence: that is, according to your own definition, you profess yourself a sceptic. But I neither said nor thought the reality of sensible things was to be defined after that manner. To me it is evident for the reasons you allow of, that sensible things .cannot exist otherwise than in a mind or spirit. Whence I conclude, not that they have no real existence, but that, seeing they depend not on my thought, and have an existence distinct from being perceived by me, *there must be some other Mind wherein they exist.* As sure, therefore, as the sensible world really exists, so sure is there an infinite omnipresent Spirit who contains and supports it.

HYL. What! This is no more than I and all Christians hold; nay, and all others too who believe there is a God, and that He knows and comprehends all things.

PHIL. Aye, but here lies the difference. Men commonly believe that all things are known or perceived by God, because they believe the being of a God; whereas I, on the other side, immediately and necessarily conclude the being of a God, because all sensible things must be perceived by Him.

HYL. But, so long as we all believe the same thing, what matter is it how we come by that belief?

PHIL. But neither do we agree in the same opinion. For

philosophers, though they acknowledge all corporeal beings to be perceived by God, yet they attribute to them an absolute subsistence distinct from their being perceived by any mind whatever; which I do not. Besides, is there no difference between saying, *There is a God, therefore He perceives all things;* and saying, *Sensible things do really exist; and, if they really exist, they are necessarily perceived by an infinite Mind: therefore there is an infinite Mind or God?* This furnishes you with a direct and immediate demonstration, from a most evident principle, of the *being of a God.* Divines and philosophers had proved beyond all controversy, from the beauty and usefulness of the several parts of the creation, that it was the workmanship of God. But that—setting aside all help of astronomy and natural philosophy, all contemplation of the contrivance, order, and adjustment of things—an infinite Mind should be necessarily inferred from the bare *existence of the sensible world,* is an advantage to them only who have made this easy reflexion: that the sensible world is that which we perceive by our several senses; and that nothing is perceived by the senses beside ideas; and that no idea or archetype of an idea can exist otherwise than in a mind. You may now, without any laborious search into the sciences, without any subtlety of reason, or tedious length of discourse, oppose and baffle the most strenuous advocate for Atheism. Those miserable refuges, whether in an eternal succession of unthinking causes and effects, or in a fortuitous concourse of atoms; those wild imaginations of Vanini, Hobbes, and Spinoza: in a word, the whole system of Atheism, is it not entirely overthrown, by this single reflexion on the repugnancy included in supposing the whole, or any part, even the most rude and shapeless, of the visible world, to exist without a mind? Let any one of those abettors of impiety but look into his own thoughts, and there try if he can conceive how so much as a rock, a desert, a chaos, or confused jumble of atoms; how anything at all, either sensible or imaginable, can exist independent of a Mind, and he need go no farther to be convinced of his folly. Can anything be fairer than to put a dispute on such an issue, and leave it to a man himself to see if he can conceive, even in thought, what he holds to be true in fact, and from a notional to allow it a real existence?

HYL. It cannot be denied there is something highly serviceable to religion in what you advance. But do you not think it looks very like a notion entertained by some eminent moderns, of *seeing all things in God?*

PHIL. I would gladly know that opinion: pray explain it to me.

HYL. They conceive that the soul, being immaterial, is incapable of being united with material things, so as to perceive them in themselves; but that she perceives them by her union with the substance of God, which, being spiritual, is therefore purely intelligible, or capable of being the immediate object of a spirit's thought. Besides the Divine essence contains in it perfections correspondent to each created being; and which are, for that reason, proper to exhibit or represent them to the mind.

PHIL. I do not understand how our ideas, which are things altogether passive and inert, can be the essence, or any part (or like any part) of the essence or substance of God, who is an impassive, indivisible, pure, active being. Many more difficulties and objections there are which occur at first view against this hypothesis; but I shall only add that it is liable to all the absurdities of the common hypothesis, in making a created world exist otherwise than in the mind of a Spirit. Besides all which it hath this peculiar to itself; that it makes that material world serve to no purpose. And, if it pass for a good argument against other hypotheses in the sciences, that they suppose Nature, or the Divine wisdom, to make something in vain, or do that by tedious roundabout methods which might have been performed in a much more easy and compendious way, what shall we think of that hypothesis which supposes the whole world made in vain?

HYL. But what say you? Are not you too of opinion that we see all things in God? If I mistake not, what you advance comes near it.

PHIL. [² Few men think; yet all have opinions. Hence

² The passage within brackets first appeared in the third edition.

men's opinions are superficial and confused. It is nothing strange that tenets which in themselves are ever so different, should nevertheless be confounded with each other, by those who do not consider them attentively. I shall not therefore be surprised if some men imagine that I run into the enthusiasm of Malebranche; though in truth I am very remote from it. He builds on the most abstract general ideas, which I entirely disclaim. He asserts an absolute external world, which I deny. He maintains that we are deceived by our senses, and know not the real natures or the true forms and figures of extended beings; of all which I hold the direct contrary. So that upon the whole there are no Principles more fundamentally opposite than his and mine. It must be owned that] I entirely agree with what the holy Scripture saith, ' That in God we live and move and have our being.' But that we see things in His essence, after the manner above set forth, I am far from believing. Take here in brief my meaning:—It is evident that the things I perceive are my own ideas, and that no idea can exist unless it be in a mind: nor is it less plain that these ideas or things by me perceived, either themselves or their archetypes, exist independently of *my* mind, since I know myself not to be their author, it being out of my power to determine at pleasure what particular ideas I shall be affected with upon opening my eyes or ears: they must therefore exist in some other Mind, whose Will it is they should be exhibited to me. The things, I say, immediately perceived are ideas or sensations, call them which you will. But how can any idea or sensation exist in, or be produced by, anything but a mind or spirit? This indeed is inconceivable. And to assert that which is inconceivable is to talk nonsense: is it not?

HYL. Without doubt.

PHIL. But, on the other hand, it is very conceivable that they should exist in and be produced by a spirit; since this is no more than I daily experience in myself, inasmuch as I perceive numberless ideas; and, by an act of my will, can form a great variety of them, and raise them up in my imagination: though, it must be confessed, these creatures of the fancy are not altogether so distinct, so strong, vivid, and permanent, as those perceived by my senses—which latter are called *real things*. From all which I conclude, *there is a Mind which affects me every moment with all the sensible impressions I perceive*. And, from the variety, order, and manner of these, I conclude *the Author of them to be wise, powerful, and good, beyond comprehension*. Mark it well; I do not say, I see things by perceiving that which represents them in the intelligible Substance of God. This I do not understand; but I say, the things by me perceived are known by the understanding, and produced by the will of an infinite Spirit. And is not all this most plain and evident? Is there any more in it than what a little observation in our own minds, and that which passeth in them, not only enables us to conceive, but also obliges us to acknowledge.

HYL. I think I understand you very clearly; and own the proof you give of a Deity seems no less evident than it is surprising. But, allowing that God is the supreme and universal Cause of all things, yet, may there not be still a Third Nature besides Spirits and Ideas? May we not admit a subordinate and limited cause of our ideas? In a word, may there not for all that be *Matter?*

PHIL. How often must I inculcate the same thing? You allow the things immediately perceived by sense to exist nowhere without the mind; but there is nothing perceived by sense which is not perceived immediately: therefore there is nothing sensible that exists without the mind. The Matter, therefore, which you still insist on is something intelligible, I suppose; something that may be discovered by reason, and not by sense.

HYL. You are in the right.

PHIL. Pray let me know what reasoning your belief of Matter is grounded on; and what this Matter is, in your present sense of it.

HYL. I find myself affected with various ideas, whereof I know I am not the cause; neither are they the cause of themselves, or of one another, or capable of subsisting by themselves, as being altogether inactive, fleeting, dependent beings. They have therefore *some* cause distinct from me and them: of which I pretend to know no more than that it is *the cause of my ideas.* And this thing, whatever it be, I call Matter.

PHIL. Tell me, Hylas, hath every one a liberty to change the current proper signification attached to a common name in any language? For example, suppose a traveller should tell you that in a certain country men pass unhurt through the fire; and, upon explaining himself, you found he meant by the word *fire* that which others call *water.* Or, if he should assert that there are trees that walk upon two legs, meaning men by the term *trees.* Would you think this reasonable?

HYL. No; I should think it very absurd. Common custom is the standard of propriety in language. And for any man to affect speaking improperly is to pervert the use of speech, and can never serve to a better purpose than to protract and multiply disputes where there is no difference in opinion.

PHIL. And doth not *Matter,* in the common current acceptation of the word, signify an extended, solid, moveable, unthinking, inactive Substance?

HYL. It doth.

PHIL. And, hath it not been made evident that no *such* substance can possibly exist? And, though it should be allowed to exist, yet how can that which is *inactive* be a *cause;* or that which is *unthinking* be a *cause of thought?* You may, indeed, if you please, annex to the word *Matter* a contrary meaning to what is vulgarly received; and tell me you understand by it, an unextended, thinking, active being, which is the cause of our ideas. But what else is this than to play with words, and run into that very fault you just now condemned with so much reason? I do by no means find fault with your reasoning, in that you collect *a* cause from the *phenomena:* but I deny that *the* cause deducible by reason can properly be termed Matter.

HYL. There is indeed something in what you say. But I am afraid you do not thoroughly comprehend my meaning. I would by no means be thought to deny that God, or an infinite Spirit, is the Supreme Cause of all things.

All I contend for is, that, subordinate to the Supreme Agent, there is a cause of a limited and inferior nature, which *concurs* in the production of our ideas, not by any act of will, or spiritual efficiency, but by that kind of action which belongs to Matter, viz. *motion*.

PHIL. I find you are at every turn relapsing into your old exploded conceit, of a moveable, and consequently an extended, substance, existing without the mind. What! Have you already forgotten you were convinced; or are you willing I should repeat what has been said on that head? In truth this is not fair dealing in you, still to suppose the being of that which you have so often acknowledged to have no being. But, not to insist farther on what has been so largely handled, I ask whether all your ideas are not perfectly passive and inert, including nothing of action in them.

HYL. They are.

PHIL. And are sensible qualities anything else but ideas?

HYL. How often have I acknowledged that they are not.

PHIL. But is not *motion* a sensible quality?

HYL. It is.

PHIL. Consequently it is no action?

HYL. I agree with you. And indeed it is very plain that when I stir my finger, it remains passive; but my will which produced the motion is active.

PHIL. Now, I desire to know, in the first place, whether, motion being allowed to be no action, you can conceive any action besides volition: and, in the second place, whether to say something and conceive nothing be not to talk nonsense: and, lastly, whether, having considered the premises, you do not perceive that to suppose any efficient or active Cause of our ideas, other than *Spirit*, is highly absurd and unreasonable?

HYL. I give up the point entirely. But, though Matter may not be a cause, yet what hinders its being an *instrument*, subservient to the supreme Agent in the production of our ideas?

PHIL. An instrument say you; pray what may be the figure, springs, wheels, and motions, of that instrument?

HYL. Those I pretend to determine nothing of, both the substance and its qualities being entirely unknown to me.

PHIL. What? You are then of opinion it is made up of unknown parts, that it hath unknown motions, and an unknown shape?

HYL. I do not believe that it hath any figure or motion at all, being already convinced, that no sensible qualities can exist in an unperceiving substance.

PHIL. But what notion is it possible to frame of an instrument void of all sensible qualities, even extension itself?

HYL. I do not pretend to have any notion of it.

PHIL. And what reason have you to think this unknown, this inconceivable Somewhat doth exist? Is it that you imagine God cannot act as well without it; or that you find by experience the use of some such thing, when you form ideas in your own mind?

HYL. You are always teasing me for reasons of my belief. Pray what reasons have you not to believe it?

PHIL. It is to me a sufficient reason not to believe the existence of anything, if I see no reason for believing it. But, not to insist on reasons for believing, you will not so much as let me know *what it is* you would have me believe; since you say you have no manner of notion of it. After all, let me entreat you to consider whether it be like a philosopher, or even like a man of common sense, to pretend to believe you know not what, and you know not why.

HYL. Hold, Philonous. When I tell you Matter is an *instrument*, I do not mean altogether nothing. It is true I know not the particular kind of instrument; but, however, I have some notion of *instrument in general*, which I apply to it.

PHIL. But what if it should prove that there is something, even in the most general notion of *instrument*, as taken in a distinct sense from *cause*, which makes the use of it inconsistent with the Divine attributes?

HYL. Make that appear and I shall give up the point.

PHIL. What mean you by the general nature or notion **of** *instrument?*

Hyl. That which is common to all particular instruments composeth the general notion.

Phil. Is it not common to all instruments, that they are applied to the doing those things only which cannot be performed by the mere act of our wills?' Thus, for instance, I never use an instrument to move my finger, because it is done by a volition. But I should use one if I were to remove part of a rock, or tear up a tree by the roots. Are you of the same mind? Or, can you shew any example where an instrument is made use of in producing an effect *immediately* depending on the will of the agent.?

Hyl. I own I cannot.

Phil. How therefore can you suppose that an All-perfect Spirit, on whose Will all things have an absolute and immediate dependence, should need an instrument in his operations, or, not needing it, make use of it? Thus it seems to me that you are obliged to own the use of a lifeless inactive instrument to be incompatible with the infinite perfection of God; that is, by your own confession, to give up the. point.

Hyl. It doth not readily occur what I can answer you.

Phil. But, methinks you should be ready to own the truth, when it has been fairly proved to you. We indeed, who are beings of finite powers, are forced to make use of instruments. And the use of an instrument sheweth the agent to be limited by rules of another's prescription, and that he cannot obtain his end but in such a way, and by such conditions. Whence it seems a clear consequence, that the supreme unlimited Agent useth no tool or instrument at all   The will of an Omnipotent Spirit is no sooner exerted than executed, without the application of means; which, if they are employed by inferior agents, it is not upon account of any real efficacy that is in them, or necessary aptitude to produce any effect, but merely in compliance with the laws of nature, or those conditions prescribed to them by the First Cause, who is Himself above all limitation or prescription whatsoever.

Hyl. I will no longer maintain that Matter is an instrument. However, I would not be understood to give up its existence neither; since, notwithstanding what hath been said, it may still be an *occasion*.

PHIL. How many shapes is your Matter to take? Or, how often must it be proved not to exist, before you are content to part with it? But, to say no more of this (though by all the laws of disputation I may justly blame you for so frequently changing the signification of the principal term)—I would fain know what you mean by affirming that matter is an occasion, having already denied it to be a cause. And, when you have shewn in what sense you understand *occasion,* pray, in the next place, be pleased to shew me what reason induceth you to believe there is such an occasion of our ideas?

HYL. As to the first point: by *occasion* I mean an inactive unthinking being, at the presence whereof God excites ideas in our minds.

PHIL. And what may be the nature of that inactive unthinking being?

HYL. I know nothing of its nature.

PHIL. Proceed then to the second point, and assign some reason why we should allow an existence to this inactive, unthinking, unknown thing.

HYL. When we see ideas produced in our minds, after an orderly and constant manner, it is natural to think they have some fixed and regular occasions, at the presence of which they are excited.

PHIL. You acknowledge then God alone to be the cause of our ideas, and that He causes them at the presence of those occasions.

HYL. That is my opinion.

PHIL. Those things which you say are present to God, without doubt He perceives.

HYL. Certainly; otherwise they could not be to Him an occasion of acting.

PHIL. Not to insist now on your making sense of this hypothesis, or answering all the puzzling questions and difficulties it is liable to: I only ask whether the order and regularity observable in the series of our ideas, or the course of nature, be not sufficiently accounted for by the wisdom and power of God; and whether it doth not derogate from those attributes, to suppose He is influenced, directed, or put in mind, when and what He is to act, by an unthinking substance? And, lastly, whether, in case I granted all you contend for, it would make anything to your purpose; it not being easy to conceive how the external or absolute existence of an unthinking substance, distinct from its being perceived, can be inferred from my allowing that there are certain things perceived by the mind of God, which are to Him the occasion of producing ideas in us?

HYL. I am perfectly at a loss what to think, this notion of *occasion* seeming now altogether as groundless as the rest.

PHIL. Do you not at length perceive that in all these different acceptations of *Matter*, you have been only supposing you know not what, for no manner of reason, and to no kind of use?

HYL. I freely own myself less fond of my notions since they have been so accurately examined. But still, methinks, I have some confused perception that there is such a thing as *Matter*.

PHIL. Either you perceive the being of Matter immediately or mediately. If immediately, pray inform me by which of the senses you perceive it. If mediately, let me know by what reasoning it is inferred from those things which you perceive immediately. So much for the perception. Then for the Matter itself, I ask whether it is object, *substratum*, cause, instrument, or occasion? You have already pleaded for each of these, shifting your notions, and making Matter to appear sometimes in one shape, then in another. And what you have offered hath been disapproved and rejected by yourself. If you have anything new to advance I would gladly bear it.

HYL. I think I have already offered all I had to say on those heads. I am at a loss what more to urge.

PHIL. And yet you are loath to part with your old prejudice. But, to make you quit it more easily, I desire that, beside what has been hitherto suggested, you will farther consider whether, upon supposition that Matter exists, you can possibly conceive how you should be affected by it. Or, supposing it did not exist, whether it be not evident you might for all that be affected with the same ideas you now are, and consequently have the very same reasons to believe its existence that you now can have.

HYL. I acknowledge it is possible we might perceive all things just as we do now, though there was no Matter in the world; neither can I conceive, if there be Matter, how it should produce any idea in our minds. And, I do farther grant you have entirely satisfied me that it is impossible there should be such a thing as Matter in any of the fore-going acceptations. But still I cannot help supposing that there is *Matter* in some sense or other. *What that is* I do not indeed pretend to determine.

PHIL. I do not expect you should define exactly the na-ture of that unknown being. Only be pleased to tell me whether it is a Substance; and if so, whether you can suppose a Substance without accidents; or, in case you suppose it to have accidents or qualities, I desire you will let me know what those qualities are, at least what is meant by Matter's supporting them?

HYL. We have already argued on those points. I have no more to say to them. But, to prevent any farther questions, let me tell you I at present understand by *Matter* neither substance nor accident, thinking nor extended be-ing, neither cause, instrument, nor occasion, but Something entirely unknown, distinct from all these.

PHIL. It seems then you include in your present no-tion of Matter nothing but the general abstract idea of *entity*.

HYL. Nothing else; save only that I superadd to this general idea the negation of all those particular things, qualities, or ideas, that I perceive, imagine, or in anywise apprehend.

PHIL. Pray where do you suppose this unknown Matter to exist?

HYL. Oh Philonous! now you think you have entangled me; for, if I say it exists in place, then you will infer that it exists in the mind, since it is agreed that place or extension exists only in the mind. But I am not ashamed to own my ignorance. I know not where it exists;

(9) HC XXXVII

only I am sure it exists not in place. There is a negative answer for you. And you must expect no other to all the questions you put for the future about Matter.

PHIL. Since you will not tell me where it exists, be pleased to inform me after what manner you suppose it to exist, or what you mean by its *existence?*

HYL. It neither thinks nor acts, neither perceives nor is perceived.

PHIL. But what is there positive in your abstracted notion of its existence?

HYL. Upon a nice observation, I do not find I have any positive notion or meaning at all. I tell you again, I am not ashamed to own my ignorance. I know not what is meant by its *existence,* or how it exists.

PHIL. Continue, good Hylas, to act the same ingenuous part, and tell me sincerely whether you can frame a distinct idea of Entity in general, prescinded from and exclusive of all thinking and corporeal beings, all particular things whatsoever.

HYL. Hold, let me think a little——I profess, Philonous, I do not find that I can. At first glance, methought I had some dilute and airy notion of Pure Entity in abstract; but, upon closer attention, it hath quite vanished out of sight. The more I think on it, the more am I confirmed in my prudent resolution of giving none but negative answers, and not pretending to the least degree of any positive knowledge or conception of Matter, its *where,* its *how,* its *entity,* or anything belonging to it.

PHIL. When, therefore, you speak of the existence of Matter, you have not any notion in your mind?

HYL. None at all.

PHIL. Pray tell me if the case stands not thus:——At first, from a belief of material substance, you would have it that the immediate objects existed without the mind; then that they are archetypes; then causes; next instruments; then occasions: lastly *something in general,* which being interpreted proves *nothing.* So Matter comes to nothing. What think you, Hylas, is not this a fair summary of your whole proceeding?

HYL. Be that as it will, yet I still insist upon it, that *our* not being able to conceive a thing is no argument against its existence.

PHIL. That from a cause, effect, operation, sign, or other circumstance, there may reasonably be inferred the existence of a thing not immediately perceived; and that it were absurd for any man to argue against the existence of that thing, from his having no direct and positive notion of it, I freely own. But, where there is nothing of all this; where neither reason nor revelation induces us to believe the existence of a thing; where we have not even a relative notion of it; where an abstraction is made from perceiving and being perceived, from Spirit and idea: lastly, where there is not so much as the most inadequate or faint idea pretended to—I will not indeed thence conclude against the reality of any notion, or existence of anything; but my inference shall be, that you mean nothing at all; that you employ words to no manner of purpose, without any design or signification whatsoever. And I leave it to you to consider how mere jargon should be treated.

HYL. To deal frankly with you, Philonous, your arguments seem in themselves unanswerable; but they have not so great an effect on me as to produce that entire conviction, that hearty acquiescence, which attends demonstration. I find myself relapsing into an obscure surmise of I know not what, *matter*.

PHIL. But, are you not sensible, Hylas, that two things must concur to take away all scruple, and work a plenary assent in the mind? Let a visible object be set in never so clear a light, yet, if there is any imperfection in the sight, or if the eye is not directed towards it, it will not be distinctly seen. And though a demonstration be never so well grounded and fairly proposed, yet, if there is withal a stain of prejudice, or a wrong bias on the understanding, can it be expected on a sudden to perceive clearly, and adhere firmly to the truth? No; there is need of time and pains: the attention must be awakened and detained by a frequent repetition of the same thing placed oft in the same, oft in different lights. I have said it already, and find I must still repeat and inculcate, that it is an unaccountable licence you take, in pretending to maintain you know not what, for you know not what reason, to you know not what purpose. Can this be paralleled in any art or science, any sect or profession of men? Or is there anything so barefacedly groundless and unreasonable to be met with even in the lowest of common conversation? But, perhaps you will still say, Matter may exist; though at the same time you neither know *what is meant* by *Matter*, or by its *existence*. This indeed is surprising, and the more so because it is altogether voluntary [³and of your own head], you not being led to it by any one reason; for I challenge you to shew me that thing in nature which needs Matter to explain or account for it.

HYL. The *reality* of things cannot be maintained without supposing the existence of Matter. And is not this, think you, a good reason why I should be earnest in its defence?

PHIL. The reality of things! What things? sensible or intelligible?

HYL. Sensible things.

PHIL. My glove for example?

HYL. That, or any other thing perceived by the senses.

PHIL. But to fix on some particular thing. Is it not a sufficient evidence to me of the existence of this *glove,* that I see it, and feel it, and wear it? Or, if this will not do, how is it possible I should be assured of the reality of this thing, which I actually see in this place, by supposing that some unknown thing, which I never did or can see, exists after an unknown manner, in an unknown place, or in no place at all? How can the supposed reality of that which is intangible be a proof that anything tangible really exists? Or, of that which is invisible, that any visible thing, or, in general of anything which is imperceptible, that a perceptible exists? Do but explain this and I shall think nothing too hard for you.

HYL. Upon the whole, I am content to own the existence of matter is highly improbable; but the direct and absolute impossibility of it does not appear to me.

PHIL. But granting Matter to be possible, yet, upon that account merely, it can have no more claim to existence than a golden mountain, or a centaur.

³ Omitted in last edition.

HYL. I acknowledge it; but still you do not deny it is possible; and that which is possible, for aught you know, may actually exist.

PHIL. I deny it to be possible; and have, if I mistake not, evidently proved, from your own concessions, that it is not. In the common sense of the word *Matter,* is there any more implied than an extended, solid, figured, moveable substance, existing without the mind? And have not you acknowledged, over and over, that you have seen evident reason for denying the possibility of such a substance?

HYL. True, but that is only one sense of the term *Matter.*

PHIL. But is it not the only proper genuine received sense? And, if Matter, in such a sense, be proved impossible, may it not be thought with good grounds absolutely impossible? Else how could anything be proved impossible? Or, indeed, how could there be any proof at all one way or other, to a man who takes the liberty to unsettle and change the common signification of words?

HYL. I thought philosophers might be allowed to speak more accurately than the vulgar, and were not always confined to the common acceptation of a term.

PHIL. But this now mentioned is the common received sense among philosophers themselves. But, not to insist on that, have you not been allowed to take Matter in what sense you pleased? And have you not used this privilege in the utmost extent; sometimes entirely changing, at others leaving out, or putting into the definition of it whatever, for the present, best served your design, contrary to all the known rules of reason and logic? And hath not this shifting, unfair method of yours spun out our dispute to an unnecessary length; Matter having been particularly examined, and by your own confession refuted in each of those senses? And can any more be required to prove the absolute impossibility of a thing, than the proving it impossible in every particular sense that either you or any one else understands it in?

HYL. But I am not so thoroughly satisfied that you have proved the impossibility of Matter, in the last most obscure abstracted and indefinite sense.

PHIL. When is a thing shewn to be impossible?

HYL. When a repugnancy is demonstrated between the ideas comprehended in its definition.

PHIL. But where there are no ideas, there no repugnancy can be demonstrated between ideas?

HYL. I agree with you.

PHIL. Now, in that which you call the obscure indefinite sense of the word *Matter,* it is plain, by your own confession, there was included no idea at all, no sense except an unknown sense; which is the same thing as none. You are not, therefore, to expect I should prove a repugnancy between ideas, where there are no ideas; or the impossibility of Matter taken in an *unknown* sense, that is, no sense at all. My business was only to shew you meant *nothing;* and this you were brought to own. So that, in all your various senses, you have been shewed either to mean nothing at all, or, if anything, an absurdity. And if this be not sufficient to prove the impossibility of a thing, I desire you will let me know what is.

HYL. I acknowledge you have proved that Matter is impossible; nor do I see what more can be said in defence of it. But, at the same time that I give up this, I suspect all my other notions. For surely none could be more seemingly evident than this once was: and yet it now seems as false and absurd as ever it did true before. But I think we have discussed the point sufficiently for the present. The remaining part of the day I would willingly spend in running over in my thoughts the several heads of this morning's conversation, and to-morrow shall be glad to meet you here again about the same time.

PHIL. I will not fail to attend you.

# THE THIRD DIALOGUE

PHILONOUS. ¹Tell me, Hylas, what are the fruits of yesterday's meditation? Has it confirmed you in the same mind you were in at parting? or have you since seen cause to change your opinion?

HYLAS. Truly my opinion is that all our opinions are alike vain and uncertain. What we approve to-day, we condemn to-morrow. We keep a stir about knowledge, and spend our lives in the pursuit of it, when, alas! we know nothing all the while: nor do I think it possible for us ever to know anything in this life. Our faculties are too narrow and too few. Nature certainly never intended us for speculation.

PHIL. What! Say you we can know nothing, Hylas?

HYL. There is not that single thing in the world whereof we can know the real nature, or what it is in itself.

PHIL. Will you tell me I do not really know what fire or water is?

HYL. You may indeed know that fire appears hot, and water fluid; but this is no more than knowing what sensations are produced in your own mind, upon the application of fire and water to your organs of sense. Their internal constitution, their true and real nature, you are utterly in the dark as to *that*.

PHIL. Do I not know this to be a real stone that I stand on, and that which I see before my eyes to be a real tree?

HYL. *Know?* No, it is impossible you or any man alive should know it. All you know is, that you have such a certain idea or appearance in your own mind. But what is this to the real tree or stone? I tell you that colour, figure, and hardness, which you perceive, are not the real natures of those things, or in the least like them. The

¹ 'Tell me, Hylas,'—' So Hylas '—in first and second editions.

same may be said of all other real things, or corporeal substances, which compose the world. They have none of them anything of themselves, like those sensible qualities by us perceived. We should not therefore pretend to affirm or know anything of them, as they are in their own nature.

PHIL. But surely, Hylas, I can distinguish gold, for example, from iron: and how could this be, if I knew not what either truly was?

HYL. Believe me, Philonous, you can only distinguish between your own ideas. That yellowness, that weight, and other sensible qualities, think you they are really in the gold? They are only relative to the senses, and have no absolute existence in nature. And in pretending to distinguish the species of real things, by the appearances in your mind, you may perhaps act as wisely as he that should conclude two men were of a different species, because their clothes were not of the same colour.

PHIL. It seems, then, we are altogether put off with the appearances of things, and those false ones too. The very meat I eat, and the cloth I wear, have nothing in them like what I see and feel.

HYL. Even so.

PHIL. But is it not strange the whole world should be thus imposed on, and so foolish as to believe their senses? And yet I know not how it is, but men eat, and drink, and sleep, and perform all the offices of life, as comfortably and conveniently as if they really knew the things they are conversant about.

HYL. They do so: but you know ordinary practice does not require a nicety of speculative knowledge. Hence the vulgar retain their mistakes, and for all that make a shift to bustle through the affairs of life. But philosophers know better things.

PHIL. You mean, they *know* that they *know nothing.*

HYL. That is the very top and perfection of human knowledge.

PHIL. But are you all this while in earnest, Hylas; and are you seriously persuaded that you know nothing real in the world? Suppose you are going to write, would you not call for pen, ink, and paper, like another man; and do you not know what it is you call for?

HYL. How often must I tell you, that I know not the real nature of any one thing in the universe? I may indeed upon occasion make use of pen, ink, and paper. But what any one of them is in its own true nature, I declare positively I know not. And the same is true with regard to every other corporeal thing. And, what is more, we are not only ignorant of the true and real nature of things, but even of their existence. It cannot be denied that we perceive such certain appearances or ideas; but it cannot be concluded from thence that bodies really exist. Nay, now I think on it, I must, agreeably to my former concessions, farther declare that it is impossible any *real* corporeal thing should exist in nature.

PHIL. You amaze me. Was ever anything more wild and extravagant than the notions you now maintain: and is it not evident you are led into all these extravagances by the belief of *material substance?* This makes you dream of those unknown natures in everything. It is this occasions your distinguishing between the reality and sensible appearances of things. It is to this you are indebted for being ignorant of what everybody else knows perfectly well. Nor is this all: you are not only ignorant of the true nature of everything, but you know not whether anything really exists, or whether there are any true natures at all; forasmuch as you attribute to your material beings an absolute or external existence, wherein you suppose their reality consists. And, as you are forced in the end to acknowledge such an existence means either a direct repugnancy, or nothing at all, it follows that you are obliged to pull down your own hypothesis of material Substance, and positively to deny the real existence of any part of the universe. And so you are plunged into the deepest and most deplorable scepticism that ever man was. Tell me, Hylas, is it not as I say?

HYL. I agree with you. *Material substance* was no more than an hypothesis; and a false and groundless one too. I will no longer spend my breath in defence of it. But whatever hypothesis you advance, or whatsoever scheme of things you introduce in its stead, I doubt not it will appear every whit as false: let me but be allowed to question you upon it. That is, suffer me to serve you in your own kind, and I warrant it shall conduct you through as many perplexities and contradictions, to the very same state of scepticism that I myself am in at present.

PHIL. I assure you, Hylas, I do not pretend to frame any hypothesis at all. I am of a vulgar cast, simple enough to believe my senses, and leave things as I find them. To be plain, it is my opinion that the real things are those very things I see, and feel, and perceive by my senses. These I know; and, finding they answer all the necessities and purposes of life, have no reason to be solicitous about any other unknown beings. A piece of sensible bread, for instance, would stay my stomach better than ten thousand times as much of that insensible, unintelligible, real bread you speak of. It is likewise my opinion that colours and other sensible qualities are on the objects. I cannot for my life help thinking that snow is white, and fire hot. You indeed, who by *snow* and *fire* mean certain external, unperceived, unperceiving substances, are in the right to deny whiteness or heat to be affections inherent in *them*. But I, who understand by those words the things I see and feel, am obliged to think like other folks. And, as I am no sceptic with regard to the nature of things, so neither am I as to their existence. That a thing should be really perceived by my senses, and at the same time not really exist, is to me a plain contradiction; since I cannot prescind or abstract, even in thought, the existence of a sensible thing from its being perceived. Wood, stones, fire, water, flesh, iron, and the like things, which I name and discourse of, are things that I know. And I should not have known them but that I perceived them by my senses; and things perceived by the senses are immediately perceived; and things immediately perceived are ideas; and ideas cannot exist without the mind; their existence therefore consists in being perceived; when, therefore, they are actually perceived there can be no doubt of their existence. Away then with all that scepticism, all those ridiculous philosophical doubts. What a jest is it for a philosopher to question the existence of sensible things, till he hath it proved to him from the veracity of God; or to pretend our knowledge in this point falls short of intuition or demonstration! I might as well doubt of my own being, as of the being of those things I actually see and feel.

HYL. Not so fast, Philonous: you say you cannot conceive how sensible things should exist without the mind. Do you not?

PHIL. I do.

HYL. Supposing you were annihilated, cannot you conceive it possible that things perceivable by sense may still exist?

PHIL. I can; but then it must be in another mind. When I deny sensible things an existence out of the mind, I do not mean my mind in particular, but all minds. Now, it is plain they have an existence exterior to my mind; since I find them by experience to be independent of it. There is therefore some other Mind wherein they exist, during the intervals between the times of my perceiving them: as likewise they did before my birth, and would do after my supposed annihilation. And, as the same is true with regard to all other finite created spirits, it necessarily follows there is an *omnipresent eternal Mind,* which knows and comprehends all things, and exhibits them to our view in such a manner, and according to such rules, as He Himself hath ordained, and are by us termed the *laws of nature.*

HYL. Answer me, Philonous. Are all our ideas perfectly inert beings? Or have they any agency included in them?

PHIL. They are altogether passive and inert.

HYL. And is not God an agent, a being purely active?

PHIL. I acknowledge it.

HYL. No idea therefore can be like unto, or represent the nature of God?

PHIL. It cannot.

HYL. Since therefore you have no *idea* of the mind of God, how can you conceive it possible that things should exist in His mind? Or, if you can conceive the mind of God, without having an idea of it, why may not I be allowed to conceive the existence of Matter, notwithstanding I have no idea of it?

PHIL. As to your first question: I own I have properly no *idea*, either of God or any other spirit; for these being active, cannot be represented by things perfectly inert, as our ideas are. I do nevertheless know that I, who am a spirit or thinking substance, exist as certainly as I know my ideas exist. Farther, I know what I mean by the terms *I* and *myself;* and I know this immediately or intuitively, though I do not perceive it as I perceive a triangle, a colour, or a sound. The Mind, Spirit, or Soul is that indivisible unextended thing which thinks, acts, and perceives. I say *indivisible,* because unextended; and *unextended,* because extended, figured, moveable things are ideas; and that which perceives ideas, which thinks and wills, is plainly itself no idea, nor like an idea. Ideas are things inactive, and perceived. And Spirits a sort of beings altogether different from them. I do not therefore say my soul is an idea, or like an idea. However, taking the word *idea* in a large sense, my soul may be said to furnish me with an idea, that is, an image or likeness of God—though indeed extremely inadequate. For, all the notion I have of God is obtained by reflecting on my own soul, heightening its powers, and removing its imperfections. I have, therefore, though not an inactive idea, yet in *myself* some sort of an active thinking image of the Deity. And, though I perceive Him not by sense, yet I have a notion of Him, or know Him by reflexion and reasoning. My own mind and my own ideas I have an immediate knowledge of; and, by the help of these, do mediately apprehend the possibility of the existence of other spirits and ideas. Farther, from my own being, and from the dependency I find in myself and my ideas, I do, by an act of reason, necessarily infer the existence of a God, and of all created things in the mind of God. So much for your first question. For the second: I suppose by this time you can answer it yourself. For you neither perceive Matter objectively, as you do an inactive being or idea; nor know it, as you do yourself, by a reflex act, neither do you mediately apprehend it by similitude of the one or the other; nor yet collect it by reasoning from that which you know immediately. All which makes the case of *Matter* widely different from that of the *Deity*.

[²HYL. You say your own soul supplies you with some sort of an idea or image of God. But, at the same time, you acknowledge you have, properly speaking, no *idea* of your own soul. You even affirm that spirits are a sort of beings altogether different from ideas. Consequently that no idea can be like a spirit. We have therefore no idea of any spirit. You admit nevertheless that there is spiritual Substance, although you have no idea of it; while you deny there can be such a thing as material Substance, because you have no notion or idea of it. Is this fair dealing? To act consistently, you must either admit Matter or reject Spirit. What say you to this?

PHIL. I say, in the first place, that I do not deny the existence of material substance, merely because I have no notion of it, but because the notion of it is inconsistent; or, in other words, because it is repugnant that there should be a notion of it. Many things, for aught I know, may exist, whereof neither I nor any other man hath or can have any idea or notion whatsoever. But then those things must be possible, that is, nothing inconsistent must be included in their definition. I say, secondly, that, although we believe things to exist which we do not perceive, yet we may not believe that any particular thing exists, without some reason for such belief: but I have no reason for believing the existence of Matter. I have no immediate intuition thereof: neither can I immediately from my sensations, ideas, notions, actions, or passions, infer an unthinking, unperceiving, inactive Substance—either by probable deduction, or necessary consequence. Whereas the being of my Self, that is, my own soul, mind, or thinking principle, I evidently know by reflexion. You will forgive me if I repeat the same things in answer to the same ob-

---

² This important passage, printed within brackets, is not found in the first and second editions of the *Dialogues*. It is, by anticipation, Berkeley's answer to Hume's application of the objections to the reality of abstract or unperceived Matter, to the reality of the Ego or Self, of which we are aware through memory, as identical amid the changes of its successive states.—A. C. F.

jections. In the very notion or definition of *material Sub-stance,* there is included a manifest repugnance and inconsistency. But this cannot be said of the notion of Spirit. That ideas should exist in what doth not perceive, or be produced by what doth not act, is repugnant. But, it is no repugnancy to say that a perceiving thing should be the subject of ideas, or an active thing the cause of them. It is granted we have neither an immediate evidence nor a demonstrative knowledge of the existence of other finite spirits; but it will not thence follow that such spirits are on a foot with material substances: if to suppose the one be inconsistent, and it be not inconsistent to suppose the other; if the one can be inferred by no argument, and there is a probability for the other; if we see signs and effects indicating distinct finite agents like ourselves, and see no sign or symptom whatever that leads to a rational belief of Matter. I say, lastly, that I have a notion of Spirit, though I have not, strictly speaking, an idea of it. I do not perceive it as an idea, or by means of an idea, but know it by reflexion.

HYL. Notwithstanding all you have said, to me it seems that, according to your own way of thinking, and in consequence of your own principles, it should follow that *you* are only a system of floating ideas, without any substance to support them. Words are not to be used without a meaning. And, as there is no more meaning in *spiritual Substance* than in *material Substance,* the one is to be exploded as well as the other.

PHIL. How often must I repeat, that I know or am conscious of my own being; and that *I myself* am not my ideas, but somewhat else, a thinking, active principle that perceives, knows, wills, and operates about ideas. I know that I, one and the same self, perceive both colours and sounds: that a colour cannot perceive a sound, nor a sound a colour: that I am therefore one individual principle, distinct from colour and sound; and, for the same reason, from all other sensible things and inert ideas. But, I am not in like manner conscious either of the existence or essence of Matter. On the contrary, I know that nothing inconsistent can exist, and that the existence of Matter implies an inconsistency. Farther, I know what I mean when I affirm that there is a spiritual substance or support of ideas, that is, that a spirit knows and perceives ideas. But, I do not know what is meant when it is said that an unperceiving substance hath inherent in it and supports either ideas or the archetypes of ideas. There is therefore upon the whole no parity of case between Spirit and Matter.]

HYL. I own myself satisfied in this point. But, do you in earnest think the real existence of sensible things consists in their being actually perceived? If so; how comes it that all mankind distinguish between them? Ask the first man you meet, and he shall tell you, *to be perceived* is one thing, and *to exist* is another.

PHIL. I am content, Hylas, to appeal to the common sense of the world for the truth of my notion. Ask the gardener why he thinks yonder cherry-tree exists in the garden, and he shall tell you, because he sees and feels it; in a word, because he perceives it by his senses. Ask him why he thinks an orange-tree not to be there, and he shall tell you, because he does not perceive it. What he perceives by sense, that he terms a real being, and saith it *is* or *exists*; but, that which is not perceivable, the same, he saith, hath no being.

HYL. Yes, Philonous, I grant the existence of a sensible thing consists in being perceivable, but not in being actually perceived.

PHIL. And what is perceivable but an idea? And can an idea exist without being actually perceived? These are points long since agreed between us.

HYL. But, be your opinion never so true, yet surely you will not deny it is shocking, and contrary to the common sense of men. Ask the fellow whether yonder tree hath an existence out of his mind: what answer think you he would make?

PHIL. The same that I should myself, to wit, that it doth exist out of his mind. But then to a Christian it cannot surely be shocking to say, the real tree, existing without his mind, is truly known and comprehended by (that is *exists in*) the infinite mind of God. Probably he may not at first glance be aware of the direct and immediate proof there is of this; inasmuch as the very being of a tree, or any other sensible thing, implies a mind wherein it is. But the point itself he cannot deny. The question between the Materialists and me is not, whether things have a *real* existence out of the mind of this or that person, but whether they have an *absolute* existence, distinct from being perceived by God, and exterior to *all* minds. This indeed some heathens and philosophers have affirmed, but whoever entertains notions of the Deity suitable to the Holy Scriptures will be of another opinion.

HYL. But, according to your notions, what difference is there between real things, and chimeras formed by the imagination, or the visions of a dream—since they are all equally in the mind?

PHIL. The ideas formed by the imagination are faint and indistinct; they have, besides, an entire dependence on the will. But the ideas perceived by sense, that is, real things, are more vivid and clear; and, being imprinted on the mind by a spirit distinct from us, have not the like dependence on our will. There is therefore no danger of confounding these with the foregoing: and there is as little of confounding them with the visions of a dream, which are dim, irregular, and confused. And, though they should happen to be never so lively and natural, yet, by their not being connected, and of a piece with the preceding and subsequent transactions of our lives, they might easily be distinguished from realities. In short, by whatever method you distinguish *things* from *chimeras* on your scheme, the same, it is evident, will hold also upon mine. For, it must be, I presume, by some perceived difference; and I am not for depriving you of any one thing that you perceive.

HYL. But still, Philonous, you hold, there is nothing in the world but spirits and ideas. And this, you must needs acknowledge, sounds very oddly.

PHIL. I own the word *idea,* not being commonly used for *thing,* sounds something out of the way. My reason for using it was, because a necessary relation to the mind is understood to be implied by that term; and it is now commonly used by philosophers to denote the immediate objects of the understanding. But, however oddly the proposition may sound in words, yet it includes nothing so very strange or shocking in its sense; which in effect amounts to no more than this, to wit, that there are only things perceiving, and things perceived; or that every unthinking being is necessarily, and from the very nature of its existence, perceived by some mind; if not by a finite created mind, yet certainly by the infinite mind of God, in whom 'we live, and move, and have our being.' Is this as strange as to say, the sensible qualities are not on the objects: or that we cannot be sure of the existence of things, or know any thing of their real natures—though we both see and feel them, and perceive them by all our senses?

HYL. And, in consequence of this, must we not think there are no such things as physical or corporeal causes; but that a Spirit is the immediate cause of all the phenomena in nature? Can there be anything more extravagant than this?

PHIL. Yes, it is infinitely more extravagant to say—a thing which is inert operates on the mind, and which is unperceiving is the cause of our perceptions, [³ without any regard either to consistency, or the old known axiom, *Nothing can give to another that which it hath not itself*]. Besides, that which to you, I know not for what reason, seems so extravagant is no more than the Holy Scriptures assert in a hundred places. In them God is represented as the sole and immediate Author of all those effects which some heathens and philosophers are wont to ascribe to Nature, Matter, Fate, or the like unthinking principle. This is so much the constant language of Scripture that it were needless to confirm it by citations.

HYL. You are not aware, Philonous, that in making God the immediate Author of all the motions in nature, you make Him the Author of murder, sacrilege, adultery, and the like heinous sins.

PHIL. In answer to that, I observe, first, that the imputation of guilt is the same, whether a person commits an

³ The words within brackets are omitted in the third edition.

action with or without an instrument. In case therefore you suppose God to act by the mediation of an instrument or occasion, called *Matter*, you as truly make Him the author of sin as I, who think Him the immediate agent in all those operations vulgarly ascribed to Nature. I farther observe that sin or moral turpitude doth not consist in the outward physical action or motion, but in the internal deviation of the will from the laws of reason and religion. This is plain, in that the killing an enemy in a battle, or putting a criminal legally to death, is not thought sinful; though the outward act be the very same with that in the case of murder. Since, therefore, sin doth not consist in the physical action, the making God an immediate cause of all such actions is not making Him the Author of sin. Lastly, I have nowhere said that God is the only agent who produces all the motions in bodies. It is true I have denied there are any other agents besides spirits; but this is very consistent with allowing to thinking rational beings, in the production of motions, the use of limited powers, ultimately indeed derived from God, but immediately under the direction of their own wills, which is sufficient to entitle them to al' the guilt of their actions.

HYL. But the denying Matter, Philonous, or corporeal Substance; there is the point. You can never persuade me that this is not repugnant to the universal sense of mankind. Were our dispute to be determined by most voices, I am confident you would give up the point, without gathering the votes.

PHIL. I wish both our opinions were fairly stated and submitted to the judgment of men who had plain common sense, without the prejudices of a learned education. Let me be represented as one who trusts his senses, who thinks he knows the things he sees and feels, and entertains no doubts of their existence; and you fairly set forth with all your doubts, your paradoxes, and your scepticism about you, and I shall willingly acquiesce in the determination of any indifferent person. That there is no substance wherein ideas can exist beside spirit is to me evident. And that the objects immediately perceived are ideas, is on all hands agreed. And that sensible qualities are objects immediately perceived no one can deny. It is therefore evident there can be no *substratum* of those qualities but spirit; *in* which they exist, not by way of mode or property, but as a thing perceived in that which perceives it. I deny therefore that there is any unthinking *substratum* of the objects of sense, and *in that acceptation* that there is any material substance. But if by *material substance* is meant only *sensible body*—that which is seen and felt (and the unphilosophical part of the world, I dare say, mean no more)—then I am more certain of matter's existence than you or any other philosopher pretend to be. If there be anything which makes the generality of mankind averse from the notions I espouse: it is a misapprehension that I deny the reality of sensible things. But, as it is you who are guilty of that, and not I, it follows that in truth their aversion is against your notions and not mine. I do therefore assert that I am as certain as of my own being, that there are bodies or corporeal substances (meaning the things I perceive by my senses); and that, granting this, the bulk of mankind will take no thought about, nor think themselves at all concerned in the fate of those unknown natures, and philosophical quiddities, which some men are so fond of.

HYL. What say you to this? Since, according to you, men judge of the reality of things by their senses, how can a man be mistaken in thinking the moon a plain lucid surface, about a foot in diameter; or a square tower, seen at a distance, round; or an oar, with one end in the water, crooked?

PHIL. He is not mistaken with regard to the ideas he actually perceives, but in the inference he makes from his present perceptions. Thus, in the case of the oar, what he immediately perceives by sight is certainly crooked; and so far he is in the right. But if he thence conclude that upon taking the oar out of the water he shall perceive the same crookedness; or that it would affect his touch as crooked things are wont to do: in that he is mistaken. In like manner, if he shall conclude from what he perceives in one station, that, in case he advances towards the moon or tower, he should still be affected with the like ideas, he is mistaken. But his mistake lies not in what he perceives immediately, and at present, (it being a manifest contradiction to suppose he should err in respect of that) but in the wrong judgment he makes concerning the ideas he apprehends to be connected with those immediately perceived: or, concerning the ideas that, from what he perceives at present, he imagines would be perceived in other circumstances. The case is the same with regard to the Copernican system. We do not here perceive any motion of the earth: but it were erroneous thence to conclude, that, in case we were placed at as great a distance from that as we are now from the other planets, we should not then perceive its motion.

HYL. I understand you; and must needs own you say things plausible enough. But, give me leave to put you in mind of one thing. Pray, Philonous, were you not formerly as positive that Matter existed, as you are now that it does not?

PHIL. I was. But here lies the difference. Before, my positiveness was founded, without examination, upon prejudice; but now, after inquiry, upon evidence.

HYL. After all, it seems our dispute is rather about words than things. We agree in the thing, but differ in the name. That we are affected with ideas *from without* is evident; and it is no less evident that there must be (I will not say archetypes, but) Powers without the mind, corresponding to those ideas. And, as these Powers cannot subsist by themselves, there is some subject of them necessarily to be admitted; which I call *Matter,* and you call *Spirit.* This is all the difference.

PHIL. Pray, Hylas, is that powerful Being, or subject of powers, extended?

HYL. It hath not extension; but it hath the power to raise in you the idea of extension.

PHIL. It is therefore itself unextended?

HYL. I grant it.

PHIL. Is it not also active?

HYL. Without doubt. Otherwise, how could we attribute powers to it?

PHIL. Now let me ask you two questions: *First,* Whether it be agreeable to the usage either of philosophers or others

to give the name *Matter* to an unextended active being?
And, *Secondly,* Whether it be not ridiculously absurd to
misapply names contrary to the common use of language?

HYL. Well then, let it not be called Matter, since you
will have it so, but some *Third Nature* distinct from Matter
and Spirit. For what reason is there why you should call
it Spirit? Does not the notion of spirit imply that it is
thinking, as well as active and unextended?

PHIL. My reason is this: because I have a mind to have
some notion of meaning in what I say: but I have no notion
of any action distinct from volition, neither can I conceive
volition to be anywhere but in a spirit: therefore, when
I speak of an active being, I am obliged to mean a Spirit.
Beside, what can be plainer than that a thing which hath
no ideas in itself cannot impart them to me; and, if it hath
ideas, surely it must be a Spirit. To make you comprehend
the point still more clearly if it be possible, I assert as well
as you that, since we are affected from without, we must
allow Powers to be without, in a Being distinct from ourselves. So far we are agreed. But then we differ as to
the kind of this powerful Being. I will have it to be Spirit,
you Matter, or I know not what (I may add too, you know
not what) Third Nature. Thus, I prove it to be Spirit.
From the effects I see produced, I conclude there are actions;
and, because actions, volitions; and, because there are volitions, there must be a *will.* Again, the things I perceive
must have an existence, they or their archetypes, out of
*my* mind: but, being ideas, neither they nor their archetypes
can exist otherwise than in an understanding; there is therefore an *understanding.* But will and understanding constitute in the strictest sense a mind or spirit. The powerful
cause, therefore, of my ideas is in strict propriety of speech
a *Spirit.*

HYL. And now I warrant you think you have made the
point very clear, little suspecting that what you advance
leads directly to a contradiction. Is it not an absurdity
to imagine any imperfection in God?

PHIL. Without a doubt.

HYL. To suffer pain is an imperfection?

PHIL. It is.

HYL. Are we not sometimes affected with pain and uneasiness by some other Being?

PHIL. We are.

HYL. And have you not said that Being is a Spirit, and is not that Spirit God?

PHIL. I grant it.

HYL. But you have asserted that whatever ideas we perceive from without are in the mind which affects us. The ideas, therefore, of pain and uneasiness are in God; or, in other words, God suffers pain: that is to say, there is an imperfection in the Divine nature: which, you acknowledged, was absurd. So you are caught in a plain contradiction.

PHIL. That God knows or understands all things, and that He knows, among other things, what pain is, even every sort of painful sensation, and what it is for His creatures to suffer pain, I make no question. But, that God, though He knows and sometimes causes painful sensations in us, can Himself suffer pain, I positively deny. We, who are limited and dependent spirits, are liable to impressions of sense, the effects of an external Agent, which, being produced against our wills, are sometimes painful and uneasy. But God, whom no external being can affect, who perceives nothing by sense as we do; whose will is absolute and independent, causing all things, and liable to be thwarted or resisted by nothing: it is evident, such a Being as this can suffer nothing, nor be affected with any painful sensation, or indeed any sensation at all. We are chained to a body: that is to say, our perceptions are connected with corporeal motions. By the law of our nature, we are affected upon every alteration in the nervous parts of our sensible body; which sensible body, rightly considered, is nothing but a complexion of such qualities or ideas as have no existence distinct from being perceived by a mind. So that this connexion of sensations with corporeal motions means no more than a correspondence in the order of nature, between two sets of ideas, or things immediately perceivable. But God is a Pure Spirit, disengaged from all such sympathy, or natural ties. No corporeal motions are attended with the sensations of pain or pleasure in His mind. To know everything knowable, is certainly a perfection; but to endure, or suffer, or feel anything by sense, is an imperfection. The former, I say, agrees to God, but not the latter. God knows, or hath ideas; but His ideas are not conveyed to Him by sense, as ours are. Your not distinguishing, where there is so manifest a difference, makes you fancy you see an absurdity where there is none.

HYL. But, all this while you have not considered that the quantity of Matter has been demonstrated to be proportioned to the gravity of bodies. And what can withstand demonstration?

PHIL. Let me see how you demonstrate that point.

HYL. I lay it down for a principle, that the moments or quantities of motion in bodies are in a direct compounded reason of the velocities and quantities of Matter contained in them. Hence, where the velocities are equal, it follows the moments are directly as the quantity of Matter in each. But it is found by experience that all bodies (bating the small inequalities, arising from the resistance of the air) descend with an equal velocity; the motion therefore of descending bodies, and consequently their gravity, which is the cause or principle of that motion, is proportional to the quantity of Matter; which was to be demonstrated.

PHIL. You lay it down as a self-evident principle that the quantity of motion in any body is proportional to the velocity and *Matter* taken together; and this is made use of to prove a proposition from whence the existence of *Matter* is inferred. Pray is not this arguing in a circle?

HYL. In the premise I only mean that the motion is proportional to the velocity, jointly with the extension and solidity.

PHIL. But, allowing this to be true, yet it will not thence follow that gravity is proportional to *Matter*, in your philosophic sense of the word; except you take it for granted that unknown *substratum*, or whatever else you call it, is proportional to those sensible qualities; which to suppose is plainly begging the question. That there is magnitude and solidity, or resistance, perceived by sense, I readily grant; as likewise, that gravity may be proportional to those qualities

I will not dispute. But that either these qualities as perceived by us, or the powers producing them, do exist in a *material substratum;* this is what I deny, and you indeed affirm, but, notwithstanding your demonstration, have not yet proved.

HYL. I shall insist no longer on that point. Do you think, however, you shall persuade me the natural philosophers have been dreaming all this while? Pray what becomes of all their hypotheses and explications of the phenomena, which suppose the existence of Matter?

PHIL. What mean you, Hylas, by the *phenomena?*

HYL. I mean the appearances which I perceive by my senses.

PHIL. And the appearances perceived by sense, are they not ideas?

HYL. I have told you so a hundred times.

PHIL. Therefore, to explain the phenomena, is, to shew how we come to be affected with ideas, in that manner and order wherein they are imprinted on our senses. Is it not?

HYL. It is.

PHIL. Now, if you can prove that any philosopher has explained the production of any one idea in our minds by the help of *Matter,* I shall for ever acquiesce, and look on all that hath been said against it as nothing; but, if you cannot, it is vain to urge the explication of phenomena. That a Being endowed with knowledge and will should produce or exhibit ideas is easily understood. But that a Being which is utterly destitute of these faculties should be able to produce ideas, or in any sort to affect an intelligence, this I can never understand. This I say, though we had some positive conception of Matter, though we knew its qualities, and could comprehend its existence, would yet be so far from explaining things, that it is itself the most inexplicable thing in the world. And yet, for all this, it will not follow that philosophers have been doing nothing; for, by observing and reasoning upon the connexion of ideas, they discover the laws and methods of nature, which is a part of knowledge both useful and entertaining.

HYL. After all, can it be supposed God would deceive

all mankind? Do you imagine He would have induced the whole world to believe the being of Matter, if there was no such thing?

PHIL. That every epidemical opinion, arising from prejudice, or passion, or thoughtlessness, may be imputed to God, as the Author of it, I believe you will not affirm. Whatsoever opinion we father on Him, it must be either because He has discovered it to us by supernatural revelation; or because it is so evident to our natural faculties, which were framed and given us by God, that it is impossible we should withhold our assent from it. But where is the revelation? or where is the evidence that extorts the belief of Matter? Nay, how does it appear, that Matter, *taken for something distinct from what we perceive by our senses,* is thought to exist by all mankind; or indeed, by any except a few philosophers, who do not know what they would be at? Your question supposes these points are clear; and, when you have cleared them, I shall think myself obliged to give you another answer. In the meantime, let it suffice that I tell you, I do not suppose God has deceived mankind at all.

HYL. But the novelty, Philonous, the novelty! There lies the danger. New notions should always be discountenanced; they unsettle men's minds, and nobody knows where they will end.

PHIL. Why the rejecting a notion that has no foundation, either in sense, or in reason, or in Divine authority, should be thought to unsettle the belief of such opinions as are grounded on all or any of these, I cannot imagine. That innovations in government and religion are dangerous, and ought to be discountenanced, I freely own. But is there the like reason why they should be discouraged in philosophy? The making anything known which was unknown before is an innovation in knowledge: and, if all such innovations had been forbidden, men would have made a notable progress in the arts and sciences. But it is none of my business to plead for novelties and paradoxes. That the qualities we perceive are not on the objects: that we must not believe our senses: that we know nothing of the real nature of things, and can never be assured even of their existence:

that real colours and sounds are nothing but certain unknown figures and motions: that motions are in themselves
neither swift nor slow: that there are in bodies absolute ex-
tensions, without any particular magnitude or figure: that
a thing stupid, thoughtless, and inactive, operates on a spirit:
that the least particle of a body contains innumerable extended parts:—these are the novelties, these are the strange
notions which shock the genuine uncorrupted judgment of
all mankind; and being once admitted, embarrass the mind
with endless doubts and difficulties. And it is against these
and the like innovations I endeavour to vindicate Common
Sense. It is true, in doing this, I may perhaps be obliged
to use some *ambages,* and ways of speech not common. But,
if my notions are once thoroughly understood, that which
is most singular in them will, in effect, be found to amount
to no more than this:—that it is absolutely impossible, and
a plain contradiction, to suppose any unthinking Being should
exist without being perceived by a Mind. And, if this notion
be singular, it is a shame it should be so, at this time of
day, and in a Christian country.

HYL. As for the difficulties other opinions may be liable
to, those are out of the question. It is your business to
defend your own opinion. Can anything be plainer than
that you are for changing all things into ideas? You,
I say, who are not ashamed to charge me with *scepticism.*
This is so plain, there is no denying it.

PHIL. You mistake me. I am not for changing things
into ideas, but rather ideas into things; since those immediate objects of perception, which, according to you,
are only appearances of things, I take to be the real things
themselves.

HYL. Things! You may pretend what you please; but
it is certain you leave us nothing but the empty forms of
things, the outside only which strikes the senses.

PHIL. What you call the empty forms and outside of
things seem to me the very things themselves. Nor are
they empty or incomplete, otherwise than upon your supposition—that Matter is an essential part of all corporeal
things. We both, therefore, agree in this, that we perceive
only sensible forms: but herein we differ—you will have

them to be empty appearances, I real beings. In short, you do not trust your senses, I do.

HYL. You say you believe your senses; and seem to applaud yourself that in this you agree with the vulgar. According to you, therefore, the true nature of a thing is discovered by the senses. If so, whence comes that disagreement? Why is not the same figure, and other sensible qualities, perceived all manner of ways? and why should we use a microscope the better to discover the true nature of a body, if it were discoverable to the naked eye?

PHIL. Strictly speaking, Hylas, we do not see the same object that we feel; neither is the same object perceived by the microscope which was by the naked eye. But, in case every variation was thought sufficient to constitute a new kind of individual, the endless number of confusion of names would render language impracticable. Therefore, to avoid this, as well as other inconveniences which are obvious upon a little thought, men combine together several ideas, apprehended by divers senses, or by the same sense at different times, or in different circumstances, but observed, however, to have some connexion in nature, either with respect to co-existence or succession; all which they refer to one name, and consider as one thing. Hence it follows that when I examine, by my other senses, a thing I have seen, it is not in order to understand better the same object which I had perceived by sight, the object of one sense not being perceived by the other senses. And, when I look through a microscope, it is not that I may perceive more clearly what I perceived already with my bare eyes; the object perceived by the glass being quite different from the former. But, in both cases, my aim is only to know what ideas are connected together; and the more a man knows of the connexion of ideas, the more he is said to know of the nature of things. What, therefore, if our ideas are variable; what if our senses are not in all circumstances affected with the same appearances. It will not thence follow they are not to be trusted; or that they are inconsistent either with themselves or anything else: except it be with your preconceived notion of (I know not what) one single, unchanged, unperceivable, real Na-

ture, marked by each name.  Which prejudice seems to have
taken its rise from not rightly understanding the common language of men, speaking of several distinct ideas
as united into one thing by the mind.  And, indeed, there
is cause to suspect several erroneous conceits of the philosophers are owing to the same original: while they began
to build their schemes not so much on notions as on words,
which were framed by the vulgar, merely for conveniency
and dispatch in the common actions of life, without any
regard to speculation.

HYL. Methinks I apprehend your meaning.

PHIL. It is your opinion the ideas we perceive by our
senses are not real things, but images or copies of them.
Our knowledge, therefore, is no farther real than as our
ideas are the true *representations* of those *originals*.  But,
as these supposed originals are in themselves unknown, it
is impossible to know how far our ideas resemble them;
or whether they resemble them at all  We cannot, therefore, be sure we have any real knowledge.  Farther, as
our ideas are perpetually varied, without any change in the
supposed real things, it necessarily follows they cannot all
be true copies of them: or, if some are and others are not,
it is impossible to distinguish the former from the latter.
And this plunges us yet deeper in uncertainty.  Again, when
we consider the point, we cannot conceive how any idea, or
anything like an idea, should have an absolute existence out
of a mind: nor consequently, according to you, how there
should be any real thing in nature.  The result of all which
is that we are thrown into the most hopeless and abandoned
scepticism.  Now, give me leave to ask you, First, Whether
your referring ideas to certain absolutely existing unperceived substances, as their originals, be not the source of all
this scepticism?  Secondly, whether you are informed, either
by sense or reason, of the existence of those unknown originals?  And, in case you are not, whether it be not absurd
to suppose them?  Thirdly, Whether, upon inquiry, you find
there is anything distinctly conceived or meant by the *absolute or external existence of unperceiving substances?* Lastly,
Whether, the premises considered, it be not the wisest way
to follow nature, trust your senses, and, laying aside all

anxious thought about unknown natures or substances, admit with the vulgar those for real things which are perceived by the senses?

HYL. For the present, I have no inclination to the answering part. I would much rather see how you can get over what follows. Pray are not the objects perceived by the *senses* of one, likewise perceivable to others present? If there were a hundred more here, they would all see the garden, the trees, and flowers, as I see them. But they are not in the same manner affected with the ideas I frame in my *imagination*. Does not this make a difference between the former sort of objects and the latter?

PHIL. I grant it does. Nor have I ever denied a difference between the objects of sense and those of imagination. But what would you infer from thence? You cannot say that sensible objects exist unperceived, because they are perceived by many.

HYL. I own I can make nothing of that objection: but it hath led me into another. Is it not your opinion that by our senses we perceive only the ideas existing in our minds?

PHIL. It is.

HYL. But the *same* idea which is in my mind cannot be in yours, or in any other mind. Doth it not therefore follow, from your principles, that no two can see the same thing? And is not this highly absurd?

PHIL. If the term *same* be taken in the vulgar acceptation, it is certain (and not at all repugnant to the principles I maintain) that different persons may perceive the same thing; or the same thing or idea exist in different minds. Words are of arbitrary imposition; and, since men are used to apply the word *same* where no distinction or variety is perceived, and I do not pretend to alter their perceptions, it follows that, as men have said before, *several saw the same thing,* so they may, upon like occasions, still continue to use the same phrase, without any deviation either from propriety of language, or the truth of things. But, if the term *same* be used in the acceptation of philosophers, who pretend to an abstracted notion of identity, then, according **to** their sundry definitions of this notion (for it is not yet agreed wherein that philosophic identity consists), it may or may not be possible for divers persons to perceive the same thing. But whether philosophers shall think fit to *call* a thing the *same* or no, is, I conceive, of small importance. Let us suppose several men together, all endued with the same faculties, and consequently affected in like sort by their senses, and who had yet never known the use of language; they would, without question, agree in their perceptions. Though perhaps, when they came to the use of speech, some regarding the uniformness of what was perceived, might call it the *same* thing: others, especially regarding the diversity of persons who perceived, might choose the denomination of *different* things. But who sees not that all the dispute is about a word? to wit, whether what is perceived by different persons may yet have the term *same* applied to it? Or, suppose a house, whose walls or outward shell remaining unaltered, the chambers are all pulled down, and new ones built in their place; and that you should call this the *same,* and I should say it was not the *same* house:—would we not, for all this, perfectly agree in our thoughts of the house, considered in itself? And would not all the difference consist in a sound? If you should say, We differed in our notions; for that you superadded to your idea of the house the simple abstracted idea of identity, whereas I did not; I would tell you, I know not what you mean by the *abstracted idea of identity;* and should desire you to look into your own thoughts, and be sure you understood yourself.——Why so silent, Hylas? Are you not yet satisfied men may dispute about identity and diversity, without any real difference in their thoughts and opinions, abstracted from names? Take this farther reflexion with you—that whether Matter be allowed to exist or no, the case is exactly the same as to the point in hand. For the Materialists themselves acknowledge what we immediately perceive by our senses to be our own ideas. Your difficulty, therefore, that no two see the same thing, makes equally against the Materialists and me.

HYL. [⁴Ay, Philonous,] But they suppose an external

⁴ Omitted in author's last edition.

archetype, to which referring their several ideas they may truly be said to perceive the same thing.

PHIL. And (not to mention your having discarded those archetypes) so may you suppose an external archetype on my principles;—*external, I mean, to your own mind:* though indeed it must be supposed to exist in that Mind which comprehends all things; but then, this serves all the ends of *identity,* as well as if it existed out of a mind. And I am sure you yourself will not say it is less intelligible.

HYL. You have indeed clearly satisfied me—either that there is no difficulty at bottom in this point; or, if there be, that it makes equally against both opinions.

PHIL. But that which makes equally against two contradictory opinions can be a proof against neither.

HYL. I acknowledge it.

But, after all, Philonous, when I consider the substance of what you advance against *Scepticism,* it amounts to no more than this:—We are sure that we really see, hear, feel; in a word, that we are affected with sensible impressions.

PHIL. And how are *we* concerned any farther? I see this cherry, I feel it, I taste it: and I am sure *nothing* cannot be seen, or felt, or tasted: it is therefore *real.* Take away the sensations of softness, moisture, redness, tartness, and you take away the cherry, since it is not a being distinct from sensations. A cherry, I say, is nothing but a congeries of sensible impressions, or ideas perceived by various senses: which ideas are united into one thing (or have one name given them) by the mind, because they are observed to attend each other. Thus, when the palate is affected with such a particular taste, the sight is affected with a red colour, the touch with roundness, softness, &c. Hence, when I see, and feel, and taste, in such sundry certain manners, I am sure the cherry exists, or is real; its reality being in my opinion nothing abstracted from those sensations. But if by the word *cherry* you mean an unknown nature, distinct from all those sensible qualities, and by its *existence* something distinct from its being perceived; then, indeed, I own, neither you nor I, nor any one else, can be sure it exists.

Hyl. But, what would you say, Philonous, if I should bring the very same reasons against the existence of sensible things *in a mind,* which you have offered against their existing *in a material substratum?*

Phil. When I see your reasons, you shall hear what I have to say to them.

Hyl. Is the mind extended or unextended?

Phil. Unextended, without doubt.

Hyl. Do you say the things you perceive are in your mind?

Phil. They are.

Hyl. Again, have I not heard you speak of sensible impressions?

Phil. I believe you may.

Hyl. Explain to me now, O Philonous! how it is possible there should be room for all those trees and houses to exist in your mind.   Can extended things be contained in that which is unextended?   Or, are we to imagine impressions made on a thing void of all solidity?   You cannot say objects are in your mind, as books in your study: or that things are imprinted on it, as the figure of a seal upon wax.   In what sense, therefore, are we to understand those expressions?   Explain me this if you can: and I shall then be able to answer all those queries you formerly put to me about my *substratum.*

Phil. Look you, Hylas, when I speak of objects as existing in the mind, or imprinted on the senses, I would not be understood in the gross literal sense; as when bodies are said to exist in a place, or a seal to make an impression upon wax.   My meaning is only that the mind comprehends or perceives them; and that it is affected from without, or by some being distinct from itself.   This is my explication of your difficulty; and how it can serve to make your tenet of an unperceiving material *substratum* intelligible, I would fain know.

Hyl. Nay, if that be all, I confess I do not see what use can be made of it.   But are you not guilty of some abuse of language in this?

Phil. None at all.   It is no more than common custom, which you know is the rule of language, hath authorised:

nothing being more usual, than for philosophers to speak of the immediate objects of the understanding as things existing in the mind. Nor is there anything in this but what is conformable to the general analogy of language; most part of the mental operations being signified by words borrowed from sensible things; as is plain in the terms *comprehend, reflect, discourse, &c.,* which, being applied to the mind, must not be taken in their gross, original sense.

HYL. You have, I own, satisfied me in this point. But there still remains one great difficulty, which I know not how you will get over. And, indeed, it is of such importance that if you could solve all others, without being able to find a solution for this, you must never expect to make me a proselyte to your principles.

PHIL. Let me know this mighty difficulty.

HYL. The Scripture account of the creation is what appears to me utterly irreconcilable with your notions. Moses tells us of a creation: a creation of what? of ideas? No, certainly, but of things, of real things, solid corporeal substances. Bring your principles to agree with this, and I shall perhaps agree with you.

PHIL. Moses mentions the sun, moon, and stars, earth and sea, plants and animals. That all these do really exist, and were in the beginning created by God, I make no question. If by *ideas* you mean fictions and fancies of the mind, then these are no ideas. If by *ideas* you mean immediate objects of the understanding, or sensible things, which cannot exist unperceived, or out of a mind, then these things are ideas. But whether you do or do not call them *ideas,* it matters little. The difference is only about a name. And, whether that name be retained or rejected, the sense, the truth, and reality of things continues the same. In common talk, the objects of our senses are not termed *ideas,* but *things.* Call them so still: provided you do not attribute to them any absolute external existence, and I shall never quarrel with you for a word. The creation, therefore, I allow to have been a creation of things, of *real* things. Neither is this in the least inconsistent with my principles, as is evident from what I have now said;

and would have been evident to you without this, if you had not forgotten what had been so often said before. But as for solid corporeal substances, I desire you to show where Moses makes any mention of them; and, if they should be mentioned by him, or any other inspired writer, it would still be incumbent on you to shew those words were not taken in the vulgar acceptation, for things falling under our senses, but in the philosophic acceptation, for Matter, or *an unknown quiddity, with an absolute existence.* When you have proved these points, then (and not till then) may you bring the authority of Moses into our dispute.

HYL. It is in vain to dispute about a point so clear. I am content to refer it to your own conscience. Are you not satisfied there is some peculiar repugnancy between the Mosaic account of the creation and your notions?

PHIL. If all possible sense which can be put on the first chapter of Genesis may be conceived as consistently with my principles as any other, then it has no peculiar repugnancy with them. But there is no sense you may not as well conceive, believing as I do. Since, besides spirits, all you conceive are ideas; and the existence of these I do not deny. Neither do you pretend they exist without the mind.

HYL. Pray let me see any sense you can understand it in.

PHIL. Why, I imagine that if I had been present at the creation, I should have seen things produced into being— that is become perceptible—in the order prescribed by the sacred historian. I never before believed the Mosaic account of the creation, and now find no alteration in my manner of believing it. When things are said to begin or end their existence, we do not mean this with regard to God, but His creatures. All objects are eternally known by God, or, which is the same thing, have an eternal existence in His mind: but when things, before imperceptible to creatures, are, by a decree of God, perceptible to them, then are they said to begin a relative existence, with respect to created minds. Upon reading therefore the Mosaic account of the creation, I understand that the several parts of the world became gradually perceivable to finite spirits, endowed with proper faculties; so that, whoever such were present, they were in truth perceived by them. This is the literal obvious sense suggested to me by the words of the Holy Scripture: in which is included no mention, or no thought, either of *substratum,* instrument, occasion, or absolute existence. And, upon inquiry, I doubt not it will be found that most plain honest men, who believe the creation, never think of those things any more than I. What metaphysical sense you may understand it in, you only can tell.

HYL. But, Philonous, you do not seem to be aware that you allow created things, in the beginning, only a relative, and consequently hypothetical being: that is to say, upon supposition there were *men* to perceive them; without which they have no actuality of absolute existence, wherein creation might terminate. Is it not, therefore, according to you, plainly impossible the creation of any inanimate creatures should precede that of man? And is not this directly contrary to the Mosaic account?

PHIL. In answer to that, I say, first, created beings might begin to exist in the mind of other created intelligences, beside men. You will not therefore be able to prove any contradiction between Moses and my notions, unless you first shew there was no other order of finite created spirits in being, before man. I say farther, in case we conceive the creation, as we should at this time, a parcel of plants or vegetables of all sorts produced, by an invisible Power, in a desert where nobody was present—that this way of explaining or conceiving it is consistent with my principles, since they deprive you of nothing, either sensible or imaginable; that it exactly suits with the common, natural, and undebauched notions of mankind; that it manifests the dependence of all things on God; and consequently hath all the good effect or influence, which it is possible that important article of our faith should have in making men humble, thankful, and resigned to their [⁵great] Creator. I say, moreover, that, in this naked conception of things, divested of words, there will not be found any notion of what you call the *actuality of absolute existence.* You may indeed raise a dust with those terms, and so lengthen our

⁵ In the first and second editions only.

dispute to no purpose. But I entreat you calmly to look into your own thoughts, and then tell me if they are not a useless and unintelligible jargon.

HYL. I own I have no very clear notion annexed to them. But what say you to this? Do you not make the existence of sensible things consist in their being in a mind? And were not all things eternally in the mind of God? Did they not therefore exist from all eternity, according to you? And how could that which was eternal be created in time? Can anything be clearer or better connected than this?

PHIL. And are not you too of opinion, that God knew all things from eternity?

HYL. I am.

PHIL. Consequently they always had a being in the Divine intellect.

HYL. This I acknowledge.

PHIL. By your own confession, therefore, nothing is new, or begins to be, in respect of the mind of God. So we are agreed in that point.

HYL. What shall we make then of the creation?

PHIL. May we not understand it to have been entirely in respect of finite spirits; so that things, with regard to us, may properly be said to begin their existence, or be created, when God decreed they should become perceptible to intelligent creatures, in that order and manner which He then established, and we now call the laws of nature? You may call this a *relative,* or *hypothetical existence* if you please. But, so long as it supplies us with the most natural, obvious, and literal sense of the Mosaic history of the creation; so long as it answers all the religious ends of that great article; in a word, so long as you can assign no other sense or meaning in its stead; why should we reject this? Is it to comply with a ridiculous sceptical humour of making everything nonsense and unintelligible? I am sure you cannot say it is for the glory of God. For, allowing it to be a thing possible and conceivable that the corporeal world should have an absolute existence extrinsical to the mind of God, as well as to the minds of all created spirits; yet how could this set forth either the immensity or omniscience of the Deity, or the necessary and immediate dependence of all things on Him? Nay, would it not rather seem to derogate from those attributes?

HYL. Well, but as to this decree of God's, for making things perceptible, what say you, Philonous? Is it not plain, God did either execute that decree from all eternity, or at some certain time began to will what He had not actually willed before, but only designed to will? If the former, then there could be no creation, or beginning of existence, in finite things. If the latter, then we must acknowledge something new to befall the Deity; which implies a sort of change: and all change argues imperfection.

PHIL. Pray consider what you are doing. Is it not evident this objection concludes equally against a creation in any sense; nay, against every other act of the Deity, discoverable by the light of nature? None of which can *we* conceive, otherwise than as performed in time, and having a beginning. God is a Being of transcendent and unlimited perfections: His nature, therefore, is incomprehensible to finite spirits. It is not, therefore, to be expected, that any man, whether Materialist or Immaterialist, should have exactly just notions of the Deity, His attributes, and ways of operation. If then you would infer anything against me, your difficulty must not be drawn from the inadequateness of our conceptions of the Divine nature, which is unavoidable on any scheme; but from the denial of Matter, of which there is not one word, directly or indirectly, in what you have now objected.

HYL. I must acknowledge the difficulties you are concerned to clear are such only as arise from the non-existence of Matter, and are peculiar to that notion. So far you are in the right. But I cannot by any means bring myself to think there is no such peculiar repugnancy between the creation and your opinion; though indeed where to fix it, I do not distinctly know.

PHIL. What would you have? Do I not acknowledge a twofold state of things—the one ectypal or natural, the other archetypal and eternal? The former was created in time; the latter existed from everlasting in the mind of

God. Is not this agreeable to the common notions of divines? or, is any more than this necessary in order to conceive the creation? But you suspect some peculiar repugnancy, though you know not where it lies. To take away all possibility of scruple in the case, do but consider this one point. Either you are not able to conceive the creation on any hypothesis whatsoever; and, if so, there is no ground for dislike or complaint against any particular opinion on that score: or you are able to conceive it; and, if so, why not on my Principles, since thereby nothing conceivable is taken away? You have all along been allowed the full scope of sense, imagination, and reason. Whatever, therefore, you could before apprehend, either immediately or mediately by your senses, or by ratiocination from your senses; whatever you could perceive, imagine, or understand, remains still with you. If, therefore, the notion you have of the creation by other Principles be intelligible, you have it still upon mine; if it be not intelligible, I conceive it to be no notion at all; and so there is no loss of it. And indeed it seems to me very plain that the supposition of Matter, that is a thing perfectly unknown and inconceivable, cannot serve to make us conceive anything. And, I hope it need not be proved to you that if the existence of Matter doth not make the creation conceivable, the creation's being without it inconceivable can be no objection against its non-existence.

HYL. I confess, Philonous, you have almost satisfied me in this point of the creation.

PHIL. I would fain know why you are not quite satisfied. You tell me indeed of a repugnancy between the Mosaic history and Immaterialism: but you know not where it lies. Is this reasonable, Hylas? Can you expect I should solve a difficulty without knowing what it is? But, to pass by all that, would not a man think you were assured there is no repugnancy between the received notions of Materialists and the inspired writings?

HYL. And so I am.

PHIL. Ought the historical part of Scripture to be understood in a plain obvious sense, or in a sense which is metaphysical and out of the way?

HYL. In the plain sense, doubtless.

PHIL. When Moses speaks of herbs, earth, water, &c. as having been created by God; think you not the sensible things commonly signified by those words are suggested to every unphilosophical reader?

HYL. I cannot help thinking so.

PHIL. And are not all ideas, or things perceived by sense, to be denied a real existence by the doctrine of the Materialist?

HYL. This I have already acknowledged.

PHIL. The creation, therefore, according to them, was not the creation of things sensible, which have only a relative being, but of certain unknown natures, which have an absolute being, wherein creation might terminate?

HYL. True.

PHIL. Is it not therefore evident the assertors of Matter destroy the plain obvious sense of Moses, with which their notions are utterly inconsistent; and instead of it obtrude on us I know not what; something equally unintelligible to themselves and me?

HYL. I cannot contradict you.

PHIL. Moses tells us of a creation. A creation of what? of unknown quiddities, of occasions, or *substratum?* No, certainly; but of things obvious to the senses. You must first reconcile this with your notions, if you expect I should be reconciled to them.

HYL. I see you can assault me with my own weapons.

PHIL. Then as to *absolute existence;* was there ever known a more jejune notion than that? Something it is so abstracted and unintelligible that you have frankly owned you could not conceive it, much less explain anything by it. But allowing Matter to exist, and the notion of absolute existence to be clear as light; yet, was this ever known to make the creation more credible? Nay, hath it not furnished the atheists and infidels of all ages with the most plausible arguments against a creation? That a corporeal substance, which hath an absolute existence without the minds of spirits, should be produced out of nothing, by the mere will of a Spirit, hath been looked upon as a thing so contrary to all reason, so impossible and absurd, that not only the most celebrated among the ancients, but even divers modern and Christian philosophers have thought Matter co-eternal with the Deity. Lay these things together, and then judge you whether Materialism disposes men to believe the creation of things.

HYL. I own, Philonous, I think it does not. This of the *creation* is the last objection I can think of; and I must needs own it hath been sufficiently answered as well as the rest. Nothing now remains to be overcome but a sort of unaccountable backwardness that I find in myself towards your notions.

PHIL. When a man is swayed, he knows not why, to one side of the question, can this, think you, be anything else but the effect of prejudice, which never fails to attend old and rooted notions? And indeed in this respect I cannot deny the belief of Matter to have very much the advantage over the contrary opinion, with men of a learned education.

HYL. I confess it seems to be as you say.

PHIL. As a balance, therefore, to this weight of prejudice, let us throw into the scale the great advantages that arise from the belief of Immaterialism, both in regard to religion and human learning. The being of a God, and incorruptibility of the soul, those great articles of religion, are they not proved with the clearest and most immediate evidence? When I say the being of a God, I do not mean an obscure general Cause of things, whereof we have no conception, but God, in the strict and proper sense of the word. A Being whose spirituality, omnipresence, providence, omniscience, infinite power and goodness, are as conspicuous as the existence of sensible things, of which (nothwithstanding the fallacious pretences and affected scruples of Sceptics) there is no more reason to doubt than of our own being.—Then, with relation to human sciences. In Natural Philosophy, what intricacies, what obscurities, what contradictions hath the belief of Matter led men into! To say nothing of the numberless disputes about its extent, continuity, homogeneity, gravity, divisibility, &c.—do they not pretend to explain all things by bodies operating on bodies, according to the laws of motion? and yet, are they able to comprehend how one body should move another? Nay, admitting there was no difficulty in reconciling the notion of an inert being with a cause, or in conceiving how an accident might pass from one body to another; yet, by all their strained thoughts and extravagant suppositions, have they been able to reach the *mechanical* production of any one animal or vegetable body? Can they account, by the laws of motion, for sounds, tastes, smells, or colours; or for the regular course of things? Have they accounted, by physical principles, for the aptitude and contrivance even of the most inconsiderable parts of the universe? But, laying aside Matter and corporeal causes, and admitting only the efficiency of an All-perfect Mind, are not all the effects of nature easy and intelligible? If the *phenomena* are nothing else but *ideas;* God is a *spirit,* but Matter an unintelligent, unperceiving being. If they demonstrate an unlimited power in their cause; God is active and omnipotent, but Matter an inert mass. If the order, regularity, and usefulness of them can never be sufficiently admired; God is infinitely wise and provident, but Matter destitute of all contrivance and design. These surely are great advantages in *Physics.* Not to mention that the apprehension of a distant Deity naturally disposes men to a negligence in their moral actions; which they would be more cautious of, in case they thought Him immediately present, and acting on their minds, without the interposition of Matter, or unthinking second causes.—Then in *Metaphysics:* what difficulties concerning entity in abstract, substantial forms, hylarchic principles, plastic natures, substance and accident, principle of individuation, possibility of Matter's thinking, origin of ideas, the manner how two independent substances so widely different as *Spirit* and *Matter,* should mutually operate on each other? what difficulties, I say, and endless disquisitions, concerning these and innumerable other the like points, do we escape, by supposing only Spirits and ideas?—Even the *Mathematics* themselves, if we take away the absolute existence of extended things, become much more clear and easy; the most shocking paradoxes and intricate speculations in those sciences depending on the infinite divisibility of finite extension; which depends on that supposition.—But what need is there to insist on the

particular sciences? Is not that opposition to all science
whatsoever, that frenzy of the ancient and modern Sceptics,
built on the same foundation? Or can you produce so much
as one argument against the reality of corporeal things, or
in behalf of that avowed utter ignorance of their natures,
which doth not suppose their reality to consist in an external
absolute existence? Upon this supposition, indeed, the
objections from the change of colours in a pigeon's neck, or
the appearance of the broken oar in the water, must be
allowed to have weight. But these and the like objections
vanish, if we do not maintain the being of absolute external originals, but place the reality of things in ideas, fleeting indeed, and changeable;—however, not changed at random, but according to the fixed order of nature. For, herein
consists that constancy and truth of things which secures all
the concerns of life, and distinguishes that which is *real*
from the *irregular visions* of the fancy.

HYL. I agree to all you have now said, and must own
that nothing can incline me to embrace your opinion more
than the advantages I see it is attended with. I am by
nature lazy; and this would be a mighty abridgment in
knowledge. What doubts, what hypotheses, what labyrinths
of amusement, what fields of disputation, what an ocean of
false learning, may be avoided by that single notion of
*Immaterialism!*

PHIL. After all, is there anything farther remaining to
be done? You may remember you promised to embrace
that opinion which upon examination should appear most
agreeable to Common Sense and remote from Scepticism.
This, by your own confession, is that which denies Matter,
or the *absolute* existence of corporeal things. Nor is this
all; the same notion has been proved several ways, viewed
in different lights, pursued in its consequences, and all objections against it cleared. Can there be a greater evidence
of its truth? or is it possible it should have all the marks
of a true opinion and yet be false?

HYL. I own myself entirely satisfied for the present in
all respects. But, what security can I have that I shall
still continue the same full assent to your opinion, and that

no unthought-of objection or difficulty will occur hereafter?

PHIL. Pray, Hylas, do you in other cases, when a point is once evidently proved, withhold your consent on account of objections or difficulties it may be liable to? Are the difficulties that attend the doctrine of incommensurable quantities, of the angle of contact, of the asymptotes to curves, or the like, sufficient to make you hold out against mathematical demonstration? Or will you disbelieve the Providence of God, because there may be some particular things which *you* know not how to reconcile with it? If there are difficulties attending *Immaterialism,* there are at the same time direct and evident proofs of it. But for the existence of Matter there is not one proof, and far more numerous and insurmountable objections lie against it. But where are those mighty difficulties you insist on? Alas! you know not where or what they are; something which may possibly occur hereafter. If this be a sufficient pretence for withholding your full assent, you should never yield it to any proposition, how free soever from exceptions, how clearly and solidly soever demonstrated.

HYL. You have satisfied me, Philonous.

PHIL. But, to arm you against all future objections, do but consider: That which bears equally hard on two contradictory opinions can be proof against neither. Whenever, therefore, any difficulty occurs, try if you can find a solution for it on the hypothesis of the *Materialists.* Be not deceived by words; but sound your own thoughts. And in case you cannot conceive it easier by the help of *Materialism,* it is plain it can be no objection against *Immaterialism.* Had you proceeded all along by this rule, you would probably have spared yourself abundance of trouble in objecting; since of all your difficulties I challenge you to shew one that is explained by Matter: nay, which is not more unintelligible with than without that supposition; and consequently makes rather *against* than *for* it. You should consider, in each particular, whether the difficulty arises from the *non-existence of Matter.* If it doth not, you might as well argue from the infinite divisibility of extension against the Divine prescience, as from such a difficulty against *Immaterialism.* And yet, upon recollection, I believe you will find this to have been often, if not always, the case. You should likewise take heed not to argue on a *petitio principii*. One is apt to say—The unknown substances ought to be esteemed real things, rather than the ideas in our minds: and who can tell but the unthinking external substance may concur, as a cause or instrument, in the productions of our ideas? But is not this proceeding on a supposition that there are such external substances? And to suppose this, is it not begging the question? But, above all things, you should beware of imposing on yourself by that vulgar sophism which is called *ignoratio elenchi*. You talked often as if you thought I maintained the non-existence of Sensible Things. Whereas in truth no one can be more thoroughly assured of their existence than I am. And it is you who doubt; I should have said, positively deny it. Everything that is seen, felt, heard, or any way perceived by the senses, is, on the principles I embrace, a real being; but not on yours. Remember, the Matter you contend for is an Unknown Somewhat (if indeed it may be termed *somewhat*), which is quite stripped of all sensible qualities, and can neither be perceived by sense, nor apprehended by the mind. Remember I say, that it is not any object which is hard or soft, hot or cold, blue or white, round or square, &c. For all these things I affirm do exist. Though indeed I deny they have an existence distinct from being perceived; or that they exist out of all minds whatsoever. Think on these points; let them be attentively considered and still kept in view. Otherwise you will not comprehend the state of the question; without which your objections will always be wide of the mark, and, instead of mine, may possibly be directed (as more than once they have been) against your own notions.

HYL. I must needs own, Philonous, nothing seems to have kept me from agreeing with you more than this same *mistaking the question*. In denying Matter, at first glimpse I am tempted to imagine you deny the things we see and feel: but, upon reflexion, find there is no ground for it. What think you, therefore, of retaining the name *Matter*, and applying it to *sensible things?* This may be done without any change in your sentiments: and, believe me, it would be a means of reconciling them to some persons who may be more shocked at an innovation in words than in opinion.

PHIL. With all my heart: retain the word *Matter,* and apply it to the objects of sense, if you please; provided you do not attribute to them any subsistence distinct from their being perceived. I shall never quarrel with you for an expression. *Matter,* or *material substance,* are terms introduced by philosophers; and, as used by them, imply a sort of independency, or a subsistence distinct from being perceived by a mind: but are never used by common people; or, if ever, it is to signify the immediate objects of sense. One would think, therefore, so long as the names of all particular things, with the terms *sensible, substance, body, stuff,* and the like, are retained, the word *Matter* should be never missed in common talk. And in philosophical discourses it seems the best way to leave it quite out: since there is not, perhaps, any one thing that hath more favoured and strengthened the depraved bent of the mind towards Atheism than the use of that general confused term.

HYL. Well but, Philonous, since I am content to give up the notion of an unthinking substance exterior to the mind, I think you ought not to deny me the privilege of using the word *Matter* as I please, and annexing it to a collection of sensible qualities subsisting only in the mind. I freely own there is no other substance, in a strict sense, than *Spirit.* But I have been so long accustomed to the *term Matter* that I know not how to part with it: to say, there is no *Matter* in the world, is still shocking to me. Whereas to say—There is no *Matter,* if by that term be meant an unthinking substance existing without the mind; but if by *Matter* is meant some sensible thing, whose existence consists in being perceived, then there is *Matter:*—this distinction gives it quite another turn; and men will come into your notions with small difficulty, when they are proposed in that manner. For, after all, the controversy about *Matter* in the strict acceptation of it, lies altogether between you and the philosophers: whose principles, I acknowledge, are not near so natural, or so agreeable to the common sense of mankind, and Holy Scripture, as yours. There is nothing we either desire or shun but as it makes, or is apprehended to make, some part of our happiness or misery. But what hath happiness or misery, joy or grief, pleasure or pain, to do with Absolute Existence; or with unknown entities, *abstracted from all relation to us?* It is evident, things regard us only as they are pleasing or displeasing: and they can please or displease only so far forth as they are perceived. Farther, therefore, we are not concerned; and thus far you leave things as you found them. Yet still there is something new in this doctrine. It is plain, I do not now think with the Philosophers; nor yet altogether with the vulgar. I would know how the case stands in that respect; precisely, what you have added to, or altered in my former notions.

PHIL. I do not pretend to be a setter-up of new notions. My endeavours tend only to unite, and place in a clearer light, that truth which was before shared between the vulgar and the philosophers:—the former being of opinion, that *those things they immediately perceive are the real things;* and the latter, that *the things immediately perceived are ideas, which exist only in the mind.* Which two notions put together, do, in effect, constitute the substance of what I advance.

HYL. I have been a long time distrusting my senses: methought I saw things by a dim light and through false glasses. Now the glasses are removed and a new light breaks in upon my understanding. I am clearly convinced that I see things in their native forms, and am no longer in pain about their *unknown natures* or *absolute existence*. This is the state I find myself in at present; though, indeed, the course that brought me to it I do not yet thoroughly comprehend. You set out upon the same principles that Academics, Cartesians, and the like sects usually do; and for a long time it looked as if you were advancing their philosophical Scepticism: but, in the end, your conclusions are directly opposite to theirs.

PHIL. You see, Hylas, the water of yonder fountain, how it is forced upwards, in a round column, to a certain height; at which it breaks, and falls back into the basin from whence it rose: its ascent, as well as descent, proceeding from the same uniform law or principle of gravitation. Just so, the same Principles which, at first view, lead to Scepticism, pursued to a certain point, bring men back to Common Sense.

# AN ENQUIRY CONCERNING
# HUMAN UNDERSTANDING

BY
**DAVID HUME**

# INTRODUCTORY NOTE

THE main facts of the life of David Hume will be found in the introductory note to his "Standard of Taste" in the volume of "English Essays" in the Harvard Classics.

Hume's most elaborate philosophical work was his "Treatise of Human Nature," published in three volumes in 1739-40. This work had been written between the ages of twenty-one and twenty-five; and in the "Advertisement" prefixed to the edition of his "Collected Essays," published the year after his death, he spoke slightingly of the "Treatise" as a juvenile work, marred by negligences both in reasoning and expression; and desired that the "Enquiry Concerning Human Understanding" and the "Enquiry Concerning the Principles of Morals" should "alone be regarded as containing his philosophical sentiments and principles."

While it is possible to take this depreciation of the "Treatise" too seriously, since it contains much of great philosophic importance which does not appear in the "Enquiries," yet the later works do represent his more mature thinking, and have the advantage of a much better style, at once more precise and more easily intelligible. To understand fully Hume's place in the history of European philosophy, it is still necessary to study the "Treatise"; but from the "Enquiry Concerning Human Understanding" one can gather much of his general attitude and method of thinking; while in such sections as that on "Miracles" we have an explanation of the bitter animosity that he roused in orthodox circles.

# AN ENQUIRY
# CONCERNING HUMAN
# UNDERSTANDING

## SECTION I

### OF THE DIFFERENT SPECIES OF PHILOSOPHY.

**M**ORAL philosophy, or the science of human nature, may be treated after two different manners; each of which has its peculiar merit, and may contribute to the entertainment, instruction, and reformation of mankind. The one considers man chiefly as born for action; and as influenced in his measures by taste and sentiment; pursuing one object, and avoiding another, according to the value which these objects seem to possess, and according to the light in which they present themselves. As virtue, of all objects, is allowed to be the most valuable, this species of philosophers paint her in the most amiable colours; borrowing all helps from poetry and eloquence, and treating their subject in an easy and obvious manner, and such as is best fitted to please the imagination, and engage the affections. They select the most striking observations and instances from common life; place opposite characters in a proper contrast; and alluring us into the paths of virtue by the views of glory and happiness, direct our steps in these paths by the soundest precepts and most illustrious examples. They make us *feel* the difference between vice and virtue; they excite and regulate our sentiments; and so they can but bend our hearts to the love of probity and true honour, they think, that they have fully attained the end of all their labours.

The other species of philosophers consider man in the

light of a reasonable rather than an active being, and endeavour to form his understanding more than cultivate his manners. They regard human nature as a subject of speculation; and with a narrow scrutiny examine it, in order to find those principles, which regulate our understanding, excite our sentiments, and make us approve or blame any particular object, action, or behaviour. They think it a reproach to all literature, that philosophy should not yet have fixed, beyond controversy, the foundation of morals, reasoning, and criticism; and should for ever talk of truth and falsehood, vice and virtue, beauty and deformity, without being able to determine the source of these distinctions. While they attempt this arduous task, they are deterred by no difficulties; but proceeding from particular instances to general principles, they still push on their enquiries to principles more general, and rest not satisfied till they arrive at those original principles, by which, in every science, all human curiosity must be bounded. Though their speculations seem abstract, and even unintelligible to common readers, they aim at the approbation of the learned and the wise; and think themselves sufficiently compensated for the labour of their whole lives, if they can discover some hidden truths, which may contribute to the instruction of posterity.

It is certain that the easy and obvious philosophy will always, with the generality of mankind, have the preference above the accurate and abstruse; and by many will be recommended, not only as more agreeable, but more useful than the other. It enters more into common life; moulds the heart and affections; and, by touching those principles which actuate men, reforms their conduct, and brings them nearer to that model of perfection which it describes. On the contrary, the abstruse philosophy, being founded on a turn of mind, which cannot enter into business and action, vanishes when the philosopher leaves the shade, and comes into open day; nor can its principles easily retain any influence over our conduct and behaviour. The feelings of our heart, the agitation of our passions, the vehemence of our affections, dissipate all its conclusions, and reduce the profound philosopher to a mere plebeian.

This also must be confessed, that the most durable, as well as justest fame, has been acquired by the easy philosophy, and that abstract reasoners seem hitherto to have enjoyed only a momentary reputation, from the caprice or ignorance of their own age, but have not been able to support their renown with more equitable posterity. It is easy for a profound philosopher to commit a mistake in his subtile reasonings; and one mistake is the necessary parent of another, while he pushes on his consequences, and is not deterred from embracing any conclusion, by its unusual appearance, or its contradiction to popular opinion. But a philosopher, who purposes only to represent the common sense of mankind in more beautiful and more engaging colours, if by accident he falls into error, goes no farther; but renewing his appeal to common sense, and the natural sentiments of the mind, returns into the right path, and secures himself from any dangerous illusions. The fame of Cicero flourishes at present; but that of Aristotle is utterly decayed. La Bruyere passes the seas, and still maintains his reputation: but the glory of Malebranche is confined to his own nation, and to his own age. And Addison, perhaps, will be read with pleasure, when Locke shall be entirely forgotten.

The mere philosopher is a character, which is commonly but little acceptable in the world, as being supposed to contribute nothing either to the advantage or pleasure of society; while he lives remote from communication with mankind, and is wrapped up in principles and notions equally remote from their comprehension. On the other hand, the mere ignorant is still more despised; nor is any thing deemed a surer sign of an illiberal genius in an age and nation where the sciences flourish, than to be entirely destitute of all relish for those noble entertainments. The most perfect character is supposed to lie between those extremes; retaining an equal ability and taste for books, company, and business; preserving in conversation that discernment and delicacy which arise from polite letters; and in business, that probity and accuracy which are the natural result of a just philosophy. In order to diffuse and cultivate so accomplished a character, nothing can be more useful than compositions of the easy style and manner, which draw not too much from life, require no deep application or retreat to be comprehended, and send back the student among mankind full of noble sentiments and wise precepts, applicable to every exigence of human life. By means of such compositions, virtue becomes amiable, science agreeable, company instructive, and retirement entertaining.

Man is a reasonable being; and as such, receives from science his proper food and nourishment: But so narrow are the bounds of human understanding, that little satisfaction can be hoped for in this particular, either from the extent of security or his acquisitions. Man is a sociable, no less than a reasonable being: but neither can he always enjoy company agreeable and amusing, or preserve the proper relish for them. Man is also an active being; and from that disposition, as well as from the various necessities of human life, must submit to business and occupation: but the mind requires some relaxation, and cannot always support its bent to care and industry. It seems, then, that nature has pointed out a mixed kind of life as most suitable to the human race, and secretly admonished them to allow none of these biases to *draw* too much, so as to incapacitate them for other occupations and entertainments. Indulge your passion for science, says she, but let your science be human, and such as may have a direct reference to action and society. Abstruse thought and profound researches I prohibit, and will severely punish, by the pensive melancholy which they introduce, by the endless uncertainty in which they involve you, and by the cold reception which your pretended discoveries shall meet with, when communicated. Be a philosopher; but, amidst all your philosophy, be still a man.

Were the generality of mankind contented to prefer the easy philosophy to the abstract and profound, without throwing any blame or contempt on the latter, it might not be improper, perhaps, to comply with this general opinion, and allow every man to enjoy, without opposition, his own taste and sentiment. But as the matter is often carried farther, even to the absolute rejecting of all profound reasonings, or what is commonly called *metaphysics*, we shall now proceed to consider what can reasonably be pleaded in their behalf.

We may begin with observing, that one considerable advantage, which results from the accurate and abstract philosophy, is, its subserviency to the easy and humane; which, without the former, can never attain a sufficient degree of exactness in its sentiments, precepts, or reasonings. All polite letters are nothing but pictures of human life in various attitudes and situations; and inspire us with different sentiments, of praise or blame, admiration or ridicule, according to the qualities of the object, which they set before us. An artist must be better qualified to succeed in this undertaking, who, besides a delicate taste and a quick apprehension, possesses an accurate knowledge of the internal fabric, the operations of the understanding, the workings of the passions, and the various species of sentiment which discriminate vice and virtue. How painful soever this inward search or enquiry may appear, it becomes, in some measure, requisite to those, who would describe with success the obvious and outward appearances of life and manners. The anatomist presents to the eye the most hideous and disagreeable objects; but his science is useful to the painter in delineating even a Venus or an Helen. While the latter employs all the richest colours of his art, and gives his figures the most graceful and engaging airs; he must still carry his attention to the inward structure of the human body, the position of the muscles, the fabric of the bones, and the use and figure of every part or organ. Accuracy is, in every case, advantageous to beauty, and just reasoning to delicate sentiment. In vain would we exalt the one by depreciating the other.

Besides, we may observe, in every art or profession, even those which most concern life or action, that a spirit of accuracy, however acquired, carries all of them nearer their perfection, and renders them more subservient to the interests of society. And though a philosopher may live remote from business, the genius of philosophy, if carefully cultivated by several, must gradually diffuse itself throughout the whole society, and bestow a similar correctness on every art and calling. The politician will acquire greater foresight and subtility, in the subdividing and balancing of power; the lawyer more method and finer principles in his reasonings; and the general more regularity in his discipline, and more caution in his plans and operations. The stability of modern governments above the ancient, and the accuracy of modern philosophy, have improved, and probably will still improve, by similar gradations.

Were there no advantage to be reaped from these studies, beyond the gratification of an innocent curiosity, yet ought not even this to be despised; as being one accession to those few safe and harmless pleasures, which are bestowed on the human race. The sweetest and most inoffensive path of life leads through the avenues of science and learning; and whoever can either remove any obstructions in this way, or open up any new prospect, ought so far to be esteemed a benefactor to mankind. And though these researches may appear painful and fatiguing, it is with some minds as with some bodies, which being endowed with vigorous and florid health, require severe exercise, and reap a pleasure from what, to the generality of mankind, may seem burdensome and laborious. Obscurity, indeed, is painful to the mind as well as to the eye; but to bring light from obscurity, by whatever labour, must needs be delightful and rejoicing.

But this obscurity in the profound and abstract philosophy, is objected to, not only as painful and fatiguing, but as the inevitable source of uncertainty and error. Here indeed lies the justest and most plausible objection against a considerable part of metaphysics, that they are not properly a science; but arise either from the fruitless efforts of human vanity, which would penetrate into subjects utterly inaccessible to the understanding, or from the craft of popular superstitions, which, being unable to defend themselves on fair ground, raise these intangling brambles to cover and protect their weakness. Chaced from the open country, these robbers fly into the forest, and lie in wait to break in upon every unguarded avenue of the mind, and overwhelm it with religious fears and prejudices. The stoutest antagonist, if he remit his watch a moment, is oppressed. And many, through cowardice and folly, open the gates to the enemies, and willingly receive them with reverence and submission, as their legal sovereigns.

But is this a sufficient reason, why philosophers should desist from such researches, and leave superstition still in possession of her retreat? Is it not proper to draw an opposite conclusion, and perceive the necessity of carrying the war into the most secret recesses of the enemy? In vain do we hope, that men, from frequent disappointment, will at last abandon such airy sciences, and discover the proper province of human reason. For, besides, that many persons find too sensible an interest in perpetually recalling such topics; besides this, I say, the motive of blind despair can never reasonably have place in the sciences; since, however unsuccessful former attempts may have proved, there is still room to hope, that the industry, good fortune, or improved sagacity of succeeding generations may reach discoveries unknown to former ages. Each adventurous genius will still leap at the arduous prize, and find himself stimulated, rather than discouraged, by the failures of his predecessors; while he hopes that the glory of achieving so hard an adventure is reserved for him alone. The only method of freeing learning, at once, from these abstruse questions, is to enquire seriously into the nature of human understanding, and show, from an exact analysis of its powers and capacity, that it is by no means fitted for such remote and abstruse subjects. We must submit to this fatigue in order to live at ease ever after: and must cultivate true metaphysics with some care, in order to destroy the false and adulterate. Indolence, which, to some persons, affords a safeguard against this deceitful philosophy, is, with others, overbalanced by curiosity; and despair, which, at some moments, prevails, may give place afterwards to sanguine hopes and expectations. Accurate and just reasoning is the only catholic remedy, fitted for all persons and all dispositions; and is alone able to subvert that abstruse philosophy and metaphysical jargon, which being mixed up with popular superstition, renders it in a manner impenetrable to careless reasoners, and gives it the air of science and wisdom.

Besides this advantage of rejecting, after deliberate en.
quiry, the most uncertain and disagreeable part of learning,
there are many positive advantages, which result from an
accurate scrutiny into the powers and faculties of human
nature. It is remarkable concerning the operations of the
mind, that, though most intimately present to us, yet,
whenever they become the object of reflexion, they seem
involved in obscurity; nor can the eye readily find those
lines and boundaries, which discriminate and distinguish
them. The objects are too fine to remain long in the same
aspect or situation; and must be apprehended in an instant, by a superior penetration, derived from nature, and
improved by habit and reflexion. It becomes, therefore,
no inconsiderable part of science barely to know the different
operations of the mind, to separate them from each other, to
class them under their proper heads, and to correct all that
seeming disorder, in which they lie involved, when made
the object of reflexion and enquiry. This talk of ordering
and distinguishing, which has no merit, when performed
with regard to external bodies, the objects of our senses,
rises in its value, when directed towards the operations
of the mind, in proportion to the difficulty and labour,
which we meet with in performing it. And if we can go no
farther than this mental geography, or delineation of the
distinct parts and powers of the mind, it is at least a satisfaction to go so far; and the more obvious this science
may appear (and it is by no means obvious) the more contemptible still must the ignorance of it be esteemed, in all
pretenders to learning and philosophy.

Nor can there remain any suspicion, that this science
is uncertain and chimerical; unless we should entertain
such a scepticism as is entirely subversive of all speculation,
and even action. It cannot be doubted, that the mind
is endowed with several powers and faculties, that these
powers are distinct from each other, that what is really
distinct to the immediate perception may be distinguished
by reflexion; and consequently, that there is a truth and
falsehood in all propositions on this subject, and a truth
and falsehood, which lie not beyond the compass of human
understanding. There are many obvious distinctions of

this kind, such as those between the will and understanding, the imagination and passions, which fall within the comprehension of every human creature; and the finer and more philosophical distinctions are no less real and certain, though more difficult to be comprehended. Some instances, especially late ones, of success in these enquiries, may give us a juster notion of the certainty and solidity of this branch of learning. And shall we esteem it worthy the labour of a philosopher to give us a true system of the planets, and adjust the position and order of those remote bodies; while we affect to overlook those, who, with so much success, delineate the parts of the mind, in which we are so intimately concerned?

But may we not hope, that philosophy, cultivated with care, and encouraged by the attention of the public, may carry its researches still farther, and discover, at least in some degree, the secret springs and principles, by which the human mind is actuated in its operations? Astronomers had long contented themselves with proving, from the phaenomena, the true motions, order, and magnitude of the heavenly bodies: till a philosopher, at last, arose, who seems, from the happiest reasoning, to have also determined the laws and forces, by which the revolutions of the planets are governed and directed. The like has been performed with regard to other parts of nature. And there is no reason to despair of equal success in our enquiries concerning the mental powers and economy, if prosecuted with equal capacity and caution. It is probable, that one operation and principle of the mind depends on another; which, again, may be resolved into one more general and universal: and how far these researches may possibly be carried, it will be difficult for us, before, or even after, a careful trial, exactly to determine. This is certain, that attempts of this kind are every day made even by those who philosophize the most negligently: and nothing can be more requisite than to enter upon the enterprize with thorough care and attention; that, if it lie within the compass of human understanding, it may at last be happily achieved; if not, it may, however, be rejected with some confidence and security. This last conclusion, surely, is not desirable; nor ought it to be embraced too rashly. For how much must we diminish from the beauty and value of this species of philosophy, upon such a supposition? Moralists have hitherto been accustomed, when they considered the vast multitude and diversity of those actions that excite our approbation or dislike, to search for some common principle, on which this variety of sentiments might depend. And though they have sometimes carried the matter too far, by their passion for some one general principle; it must, however, be confessed, that they are excusable in expecting to find some general principles, into which all the vices and virtues were justly to be resolved. The like has been the endeavour of critics, logicians, and even politicians: nor have their attempts been wholly unsuccessful; though perhaps longer time, greater accuracy, and more ardent application may bring these sciences still nearer their perfection. To throw up at once all pretensions of this kind may justly be deemed more rash, precipitate, and dogmatical, than even the boldest and most affirmative philosophy, that has ever attempted to impose its crude dictates and principles on mankind.

What though these reasonings concerning human nature seem abstract, and of difficult comprehension? This affords no presumption of their falsehood. On the contrary, it seems impossible, that what has hitherto escaped so many wise and profound philosophers can be very obvious and easy. And whatever pains these researches may cost us, we may think ourselves sufficiently rewarded, not only in point of profit but of pleasure, if, by that means, we can make any addition to our stock of knowledge, in subjects of such unspeakable importance.

But as, after all, the abstractedness of these speculations is no recommendation, but rather a disadvantage to them, and as this difficulty may perhaps be surmounted by care and art, and the avoiding of all unnecessary detail, we have, in the following enquiry, attempted to throw some light upon subjects, from which uncertainty has hitherto deterred the wise, and obscurity the ignorant. Happy, if we can unite the boundaries of the different species of philosophy, by reconciling profound enquiry with clearness, and truth with novelty! And still more happy, if, reasoning in this easy manner, we can undermine the foundations of an abstruse philosophy, which seems to have hitherto served only as a shelter to superstition, and a cover to absurdity and error!

# SECTION II

## OF THE ORIGIN OF IDEAS

EVERY one will readily allow, that there is a considerable difference between the perceptions of the mind, when a man feels the pain of excessive heat, or the pleasure of moderate warmth, and when he afterwards recalls to his memory this sensation, or anticipates it by his imagination. These faculties may mimic or copy the perceptions of the senses; but they never can entirely reach the force and vivacity of the original sentiment. The utmost we say of them, even when they operate with greatest vigour, is, that they represent their object in so lively a manner, that we could *almost* say we feel or see it: But, except the mind be disordered by disease or madness, they never can arrive at such a pitch of vivacity, as to render these perceptions altogether undistinguishable. All the colours of poetry, however splendid, can never paint natural objects in such a manner as to make the description be taken for a real landskip. The most lively thought is still inferior to the dullest sensation.

We may observe a like distinction to run through all the other perceptions of the mind. A man in a fit of anger, is actuated in a very different manner from one who only thinks of that emotion. If you tell me, that any person is in love, I easily understand your meaning, and from a just conception of his situation; but never can mistake that conception for the real disorders and agitations of the passion. When we reflect on our past sentiments and affections, our thought is a faithful mirror, and copies its objects truly; but the colours which it employs are faint and dull, in comparison of those in which our original perceptions were clothed. It requires no nice discernment or metaphysical head to mark the distinction between them.

316

Here therefore we may divide all the perceptions of the mind into two classes or species, which are distinguished by their different degrees of force and vivacity. The less forcible and lively are commonly denominated *Thoughts* or *Ideas*. The other species want a name in our language, and in most others; I suppose, because it was not requisite for any, but philosophical purposes, to rank them under a general term or appellation. Let us, therefore, use a little freedom, and call them *Impressions;* employing that word in a sense somewhat different from the usual. By the term *impression,* then, I mean all our more lively perceptions, when we hear, or see, or feel, or love, or hate, or desire, or will. And impressions are distinguished from ideas, which are the less lively perceptions, of which we are conscious, when we reflect on any of those sensations or movements above mentioned.

Nothing, at first view, may seem more unbounded than the thought of man, which not only escapes all human power and authority, but is not even restrained within the limits of nature and reality. To form monsters, and join incongruous shapes and appearances, costs the imagination no more trouble than to conceive the most natural and familiar objects. And while the body is confined to one planet, along which it creeps with pain and difficulty; the thought can in an instant transport us into the most distant regions of the universe; or even beyond the universe, into the unbounded chaos, where nature is supposed to lie in total confusion. What never was seen, or heard of, may yet be conceived; nor is any thing beyond the power of thought, except what implies an absolute contradiction.

But though our thought seems to possess this unbounded liberty, we shall find, upon a nearer examination, that it is really confined within very narrow limits, and that all this creative power of the mind amounts to no more than the faculty of compounding, transposing, augmenting, or diminishing the materials afforded us by the senses and experience. When we think of a golden mountain, we only join two consistent ideas, *gold,* and *mountain,* with which we were formerly acquainted. A virtuous horse we

can conceive; because, from our own feeling, we can
conceive virtue; and this we may unite to the figure and
shape of a horse, which is an animal familiar to us. In
short, all the materials of thinking are derived either from
our outward or inward sentiment: the mixture and composition of these belongs alone to the mind and will. Or,
to express myself in philosophical language, all our ideas or
more feeble perceptions are copies of our impressions or
more lively ones.

To prove this, the two following arguments will, I hope,
be sufficient. First, when we analyze our thoughts or ideas,
however compounded or sublime, we always find that they
resolve themselves into such simple ideas as were copied
from a precedent feeling or sentiment. Even those ideas,
which, at first view, seem the most wide of this origin, are
found, upon a nearer scrutiny, to be derived from it. The
idea of God, as meaning an infinitely intelligent, wise, and
good Being, arises from reflecting on the operations of our
own mind, and augmenting, without limit, those qualities
of goodness and wisdom. We may prosecute this enquiry
to what length we please; where we shall always find, that
every idea which we examine is copied from a similar
impression. Those who would assert that this position is
not universally true nor without exception, have only one,
and that an easy method of refuting it; by producing that
idea, which, in their opinion, is not derived from this source.
It will then be incumbent on us, if we would maintain our
doctrine, to produce the impression, or lively perception,
which corresponds to it.

Secondly. If it happen, from a defect of the organ,
that a man is not susceptible of any species of sensation,
we always find that he is as little susceptible of the correspondent ideas. A blind man can form no notion of
colours; a deaf man of sounds. Restore either of them
that sense in which he is deficient; by opening this new
inlet for his sensations, you also open an inlet for the ideas;
and he finds no difficulty in conceiving these objects. The
case is the same, if the object, proper for exciting any
sensation, has never been applied to the organ. A Lap-
lander or Negro has no notion of the relish of wine.

And though there are few or no instances of a like deficency in the mind, where a person has never felt or is wholly incapable of a sentiment or passion that belongs to his species; yet we find the same observation to take place in a less degree. A man of mild manners can form no idea of inveterate revenge or cruelty; nor can a selfish heart easily conceive the heights of friendship and generosity. It is readily allowed, that other beings may possess many senses of which we can have no conception; because the ideas of them have never been introduced to us in the only manner by which an idea can have access to the mind, to wit, by the actual feeling and sensation.

There is, however, one contradictory phenomenon, which may prove that it is not absolutely impossible for ideas to arise, independent of their correspondent impressions. I believe it will readily be allowed, that the several distinct ideas of colour, which enter by the eye, or those of sound, which are conveyed by the ear, are really different from each other; though, at the same time, resembling. Now if this be true of different colours, it must be no less so of the different shades of the same colour; and each shade produces a distinct idea, independent of the rest. For if this should be denied, it is possible, by the continual gradation of shades, to run a colour insensibly into what is most remote from it; and if you will not allow any of the means to be different, you cannot, without absurdity, deny the extremes to be the same. Suppose, therefore, a person to have enjoyed his sight for thirty years, and to have become perfectly acquainted with colours of all kinds except one particular shade of blue, for instance, which it never has been his fortune to meet with. Let all the different shades of that colour, except that single one, be placed before him, descending gradually from the deepest to the lightest; it is plain that he will perceive a blank, where that shade is wanting, and will be sensible that there is a greater distance in that place between the contiguous colour than in any other. Now I ask, whether it be possible for him, from his own imagination, to supply this deficiency, and raise up to himself the idea of that particular shade, though it had never been conveyed to him by his senses? I believe there are few but will be of opinion that he can: and this may serve as a proof that the simple ideas are not always, in every instance, derived from the correspondent impressions; though this instance is so singular, that it is scarcely worth our observing, and does not merit that for it alone we should alter our general maxim.

Here, therefore, is a proposition, which not only seems, in itself, simple and intelligible; but, if a proper use were made of it, might render every dispute equally intelligible, and banish all that jargon, which has so long taken possession of metaphysical reasonings, and drawn disgrace upon them. All ideas, especially abstract ones, are naturally faint and obscure: the mind has but a slender hold of them: they are apt to be confounded with other resembling ideas; and when we have often employed any term, though without a distinct meaning, we are apt to imagine it has a determinate idea annexed to it. On the contrary, all impressions, that is, all sensations, either outward or inward, are strong and vivid: the limits between them are more exactly determined: nor is it easy to fall into any error or mistake with regard to them. When we entertain, therefore, any suspicion that a philosophical term is employed without any meaning or idea (as is but too frequent), we need but enquire, *from what impression is that supposed idea derived?* And if it be impossible to assign any, this will serve to confirm our suspicion. By bringing ideas into so clear a light we may reasonably hope to remove all dispute, which may arise, concerning their nature and reality.[1]

---

[1] It is probable that no more was meant by those, who denied innate ideas, than that all ideas were copies of our impressions; though it must be confessed, that the terms, which they employed, were not chosen with such caution, nor so exactly defined, as to prevent all mistakes about their doctrine. For what is meant by *innate?* If innate be equivalent to natural, then all the perceptions and ideas of the mind must be allowed to be innate or natural, in whatever sense we take the latter word, whether in opposition to what is uncommon, artificial, or miraculous. If by innate be meant, contemporary to our birth, the dispute seems to be frivolous; nor is it worth while to enquire at what time thinking begins, whether before, at, or after our birth. Again, the word *idea,* seems to be commonly taken in a very loose sense, by LOCKE and others; as standing for any of our perceptions, our sensations and passions, as well as thoughts. Now in this sense, I should desire to know, what can be meant by asserting, that self-love, or resentment of injuries, or the passion between the sexes is not innate? But admitting these terms, *impressions* and *ideas,* in the sense above explained, and understanding by *innate,* what is original or copied from

no precedent perception, then may we assert that all our impressions are innate, and our ideas not innate.

To be ingenuous, I must own it to be my opinion, that LOCKE was betrayed into this question by the schoolmen, who, making use of undefined terms, draw out their disputes to a tedious length, without ever touching the point in question. A like ambiguity and circumlocution seem to run through that philosopher's reasonings on this as well as most other subjects.

# SECTION III

## OF THE ASSOCIATION OF IDEAS

IT IS evident that there is a principle of connexion between the different thoughts or ideas of the mind, and that in their appearance to the memory or imagination, they introduce each other with a certain degree of method and regularity. In our more serious thinking or discourse this is so observable that any particular thought, which breaks in upon the regular tract or chain of ideas, is immediately remarked and rejected. And even in our wildest and most wandering reveries, nay in our very dreams, we shall find, if we reflect, that the imagination ran not altogether at adventures, but that there was still a connexion upheld among the different ideas, which succeeded each other. Were the loosest and freest conversation to be transcribed, there would immediately be observed something which connected it in all its transitions. Or where this is wanting, the person who broke the thread of discourse might still inform you, that there had secretly revolved in his mind a succession of thought, which had gradually led him from the subject of conversation. Among different languages, even where we cannot suspect the least connexion or communication, it is found, that the words, expressive of ideas, the most compounded, do yet nearly correspond to each other: a certain proof that the simple ideas, comprehended in the compound ones, were bound together by some universal principle, which had an equal influence on all mankind.

Though it be too obvious to escape observation, that different ideas are connected together; I do not find that any philosopher has attempted to enumerate or class all the principles of association; a subject, however, that seems worthy of curiosity. To me, there appear to be only three principles of connexion among ideas, namely, *Resemblance, Contiguity* in time or place, and *Cause* or *Effect*.

That these principles serve to connect ideas will not, I believe, be much doubted. A picture naturally leads our thoughts to the original:[1] the mention of one apartment in a building naturally introduces an enquiry or discourse concerning the others:[2] and if we think of a wound, we can scarcely forbear reflecting on the pain which follows it.[3] But that this enumeration is complete, and that there are no other principles of association except these, may be difficult to prove to the satisfaction of the reader, or even to a man's own satisfaction. All we can do, in such cases, is to run over several instances, and examine carefully the principle which binds the different thoughts to each other, never stopping till we render the principle as general as possible.[4] The more instances we examine, and the more care we employ, the more assurance shall we acquire, that the enumeration, which we form from the whole, is complete and entire.

[1] Resemblance.  [2] Contiguity.  [3] Cause and effect.
[4] For instance, Contrast or Contrariety is also a connexion among Ideas: but it may, perhaps, be considered as a mixture of *Causation* and *Resemblance*. Where two objects are contrary, the one destroys the other; that is, the cause of its annihilation, and the idea of the annihilation of an object, implies the idea of its former existence.

# SECTION IV

## Part I

ALL the objects of human reason or enquiry may
naturally be divided into two kinds, to wit, *Relations of Ideas,* and *Matters of Fact.* Of the first
kind are the sciences of ¡Geometry, Algebra, and Arithmetic;
and in short, every affirmation which is either intuitively or
demonstratively certain. *That the square of the hypothenuse
is equal to the square of the two sides,* is a proposition
which expresses a relation between these figures. *That
three times five is equal to the half of thirty,* expresses a
relation between these numbers. Propositions of this kind
are discoverable by the mere operation of thought, without
dependence on what is anywhere existent in the universe.
Though there never were a circle or triangle in nature, the
truths demonstrated by Euclid would for ever retain their
certainty and evidence.

Matters of fact, which are the second objects of human
reason, are not ascertained in the same manner; nor is our
evidence of their truth, however great, of a like nature with
the foregoing. The contrary of every matter of fact is still
possible; because it can never imply a contradiction, and
is conceived by the mind with the same facility and distinctness, as if ever so conformable to reality. *That the
sun will not rise to-morrow* is no less intelligible a proposition, and implies no more contradiction than the affirmation, *that it will rise.* We should in vain, therefore, attempt
to demonstrate its falsehood. Were it demonstratively false,
it would imply a contradiction, and could never be distinctly conceived by the mind.

It may, therefore, be a subject worthy of curiosity, to
enquire what is the nature of that evidence which assures

us of any real existence and matter of fact, beyond the present testimony of our senses, or the records of our memory. This part of philosophy, it is observable, has been little cultivated, either by the ancients or moderns; and therefore our doubts and errors, in the prosecution of so important an enquiry, may be the more excusable; while we march through such difficult paths without any guide or direction. They may even prove useful, by exciting curiosity, and destroying that implicit faith and security, which is the bane of all reasoning and free enquiry. The discovery of defects in the common philosophy, if any such there be, will not, I presume, be a discouragement, but rather an incitement, as is usual, to attempt something more full and satisfactory than has yet been proposed to the public.

All reasonings concerning matter of fact seem to be founded on the relation of *Cause and Effect*. By means of that relation alone we can go beyond the evidence of our memory and senses. If you were to ask a man, why he believes any matter of fact, which is absent; for instance, that his friend is in the country, or in France; he would give you a reason; and this reason would be some other fact; as a letter received from him, or the knowledge of his former resolutions and promises. A man finding a watch or any other machine in a desert island, would conclude that there had once been men in that island. All our reasonings concerning fact are of the same nature. And here it is constantly supposed that there is a connexion between the present fact and that which is inferred from it. Were there nothing to bind them together, the inference would be entirely precarious. The hearing of an articulate voice and rational discourse in the dark assures us of the presence of some person: Why? because these are the effects of the human make and fabric, and closely connected with it. If we anatomize all the other reasonings of this nature, we shall find that they are founded on the relation of cause and effect, and that this relation is either near or remote, direct or collateral. Heat and light are collateral effects of fire, and the one effect may justly be inferred from the other.

If we would satisfy ourselves, therefore, concerning the nature of that evidence, which assures us of matters of fact, we must enquire how we arrive at the knowledge of cause and effect.

I shall venture to affirm, as a general proposition, which admits of no exception, that the knowledge of this relation is not, in any instance, attained by reasonings *a priori;* but arises entirely from experience, when we find that any particular objects are constantly conjoined with each other. Let an object be presented to a man of ever so strong natural reason and abilities; if that object be entirely new to him, he will not be able, by the most accurate examination of its sensible qualities, to discover any of its causes or effects. Adam, though his rational faculties be supposed, at the very first, entirely perfect, could not have inferred from the fluidity and transparency of water that it would suffocate him, or from the light and warmth of fire that it would consume him. No object ever discovers, by the qualities which appear to the senses, either the causes which produced it, or the effects which will arise from it; nor can our reason, unassisted by experience, ever draw any inference concerning real existence and matter of fact.

This proposition, *that causes and effects are discoverable, not by reason but by experience,* will readily be admitted with regard to such objects, as we remember to have once been altogether unknown to us; since we must be conscious of the utter inability, which we then lay under, of foretelling what would arise from them. Present two smooth pieces of marble to a man who has no tincture of natural philosophy; he will never discover that they will adhere together in such a manner as to require great force to separate them in a direct line, while they make so small a resistance to a lateral pressure. Such events, as bear little analogy to the common course of nature, are also readily confessed to be known only by experience; nor does any man imagine that the explosion of gunpowder, or the attraction of a loadstone, could ever be discovered by arguments *a priori.* In like manner, when an effect is supposed to depend upon an intricate machinery or secret structure of parts, we make no difficulty in attributing all our knowledge of it to experience.

Who will assert that he can give the ultimate reason, why milk or bread is proper nourishment for a man, not for a lion or a tiger?

But the same truth may not appear, at first sight, to have the same evidence with regard to events, which have become familiar to us from our first appearance in the world, which bear a close analogy to the whole course of nature, and which are supposed to depend on the simple qualities of objects, without any secret structure of parts. We are apt to imagine that we could discover these effects by the mere operation of our reason, without experience. We fancy, that were we brought on a sudden into this world, we could at first have inferred that one Billiard-ball would communicate motion to another upon impulse; and that we needed not to have waited for the event, in order to pronounce with certainty concerning it. Such is the influence of custom, that, where it is strongest, it not only covers our natural ignorance, but even conceals itself, and seems not to take place, merely because it is found in the highest degree.

But to convince us that all the laws of nature, and all the operations of bodies without exception, are known only by experience, the following reflections may, perhaps, suffice. Were any object presented to us, and were we required to pronounce concerning the effect, which will result from it, without consulting past observation; after what manner, I beseech you, must the mind proceed in this operation? It must invent or imagine some event, which it ascribes to the object as its effect; and it is plain that this invention must be entirely arbitrary. The mind can never possibly find the effect in the supposed cause, by the most accurate scrutiny and examination. For the effect is totally different from the cause, and consequently can never be discovered in it. Motion in the second Billiard-ball is a quite distinct event from motion in the first; nor is there anything in the one to suggest the smallest hint of the other. A stone or piece of metal raised into the air, and left without any support, immediately falls: but to consider the matter *a priori,* is there anything we discover in this situation which can beget the idea of a downward, rather than an upward, or any other motion, in the stone or metal?

And as the first imagination or invention of a particular effect, in all natural operations, is arbitrary, where we consult not experience; so must we also esteem the supposed tie or connexion between the cause and effect, which binds them together, and renders it impossible that any other effect could result from the operation of that cause. When I see, for instance, a Billiard-ball moving in a straight line towards another; even suppose motion in the second ball should by accident be suggested to me, as the result of their contact or impulse; may I not conceive, that a hundred different events might as well follow from that cause? May not both these balls remain at absolute rest? May not the first ball return in a straight line, or leap off from the second in any line or direction? All these suppositions are consistent and conceivable. Why then should we give the preference to one, which is no more consistent or conceivable than the rest? All our reasonings *a priori* will never be able to show us any foundation for this preference.

In a word, then, every effect is a distinct event from its cause. It could not, therefore, be discovered in the cause, and the first invention or conception of it, *a priori,* must be entirely arbitrary. And even after it is suggested, the conjunction of it with the cause must appear equally arbitrary; since there are always many other effects, which, to reason, must seem fully as consistent and natural. In vain, therefore, should we pretend to determine any single event, or infer any cause or effect, without the assistance of observation and experience.

Hence we may discover the reason why no philosopher, who is rational and modest, has ever pretended to assign the ultimate cause of any natural operation, or to show distinctly the action of that power, which produces any single effect in the universe. It is confessed, that the utmost effort of human reason is to reduce the principles, productive of natural phenomena, to a greater simplicity, and to resolve the many particular effects into a few general causes, by means of reasonings from analogy, experience, and observation. But as to the causes of these general causes, we should in vain attempt their discovery; nor shall we ever be able to satisfy ourselves, by any particular explication of them. These ultimate springs and principles are totally shut up from human curiosity and enquiry. Elasticity, gravity, cohesion of parts, communication of motion by impulse; these are probably the ultimate causes and principles which we shall ever discover in nature; and we may esteem ourselves sufficiently happy, if, by accurate enquiry and reasoning, we can trace up the particular phenomena to, or near to, these general principles. The most perfect philosophy of the natural kind only staves off our ignorance a little longer: as perhaps the most perfect philosophy of the moral or metaphysical kind serves only to discover larger portions of it. Thus the observation of human blindness and weakness is the result of all philosophy, and meets us at every turn, in spite of our endeavours to elude or avoid it.

Nor is geometry, when taken into the assistance of natural philosophy, ever able to remedy this defect, or lead us into the knowledge of ultimate causes, by all that accuracy of reasoning for which it is so justly celebrated. Every part of mixed mathematics proceeds upon the supposition that certain laws are established by nature in her operations; and abstract reasonings are employed, either to assist experience in the discovery of these laws, or to determine their influence in particular instances, where it depends upon any precise degree of distance and quantity. Thus, it is a law of motion, discovered by experience, that the moment or force of any body in motion is in the compound ratio or proportion of its solid contents and its velocity; and consequently, that a small force may remove the greatest obstacle or raise the greatest weight, if, by any contrivance or machinery, we can increase the velocity of that force, so as to make it an overmatch for its antagonist. Geometry assists us in the application of this law, by giving us the just dimensions of all the parts and figures which can enter into any species of machine; but still the discovery of the law itself is owing merely to experience, and all the abstract reasonings in the world could never lead us one step towards the knowledge of it. When we reason *a priori,* and consider merely any object or cause, as it appears to the mind, independent of all observation, it never could suggest to us the notion of any distinct object, such as its effect; much less, show us the inseparable and inviolable connexion between them. A man must be very sagacious who could discover by reasoning that crystal is the effect of heat, and ice of cold, without being previously acquainted with the operation of these qualities.

## Part II

BUT we have not yet attained any tolerable satisfaction with regard to the question first proposed. Each solution still gives rise to a new question as difficult as the foregoing, and leads us on to farther enquiries. When it is asked, *What is the nature of all our reasonings concerning matter of fact?* the proper answer seems to be, that they are founded on the relation of cause and effect. When again it is asked, *What is the foundation of all our reasonings and conclusions concerning that relation?* it may be replied in one word, Experience. But if we still carry on our sifting humour, and ask, *What is the foundation of all conclusions from experience?* this implies a new question, which may be of more difficult solution and explication. Philosophers, that give themselves airs of superior wisdom and sufficiency, have a hard task when they encounter persons of inquisitive dispositions, who push them from every corner to which they retreat, and who are sure at last to bring them to some dangerous dilemma. The best expedient to prevent this confusion, is to be modest in our pretensions; and even to discover the difficulty ourselves before it is objected to us. By this means, we may make a kind of merit of our very ignorance.

I shall content myself, in this section, with an easy task, and shall pretend only to give a negative answer to the question here proposed. I say then, that even after we have experience of the operations of cause and effect, our conclusions from that experience are *not* founded on reasoning, or any process of the understanding. This answer we must endeavour both to explain and to defend.

It must certainly be allowed, that nature has kept us at a great distance from all her secrets, and has afforded us only the knowledge of a few superficial qualities of objects; while she conceals from us those powers and principles on which the influence of those objects entirely depends. Our senses inform us of the colour, weight, and consistence of bread; but neither sense nor reason can ever inform us of those qualities which fit it for the nourishment and support of a human body. Sight or feeling conveys an idea of the actual motion of bodies; but as to that wonderful force or power, which would carry on a moving body for ever in a continued change of place, and which bodies never lose but by communicating it to others; of this we cannot form the most distant conception. But notwithstanding this ignorance of natural powers[1] and principles, we always presume, when we see like sensible qualities, that they have like secret powers, and expect that effects, similar to those which we have experienced, will follow from them. If a body of like colour and consistence with that bread, which we have formerly eat, be presented to us, we make no scruple of repeating the experiment, and foresee, with certainty, like nourishment and support. Now this is a process of the mind or thought, of which I would willingly know the foundation. It is allowed on all hands that there is no known connexion between the sensible qualities and the secret powers; and consequently, that the mind is not led to form such a conclusion concerning their constant and regular conjunction, by anything which it knows of their nature. As to past *Experience,* it can be allowed to give *direct* and *certain* information of those precise objects only, and that precise period of time, which fell under its cognizance: but why this experience should be extended to future times, and to other objects, which for aught we know, may be only in appearance similar; this is the main question on which I would insist. The bread, which I formerly eat, nourished me; that is, a body of such sensible qualities was, at that time, endued with such secret powers: but does it follow, that other bread must also nourish me at another time, and that like sensible qualities must always be attended with like secret powers? The consequence seems nowise necessary. At least, it must be acknowledged that there is here

[1] The word, Power, is here used in a loose and popular sense. The more accurate explication of it would give additional evidence to this argument. See Sect. 7.

a consequence drawn by the mind; that there is a certain step taken; a process of thought, and an inference, which wants to be explained. These two propositions are far from being the same. *I have found that such an object has always been attended with such an effect,* and *I foresee, that other objects, which are, in appearance, similar, will be attended with similar effects.* I shall allow, if you please, that the one proposition may justly be inferred from the other: I know, in fact, that it always is inferred. But if you insist that the inference is made by a chain of reasoning, I desire you to produce that reasoning. The connexion between these propositions is not intuitive. There is required a medium, which may enable the mind to draw such an inference, if indeed it be drawn by reasoning and argument. What that medium is, I must confess, passes my comprehension; and it is incumbent on those to produce it, who asert that it really exists, and is the origin of all our conclusions concerning matter of fact.

This negative argument must certainly, in process of time, become altogether convincing, if many penetrating and able philosophers shall turn their enquiries this way and no one be ever able to discover any connecting proposition or intermediate step, which supports the understanding in this conclusion. But as the question is yet new, every reader may not trust so far to his own penetration, as to conclude, because an argument escapes his enquiry, that therefore it does not really exist. For this reason it may be requisite to venture upon a more difficult task; and enumerating all the branches of human knowledge, endeavour to show that none of them can afford such an argument.

All reasonings may be divided into two kinds, namely, demonstrative reasoning, or that concerning relations of ideas, and moral reasoning, or that concerning matter of fact and existence. That there are no demonstrative arguments in the case seems evident; since it implies no contradiction that the course of nature may change, and that an object, seemingly like those which we have experienced, may be attended with different or contrary effects. May I not clearly and distinctly conceive that a body, falling from the clouds, and which, in all other respects, resembles snow, has yet the taste of salt or feeling of fire? Is there any more intelligible proposition than to affirm, that all the trees will flourish in December and January, and decay in May and June? Now whatever is intelligible, and can be distinctly conceived, implies no contradiction, and can never be proved false by any demonstrative argument or abstract reasoning *à priori*.

If we be, therefore, engaged by arguments to put trust in past experience, and make it the standard of our future judgment, these arguments must be probable only, or such as regard matter of fact and real existence according to the division above mentioned. But that there is no argument of this kind, must appear, if our explication of that species of reasoning be admitted as solid and satisfactory. We have said that all arguments concerning existence are founded on the relation of cause and effect; that our knowledge of that relation is derived entirely from experience; and that all our experimental conclusions proceed upon the supposition that the future will be conformable to the past. To endeavour, therefore, the proof of this last supposition by probable arguments, or arguments regarding existence, must be evidently going in a circle, and taking that for granted, which is the very point in question.

In reality, all arguments from experience are founded on the similarity which we discover among natural objects, and by which we are induced to expect effects similar to those which we have found to follow from such objects. And though none but a fool or madman will ever pretend to dispute the authority of experience, or to reject that great guide of human life, it may surely be allowed a philosopher to have so much curiosity at least as to examine the principle of human nature, which gives this mighty authority to experience, and makes us draw advantage from that similarity which nature has placed among different objects. From causes which appear *similar* we expect similar effects. This is the sum of all our experimental conclusions. Now it seems evident that, if this conclusion were formed by reason, it would be as perfect at first, and upon one instance, as after ever so long a course of experience. But the case is far otherwise. Nothing so like as eggs; yet no one, on account of this appearing similarity, expects the same taste and relish in all of them. It is only after a long course of uniform experiments in any kind, that we attain a firm reliance and security with regard to a particular event. Now where is that process of reasoning which, from one instance, draws a conclusion, so different from that which it infers from a hundred instances that are nowise different from that single one? This question I propose as much for the sake of information, as with an intention of raising difficulties. I cannot find, I cannot imagine any such reasoning. But I keep my mind still open to instruction, if any one will vouchsafe to bestow it on me.

Should it be said that, from a number of uniform experiments, we *infer* a connexion between the sensible qualities and the secret powers; this, I must confess, seems the same difficulty, couched in different terms. The question still recurs, on what process of argument this *inference* is founded? Where is the medium, the interposing ideas, which join propositions so very wide of each other? It is confessed that the colour, consistence, and other sensible qualities of bread appear not, of themselves, to have any connexion with the secret powers of nourishment and support. For otherwise we could infer these secret powers from the first appearance of these sensible qualities, without the aid of experience; contrary to the sentiment of all philosophers, and contrary to plain matter of fact. Here, then, is our natural state of ignorance with regard to the powers and influence of all objects. How is this remedied by experience? It only shows us a number of uniform effects, resulting from certain objects, and teaches us that those particular objects, at that particular time, were endowed with such powers and forces. When a new object, endowed with similar sensible qualities, is produced, we expect similar powers and forces, and look for a like effect. From a body of like colour and consistence with bread we expect like nourishment and support. But this surely is a step or progress of the mind, which wants to be explained. When a man says, *I have found, in all past instances, such sensible qualities conjoined with such secret powers:* And when he says, *Similar sensible qualities will always be conjoined with similar secret powers,* he is not guilty of a tautology, nor are these propositions in any respect the same. You say that the one proposition is an inference from the other. But you must confess that the inference is not intuitive; neither is it demonstrative: Of what nature is it, then? To say it is experimental, is begging the question. For all inferences from experience suppose, as their foundation, that the future will resemble the past, and that similar powers will be conjoined with similar sensible qualities. If there be any suspicion that the course of nature may change, and that the past may be no rule for the future, all experience becomes useless, and can give rise to no inference or conclusion. It is impossible, therefore, that any arguments from experience can prove this resemblance of the past to the future; since all these arguments are founded on the supposition of that resemblance. Let the course of things be allowed hitherto ever so regular; that alone, without some new argument or inference, proves not that, for the future, it will continue so. In vain do you pretend to have learned the nature of bodies from your past experience. Their secret nature, and consequently all their effects and influence, may change, without any change in their sensible qualities. This happens sometimes, and with regard to some objects: Why may it not happen always, and with regard to all objects? What logic, what process or argument secures you against this supposition? My practice, you say, refutes my doubts. But you mistake the purport of my question. As an agent, I am quite satisfied in the point; but as a philosopher, who has some share of curiosity, I will not say scepticism, I want to learn the foundation of this inference. No reading, no enquiry has yet been able to remove my difficulty, or give me satisfaction in a matter of such importance. Can I do better than propose the difficulty to the public, even though, perhaps, I have small hopes of obtaining a solution? We shall at least, by this means, be sensible of our ignorance, if we do not augment our knowledge.

I must confess that a man is guilty of unpardonable

arrogance who concludes, because an argument has escaped his own investigation, that therefore it does not really exist. I must also confess that, though all the learned, for several ages, should have employed themselves in fruitless search upon any subject, it may still, perhaps, be rash to conclude positively that the subject must, therefore, pass all human comprehension. Even though we examine all the sources of our knowledge, and conclude them unfit for such a subject, there may still remain a suspicion, that the enumeration is not complete, or the examination not accurate. But with regard to the present subject, there are some considerations which seem to remove all this accusation of arrogance or suspicion of mistake.

It is certain that the most ignorant and stupid peasants—nay infants, nay even brute beasts—improve by experience, and learn the qualities of natural objects, by observing the effects which result from them. When a child has felt the sensation of pain from touching the flame of a candle, he will be careful not to put his hand near any candle; but will expect a similar effect from a cause which is similar in its sensible qualities and appearance. If you assert, therefore, that the understanding of the child is led into this conclusion by any process of argument or ratiocination, I may justly require you to produce that argument; nor have you any pretence to refuse so equitable a demand. You cannot say that the argument is abstruse, and may possibly escape your enquiry; since you confess that it is obvious to the capacity of a mere infant. If you hesitate, therefore, a moment, or if, after reflection, you produce any intricate or profound argument, you, in a manner, give up the question, and confess that it is not reasoning which engages us to suppose the past resembling the future, and to expect similar effects from causes which are, to appearance, similar. This is the proposition which I intended to enforce in the present section. If I be right, I pretend not to have made any mighty discovery. And if I be wrong, I must acknowledge myself to be indeed a very backward scholar; since I cannot now discover an argument which, it seems, was perfectly familiar to me long before I was out of my cradle.

# SECTION V

## SCEPTICAL SOLUTION OF THESE DOUBTS

### PART I

THE passion for philosophy, like that for religion, seems liable to this inconvenience, that, though it aims at the correction of our manners, and extirpation of our vices, it may only serve, by imprudent management, to foster a predominant inclination, and push the mind, with more determined resolution, towards that side which already *draws* too much, by the bias and propensity of the natural temper. It is certain that, while we aspire to the magnanimous firmness of the philosophic sage, and endeavour to confine our pleasures altogether within our own minds, we may, at last, render our philosophy like that of Epictetus, and other *Stoics,* only a more refined system of selfishness, and reason ourselves out of all virtue as well as social enjoyment. While we study with attention the vanity of human life, and turn all our thoughts towards the empty and transitory nature of riches and honours, we are, perhaps, all the while flattering our natural indolence, which, hating the bustle of the world, and drudgery of business, seeks a pretence of reason to give itself a full and uncontrolled indulgence. There is, however, one species of philosophy which seems little liable to this inconvenience, and that because it strikes in with no disorderly passion of the human mind, nor can mingle itself with any natural affection or propensity; and that is the Academic or Sceptical philosophy. The academics always talk of doubt and suspense of judgment, of danger in hasty determinations, of confining to very narrow bounds the enquiries of the understanding, and of renouncing all speculations which lie not within the limits of common life and practice. Nothing, therefore, can be more contrary than such a philosophy to the supine indolence of the mind, its rash arrogance, its lofty pretensions, and its superstitious credulity. Every passion is mortified by it, except the love of truth; and that passion never is, nor can be, carried to too high a degree. It is surprising, therefore, that this philosophy, which, in almost every instance, must be harmless and innocent, should be the subject of so much groundless reproach and obloquy. But, perhaps, the very circumstance which renders it so innocent is what chiefly exposes it to the public hatred and resentment. By flattering no irregular passion, it gains few partizans: By opposing so many vices and follies, it raises to itself abundance of enemies, who stigmatize it as libertine, profane, and irreligious.

Nor need we fear that this philosophy, while it endeavours to limit our enquiries to common life, should ever undermine the reasonings of common life, and carry its doubts so far as to destroy all action, as well as speculation. Nature will always maintain her rights, and prevail in the end over any abstract reasoning whatsoever. Though we should conclude, for instance, as in the foregoing section, that, in all reasonings from experience, there is a step taken by the mind which is not supported by any argument or process of the understanding; there is no danger that these reasonings, on which almost all knowledge depends, will ever be affected by such a discovery. If the mind be not engaged by argument to make this step, it must be induced by some other principle of equal weight and authority; and that principle will preserve its influence as long as human nature remains the same. What that principle is may well be worth the pains of enquiry.

Suppose a person, though endowed with the strongest faculties of reason and reflection, to be brought on a sudden into this world; he would, indeed, immediately observe a continual succession of objects, and one event following another; but he would not be able to discover anything farther. He would not, at first, by any reasoning, be able to reach the idea of cause and effect; since the particular powers, by which all natural operations are performed, never appear to the senses; nor is it reasonable to conclude, merely because one event, in one instance, precedes another, that therefore the one is the cause, the other the effect. Their conjunction may be arbitrary and casual. There may be no reason to infer the existence of one from the appearance of the other. And in a word, such a person, without more experience, could never employ his conjecture or reasoning concerning any matter of fact, or be assured of anything beyond what was immediately present to his memory and senses.

Suppose, again, that he has acquired more experience, and has lived so long in the world as to have observed familiar objects or events to be constantly conjoined together; what is the consequence of this experience? He immediately infers the existence of one object from the appearance of the other. Yet he has not, by all his experience, acquired any idea or knowledge of the secret power by which the one object produces the other; nor is it by any process of reasoning, he is engaged to draw this inference. But still he finds himself determined to draw it: and though he should be convinced that his understanding has no part in the operation, he would nevertheless continue in the same course of thinking. There is some other principle which determines him to form such a conclusion.

This principle is Custom or Habit. For wherever the repetition of any particular act or operation produces a propensity to renew the same act or operation, without being impelled by any reasoning or process of the understanding, we always say, that this propensity is the effect of *Custom*. By employing that word, we pretend not to have given the ultimate reason of such a propensity. We only point out a principle of human nature, which is universally acknowledged, and which is well known by its effects. Perhaps we can push our enquiries no farther, or pretend to give the cause of this cause; but must rest contented with it as the ultimate principle, which we can assign, of all our conclusions from experience. It is sufficient satisfaction, that we can go so far, without repining at the narrowness of our faculties because they will carry us no farther. And it is certain we here advance a very intelligible proposition at least, if not a true one, when we assert that, after the constant conjunction of two objects—heat and flame, for instance, weight and solidity—we are determined by custom alone to expect the one from the appearance of the other. This hypothesis seems even the only one which explains the difficulty, why we draw, from a thousand instances, an inference which we are not able to draw from one instance, that is, in no respect, different from them. Reason is incapable of any such variation. The conclusions which it draws from considering one circle are the same which it would form upon surveying all the circles in the universe. But no man, having seen only one body move after being impelled by another, could infer that every other body will move after a like impulse. All inferences from experience, therefore, are effects of custom, not of reasoning[1].

[1] Nothing is more useful than for writers, even, on *moral, political,* or *physical* subjects, to distinguish between *reason* and *experience,* and to suppose, that these species of argumentation are entirely different from each other. The former are taken for the mere result of our intellectual faculties, which, by considering *à priori* the nature of things, and examining the effects, that must follow from their operation, establish particular principles of science and philosophy. The latter are supposed to be derived entirely from sense and observation, by which we learn what has actually resulted from the operation of particular objects, and are thence able to infer, what will, for the future, result from them. Thus, for instance, the limitations and restraints of civil government, and a legal constitution, may be defended, either from *reason,* which reflecting on the great frailty and corruption of human nature, teaches, that no man can safely be trusted with unlimited authority; or from *experience* and history, which inform us of the enormous abuses, that ambition, in every age and country, has been found to make of so imprudent a confidence.

The same distinction between reason and experience is maintained in all our deliberations concerning the conduct of life; while the experienced statesman, general, physician, or merchant is trusted and followed; and the unpractised novice, with whatever natural talents endowed, neglected and despised. Though it be allowed, that reason may form very plausible conjectures with regard to the consequences of such a particular conduct in such particular circumstances; it is still supposed imperfect, without the assistance of experience, which is alone able to give stability and certainty to the maxims, derived from study and reflection.

But notwithstanding that this distinction be thus universally received, both in the active and speculative scenes of life, I shall not scruple to pronounce, that it is, at bottom, erroneous, at least, superficial.

If we examine those arguments, which, in any of the sciences above mentioned, are supposed to be the mere effects of reasoning and reflection, they will be found to terminate, at last, in some general principle or conclusion, for which we can assign no reason but observation and experience. The only difference between them and those maxims, which are vulgarly esteemed the result of pure experience, is, that the former cannot be established without some process of thought, and some reflection on what we have observed, in order to distinguish its circumstances, and trace its consequences: Whereas in the latter, the experienced event is exactly and fully familiar to that which we infer as the result of any particular situation.

Custom, then, is the great guide of human life. It is that principle alone which renders our experience useful to us, and makes us expect, for the future, a similar train of events with those which have appeared in the past. Without the influence of custom, we should be entirely ignorant of every matter of fact beyond what is immediately present to the memory and senses. We should never know how to adjust means to ends, or to employ our natural powers in the production of any effect. There would be an end at once of all action, as well as of the chief part of speculation.

But here it may be proper to remark, that though our conclusions from experience carry us beyond our memory and senses, and assure us of matters of fact which happened in the most distant places and most remote ages, yet some fact must always be present to the senses or memory, from which we may first proceed in drawing these conclusions. A man, who should find in a desert country the remains of pompous buildings, would conclude that the country had, in ancient times, been cultivated by civilized inhabitants; but did nothing of this nature occur to him, he could never form such an inference. We learn the events of former ages from history; but then we must peruse the volumes in which this instruction is contained, and thence carry up our inferences from one testimony to

---

The history of a TIBERIUS or a NERO makes us dread a like tyranny, were our monarchs freed from the restraints of laws and senates: But the observation of any fraud or cruelty in private life is sufficient, with the aid of a little thought, to give us the same apprehension; while it serves as an instance of the general corruption of human nature, and shows us the danger which we must incur by reposing an entire confidence in mankind. In both cases, it is experience which is ultimately the foundation of our inference and conclusion.

There is no man so young and unexperienced, as not to have formed, from observation, many general and just maxims concerning human affairs and the conduct of life; but it must be confessed, that, when a man comes to put these in practice, he will be extremely liable to error, till time and farther experience both enlarge these maxims, and teach him their proper use and application. In every situation or incident, there are many particular and seemingly minute circumstances, which the man of greatest talent is, at first, apt to overlook, though on them the justness of his conclusions, and consequently the prudence of his conduct, entirely depend. Not to mention, that, to a young beginner, the general observations and maxims occur not always on the proper occasions, nor can be immediately applied with due calmness and distinction. The truth is, an unexperienced reasoner could be no reasoner at all, were he absolutely unexperienced; and when we assign that character to any one, we mean it only in a comparative sense, and suppose him possessed of experience, in a smaller and more imperfect degree.

another, till we arrive at the eyewitnesses and spectators of these distant events. In a word, if we proceed not upon some fact, present to the memory or senses, our reasonings would be merely hypothetical; and however the particular links might be connected with each other, the whole chain of inferences would have nothing to support it, nor could we ever, by its means, arrive at the knowledge of any real existence. If I ask why you believe any particular matter of fact, which you relate, you must tell me some reason; and this reason will be some other fact, connected with it. But as you cannot proceed after this manner, *in infinitum,* you must at last terminate in some fact, which is present to your memory or senses; or must allow that your belief is entirely without foundation.

What, then, is the conclusion of the whole matter? A simple one; though, it must be confessed, pretty remote from the common theories of philosophy. All belief of matter of fact or real existence is derived merely from some object, present to the memory or senses, and a customary conjunction between that and some other object. Or in other words; having found, in many instances, that any two kinds of objects—flame and heat, snow and cold—have always been conjoined together; if flame or snow be presented anew to the senses, the mind is carried by custom to expect heat or cold, and to *believe* that such a quality does exist, and will discover itself upon a nearer approach. This belief is the necessary result of placing the mind in such circumstances. It is an operation of the soul, when we are so situated, as unavoidable as to feel the passion of love, when we receive benefits; or hatred, when we meet with injuries. All these operations are a species of natural instincts, which no reasoning or process of the thought and understanding is able either to produce or to prevent.

At this point, it would be very allowable for us to stop our philosophical researches. In most questions we can never make a single step farther; and in all questions we must terminate here at last, after our most restless and curious enquiries. But still our curiosity will be pardonable, perhaps commendable, if it carry us on to still farther researches, and make us examine more accurately the nature of this *belief,* and of the *customary conjunction,* whence it is derived. By this means we may meet with some explications and analogies that will give satisfaction; at least to such as love the abstract sciences, and can be entertained with speculations, which, however accurate, may still retain a degree of doubt and uncertainty. As to readers of a different taste; the remaining part of this section is not calculated for them, and the following enquiries may well be understood, though it be neglected.

## Part II

NOTHING is more free than the imagination of man; and though it cannot exceed that original stock of ideas furnished by the internal and external senses, it has unlimited power of mixing, compounding, separating, and dividing these ideas, in all the varieties of fiction and vision. It can feign a train of events, with all the appearance of reality, ascribe to them a particular time and place, conceive them as existent, and paint them out to itself with every circumstance, that belongs to any historical fact, which it believes with the greatest certainty. Wherein, therefore, consists the difference between such a fiction and belief? It lies not merely in any peculiar idea, which is annexed to such a conception as commands our assent, and which is wanting to every known fiction. For as the mind has authority over all its ideas, it could voluntarily annex this particular idea to any fiction, and consequently be able to believe whatever it pleases; contrary to what we find by daily experience. We can, in our conception, join the head of a man to the body of a horse; but it is not in our power to believe that such an animal has ever really existed.

It follows, therefore, that the difference between *fiction* and *belief* lies in some sentiment or feeling, which is annexed to the latter, not to the former, and which depends not on the will, nor can be commanded at pleasure. It must be excited by nature, like all other sentiments; and must arise from the particular situation, in which the mind is placed at any particular juncture. Whenever any object is presented to the memory or senses, it immediately, by the force of custom, carries the imagination to conceive that object, which is usually conjoined to it; and this conception is attended with a feeling or sentiment, different from the loose reveries of the fancy. In this consists the whole nature of belief. For as there is no matter of fact which we believe so firmly that we cannot conceive the contrary, there would be no difference between the conception assented to and that which is rejected, were it not for some sentiment which distinguishes the one from the other. If I see a billiard-ball moving toward another, on a smooth table, I can easily conceive it to stop upon contact. This conception implies no contradiction; but still it feels very differently from that conception by which I represent to myself the impulse and the communication of motion from one ball to another.

Were we to attempt a *definition* of this sentiment, we should, perhaps, find it a very difficult, if not an impossible task; in the same manner as if we should endeavour to define the feeling of cold or passion of anger, to a creature who never had any experience of these sentiments. Belief is the true and proper name of this feeling; and no one is ever at a loss to know the meaning of that term; because every man is every moment conscious of the sentiment represented by it. It may not, however, be improper to attempt a description of this sentiment; in hopes we may, by that means, arrive at some analogies, which may afford a more perfect explication of it. I say, then, that belief is nothing but a more vivid, lively, forcible, firm, steady conception of an object, than what the imagination alone is ever able to attain. This variety of terms, which may seem so unphilosophical, is intended only to express that act of the mind, which renders realities, or what is taken for such, more present to us than fictions, causes them to weigh more in the thought, and gives them a superior influence on the passions and imagination. Provided we agree about the thing, it is needless to dispute about the terms. The imagination has the command over all its ideas, and can join and mix and vary them, in all the ways possible. It may conceive fictitious objects with all the circumstances of place and time. It may set them, in a manner, before our eyes, in their true colours, just as they might have existed. But as it is impossible that this faculty of imagination can ever, of itself, reach belief, it is evident that belief consists not in the peculiar nature or order of ideas, but in the *manner* of their conception, and in their *feeling* to the mind. I confess, that it is impossible perfectly to explain this feeling or manner of conception. We may make use of words which express something near it. But its true and proper name, as we observed before, is *belief;* which is a term that every one sufficiently understands in common life. And in philosophy, we can go no farther than assert, that *belief* is something felt by the mind, which distinguishes the ideas of the judgement from the fictions of the imagination. It gives them more weight and influence; makes them appear of greater importance; enforces them in the mind; and renders them the governing principle of our actions. I hear at present, for instance, a person's voice, with whom I am acquainted; and the sound comes as from the next room. This impression of my senses immediately conveys my thought to the person, together with all the surrounding objects. I paint them out to myself as existing at present, with the same qualities and relations, of which I formerly knew them possessed. These ideas take faster hold of my mind than ideas of an enchanted castle. They are very different to the feeling, and have a much greater influence of every kind, either to give pleasure or pain, joy or sorrow.

Let us, then, take in the whole compass of this doctrine, and allow, that the sentiment of belief is nothing but a conception more intense and steady than what attends the mere fictions of the imagination, and that this *manner* of conception arises from a customary conjunction of the object with something present to the memory or senses: I believe that it will not be difficult, upon these suppositions, to find other operations of the mind analogous to it, and to trace up these phenomena to principles still more general.

We have already observed that nature has established connexions among particular ideas, and that no sooner one idea occurs to our thoughts than it introduces its correlative, and carries our attention towards it, by a gentle and insensible movement.   These principles of connexion or association we have reduced to three, namely, *Resemblance, Contiguity and Causation;* which are the only bonds that unite our thoughts together, and beget that regular train of reflection or discourse, which, in a greater or less degree, takes place among all mankind.   Now here arises a question, on which the solution of the present difficulty will depend.   Does it happen, in all these relations, that, when one of the objects is presented to the senses or memory, the mind is not only carried to the conception of the correlative, but reaches a steadier and stronger conception of it than what otherwise it would have been able to attain?   This seems to be the case with that belief which arises from the relation of cause and effect. And if the case be the same with the other relations or principles of associations, this may be established as a general law, which takes place in all the operations of the mind.

We may, therefore, observe, as the first experiment to our present purpose, that, upon the appearance of the picture of an absent friend, our idea of him is evidently enlivened by the *resemblance,* and that every passion, which that idea occasions, whether of joy or sorrow, acquires new force and vigour.   In producing this effect, there concur both a relation and a present impression.   Where the picture bears him no resemblance, at least was not intended for him, it never so much as conveys our thought to him: and where it is absent, as well as the person, though the mind may pass from the thought of the one to that of the other, it feels its idea to be rather weakened than enlivened by that transition.   We take a pleasure in viewing the picture of a friend, when it is set before us; but when it is removed, rather choose to consider him directly than by reflection in an image, which is equally distant and obscure.

The ceremonies of the Roman Catholic religion may be considered as instances of the same nature.   The devotees of that superstition usually plead in excuse for the mummeries, with which they are upbraided, that they feel the good effect of those external motions, and postures, and actions, in enlivening their devotion and quickening their fervour, which otherwise would decay, if directed entirely to distant and immaterial objects. We shadow out the objects of our faith, say they, in sensible types and images, and render them more present to us by the immediate presence of these types, than it is possible for us to do merely by an intellectual view and contemplation. Sensible objects have always a greater influence on the fancy than any other; and this influence they readily convey to those ideas to which they are related, and which they resemble. I shall only infer from these practices, and this reasoning, that the effect of resemblance in enlivening the ideas is very common; and as in every case a resemblance and a present impression must concur, we are abundantly supplied with experiments to prove the reality of the foregoing principle.

We may add force to these experiments by others of a different kind, in considering the effects of *contiguity* as well as of *resemblance*. It is certain that distance diminishes the force of every idea, and that, upon our approach to any object; though it does not discover itself to our senses; it operates upon the mind with an influence, which imitates an immediate impression. The thinking on any object readily transports the mind to what is contiguous; but it is only the actual presence of an object, that transports it with a superior vivacity. When I am a few miles from home, whatever relates to it touches me more nearly than when I am two hundred leagues distant; though even at that distance the reflecting on any thing in the neighbourhood of my friends or family naturally produces an idea of them. But as in this latter case, both the objects of the mind are ideas; notwithstanding there is an easy transition between them; that transition alone is not able to give a superior vivacity to any of the ideas, for want of some immediate impression.[2]

[2] 'Naturane nobis, inquit, datum dicam, an errore quodam, ut, cum ea loca videamus, in quibus memoria dignos viros acceperimus multum esse versatos, magis moveamur, quam siquando eorum ipsorum aut facta audiamus aut scriptum aliquod legamus? Velut ego nunc moveor. Venit enim mihi

No one can doubt but causation has the same influence as the other two relations of resemblance and contiguity. Superstitious people are fond of the reliques of saints and holy men, for the same reason, that they seek after types or images, in order to enliven their devotion, and give them a more intimate and strong conception of those exemplary lives, which they desire to imitate. Now it is evident, that one of the best reliques, which a devotee could procure, would be the handywork of a saint; and if his cloaths and furniture are ever to be considered in this light, it is because they were once at his disposal, and were moved and affected by him; in which respect they are to be considered as imperfect effects, and as connected with him by a shorter chain of consequences than any of those, by which we learn the reality of his existence.

Suppose, that the son of a friend, who had been long dead or absent, were presented to us; it is evident, that this object would instantly revive its correlative idea, and recall to our thoughts all past intimacies and familiarities, in more lively colours than they would otherwise have appeared to us. This is another phaenomenon, which seems to prove the principle above mentioned.

We may observe, that, in these phaenomena, the belief of the correlative object is always presupposed; without which the relation could have no effect. The influence of the picture supposes, that we *believe* our friend to have once existed. Contiguity to home can never excite our ideas of home, unless we *believe* that it really exists. Now I assert, that this belief, where it reaches beyond the memory or senses, is of a similar nature, and arises from similar causes, with the transition of thought and vivacity of conception here explained. When I throw a piece of dry wood into a fire, my mind is immediately carried to conceive, that it augments, not extinguishes the flame. This

Plato in mentem, quem accepimus primum hic disputare solitum: cuius etiam illi hortuli propinqui non memoriam solum mihi afferunt, sed ipsum videntur in conspectu meo hic ponere. Hic Speusippus, hic Xenocrates, hic eius auditor Polemo; cuius ipsa illa sessio fuit, quam videmus. Equidem etiam curiam nostram, Hostiliam dico, non hanc novam, quae mihi minor esse videtur postquam est maior, solebam intuens, Scipionem, Catonem, Laelium, nostrum vero in primis avum cogitare. Tanta vis admonitionis est in locis; ut non sine causa ex his memoriae deducta sit disciplina.'— *Cicero de Finibus.* Lib. v.

transition of thought from the cause to the effect proceeds not from reason. It derives its origin altogether from custom and experience. And as it first begins from an object, present to the senses, it renders the idea or conception of flame more strong and lively than any loose, floating reverie of the imagination. That idea arises immediately. The thought moves instantly towards it, and conveys to it all that force of conception, which is derived from the impression present to the senses. When a sword is levelled at my breast, does not the idea of wound and pain strike me more strongly, than when a glass of wine is presented to me, even though by accident this idea should occur after the appearance of the latter object? But what is there in this whole matter to cause such a strong conception, except only a present object and a customary transition of the idea of another object, which we have been accustomed to conjoin with the former? This is the whole operation of the mind, in all our conclusions concerning matter of fact and existence; and it is a satisfaction to find some analogies, by which it may be explained. The transition from a present object does in all cases give strength and solidity to the related idea.

Here, then, is a kind of pre-established harmony between the course of nature and the succession of our ideas; and though the powers and forces, by which the former is governed, be wholly unknown to us; yet our thoughts and conceptions have still, we find, gone on in the same train with the other works of nature. Custom is that principle, by which this correspondence has been effected; so necessary to the subsistence of our species, and the regulation of our conduct, in every circumstance and occurrence of human life. Had not the presence of an object, instantly excited the idea of those objects, commonly conjoined with it, all our knowledge must have been limited to the narrow sphere of our memory and senses; and we should never have been able to adjust means to ends, or employ our natural powers, either to the producing of good, or avoiding of evil. Those, who delight in the discovery and contemplation of *final causes,* have here ample subject to employ their wonder and admiration. ·

I shall add, for a further confirmation of the foregoing theory, that, as this operation of the mind, by which we infer like effects from like causes, and *vice versa,* is so essential to the subsistence of all human creatures, it is not probable, that it could be trusted to the fallacious deductions of our reason, which is slow in its operations; appears not, in any degree, during the first years of infancy; and at best is, in every age and period of human life, extremely liable to error and mistake. It is more conformable to the ordinary wisdom of nature to secure so necessary an act of the mind, by some instinct or mechanical tendency, which may be infallible in its operations, may discover itself at the first appearance of life and thought, and may be independent of all the laboured deductions of the understanding. As nature has taught us the use of our limbs, without giving us the knowledge of the muscles and nerves, by which they are actuated; so has she implanted in us an instinct, which carries forward the thought in a correspondent course to that which she has established among external objects; though we are ignorant of those powers and forces, on which this regular course and succession of objects totally depends.

# SECTION VI

## OF PROBABILITY[1]

THOUGH there be no such thing as *Chance* in the world; our ignorance of the real cause of any event has the same influence on the understanding, and begets a like species of belief or opinion.

There is certainly a probability, which arises from a superiority of chances on any side; and according as this superiority increases, and surpasses the opposite chances, the probability receives a proportionable increase, and begets still a higher degree of belief or assent to that side, in which we discover the superiority. If a dye were marked with one figure or number of spots on four sides, and with another figure or number of spots on the two remaining sides, it would be more probable, that the former would turn up than the latter; though, if it had a thousand sides marked in the same manner, and only one side different, the probability would be much higher, and our belief or expectation of the event more steady and secure. This process of the thought or reasoning may seem trivial and obvious; but to those who consider it more narrowly, it may, perhaps, afford matter for curious speculation.

It seems evident, that, when the mind looks forward to discover the event, which may result from the throw of such a dye, it considers the turning up of each particular side as alike probable; and this is the very nature of chance, to render all the particular events, comprehended in it, entirely equal. But finding a greater number of sides concur in the one event than in the other, the mind is carried more frequently to that event, and meets it oftener, in revolving

[1] Mr. Locke divides all arguments into demonstrative and probable. In this view, we must say, that it is only probable all men must die, or that the sun will rise to-morrow. But to conform our language more to common use, we ought to divide arguments into *demonstrations, proofs,* and *probabilities.* By proofs meaning such arguments from experience as leave no room for doubt or opposition.

the various possibilities or chances, on which the ultimate result depends. This concurrence of several views in one particular event begets immediately, by an inexplicable contrivance of nature, the sentiment of belief, and gives that event the advantage over its antagonist, which is supported by a smaller number of views, and recurs less frequently to the mind. If we allow, that belief is nothing but a firmer and stronger conception of an object than what attends the mere fictions of the imagination, this operation may, perhaps, in some measure, be accounted for. The concurrence of these several views or glimpses imprints the idea more strongly on the imagination; gives it superior force and vigour; renders its influence on the passions and affections more sensible; and in a word, begets that reliance or security, which constitutes the nature of belief and opinion.

The case is the same with the probability of causes, as with that of chance. There are some causes, which are entirely uniform and constant in producing a particular effect; and no instance has ever yet been found of any failure or irregularity in their operation. Fire has always burned, and water suffocated every human creature: the production of motion by impulse and gravity is an universal law, which has hitherto admitted of no exception. But there are other causes, which have been found more irregular and uncertain; nor has rhubarb always proved a purge, or opium a soporific to every one, who has taken these medicines. It is true, when any cause fails of producing its usual effect, philosophers ascribe not this to any irregularity in nature; but suppose, that some secret causes, in the particular structure of parts, have prevented the operation. Our reasonings, however, and conclusions concerning the event are the same as if this principle had no place. Being determined by custom to transfer the past to the future, in all our inferences; where the past has been entirely regular and uniform, we expect the event with the greatest assurance, and leave no room for any contrary supposition. But where different effects have been found to follow from causes, which are to *appearance* exactly similar, all these various effects must occur to the mind in transferring the past to the future, and enter into our consideration, when we determine the probability of the event. Though we give the preference to that which has been found most usual, and believe that this effect will exist, we must not overlook the other effects, but must assign to each of them a particular weight and authority, in proportion as we have found it to be more or less frequent. It is more probable, in almost every country of Europe, that there will be frost sometime in January, than that the weather will continue open throughout that whole month; though this probability varies according to the different climates, and approaches to a certainty in the more northern kingdoms. Here then it seems evident, that, when we transfer the past to the future, in order to determine the effect, which will result from any cause, we transfer all the different events, in the same proportion as they have appeared in the past, and conceive one to have existed a hundred times, for instance, another ten times, and another once. As a great number of views do here concur in one event, they fortify and confirm it to the imagination, beget that sentiment which we call *belief,* and give its object the preference above the contrary event, which is not supported by an equal number of experiments, and recurs not so frequently to the thought in transferring the past to the future. Let any one try to account for this operation of the mind upon any of the received systems of philosophy, and he will be sensible of the difficulty. For my part, I shall think it sufficient, if the present hints excite the curiosity of philosophers, and make them sensible how defective all common theories are in treating of such curious and such sublime subjects.

# SECTION VII

## OF THE IDEA OF NECESSARY CONNEXION

### PART I

THE great advantage of the mathematical sciences above the moral consists in this, that the ideas of the former, being sensible, are always clear and determinate, the smallest distinction between them is immediately perceptible, and the same terms are still expressive of the same ideas, without ambiguity or variation. An oval is never mistaken for a circle, nor an hyperbola for an ellipsis. The isosceles and scalenum are distinguished by boundaries more exact than vice and virtue, right and wrong. If any term be defined in geometry, the mind readily, of itself, substitutes, on all occasions, the definition for the term defined: or even when no definition is employed, the object itself may be presented to the senses, and by that means be steadily and clearly apprehended. But the finer sentiments of the mind, the operations of the understanding, the various agitations of the passions, though really in themselves distinct, easily escape us, when surveyed by reflection; nor is it in our power to recall the original object, as often as we have occasion to contemplate it. Ambiguity, by this means, is gradually introduced into our reasonings: similar objects are readily taken to be the same: and the conclusion becomes at last very wide of the premises.

One may safely, however, affirm, that, if we consider these sciences in a proper light, their advantages and disadvantages nearly compensate each other, and reduce both of them to a state of equality. If the mind, with greater facility, retains the ideas of geometry clear and determinate, it must carry on a much longer and more intricate chain of reasoning, and compare ideas much wider of each other, in order to reach the abstruser truths of that science. And if moral ideas are apt, without extreme care, to fall into obscurity and confusion, the inferences are always much shorter in these disquisitions, and the intermediate steps, which lead to the conclusion, much fewer than in the sciences which treat of quantity and number. In reality, there is scarcely a proposition in Euclid so simple, as not to consist of more parts, than are to be found in any moral reasoning which runs not into chimera and conceit. Where we trace the principles of the human mind through a few steps, we may be very well satisfied with our progress; considering how soon nature throws a bar to all our enquiries concerning causes, and reduces us to an acknowledgment of our ignorance. The chief obstacle, therefore, to our improvement in the moral or metaphysical sciences is the obscurity of the ideas, and ambiguity of the terms. The principal difficulty in the mathematics is the length of inferences and compass of thought, requisite to the forming of any conclusion. And, perhaps, our progress in natural philosophy is chiefly retarded by the want of proper experiments and phænomena, which are often discovered by chance, and cannot always be found, when requisite, even by the most diligent and prudent enquiry. As moral philosophy seems hitherto to have received less improvement than either geometry or physics, we may conclude, that, if there be any difference in this respect among these sciences, the difficulties, which obstruct the progress of the former, require superior care and capacity to be surmounted.

There are no ideas, which occur in metaphysics, more obscure and uncertain, than those of *power, force, energy* or *necessary connexion,* of which it is every moment necessary for us to treat in all our disquisitions. We shall, therefore, endeavour, in this section, to fix, if possible, the precise meaning of these terms, and thereby remove some part of that obscurity, which is so much complained of in this species of philosophy.

It seems a proposition, which will not admit of much dispute, that all our ideas are nothing but copies of our impressions, or, in other words, that it is impossible for us to *think* of anything, which we have not antecedently *felt,* either by our external or internal senses. I have endeavoured[1] to

[1] Section II.

explain and prove this proposition, and have expressed my
hopes, that, by a proper application of it, men may reach
a greater clearness and precision in philosophical reasonings,
than what they have hitherto been able to attain. Complex
ideas, may, perhaps, be well known by definition, which is
nothing but an enumeration of those parts or simple ideas,
that compose them. But when we have pushed up definitions to the most simple ideas, and find still more ambiguity
and obscurity; what resource are we then possessed of? By
what invention can we throw light upon these ideas, and
render them altogether precise and determinate to our intellectual view? Produce the impressions or original sentiments, from which the ideas are copied. These impressions
are all strong and sensible. They admit not of ambiguity.
They are not only placed in a full light themselves, but may
throw light on their correspondent ideas, which lie in obscurity. And by this means, we may, perhaps, attain a new
microscope or species of optics, by which, in the moral
sciences, the most minute, and most simple ideas may be so
enlarged as to fall readily under our apprehension, and be
equally known with the grossest and most sensible ideas, that
can be the object of our enquiry.

To be fully acquainted, therefore, with the idea of power
or necessary connexion, let us examine its impression; and
in order to find the impression with greater certainty, let us
search for it in all the sources, from which it may possibly
be derived.

When we look about us towards external objects, and
consider the operation of causes, we are never able, in
a single instance, to discover any power or necessary connexion; any quality, which binds the effect to the cause,
and renders the one an infallible consequence of the other.
We only find, that the one does actually, in fact, follow the
other. The impulse of one billiard-ball is attended with
motion in the second. This is the whole that appears to
the *outward* senses. The mind feels no sentiment or *inward*
impression from this succession of objects: consequently,
there is not, in any single, particular instance of cause and
effect, any thing which can suggest the idea of power or
necessary connexion.

From the first appearance of an object, we never can conjecture what effect will result from it. But were the power or energy of any cause discoverable by the mind, we could foresee the effect, even without experience; and might, at first, pronounce with certainty concerning it, by mere dint of thought and reasoning.

In reality, there is no part of matter, that does ever, by its sensible qualities, discover any power or energy, or give us ground to imagine, that it could produce any thing, or be followed by any other object, which we could denominate its effect. Solidity, extension, motion; these qualities are all complete in themselves, and never point out any other event which may result from them. The scenes of the universe are continually shifting, and one object follows another in an uninterrupted succession; but the power of force, which actuates the whole machine, is entirely concealed from us, and never discovers itself in any of the sensible qualities of body. We know that, in fact, heat is a constant attendant of flame; but what is the connexion between them, we have no room so much as to conjecture or imagine. It is impossible, therefore, that the idea of power can be derived from the contemplation of bodies, in single instances of their operation; because no bodies ever discover any power, which can be the original of this idea.[2]

Since, therefore, external objects as they appear to the senses, give us no idea of power or necessary connexion, by their operation in particular instances, let us see, whether this idea be derived from reflection on the operations of our own minds, and be copied from any internal impression. It may be said, that we are every moment conscious of internal power; while we feel, that, by the simple command of our will, we can move the organs of our body, or direct the faculties of our mind. An act of volition produces motion in our limbs, or raises a new idea in our imagination. This influence of the will we know by consciousness. Hence we acquire the idea of power or energy; and are certain,

[2] Mr. Locke, in his chapter of power, says that, finding from experience, that there are several new productions in matter, and concluding that there must somewhere be a power capable of producing them, we arrive at last by this reasoning at the idea of power. But no reasoning can ever give us a new, original, simple idea; as this philosopher himself confesses. This, therefore, can never be the origin of that idea.

that we ourselves and all other intelligent beings are possessed of power. This idea, then, is an idea of reflection,
since it arises from reflecting on the operations of our own
mind, and on the command which is exercised by will, both
over the organs of the body and faculties of the soul.

We shall proceed to examine this pretension; and first
with regard to the influence of volition over the organs of
the body. This influence, we may observe, is a fact, which,
like all other natural events, can be known only by experience, and can never be foreseen from any apparent energy
or power in the cause, which connects it with the effect, and
renders the one an infallible consequence of the other.
The motion of our body follows upon the command of our
will. Of this we are every moment conscious. But the
means, by which this is effected; the energy, by which the
will performs so extraordinary an operation; of this we are
so far from being immediately conscious, that it must for
ever escape our most diligent enquiry.

For *first:* Is there any principle in all nature more
mysterious than the union of soul with body; by which a
supposed spiritual substance acquires such an influence over
a material one, that the most refined thought is able to
actuate the grossest matter? Were we empowered, by a
secret wish, to remove mountains, or control the planets in
their orbit; this extensive authority would not be more
extraordinary, nor more beyond our comprehension. But
if by consciousness we perceived any power or energy in the
will, we must know this power; we must know its connexion
with the effect; we must know the secret union of soul and
body, and the nature of both these substances; by which
the one is able to operate, in so many instances, upon the
other.

*Secondly,* We are not able to move all the organs of the
body with a like authority; though we cannot assign any
reason besides experience, for so remarkable a difference
between one and the other. Why has the will an influence
over the tongue and fingers, not over the heart or liver?
This question would never embarrass us, were we conscious
of a power in the former case, not in the latter. We should
then perceive, independent of experience, why the authority

of will over the organs of the body is circumscribed within such particular limits. Being in that case fully acquainted with the power or force, by which it operates, we should also know, why its influence reaches precisely to such boundaries, and no farther.

A man, suddenly struck with palsy in the leg or arm, or who had newly lost those members, frequently endeavours, at first to move them, and employ them, in their usual offices. Here he is as much conscious of power to command such limbs, as a man in perfect health is conscious of power to actuate any member which remains in its natural state and condition. But consciousness never deceives. Consequently, neither in the one case nor in the other, are we ever conscious of any power. We learn the influence of our will from experience alone. And experience only teaches us, how one event constantly follows another; without instructing us in the secret connexion, which binds them together, and renders them inseparable.

*Thirdly,* We learn from anatomy, that the immediate object of power in voluntary motion, is not the member itself which is moved, but certain muscles, and nerves, and animal spirits, and, perhaps, something still more minute and more unknown, through which the motion is successively propagated, ere it reach the member itself whose motion is the immediate object of volition. Can there be a more certain proof, that the power, by which this whole operation is performed, so far from being directly and fully known by an inward sentiment or consciousness is, to the last degree, mysterious and unintelligible? Here the mind wills a certain event. Immediately another event, unknown to ourselves, and totally different from the one intended, is produced: This event produces another, equally unknown: till at last, through a long succession, the desired event is produced. But if the original power were felt, it must be known: were it known, its effect also must be known; since all power is relative to its effect. And *vice versa,* if the effect be not known, the power cannot be known nor felt. How indeed can we be conscious of a power to move our limbs, when we have no such power; but only that to move certain animal spirits, which, though they produce at last the motion

of our limbs, yet operate in such a manner as is wholly
beyond our comprehension?

We may, therefore, conclude from the whole, I hope,
without any temerity, though with assurance; that our idea
of power is not copied from any sentiment or consciousness
of power within ourselves, when we give rise to animal
motion, or apply our limbs to their proper use and office.
That their motion follows the command of the will is a
matter of common experience, like other natural events:
But the power or energy by which this is effected, like that
in other natural events, is unknown and inconceivable.[3]

Shall we then assert, that we are conscious of a power or
energy in our own minds, when, by an act or command of
our will, we raise up a new idea, fix the mind to the contemplation of it, turn it on all sides, and at last dismiss it
for some other idea, when we think that we have surveyed it
with sufficient accuracy?  I believe the same arguments will
prove, that even this command of the will gives us no real
idea of force or energy.

*First,* It must be allowed, that, when we know a power,
we know that very circumstance in the cause, by which it is
enabled to produce the effect: for these are supposed to be
synonymous.  We must, therefore, know both the cause and
effect, and the relation between them.  But do we pretend
to be acquainted with the nature of the human soul and the
nature of an idea, or the aptitude of the one to produce the
other?  This is a real creation; a production of something
out of nothing: which implies a power so great, that it may
seem, at first sight, beyond the reach of any being, less than
infinite.  At least it must be owned, that such a power is

---

[3] It may be pretended, that the resistance which we meet with in bodies,
obliging us frequently to exert our force, and call up all our power, this
gives us the idea of force and power.  It is this *nisus,* or strong endeavour,
of which we are conscious, that is the original impression from which this
idea is copied.  But, first, we attribute power to a vast number of objects,
where we never can suppose this resistance or exertion of force to take
place; to the Supreme Being, who never meets with any resistance; to
the mind in its command over its ideas and limbs, in common thinking
and motion, where the effect follows immediately upon the will, without
any exertion or summoning up of force; to inanimate matter, which is not
capable of this sentiment.  *Secondly,* This sentiment of an endeavour to
overcome resistance has no known connexion with any event: What follows
it, we know by experience; but could not know it *à priori.*  It must, however, be confessed, that the animal *nisus,* which we experience, though it
can afford no accurate precise idea of power, enters very much into that
vulgar, inaccurate idea, which is formed of it.

not felt, nor known, nor even conceivable by the mind. We only feel the event, namely, the existence of an idea, consequent to a command of the will: but the manner, in which this operation is performed, the power by which it is produced, is entirely beyond our comprehension.

*Secondly,* The command of the mind over itself is limited, as well as its command over the body; and these limits are not known by reason, or any acquaintance with the nature of cause and effect, but only by experience and observation, as in all other natural events and in the operation of external objects. Our authority over our sentiments and passions is much weaker than that over our ideas; and even the latter authority is circumscribed within very narrow boundaries. Will any one pretend to assign the ultimate reason of these boundaries, or show why the power is deficient in one case, not in another.

*Thirdly,* This self-command is very different at different times. A man in health possesses more of it than one languishing with sickness. We are more master of our thoughts in the morning than in the evening: fasting, than after a full meal. Can we give any reason for these variations, except experience? Where then is the power, of which we pretend to be conscious? Is there not here, either in a spiritual or material substance, or both, some secret mechanism or structure of parts, upon which the effect depends, and which, being entirely unknown to us, renders the power or energy of the will equally unknown and incomprehensible?

Volition is surely an act of the mind, with which we are sufficiently acquainted. Reflect upon it. Consider it on all sides. Do you find anything in it like this creative power, by which it raises from nothing a new idea, and with a kind of *Fiat,* imitates the omnipotence of its Maker, if I may be allowed so to speak, who called forth into existence all the various scenes of nature? So far from being conscious of this energy in the will, it requires as certain experience as that of which we are possessed, to convince us that such extraordinary effects do ever result from a simple act of volition.

The generality of mankind never find any difficulty in

accounting for the more common and familiar operations of nature—such as the descent of heavy bodies, the growth of plants, the generation of animals, or the nourishment of bodies by food: but suppose that, in all these cases, they perceive the very force or energy of the cause, by which it is connected with its effect, and is for ever infallible in its operation. They acquire, by long habit, such a turn of mind, that, upon the appearance of the cause, they immediately expect with assurance its usual attendant, and hardly conceive it possible that any other event could result from it. It is only on the discovery of extraordinary phaenomena, such as earthquakes, pestilence, and prodigies of any kind, that they find themselves at a loss to assign a proper cause, and to explain the manner in which the effect is produced by it. It is usual for men, in such difficulties, to have recourse to some invisible intelligent principle[4] as the immediate cause of that event which surprises them, and which, they think, cannot be accounted for from the common powers of nature. But philosophers, who carry their scrutiny a little farther, immediately perceive that, even in the most familiar events, the energy of the cause is as unintelligible as in the most unusual, and that we only learn by experience the frequent *Conjunction* of objects, without being ever able to comprehend anything like *Connexion* between them. Here, then, many philosophers think themselves obliged by reason to have recourse, on all occasions, to the same principle, which the vulgar never appeal to but in cases that appear miraculous and supernatural. They acknowledge mind and intelligence to be, not only the ultimate and original cause of all things, but the immediate and sole cause of every event which appears in nature. They pretend that those objects which are commonly denominated *causes,* are in reality nothing but *occasions;* and that the true and direct principle of every effect is not any power or force in nature, but a volition of the Supreme Being, who wills that such particular objects should for ever be conjoined with each other. Instead of saying that one billiard-ball moves another by a force which it has derived from the author of nature, it is the Deity himself, they say, who, by a particular

---

[4] Θεὸς ἀπὸ μηχανῆς.

volition, moves the second ball, being determined to this operation by the impulse of the first ball, in consequence of those general laws which he has laid down to himself in the government of the universe. But philosophers advancing still in their inquiries, discover that, as we are totally ignorant of the power on which depends the mutual operation of bodies, we are no less ignorant of that power on which depends the operation of mind on body, or of body on mind, nor are we able, either from our senses or consciousness, to assign the ultimate principle in one case more than in the other. The same ignorance, therefore, reduces them to the same conclusion. They assert that the Deity is the immediate cause of the union between soul and body; and that they are not the organs of sense, which, being agitated by external objects, produce sensations in the mind; but that it is a particular volition of our omnipotent Maker, which excites such a sensation, in consequence of such a motion in the organ. In like manner, it is not any energy in the will that produces local motion in our members: it is God himself, who is pleased to second our will, in itself impotent, and to command that motion which we erroneously attribute to our own power and efficacy. Nor do philosophers stop at this conclusion. They sometimes extend the same inference to the mind itself, in its internal operations. Our mental vision or conception of ideas is nothing but a revelation made to us by our Maker. When we voluntarily turn our thoughts to any object, and raise up its image in the fancy, it is not the will which creates that idea: it is the universal Creator, who discovers it to the mind, and renders it present to us.

Thus, according to these philosophers, every thing is full of God. Not content with the principle, that nothing exists but by his will, that nothing possesses any power but by his concession: they rob nature, and all created beings, of every power, in order to render their dependence on the Deity still more sensible and immediate. They consider not that, by this theory, they diminish, instead of magnifying, the grandeur of those attributes, which they affect so much to celebrate. It argues surely more power in the Deity to delegate a certain degree of power to inferior creatures than to produce every thing by his own immediate volition. It argues more wisdom to contrive at first the fabric of the world with such perfect foresight that, of itself, and by its proper operation, it may serve all the purposes of providence, than if the great Creator were obliged every moment to adjust its parts, and animate by his breath all the wheels of that stupendous machine.

But if we would have a more philosophical confutation of this theory, perhaps the two following reflections may suffice:

*First,* it seems to me that this theory of the universal energy and operation of the Supreme Being is too bold ever to carry conviction with it to a man, sufficiently apprized of the weakness of human reason, and the narrow limits to which it is confined in all its operations. Though the chain of arguments which conduct to it were ever so logical, there must arise a strong suspicion, if not an absolute assurance, that it has carried us quite beyond the reach of our faculties, when it leads to conclusions so extraordinary, and so remote from common life and experience. We are got into fairy land, long ere we have reached the last steps of our theory; and *there* we have no reason to trust our common methods of argument, or to think that our usual analogies and probabilities have any authority. Our line is too short to fathom such immense abysses. And however we may flatter ourselves that we are guided, in every step which we take, by a kind of verisimilitude and experience, we may be assured that this fancied experience has no authority when we thus apply it to subjects that lie entirely out of the sphere of experience. But on this we shall have occasion to touch afterwards.[6]

*Secondly,* I cannot perceive any force in the arguments on which this theory is founded. We are ignorant, it is true, of the manner in which bodies operate on each other: their force or energy is entirely incomprehensible: but are we not equally ignorant of the manner or force by which a mind, even the supreme mind, operates either on itself or on body? Whence, I beseech you, do we acquire any idea

[6] Section XII.

of it? We have no sentiment or consciousness of this power in ourselves. We have no idea of the Supreme Being but what we learn from reflection on our own faculties. Were our ignorance, therefore, a good reason for rejecting any thing, we should be led into that principle of denying all energy in the Supreme Being as much as in the grossest matter. We surely comprehend as little the operations of one as of the other. Is it more difficult to conceive that motion may arise from impulse than that it may arise from volition? All we know is our profound ignorance in both cases.[6]

## PART II

BUT to hasten to a conclusion of this argument, which is already drawn out to too great a length: we have sought in vain for an idea of power or necessary connexion in all the sources from which we could suppose it to be derived. It appears that, in single instances of the operation of bodies, we never can, by our utmost scrutiny, discover any thing but one event following another, without being able to comprehend any force or power by which the cause operates, or any connexion between it and its supposed effect. The same difficulty occurs in contemplating the operations of mind on body—where we observe the motion of the latter to follow upon the volition of the former, but are not able to observe or conceive the tie which binds together the motion and volition, or the energy by which the mind produces this

[6] I need not examine at length the *vis inertiae* which is so much talked of in the new philosophy, and which is ascribed to matter. We find by experience, that a body at rest or in motion continues for ever in its present state, till put from it by some new cause; and that a body impelled takes as much motion from the impelling body as it acquires itself. These are facts. When we call this a *vis inertiae*, we only mark these facts, without pretending to have any idea of the inert power; in the same manner as, when we talk of gravity, we mean certain effects, without comprehending that active power. It was never the meaning of Sir ISAAC NEWTON to rob second causes of all force or energy; though some of his followers have endeavoured to establish that theory upon his authority. On the contrary, that great philosopher had recourse to an etherial active fluid to explain his universal attraction; though he was so cautious and modest as to allow, that it was a mere hypothesis, not to be insisted on, without more experiments. I must confess, that there is something in the fate of opinions a little extraordinary. DES CARTES insinuated that doctrine of the universal and sole efficacy of the Deity, without insisting on it. MALEBRANCHE and other CARTESIANS made it the foundation of all their philosophy. It had, however, no authority in England. LOCKE, CLARKE, and CUDWORTH, never so much as take notice of it, but suppose all along, that matter has a real, though subordinate and derived power. By what means has it become so prevalent among our modern metaphysicians?

effect.  The authority of the will over its own faculties and
ideas is not a whit more comprehensible: so that, upon the
whole, there appears not, throughout all nature, any one instance of connexion which is conceivable by us.  All events
seem entirely loose and separate.  One event follows another; but we never can observe any tie between them.  They
seem *conjoined,* but never *connected.*  And as we can have
no idea of any thing which never appeared to our outward
sense or inward sentiment, the necessary conclusion *seems* to
be that we have no idea of connexion or power at all, and
that these words are absolutely, without any meaning, when
employed either in philosophical reasonings or common life.

But there still remains one method of avoiding this conclusion, and one source which we have not yet examined.
When any natural object or event is presented, it is impossible for us, by any sagacity or penetration, to discover,
or even conjecture, without experience, what event will
result from it, or to carry our foresight beyond that object
which is immediately present to the memory and senses.
Even after one instance or experiment where we have observed a particular event to follow upon another, we are not
entitled to form a general rule, or foretell what will happen
in like cases; it being justly esteemed an unpardonable
temerity to judge of the whole course of nature from one
single experiment, however accurate or certain.  But when
one particular species of event has always, in all instances,
been conjoined with another, we make no longer any scruple
of foretelling one upon the appearance of the other, and of
employing that reasoning, which can alone assure us of any
matter of fact or existence.  We then call the one object,
*Cause;* the other, *Effect.*  We suppose that there is some
connexion between them; some power in the one, by which
it infallibly produces the other, and operates with the greatest certainty and strongest necessity.

It appears, then, that this idea of a necessary connexion
among events arises from a number of similar instances
which occur of the constant conjunction of these events;
nor can that idea ever be suggested by any one of these
instances, surveyed in all possible lights and positions.  But
there is nothing in a number of instances, different from

every single instance, which is supposed to be exactly similar; except only, that after a repetition of similar instances, the mind is carried by habit, upon the appearance of one event, to expect its usual attendant, and to believe that it will exist. This connexion, therefore, which we *feel* in the mind, this customary transition of the imagination from one object to its usual attendant, is the sentiment or impression from which we form the idea of power or necessary connexion. Nothing farther is in the case. Contemplate the subject on all sides; you will never find any other origin of that idea. This is the sole difference between one instance, from which we can never receive the idea of connexion, and a number of similar instances, by which it is suggested. The first time a man saw the communication of motion by impulse, as by the shock of two billiard balls, he could not pronounce that the one event was *connected:* but only that it was *conjoined* with the other. After he has observed several instances of this nature, he then pronounces them to be *connected.* What alteration has happened to give rise to this new idea of *connexion?* Nothing but that he now *feels* these events to be connected in his imagination, and can readily foretell the existence of one from the appearance of the other. When we say, therefore, that one object is connected with another, we mean only that they have acquired a connexion in our thought, and give rise to this inference, by which they become proofs of each other's existence: A conclusion which is somewhat extraordinary, but which seems founded on sufficient evidence. Nor will its evidence be weakened by any general diffidence of the understanding, or sceptical suspicion concerning every conclusion which is new and extraordinary. No conclusions can be more agreeable to scepticism than such as make discoveries concerning the weakness and narrow limits of human reason and capacity.

And what stronger instance can be produced of the surprising ignorance and weakness of the understanding than the present. For surely, if there be any relation among objects which it imports to us to know perfectly, it is that of cause and effect. On this are founded all our reasonings concerning matter of fact or existence. By means of it alone we attain any assurance concerning objects which are removed from the present testimony of our memory and senses. The only immediate utility of all sciences, is to teach us, how to control and regulate future events by their causes. Our thoughts and enquiries are, therefore, every moment, employed about this relation: yet so imperfect are the ideas which we form concerning it, that it is impossible to give any just definition of cause, except what is drawn from something extraneous and foreign to it. Similar objects are always conjoined with similar. Of this we have experience. Suitably to this experience, therefore, we may define a cause to be *an object, followed by another, and where all the objects similar to the first are followed by objects similar to the second.* Or in other words *where, if the first object had not been, the second never had existed.* The appearance of a cause always conveys the mind, by a customary transition, to the idea of the effect. Of this also we have experience. We may, therefore, suitably to this experience, form another definition of cause, and call it, *an object followed by another, and whose appearance always conveys the thought to that other.* But though both these definitions be drawn from circumstances foreign to the cause, we cannot remedy this inconvenience, or attain any more perfect definition, which may point out that circumstance in the cause, which gives it a connexion with its effect. We have no idea of this connexion, nor even any distant notion what it is we desire to know, when we endeavour at a conception of it. We say, for instance, that the vibration of this string is the cause of this particular sound. But what do we mean by that affirmation? We either mean *that this vibration is followed by this sound, and that all similar vibrations have been followed by similar sounds* · or, *that this vibration is followed by this sound, and that upon the appearance of one the mind anticipates the senses, and forms immediately an idea of the other.* We may consider the relation of cause and effect in either of these two lights; but beyond these, we have no idea of it.[7]

To recapitulate, therefore, the reasonings of this section:

[7] According to these explications and definitions, the idea of *power* is relative as much as that of *cause;* and both have a reference to an effect, or some other event constantly conjoined with the former. When we consider

Every idea is copied from some preceding impression or sentiment; and where we cannot find any impression, we may be certain that there is no idea. In all single instances of the operation of bodies or minds, there is nothing that produces any impression, nor consequently can suggest any idea of power or necessary connexion. But when many uniform instances appear, and the same object is always followed by the same event; we then begin to entertain the notion of cause and connexion. We then *feel* a new sentiment or impression, to wit, a customary connexion in the thought or imagination between one object and its usual attendant; and this sentiment is the original of that idea which we seek for. For as this idea arises from a number of similar instances, and not from any single instance, it must arise from that circumstance, in which the number of instances differ from every individual instance. But this customary connexion or transition of the imagination is the only circumstance in which they differ. In every other particular they are alike. The first instance which we saw of motion communicated by the shock of two billiard balls (to return to this obvious illustration) is exactly similar to any instance that may, at present, occur to us; except only, that we could not, at first, *infer* one event from the other; which we are enabled to do

the *unknown* circumstance of an object, by which the degree or quantity of its effect is fixed and determined, we call that its power: and accordingly, it is allowed by all philosophers, that the effect is the measure of the power. But if they had any idea of power, as it is in itself, why could not they Measure it in itself? The dispute whether the force of a body in motion be as its velocity, or the square of its velocity; this dispute, I say, need not be decided by comparing its effects in equal or unequal times; but by a direct mensuration and comparison.

As to the frequent use of the words, Force, Power, Energy, &c., which every where occur in common conversation, as well as in philosophy; that is no proof, that we are acquainted, in any instance, with the connecting principle between cause and effect, or can account ultimately for the production of one thing to another. These words, as commonly used, have very loose meanings annexed to them; and their ideas are very uncertain and confused. No animal can put external bodies in motion without the sentiment of a *nisus* or endeavour; and every animal has a sentiment or feeling from the stroke or blow of an external object, that is in motion. These sensations, which are merely animal, and from which we can *à priori* draw no inference, we are apt to transfer to inanimate objects, and to suppose, that they have some such feelings, whenever they transfer or receive motion. With regard to energies, which are exerted, without our annexing to them any idea of communicated motion, we consider only the constant experienced conjunction of the events; and as we *feel* a customary connexion between the ideas, we transfer that feeling to the objects; as nothing is more usual than to apply to external bodies every internal sensation, which they occasion.

at present, after so long a course of uniform experience. I know not whether the reader will readily apprehend this reasoning. I am afraid that, should I multiply words about it, or throw it into a greater variety of lights, it would only become more obscure and intricate. In all abstract reasonings there is one point of view which, if we can happily hit, we shall go farther towards illustrating the subject than by all the eloquence and copious expression in the world. This point of view we should endeavour to reach, and reserve the flowers of rhetoric for subjects which are more adapted to them.

# SECTION VIII

## OF LIBERTY AND NECESSITY

### PART I

IT might reasonably be expected in questions which have been canvassed and disputed with great eagerness, since the first origin of science, and philosophy, that the meaning of all the terms, at least, should have been agreed upon among the disputants; and our enquiries, in the course of two thousand years, been able to pass from words to the true and real subject of the controversy. For how easy may it seem to give exact definitions of the terms employed in reasoning, and make these definitions, not the mere sound of words, the object of future scrutiny and examination? But if we consider the matter more narrowly, we shall be apt to draw a quite opposite conclusion. From this circumstance alone, that a controversy has been long kept on foot, and remains still undecided, we may presume that there is some ambiguity in the expression, and that the disputants affix different ideas to the terms employed in the controversy. For as the faculties of the mind are supposed to be naturally alike in every individual; otherwise nothing could be more fruitless than to reason or dispute together; it were impossible, if men affix the same ideas to their terms, that they could so long form different opinions of the same subject; especially when they communicate their views, and each party turn themselves on all sides, in search of arguments which may give them the victory over their antagonists. It is true, if men attempt the discussion of questions which lie entirely beyond the reach of human capacity, such as those concerning the origin of worlds, or the economy of the intellectual system or region of spirits, they may long beat the air in their fruitless contests, and never arrive at any determinate conclusion. But if the question regard any subject of common life and experience, nothing, one would think, could preserve the dispute so long undecided but some ambiguous expressions, which keep the antagonists still at a distance, and hinder them from grappling with each other.

This has been the case in the long disputed question concerning liberty and necessity; and to so remarkable a degree that, if I be not much mistaken, we shall find, that all mankind, both learned and ignorant, have always been of the same opinion with regard to this subject, and that a few intelligible definitions would immediately have put an end to the whole controversy. I own that this dispute has been so much canvassed on all hands, and has led philosophers into such a labyrinth of obscure sophistry, that it is no wonder, if a sensible reader indulge his ease so far as to turn a deaf ear to the proposal of such a question, from which he can expect neither instruction or entertainment. But the state of the argument here proposed may, perhaps, serve to renew his attention; as it has more novelty, promises at least some decision of the controversy, and will not much disturb his ease by any intricate or obscure reasoning.

I hope, therefore, to make it appear that all men have ever agreed in the doctrine both of necessity and of liberty, according to any reasonable sense, which can be put on these terms; and that the whole controversy, has hitherto turned merely upon words. We shall begin with examining the doctrine of necessity.

It is universally allowed that matter, in all its operations, is actuated by a necessary force, and that every natural effect is so precisely determined by the energy of its cause that no other effect, in such particular circumstances, could possibly have resulted from it. The degree and direction of every motion is, by the laws of nature, prescribed with such exactness that a living creature may as soon arise from the shock of two bodies as motion in any other degree or direction than what is actually produced by it. Would we, therefore, form a just and precise idea of *necessity*, we must consider whence that idea arises when we apply it to the operation of bodies.

It seems evident that, if all the scenes of nature were continually shifted in such a manner that no two events bore any resemblance to each other, but every object was entirely new, without any similitude to whatever had been seen before, we should never, in that case, have attained the least idea of necessity, or of a connexion among these objects. We might say, upon such a supposition, that one object or event has followed another; not that one was produced by the other. The relation of cause and effect must be utterly unknown to mankind. Inference and reasoning concerning the operations of nature would, from that moment, be at an end; and the memory and senses remain the only canals, by which the knowledge of any real existence could possibly have access to the mind. Our idea, therefore, of necessity and causation arises entirely from the uniformity observable in the operations of nature, where similar objects are constantly conjoined together, and the mind is determined by custom to infer the one from the appearance of the other. These two circumstances form the whole of that necessity, which we ascribe to matter. Beyond the constant *conjunction* of similar objects, and the consequent *inference* from one to the other, we have no notion of any necessity or connexion.

If it appear, therefore, that all mankind have ever allowed, without any doubt or hesitation, that these two circumstances take place in the voluntary actions of men, and in the operations of mind; it must follow, that all mankind have ever agreed in the doctrine of necessity, and that they have hitherto disputed, merely for not understanding each other.

As to the first circumstance, the constant and regular conjunction of similar events, we may possibly satisfy ourselves by the following considerations: It is universally acknowledged that there is a great uniformity among the actions of men, in all nations and ages, and that human nature remains still the same, in its principles and operations. The same motives always produce the same actions: the same events follow from the same causes. Ambition, avarice, self-love, vanity, friendship, generosity, public spirit: these passions, mixed in various degrees, and distributed through society, have been, from the beginning of the world, and still are, the source of all the actions and enterprises, which have ever been observed among mankind. Would you know the sentiments, inclinations, and course of life of the Greeks and Romans? Study well the temper and actions of the French and English: You cannot be much mistaken in transferring to the former *most* of the observations which you have made with regard to the latter. Mankind are so much the same, in all times and places, that history informs us of nothing new or strange in this particular. Its chief use is only to discover the constant and universal principles of human nature, by showing men in all varieties of circumstances and situations, and furnishing us with materials from which we may form our observations and become acquainted with the regular springs of human action and behaviour. These records of wars, intrigues, factions, and revolutions, are so many collections of experiments, by which the politician or moral philosopher fixes the principles of his science, in the same manner as the physician or natural philosopher becomes acquainted with the nature of plants, minerals, and other external objects, by the experiments which he forms concerning them. Nor are the earth, water, and other elements, examined by Aristotle, and Hippocrates, more like to those which at present lie under our observation than the men described by Polybius and Tacitus are to those who now govern the world.

Should a traveller, returning from a far country, bring us an account of men, wholly different from any with whom we were ever acquainted; men, who were entirely divested of avarice, ambition, or revenge; who knew no pleasure but friendship, generosity, and public spirit; we should immediately, from these circumstances, detect the falsehood, and prove him a liar, with the same certainty as if he had stuffed his narration with stories of centaurs and dragons, miracles and prodigies. And if we would explode any forgery in history, we cannot make use of a more convincing argument, than to prove, that the actions ascribed to any person are directly contrary to the course of nature, and that no human motives, in such circumstances, could ever induce him to such a conduct. The veracity of Quintus Curtius is as much to be suspected, when he describes the supernatural courage of Alexander, by which he was hurried on singly to attack multitudes, as when he describes his supernatural force and activity, by which he was able to resist them. So readily and universally do we acknowledge a uniformity in human motives and actions as well as in the operations of body.

Hence likewise the benefit of that experience, acquired by long life and a variety of business and company, in order to instruct us in the principles of human nature, and regulate our future conduct, as well as speculation. By means of this guide, we mount up to the knowledge of men's inclinations and motives, from their actions, expressions, and even gestures; and again descend to the interpretation of their actions from our knowledge of their motives and inclinations. The general observations treasured up by a course of experience, give us the clue of human nature, and teach us to unravel all its intricacies. Pretexts and appearances no longer deceive us. Public declarations pass for the specious colouring of a cause. And though virtue and honour be allowed their proper weight and authority, that perfect disinterestedness, so often pretended to, is never expected in multitudes and parties; seldom in their leaders; and scarcely even in individuals of any rank or station. But were there no uniformity in human actions, and were every experiment which we could form of this kind irregular and anomalous, it were impossible to collect any general observations concerning mankind; and no experience, however accurately digested by reflection, would ever serve to any purpose. Why is the aged husbandman more skilful in his calling than the young beginner but because there is a certain uniformity in the operation of the sun, rain, and earth towards the production of vegetables; and experience teaches the old practitioner the rules by which this operation is governed and directed.

We must not, however, expect that this uniformity of human actions should be carried to such a length as that all men, in the same circumstances, will always act precisely in the same manner, without making any allowance for the diversity of characters, prejudices, and opinions. Such a uniformity in every particular, is found in no part of nature. On the contrary, from observing the variety of conduct in different men, we are enabled to form a greater variety of maxims, which still suppose a degree of uniformity and regularity.

Are the manners of men different in different ages and countries? We learn thence the great force of custom and education, which mould the human mind from its infancy and form it into a fixed and established character. Is the behaviour and conduct of the one sex very unlike that of the other? Is it thence we become acquainted with the different characters which nature has impressed upon the sexes, and which she preserves with constancy and regularity? Are the actions of the same person much diversified in the different periods of his life, from infancy to old age? This affords room for many general observations concerning the gradual change of our sentiments and inclinations, and the different maxims which prevail in the different ages of human creatures. Even the characters, which are peculiar to each individual, have a uniformity in their influence; otherwise our acquaintance with the persons and our observation of their conduct could never teach us their dispositions, or serve to direct our behaviour with regard to them.

I grant it possible to find some actions, which seem to have no regular connexion with any known motives, and are exceptions to all the measures of conduct which have ever been established for the government of men. But if we would willingly know what judgment should be formed of such irregular and extraordinary actions, we may consider the sentiments commonly entertained with regard to those irregular events which appear in the course of nature, and the operations of external objects. All causes are not conjoined to their usual effects with like uniformity. An artificer, who handles only dead matter, may be disappointed of his aim, as well as the politician, who directs the conduct of sensible and intelligent agents.

The vulgar, who take things according to their first appearance, attribute the uncertainty of events to such an uncertainty in the causes as makes the latter often fail of their usual influence; though they meet with no impediment in their operation. But philosophers, observing that, almost in every part of nature, there is contained a vast variety of springs and principles, which are hid, by reason of their minuteness or remoteness, find, that it is at least possible the contrariety of events may not proceed from any contingency in the cause, but from the secret operation of contrary causes. This possibility is converted into certainty by farther observation, when they remark that, upon an exact scrutiny, a contrariety of effects always betrays a contrariety of causes, and proceeds from their mutual opposition. A peasant can give no better reason for the stopping of any clock or watch than to say that it does not commonly go right: But an artist easily perceives that the same force in the spring or pendulum has always the same influence on the wheels; but fails of its usual effects, perhaps by reason of a grain of dust, which puts a stop to the whole movement. From the observation of several parallel instances, philosophers form a maxim that the connexion between all causes and effects is equally necessary, and that its seeming uncertainty in some instances proceeds from the secret opposition of contrary causes.

Thus, for instance, in the human body, when the usual symptoms of health or sickness disappoint our expectation; when medicines operate not with their wonted powers; when irregular events follow from any particular cause; the philosopher and physician are not surprised at the matter, nor are ever tempted to deny, in general, the necessity and uniformity of those principles by which the animal economy is conducted. They know that a human body is a mighty complicated machine: That many secret powers lurk in it, which are altogether beyond our comprehension: That to us it must often appear very uncertain in its operations: And that therefore the irregular events, which outwardly discover themselves, can be no proof that the laws of nature are not observed with the greatest regularity in its internal operations and government.

The philosopher, if he be consistent, must apply the same reasoning to the actions and volitions of intelligent agents. The most irregular and unexpected resolutions of men may frequently be accounted for by those who know every particular circumstance of their character and situation. A person of an obliging disposition gives a peevish answer: But he has the toothache, or has not dined. A stupid fellow discovers an uncommon alacrity in his carriage: But he has met with a sudden piece of good fortune. Or even when an action, as sometimes happens, cannot be particularly accounted for, either by the person himself or by others; we know, in general, that the characters of men are, to a certain degree, inconstant and irregular. This is, in a manner, the constant character of human nature; though it be applicable, in a more particular manner, to some persons who have no fixed rule for their conduct, but proceed in a continued course of caprice and inconstancy. The internal principles and motives may operate in a uniform manner, notwithstanding these seeming irregularities; in the same manner as the winds, rain, cloud, and other variations of the weather are supposed to be governed by steady principles; though not easily discoverable by human sagacity and enquiry.

Thus it appears, not only that the conjunction between motives and voluntary actions is as regular and uniform as that between the cause and effect in any part of nature; but also that this regular conjunction has been universally acknowledged among mankind, and has never been the subject of dispute, either in philosophy or common life. Now, as it is from past experience that we draw all inferences concerning the future, and as we conclude that objects will always be conjoined together which we find to have always been conjoined; it may seem superfluous to prove that this experienced uniformity in human actions is a source whence we draw *inferences* concerning them. But in order to throw the argument into a greater variety of lights we shall also insist, though briefly, on this latter topic.

The mutual dependence of men is so great in all societies that scarce any human action is entirely complete in itself, or is performed without some reference to the actions of others, which are requisite to make it answer fully the intention of the agent. The poorest artificer, who labours alone, expects at least the protection of the magistrate, to ensure him the enjoyment of the fruits of his labour. He also expects that, when he carries his goods to market, and offers them at a reasonable price, he shall find purchasers, and shall be able, by the money he acquires, to engage others to supply him with those commodities which are requisite for his subsistence. In proportion as men extend their dealings, and render their intercourse with others more complicated, they always comprehend, in their schemes of life, a greater variety of voluntary actions, which they expect, from the proper motives, to co-operate with their own. In all these conclusions they take their measures from past experience, in the same manner as in their reasonings concerning external objects; and firmly believe that men, as well as all the elements, are to continue, in their operations, the same that they have ever found them. A manufacturer reckons upon the labour of his servants for the execution of any work as much as upon the tools which he employs, and would be equally surprised were his expectations disappointed. In short, this experimental inference and reasoning concerning the actions of others enters so much into human life that no man, while awake, is ever a moment without employing it. Have we not reason, therefore, to affirm that all mankind have always agreed in the doctrine of necessity according to the foregoing definition and explication of it?

Nor have philosophers even entertained a different opinion from the people in this particular. For, not to mention that almost every action of their life supposes that opinion, there are even few of the speculative parts of learning to which it is not essential. What would become of *history,* had we not a dependence on the veracity of the historian according to the experience which we have had of mankind? How could *politics* be a science, if laws and forms of government had not a uniform influence upon society? Where would be the foundation of *morals,* if particular characters had no certain or determinate power to produce particular sentiments, and if these sentiments had no constant operation on actions? And with what pretence could we employ our *criticism* upon any poet or polite author, if we could not pronounce the conduct and sentiments of his actors either natural or unnatural to such characters, and in such circumstances? It seems almost impossible, therefore, to engage either in science or action of any kind without acknowledging the doctrine of necessity, and this *inference* from motive to voluntary actions, from characters to conduct.

And indeed, when we consider how aptly *natural* and *moral* evidence link together, and form only one chain of argument, we shall make no scruple to allow that they are of the same nature, and derived from the same principles. A prisoner who has neither money nor interest, discovers the impossibility of his escape, as well when he considers the obstinacy of the gaoler, as the walls and bars with which he is surrounded; and, in all attempts for his freedom, chooses rather to work upon the stone and iron of the one, than upon the inflexible nature of the other. The same prisoner, when conducted to the scaffold, foresees his death as certainly from the constancy and fidelity of his guards, as from the operation of the axe or wheel. His mind runs along a certain train of ideas: the refusal of the soldiers to consent to his escape; the action of the executioner; the separation of the head and body; bleeding, convulsive motions, and death. Here is a connected chain of natural causes and voluntary actions; but the mind feels no difference between them in passing from one link to another: Nor is it less certain of the future event than if it were connected with the objects present to the memory or senses, by a train of causes, cemented together by what we are pleased to call a *physical* necessity. The same experienced union has the same effect on the mind, whether the united objects be motives, volition, and actions; or figure and motion. We may change the name of things; but their nature and their operation on the understanding never change.

Were a man, whom I know to be honest and opulent, and with whom I live in intimate friendship, to come into my house, where I am surrounded with my servants, I rest assured that he is not to stab me before he leaves it in order to rob me of my silver standish; and I no more suspect this event than the falling of the house itself, which is new, and solidly built and founded.—*But he may have been seized with a sudden and unknown frenzy.*—So may a sudden earthquake arise, and shake and tumble my house about my ears. I shall therefore change the suppositions. I shall say that I know with certainty that he is not to put his hand into the fire and hold it there till it be consumed: and this event, I think I can foretell with the same assurance, as that, if he throw himself out at the window, and meet with no obstruction, he will not remain a moment suspended in the air. No suspicion of an unknown frenzy can give the least possibility to the former event, which is so contrary to all the known principles of human nature. A man who at noon leaves his purse full of gold on the pavement at Charing-Cross, may as well expect that it will fly away like a feather, as that he will find it untouched an hour after. Above one half of human reasonings contain inferences of a similar nature, attended with more or less degrees of certainty proportioned to our experience of the usual conduct of mankind in such particular situations.

I have frequently considered, what could possibly be the reason why all mankind, though they have ever, without hesitation, acknowledged the doctrine of necessity in their whole practice and reasoning, have yet discovered such a reluctance to acknowledge it in words, and have rather shown a propensity, in all ages, to profess the contrary opinion. The matter, I think, may be accounted for after the following manner. If we examine the operations of body, and the production of effects from their causes, we shall find that all our faculties can never carry us farther in our knowledge of this relation than barely to observe that particular objects are *constantly conjoined* together, and that the mind is carried, by a *customary transition,* from the appearance of one to the belief of the other. But though this conclusion concerning human ignorance be the result of the strictest scrutiny of this subject, men still entertain a strong propensity to believe that they penetrate farther into the powers of nature, and perceive something like a necessary connexion between the cause and the effect. When again they turn their reflections towards the operations of their own minds, and *feel* no such connexion of the motive and the action; they are thence apt to suppose, that there is a difference between the effects which result from material force, and those which arise from thought and intelligence. But being once convinced that we know nothing farther of causation of any kind than merely the *constant conjunction* of objects, and the consequent *inference* of the mind from one to another, and finding that these two circumstances are universally allowed to have place in voluntary actions; we may be more easily led to own the same necessity common to all causes. And though this reasoning may contradict the systems of many philosophers, in ascribing necessity to the determinations of the will, we shall find, upon reflection, that they dissent from it in words only, not in their real sentiment. Necessity, according to the sense in which it is here taken, has never yet been rejected, nor can ever, I think, be rejected by any philosopher. It may only, perhaps, be pretended that the mind can perceive, in the operations of matter, some farther connexion between the cause and effect; and connexion that has not place in voluntary actions of intelligent beings. Now whether it be so or not, can only appear upon examination; and it is incumbent on these philosophers to make good their assertion, by defining or describing that necessity, and pointing it out to us in the operations of material causes.

It would seem, indeed, that men begin at the wrong end of this question concerning liberty and necessity, when they enter upon it by examining the faculties of the soul, the influence of the understanding, and the operations of the will. Let them first discuss a more simple question, namely, the operations of body and of brute unintelligent matter; and try whether they can there form any idea of causation and necessity, except that of a constant conjunction of objects, and subsequent inference of the mind from one to another. If these circumstances form, in reality, the whole of that necessity, which we conceive in matter, and if these circumstances be also universally acknowledged to take place in the operations of the mind, the dispute is at an end; at least, must be owned to be thenceforth merely verbal. But as long as we will rashly suppose, that we have some farther idea of necessity and causation in the operations of external objects; at the same time, that we can find nothing farther in the voluntary actions of the mind; there is no possibility of bringing the question to any determinate issue, while we proceed upon so erroneous a supposition. The only method of undeceiving us is to mount up higher; to examine the narrow extent of science when applied to material causes; and to convince ourselves that all we know of them is the constant conjunction and inference above mentioned. We may, perhaps, find that it is with difficulty we are induced to fix such narrow limits to human understanding: but we can afterwards find no difficulty when we come to apply this doctrine to the actions of the will. For as it is evident that these have a regular conjunction with motives and circumstances and characters, and as we always draw inferences from one to the other, we must be obliged to acknowledge in words that necessity, which we have already avowed, in every deliberation of our lives, and in every step of our conduct and behaviour.[1]

But to proceed in this reconciling project with regard to the question of liberty and necessity; the most contentious question of metaphysics, the most contentious science; it will not require many words to prove, that all mankind

[1] The prevalence of the doctrine of liberty may be accounted for, from another cause, viz. a false sensation or seeming experience which we have, or may have, of liberty or indifference, in many of our actions. The necessity of any action, whether of matter or of mind, is not, properly speaking, a quality in the agent, but in any thinking or intelligent being, who may consider the action; and it consists chiefly in the determination of his thoughts to infer the existence of that action from some preceding objects; as liberty, when opposed to necessity, is nothing but the want of that determination, and a certain looseness or indifference, which we feel, in passing, or not passing, from the idea of one object to that of any succeeding one. Now we may observe, that, though, in *reflecting* on human actions, we seldom feel such a looseness, or indifference, but are commonly able to infer them with considerable certainty from their motives, and from the dispositions of the agent; yet it frequently happens, that, in *performing* the actions themselves, we are sensible of something like it: And as all resembling objects are readily taken for each other, this has been employed as a demonstrative and even intuitive proof of human liberty. We feel, that our actions are subject to our will, on most occasions; and imagine we feel, that the will itself is subject to nothing, because, when by a denial of it we are provoked to try, we feel, that it moves easily every way, and produces an image of itself (or a *Velleity*, as it is called in the schools) even on that side, on which it did not settle. This image, or faint motion, we persuade ourselves, could, at that time, have been compleated into the thing itself; because, should that be denied, we find, upon a second trial, that, at present, it can. We consider not, that the fantastical desire of shewing liberty, is here the motive of our actions. And it seems certain, that, however we may imagine we feel a liberty within ourselves, a spectator can commonly infer our actions from our motives and character; and even where he cannot, he concludes in general, that he might, were he perfectly acquainted with every circumstance of our situation and temper, and the most secret springs of our complexion and disposition. Now this is the very essence of necessity, according to the foregoing doctrine.

have ever agreed in the doctrine of liberty as well as in that of necessity, and that the whole dispute, in this respect also, has been hitherto merely verbal. For what is meant by liberty, when applied to voluntary actions? We cannot surely mean that actions have so little connexion with motives, inclinations, and circumstances, that one does not follow with a certain degree of uniformity from the other, and that one affords no inference by which we can conclude the existence of the other. For these are plain and acknowledged matters of fact. By liberty, then, we can only mean *a power of acting or not acting, according to the determinations of the will;* this is, if we choose to remain at rest, we may; if we choose to move, we also may. Now this hypothetical liberty is universally allowed to belong to every one who is not a prisoner and in chains. Here, then, is no subject of dispute.

Whatever definition we may give of liberty, we should be careful to observe two requisite circumstances; *First,* that it be consistent with plain matter of fact; *secondly,* that it be consistent with itself. If we observe these circumstances, and render our definition intelligible, I am persuaded that all mankind will be found of one opinion with regard to it.

It is universally allowed that nothing exists without a cause of its existence, and that chance, when strictly examined, is a mere negative word, and means not any real power which has anywhere a being in nature. But it is pretended that some causes are necessary, some not necessary. Here then is the advantage of definitions. Let any one *define* a cause, without comprehending, as a part of the definition, a *necessary connexion* with its effect; and let him show distinctly the origin of the idea, expressed by the definition; and I shall readily give up the whole controversy. But if the foregoing explication of the matter be received, this must be absolutely impracticable. Had not objects a regular conjunction with each other, we should never have entertained any notion of cause and effect; and this regular conjunction produces that inference of the understanding, which is the only connexion, that we can have any comprehension of. Whoever attempts a defi-

nition of cause, exclusive of these circumstances, will be
obliged either to employ unintelligible terms or such as
are synonymous to the term which he endeavours to define.[2]
And if the definition above mentioned be admitted; liberty,
when opposed to necessity, not to constraint, is the same
thing with chance; which is universally allowed to have no
existence.

## PART II

THERE is no method of reasoning more common, and
yet none more blameable, than, in philosophical disputes,
to endeavour the refutation of any hypothesis, by a pretence of its dangerous consequences to religion and morality. When any opinion leads to absurdities, it is certainly false; but it is not certain that an opinion is false,
because it is of dangerous consequence. Such topics, therefore, ought entirely to be forborne; as serving nothing to
the discovery of truth, but only to make the person of an
antagonist odious. This I observe in general, without pretending to draw any advantage from it. I frankly submit
to an examination of this kind, and shall venture to affirm
that the doctrines, both of necessity and of liberty, as above
explained, are not only consistent with morality, but are
absolutely essential to its support.

Necessity may be defined two ways, conformably to the
two definitions of *cause,* of which it makes an essential part.
It consists either in the constant conjunction of like objects,
or in the inference of the understanding from one object
to another. Now necessity, in both these senses, (which,
indeed, are at bottom the same) has universally, though
tacitly, in the schools, in the pulpit, and in common life,
been allowed to belong to the will of man; and no one
has ever pretended to deny that we can draw inferences
concerning human actions, and that those inferences are
founded on the experienced union of like actions, with like

[2] Thus, if a cause be defined, *that which produces any thing;* it is easy
to observe, that *producing* is synonymous to *causing.* In like manner, if a
cause be defined, *that by which any thing exists;* this is liable to the same
objection. For what is meant by these words, *by which?* Had it been
said, that a cause is *that* after which *any thing constantly exists;* we should
have understood the terms. For this is, indeed, all we know of the matter. And this constancy forms the very essence of necessity, nor have we
any other idea of it.

motives, inclinations, and circumstances. The only particular in which any one can differ, is, that either, perhaps, he will refuse to give the name of necessity to this property of human actions: but as long as the meaning is understood, I hope the word can do no harm: or that he will maintain it possible to discover something farther in the operations of matter. But this, it must be acknowledged, can be of no consequence to morality or religion, whatever it may be to natural philosophy or metaphysics. We may here be mistaken in asserting that there is no idea of any other necessity or connexion in the actions of body: But surely we ascribe nothing to the actions of the mind, but what everyone does, and must readily allow of. We change no circumstance in the received orthodox system with regard to the will, but only in that with regard to material objects and causes. Nothing, therefore, can be more innocent, at least, than this doctrine.

All laws being founded on rewards and punishments, it is supposed as a fundamental principle, that these motives have a regular and uniform influence on the mind, and both produce the good and prevent the evil actions. We may give to this influence what name we please; but, as it is usually conjoined with the action, it must be esteemed a *cause,* and be looked upon as an instance of that necessity, which we would here establish.

The only proper object of hatred or vengeance is a person or creature, endowed with thought and consciousness; and when any criminal or injurious actions excite that passion, it is only by their relation to the person, or connexion with him. Actions are, by their very nature, temporary and perishing; and where they proceed not from some *cause* in the character and disposition of the person who performed them, they can neither redound to his honour, if good; nor infamy, if evil. The actions themselves may be blameable; they may be contrary to all the rules of morality and religion: but the person is not answerable for them; and as they proceeded from nothing in him that is durable and constant, and leave nothing of that nature behind them, it is impossible he can, upon their account, become the object of punishment or vengeance.

According to the principle, therefore, which denies necessity, and consequently causes, a man is as pure and untainted, after having committed the most horrid crime, as at the first moment of his birth, nor is his character anywise concerned in his actions, since they are not derived from it, and the wickedness of the one can never be used as a proof of the depravity of the other.

Men are not blamed for such actions as they perform ignorantly and casually, whatever may be the consequences. Why? but because the principles of these actions are only momentary, and terminate in them alone. Men are less blamed for such actions as they perform hastily and unpremeditatedly than for such as proceed from deliberation. For what reason? but because a hasty temper, though a constant cause or principle in the mind, operates only by intervals, and infects not the whole character. Again, repentance wipes off every crime, if attended with a reformation of life and manners. How is this to be accounted for? but by asserting that actions render a person criminal merely as they are proofs of criminal principles in the mind; and when, by an alteration of these principles, they cease to be just proofs, they likewise cease to be criminal. But, except upon the doctrine of necessity, they never were just proofs, and consequently never were criminal.

It will be equally easy to prove, and from the same arguments, that *liberty,* according to that definition above mentioned, in which all men agree, is also essential to morality, and that no human actions, where it is wanting, are susceptible of any moral qualities, or can be the objects either of approbation or dislike. For as actions are objects of our moral sentiment, so far only as they are indications of the internal character, passions, and affections; it is impossible that they can give rise either to praise or blame, where they proceed not from these principles, but are derived altogether from external violence.

I pretend not to have obviated or removed all objections to this theory, with regard to necessity and liberty. I can foresee other objections, derived from topics which have not here been treated of. It may be said, for instance, that, if voluntary actions be subjected to the same laws of necessity with the operations of matter, there is a continued chain of necessary causes, pre-ordained and pre-determined, reaching from the original cause of all to every single volition of every human creature. No contingency anywhere in the universe; no indifference; no liberty. While we act, we are, at the same time, acted upon. The ultimate Author of all our volitions is the Creator of the world, who first bestowed motion on this immense machine, and placed all beings in that particular position, whence every subsequent event, by an inevitable necessity, must result. Human actions, therefore, either can have no moral turpitude at all, as proceeding from so good a cause; or if they have any turpitude, they must involve our Creator in the same guilt, while he is acknowledged to be their ultimate cause and author. For as a man, who fired a mine, is answerable for all the consequences whether the train he employed be long or short; so wherever a continued chain of necessary causes is fixed, that Being, either finite or infinite, who produces the first, is likewise the author of all the rest, and must both bear the blame and acquire the praise which belong to them. Our clear and unalterable ideas of morality establish this rule, upon unquestionable reasons, when we examine the consequences of any human action; and these reasons must still have greater force when applied to the volitions and intentions of a Being infinitely wise and powerful. Ignorance or impotence may be pleaded for so limited a creature as man; but those imperfections have no place in our Creator. He foresaw, he ordained, he intended all those actions of men, which we so rashly pronounce criminal. And we must therefore conclude, either that they are not criminal, or that the Deity, not man, is accountable for them. But as either of these positions is absurd and impious, it follows, that the doctrine from which they are deduced cannot possibly be true, as being liable to all the same objections. An absurd consequence, if necessary, proves the original doctrine to be absurd; in the same manner as criminal actions render criminal the original cause, if the connexion between them be necessary and inevitable.

This objection consists of two parts, which we shall

examine separately; *First,* that, if human actions can be traced up, by a necessary chain, to the Deity, they can never be criminal; on account of the infinite perfection of that Being from whom they are derived, and who can intend nothing but what is altogether good and laudable. Or, *Secondly,* if they be criminal, we must retract the attribute of perfection, which we ascribe to the Deity, and must acknowledge him to be the ultimate author of guilt and moral turpitude in all his creatures.

The answer to the first objection seems obvious and convincing. There are many philosophers who, after an exact scrutiny of all the phenomena of nature, conclude, that the WHOLE, considered as one system, is, in every period of its existence, ordered with perfect benevolence; and that the utmost possible happiness will, in the end, result to all created beings, without any mixture of positive or absolute ill or misery. Every physical ill, say they, makes an essential part of this benevolent system, and could not possibly be removed, even by the Deity himself, considered as a wise agent, without giving entrance to greater ill, or excluding greater good, which will result from it. From this theory, some philosophers, and the ancient *Stoics* among the rest, derived a topic of consolation under all afflictions, while they taught their pupils that those ills under which they laboured were, in reality, goods to the universe; and that to an enlarged view, which could comprehend the whole system of nature, every event became an object of joy and exultation. But though this topic be specious and sublime, it was soon found in practice weak and ineffectual. You would surely more irritate than appease a man lying under the racking pains of the gout by preaching up to him the rectitude of those general laws, which produced the malignant humours in his body, and led them through the proper canals, to the sinews and nerves, where they now excite such acute torments. These enlarged views may, for a moment, please the imagination of a speculative man, who is placed in ease and security; but neither can they dwell with constancy on his mind, even though undisturbed by the emotions of pain or passion; much less can they maintain their ground when attacked by such powerful antagonists. The affections take a narrower and more natural survey of their object; and by an economy, more suitable to the infirmity of human minds, regard alone the beings around us, and are actuated by such events as appear good or ill to the private system.

The case is the same with *moral* as with *physical* ill. It cannot reasonably be supposed, that those remote considerations, which are found of so little efficacy with regard to one, will have a more powerful influence with regard to the other. The mind of man is so formed by nature that, upon the appearance of certain characters, dispositions, and actions, it immediately feels the sentiment of approbation or blame; nor are there any emotions more essential to its frame and constitution. The characters which engage our approbation are chiefly such as contribute to the peace and security of human society; as the characters which excite blame are chiefly such as tend to public detriment and disturbance: whence it may reasonably be presumed, that the moral sentiments arise, either mediately or immediately, from a reflection of these opposite interests. What though philosophical meditations establish a different opinion or conjecture; that everything is right with regard to the WHOLE, and that the qualities, which disturb society, are, in the main, as beneficial, and are as suitable to the primary intention of nature as those which more directly promote its happiness and welfare? Are such remote and uncertain speculations able to counterbalance the sentiments which arise from the natural and immediate view of the objects? A man who is robbed of a considerable sum; does he find his vexation for the loss anywise diminished by these sublime reflections? Why then should his moral resentment against the crime be supposed incompatible with them? Or why should not the acknowledgment of a real distinction between vice and virtue be reconcileable to all speculative systems of philosophy, as well as that of a real distinction between personal beauty and deformity? Both these distinctions are founded in the natural sentiments of the human mind: And these sentiments are not to be controuled or altered by any philosophical theory or speculation whatsoever.

The *second* objection admits not of so easy and satisfactory an answer; nor is it possible to explain distinctly, how the Deity can be the mediate cause of all the actions of men, without being the author of sin and moral turpitude. These are mysteries, which mere natural and unassisted reason is very unfit to handle; and whatever system she embraces, she must find herself involved in inextricable difficulties, and even contradictions, at every step which she takes with regard to such subjects. To reconcile the indifference and contingency of human actions with prescience; or to defend absolute decrees, and yet free the Deity from being the author of sin, has been found hitherto to exceed all the power of philosophy. Happy, if she be thence sensible of her temerity, when she pries into these sublime mysteries; and leaving a scene so full of obscurities and perplexities, return, with suitable modesty, to her true and proper province, the examination of common life; where she will find difficulties enough to employ her enquiries, without launching into so boundless an ocean of doubt, uncertainty, and contradiction!

# SECTION IX

## OF THE REASON OF ANIMALS

ALL our reasonings concerning matter of fact are founded on a species of Analogy, which leads us to expect from any cause the same events, which we have observed to result from similar causes. Where the causes are entirely similar, the analogy is perfect, and the inference, drawn from it, is regarded as certain and conclusive: nor does any man ever entertain a doubt, where he sees a piece of iron, that it will have weight and cohesion of parts; as in all other instances, which have ever fallen under his observation. But where the objects have not so exact a similarity, the analogy is less perfect, and the inference is less conclusive; though still it has some force, in proportion to the degree of similarity and resemblance. The anatomical observations, formed upon one animal, are, by this species of reasoning, extended to all animals; and it is certain, that when the circulation of the blood, for instance, is clearly proved to have place in one creature, as a frog, or fish, it forms a strong presumption, that the same principle has place in all. These analogical observations may be carried farther, even to this science, of which we are now treating; and any theory, by which we explain the operations of the understanding, or the origin and connexion of the passions in man, will acquire additional authority, if we find, that the same theory is requisite to explain the same phenomena in all other animals. We shall make trial of this, with regard to the hypothesis, by which we have, in the foregoing discourse, endeavoured to account for all experimental reasonings; and it is hoped, that this new point of view will serve to confirm all our former observations.

*First,* It seems evident, that animals as well as men learn many things from experience, and infer, that the same events will always follow from the same causes. By this principle they become acquainted with the more obvious properties of external objects, and gradually, from their birth, treasure up a knowledge of the nature of fire, water, earth, stones, heights, depths, &c., and of the effects which result from their operation. The ignorance and inexperience of the young are here plainly distinguishable from the cunning and sagacity of the old, who have learned, by long observation, to avoid what hurt them, and to pursue what gave ease or pleasure. A horse, that has been accustomed to the field, becomes acquainted with the proper height which he can leap, and will never attempt what exceeds his force and ability. An old greyhound will trust the more fatiguing part of the chace to the younger, and will place himself so as to meet the hare in her doubles; nor are the conjectures, which he forms on this occasion, founded in any thing but his observation and experience.

This is still more evident from the effects of discipline and education on animals, who, by the proper application of rewards and punishments, may be taught any course of action, and most contrary to their natural instincts and propensities. Is it not experience, which renders a dog apprehensive of pain, when you menace him, or lift up the whip to beat him? Is it not even experience, which makes him answer to his name, and infer, from such an arbitrary sound, that you mean him rather than any of his fellows, and intend to call him, when you pronounce it in a certain manner, and with a certain tone and accent?

In all these cases, we may observe, that the animal infers some fact beyond what immediately strikes his senses; and that this inference is altogether founded on past experience, while the creature expects from the present object the same consequences, which it has always found in its observation to result from similar objects.

*Secondly,* It is impossible, that this inference of the animal can be founded on any process of argument or reasoning, by which he concludes, that like events must follow like objects, and that the course of nature will always be regular in its operations. For if there be in reality any arguments of this nature, they surely lie too abstruse for the observation of such imperfect understandings; since it may well employ the utmost care and attention of a philosophic genius to discover and observe them. Animals, therefore are not guided in these inferences by reasoning: neither are children; neither are the generality of mankind, in their ordinary actions and conclusions: neither are philosophers themselves, who, in all the active parts of life, are, in the main, the same with the vulgar, and are governed by the same maxims. Nature must have provided some other principle, of more ready, and more general use and application; nor can an operation of such immense consequence in life, as that of inferring effects from causes, be trusted to the uncertain process of reasoning and argumentation. Were this doubtful with regard to men, it seems to admit of no question with regard to the brute creation; and the conclusion being once firmly established in the one, we have a strong presumption, from all the rules of analogy, that it ought to be universally admitted, without any exception or reserve. It is custom alone, which engages animals, from every object, that strikes their senses, to infer its usual attendant, and carries their imagination, from the appearance of the one, to conceive the other, in that particular manner, which we denominate *belief*. No other explication can be given of this operation, in all the higher, as well as lower classes of sensitive beings, which fall under our notice and observation.[1]

[1] Since all reasoning concerning facts or causes is derived merely from custom, it may be asked how it happens, that men so much surpass animals in reasoning, and one man so much surpasses another? Has not the same custom the same influence on all?

We shall here endeavour briefly to explain the great difference in human understandings: After which the reason of the difference between men and animals will easily be comprehended.

1. When we have lived any time, and have been accustomed to the uniformity of nature, we acquire a general habit, by which we always transfer the known to the unknown, and conceive the latter to resemble the former. By means of this general habitual principle, we regard even one experiment as the foundation of reasoning, and expect a similar event with some degree of certainty, where the experiment has been made accurately, and free from all foreign circumstances. It is therefore considered as a matter of great importance to observe the consequences of things; and as one man may very much surpass another in attention and memory and observation, this will make a very great difference in their reasoning.

2. Where there is a complication of causes to produce any effect, one mind may be much larger than another, and better able to comprehend the whole system of objects, and to infer justly their consequences.

3. One man is able to carry on a chain of consequences to a greater length than another.

4. Few men can think long without running into a confusion of ideas, and mistaking one for another; and there are various degrees of this infirmity.

But though animals learn many parts of their knowledge from observation, there are also many parts of it, which they derive from the original hand of nature; which much exceed the share of capacity they possess on ordinary occasions; and in which they improve, little or nothing, by the longest practice and experience. These we denominate Instincts, and are so apt to admire as something very extraordinary, and inexplicable by all the disquisitions of human understanding. But our wonder will, perhaps, cease or diminish, when we consider, that the experimental reasoning itself, which we possess in common with beasts, and on which the whole conduct of life depends, is nothing but a species of instinct or mechanical power, that acts in us unknown to ourselves; and in its chief operations, is not directed by any such relations or comparisons of ideas, as are the proper objects of our intellectual faculties. Though the instinct be different, yet still it is an instinct, which teaches a man to avoid the fire; as much as that, which teaches a bird, with such exactness, the art of incubation, and the whole economy and order of its nursery.

5. The circumstance, on which the effect depends, is frequently involved in other circumstances, which are foreign and extrinsic. The separation of it often requires great attention, accuracy, and subtility.

6. The forming of general maxims from particular observation is a very nice operation; and nothing is more usual, from haste or a narrowness of mind, which sees not on all sides, than to commit mistakes in this particular.

7. When we reason from analogies, the man, who has the greater experience or the greater promptitude of suggesting analogies, will be the better reasoner.

8. Biases from prejudice, education, passion, party, &c. hang more upon one mind than another.

9. After we have acquired a confidence in human testimony, books and conversation enlarge much more the sphere of one man's experience and thought than those of another.

It would be easy to discover many other circumstances that make a difference in the understandings of men.

# SECTION X

## OF MIRACLES

### PART I

THERE is, in Dr. Tillotson's writings, an argument against the *real presence,* which is as concise, and elegant, and strong as any argument can possibly be supposed against a doctrine, so little worthy of a serious refutation. It is acknowledged on all hands, says that learned prelate, that the authority, either of the scripture or of tradition, is founded merely in the testimony of the Apostles, who were eye-witnesses to those miracles of our Saviour, by which he proved his divine mission. Our evidence, then, for, the truth of the *Christian* religion is less than the evidence for the truth of our senses; because, even in the first authors of our religion, it was no greater; and it is evident it must diminish in passing from them to their disciples; nor can any one rest such confidence in their testimony, as in the immediate object of his senses. But a weaker evidence can never destroy a stronger; and therefore, were the doctrine of the real presence ever so clearly revealed in scripture, it were directly contrary to the rules of just reasoning to give our assent to it. It contradicts sense, though both the scripture and tradition, on which it is supposed to be built, carry not such evidence with them as sense; when they are considered merely as external evidences, and are not brought home to every one's breast, by the immediate operation of the Holy Spirit.

Nothing is so convenient as a decisive argument of this kind, which must at least *silence* the most arrogant bigotry and superstition, and free us from their impertinent solicitations. I flatter myself, that I have discovered an argument of a like nature, which, if just, will, with the wise and learned, be an everlasting check to all kinds of superstitious delusion, and consequently, will be useful as long as the world endures. For so long, I presume, will the accounts of miracles and prodigies be found in all history, sacred and profane.

Though experience be our only guide in reasoning concerning matters of fact; it must be acknowledged, that this guide is not altogether infallible, but in some cases is apt to lead us into errors. One, who in our climate, should expect better weather in any week of June than in one of December, would reason justly, and conformably to experience; but it is certain, that he may happen, in the event, to find himself mistaken. However, we may observe, that, in such a case, he would have no cause to complain of experience; because it commonly informs us beforehand of the uncertainty, by that contrariety of events, which we may learn from a diligent observation. All effects follow not with like certainty from their supposed causes. Some events are found, in all countries and all ages, to have been constantly conjoined together: Others are found to have been more variable, and sometimes to disappoint our expectations; so that, in our reasonings concerning matter of fact, there are all imaginable degrees of assurance, from the highest certainty to the lowest species of moral evidence.

A wise man, therefore, proportions his belief to the evidence. In such conclusions as are founded on an infallible experience, he expects the event with the last degree of assurance, and regards his past experience as a full *proof* of the future existence of that event. In other cases, he proceeds with more caution: he weighs the opposite experiments: he considers which side is supported by the greater number of experiments: to that side he inclines, with doubt and hesitation; and when at last he fixes his judgement, the evidence exceeds not what we properly call *probability*. All probability, then, supposes an opposition of experiments and observations, where the one side is found to overbalance the other, and to produce a degree of evidence, proportioned to the superiority. A hundred instances or experiments on one side, and fifty on another, afford a doubtful expectation of any event; though a hundred uniform experiments, with only one that is contradictory, reasonably beget a pretty strong degree of assurance. In all cases, we must balance the opposite experiments, where they are opposite, and deduct the smaller number from the greater, in order to know the exact force of the superior evidence.

To apply these principles to a particular instance; we may observe, that there is no species of reasoning more common, more useful, and even necessary to human life, than that which is derived from the testimony of men, and the reports of eye-witnesses and spectators. This species of reasoning, perhaps, one may deny to be founded on the relation of cause and effect. I shall not dispute about a word. It will be sufficient to observe that our assurance in any argument of this kind is derived from no other principle than our observation of the veracity of human testimony, and of the usual conformity of facts to the reports of witnesses. It being a general maxim, that no objects have any discoverable connexion together, and that all the inferences, which we can draw from one to another, are founded merely on our experience of their constant and regular conjunction; it is evident, that we ought not to make an exception to this maxim in favour of human testimony, whose connexion with any event seems, in itself, as little necessary as any other. Were not the memory tenacious to a certain degree; had not men commonly an inclination to truth and a principle of probity; were they not sensible to shame, when detected in a falsehood: were not these, I say, discovered by *experience* to be qualities, inherent in human nature, we should never repose the least confidence in human testimony. A man delirious, or noted for falsehood and villainy, has no manner of authority with us.

And as the evidence, derived from witnesses and human testimony, is founded on past experience, so it varies with the experience, and is regarded either as a *proof* or a *probability,* according as the conjunction between any particular kind of report and any kind of object has been found to be constant or variable. There are a number of circumstances to be taken into consideration in all judgements of this kind; and the ultimate standard, by which we determine all disputes, that may arise concerning them, is always derived from experience and observation. Where this experience is not entirely uniform on any side, it is attended with an unavoidable contrariety in our judgements, and with the same opposition and mutual destruction of argument as in every other kind of evidence. We frequently hesitate concerning the reports of others. We balance the opposite circumstances, which cause any doubt or uncertainty; and when we discover a superiority on any side, we incline to it; but still with a diminution of assurance, in proportion to the force of its antagonist.

This contrariety of evidence, in the present case, may be derived from several different causes; from the opposition of contrary testimony; from the character or number of the witnesses; from the manner of their delivering their testimony; or from the union of all these circumstances. We entertain a suspicion concerning any matter of fact, when the witnesses contradict each other; when they are but few, or of a doubtful character; when they have an interest in what they affirm; when they deliver their testimony with hesitation, or on the contrary, with too violent asseverations. There are many other particulars of the same kind, which may diminish or destroy the force of any argument, derived from human testimony.

Suppose, for instance, that the fact, which the testimony endeavours to establish, partakes of the extraordinary and the marvellous; in that case, the evidence, resulting from the testimony, admits of a diminution, greater or less, in proportion as the fact is more or less unusual. The reason why we place any credit in witnesses and historians, is not derived from any *connexion,* which we perceive *à priori,* between testimony and reality, but because we are accustomed to find a conformity between them. But when the fact attested is such a one as has seldom fallen under our observation, here is a contest of two opposite experiences; of which the one destroys the other, as far as its force goes, and the superior can only operate on the mind by the force, which remains. The very same principle of experience, which gives us a certain degree of assurance in the testimony of witnesses, gives us also, in this case, another degree of assurance against the fact, which they endeavour to establish; from which contradiction there necessarily arises a counterpoize, and mutual destruction of belief and authority.

*I should not believe such a story were it told me by Cato,* was a proverbial saying in Rome, even during the lifetime of that philosophical patriot.[1]   The incredibility of a fact, it was allowed, might invalidate so great an authority.

The Indian prince, who refused to believe the first relations concerning the effects of frost, reasoned justly; and it naturally required very strong testimony to engage his assent to facts, that arose from a state of nature, with which he was unacquainted, and which bore so little analogy to those events, of which he had had constant and uniform experience.  Though they were not contrary to his experience, they were not conformable to it.[2]

But in order to encrease the probability against the testimony of witnesses, let us suppose, that the fact, which they affirm, instead of being only marvellous, is really miraculous; and suppose also, that the testimony considered apart and in itself, amounts to an entire proof; in that case, there is proof against proof, of which the strongest must prevail, but still with a diminution of its force, in proportion to that of its antagonist.

A miracle is a violation of the laws of nature; and as a firm and unalterable experience has established these laws, the proof against a miracle, from the very nature of the fact, is as entire as any argument from experience can possibly

[1] Plutarch, in vita Catonis.

[2] No Indian, it is evident, could have experience that water did not freeze in cold climates.  This is placing nature in a situation quite unknown to him; and it is impossible for him to tell *à priori* what will result from it. It is making a new experiment, the consequence of which is always uncertain.   One may sometimes conjecture from analogy what will follow; but still this is but conjecture.  And it must be confessed, that, in the present case of freezing, the event follows contrary to the rules of analogy, and is such as a rational Indian would not look for.  The operations of cold upon water are not gradual, according to the degrees of cold; but whenever it comes to the freezing point, the water passes in a moment, from the utmost liquidity to perfect hardness.  Such an event, therefore, may be denominated *extraordinary,* and requires a pretty strong testimony, to render it credible to people in a warm climate:  But still it is not *miraculous,* nor contrary to uniform experience of the course of nature in cases where all the circumstances are the same.  The inhabitants of Sumatra have always seen water fluid in their own climate, and the freezing of their rivers ought to be deemed a prodigy:  But they never saw water in Muscovy during the winter; and therefore they cannot reasonably be positive what would there be the consequence.

be imagined. Why is it more than probable, that all men must die; that lead cannot, of itself, remain suspended in the air; that fire consumes wood, and is extinguished by water; unless it be, that these events are found agreeable to the laws of nature, and there is required a violation of these laws, or in other words, a miracle to prevent them? Nothing is esteemed a miracle, if it ever happen in the common course of nature. It is no miracle that a man, seemingly in good health, should die on a sudden: because such a kind of death, though more unusual than any other, has yet been frequently observed to happen. But it is a miracle, that a dead man should come to life; because that has never been observed in any age or country. There must, therefore, be a uniform experience against every miraculous event, otherwise the event would not merit that appellation. And as a uniform experience amounts to a proof, there is here a direct and full *proof,* from the nature of the fact, against the existence of any miracle; nor can such a proof be destroyed, or the miracle rendered credible, but by an opposite proof, which is superior.[3]

The plain consequence is (and it is a general maxim worthy of our attention), ' that no testimony is sufficient to establish a miracle, unless the testimony be of such a kind, that its falsehood would be more miraculous, than the fact, which it endeavors to establish; and even in that case there is a mutual destruction of arguments, and the superior only gives us an assurance suitable to that

[3] Sometimes an event may not, *in itself, seem* to be contrary to the laws of nature, and yet, if it were real, it might, by reason of some circumstances, be denominated a miracle; because, in *fact,* it is contrary to these laws. Thus if a person, claiming a divine authority, should command a sick person to be well, a healthful man to fall down dead, the clouds to pour rain, the winds to blow, in short, should order many natural events, which immediately follow upon his command; these might justly be esteemed miracles, because they are really, in this case, contrary to the laws of nature. For if any suspicion remain, that the event and command concurred by accident, there is no miracle and no transgression of the laws of nature. If this suspicion be removed, there is evidently a miracle, and a transgression of these laws; because nothing can be more contrary to nature than that the voice or command of a man should have such an influence. A miracle may be accurately defined, *a transgression of a law of nature by a particular volition of the Deity, or by the interposition of some invisible agent.* A miracle may either be discoverable by men or not. This alters not its nature and essence. The raising of a house or ship into the air is a visible miracle. The raising of a feather, when the wind wants ever so little of a force requisite for that purpose, is as real a miracle, though not so sensible with regard to us.

degree of force, which remains, after deducting the inferior.' When anyone tells me, that he saw a dead man restored to life, I immediately consider with myself, whether it be more probable, that this person should either deceive or be deceived, or that the fact, which he relates, should really have happened. I weigh the one miracle against the other; and according to the superiority, which I discover, I pronounce my decision, and always reject the greater miracle If the falsehood of his testimony would be more miraculous, than the event which he relates; then, and not till then, can he pretend to command my belief or opinion.

## PART II

In the foregoing reasoning we have supposed, that the testimony, upon which a miracle is founded, may possibly amount to an entire proof, and that the falsehood of that testimony would be a real prodigy: but it is easy to shew, that we have been a great deal too liberal in our concession, and that there never was a miraculous event established on so full an evidence.

For *first*, there is not to be found, in all history, any miracle attested by a sufficient number of men, of such unquestioned good-sense, education, and learning, as to secure us against all delusion in themselves; of such undoubted integrity, as to place them beyond all suspicion of any design to deceive others; of such credit and reputation in the eyes of mankind, as to have a great deal to lose in case of their being detected in any falsehood; and at the same time, attesting facts performed in such a public manner and in so celebrated a part of the world, as to render the detection unavoidable: all which circumstances are requisite to give us a full assurance in the testimony of men.

*Secondly.* We may observe in human nature a principle which, if strictly examined, will be found to diminish extremely the assurance, which we might, from human testimony, have in any kind of prodigy. The maxim, by which we commonly conduct ourselves in our reasonings, is, that the objects, of which we have no experience, resembles those, of which we have; that what we have found to be most usual is always most probable; and that where there is an opposition of arguments, we ought to give the preference to such as are founded on the greatest number of past observations. But though, in proceeding by this rule, we readily reject any fact which is unusual and incredible in an ordinary degree; yet in advancing farther, the mind observes not always the same rule; but when anything is affirmed utterly absurd and miraculous, it rather the more readily admits of such a fact, upon account of that very circumstance, which ought to destroy all its authority. The passion of *surprise* and *wonder,* arising from miracles, being an agreeable emotion, gives a sensible tendency towards the belief of those events, from which it is derived. And this goes so far, that even those who cannot enjoy this pleasure immediately, nor can believe those miraculous events, of which they are informed, yet love to partake of the satisfaction at second-hand or by rebound, and place a pride and delight in exciting the admiration of others.

With what greediness are the miraculous accounts of travellers received, their descriptions of sea and land monsters, their relations of wonderful adventures, strange men, and uncouth manners? But if the spirit of religion join itself to the love of wonder, there is an end of common sense; and human testimony, in these circumstances, loses all pretensions to authority. A religionist may be an enthusiast, and imagine he sees what has no reality: he may know his narrative to be false, and yet persevere in it, with the best intentions in the world, for the sake of promoting so holy a cause: or even where this delusion has not place, vanity, excited by so strong a temptation, operates on him more powerfully than on the rest of mankind in any other circumstances; and self-interest with equal force. His auditors may not have, and commonly have not, sufficient judgement to canvass his evidence: what judgement they have, they renounce by principle, in these sublime and mysterious subjects: or if they were ever so willing to employ it, passion and a heated imagination disturb the regularity of its operations. their credulity increases his impudence: and his impudence overpowers their credulity.

Eloquence, when at its highest pitch, leaves little room

for reason or reflection; but addressing itself entirely to the fancy or the affections, captivates the willing hearers, and subdues their understanding. Happily, this pitch it seldom attains. But what a Tully or a Demosthenes could scarcely effect over a Roman or Athenian audience, every *Capuchin,* every itinerant or stationary teacher can perform over the generality of mankind, and in a higher degree, by touching such gross and vulgar passions.

The many instances of forged miracles, and prophecies, and supernatural events, which, in all ages, have either been detected by contrary evidence, or which detect themselves by their absurdity, prove sufficiently the strong propensity of mankind to the extraordinary and the marvellous, and ought reasonably to beget a suspicion against all relations of this kind. This is our natural way of thinking, even with regard to the most common and most credible events. For instance: There is no kind of report which rises so easily, and spreads so quickly, especially in country places and provincial towns, as those concerning marriages; insomuch that two young persons of equal condition never see each other twice, but the whole neighbourhood immediately join them together. The pleasure of telling a piece of news so interesting, of propagating it, and of being the first reporters of it, spreads the intelligence. And this is so well known, that no man of sense gives attention to these reports, till he find them confirmed by some greater evidence. Do not the same passions, and others still stronger, incline the generality of mankind to believe and report, with the greatest vehemence and assurance, all religious miracles?

*Thirdly.* It forms a strong presumption against all supernatural and miraculous relations, that they are observed chiefly to abound among ignorant and barbarous nations; or if a civilized people has ever given admission to any of them, that people will be found to have received them from ignorant and barbarous ancestors, who transmitted them with that inviolable sanction and authority, which always attend received opinions  When we peruse the first histories of all nations, we are apt to imagine ourselves transported into some new world; where the whole frame of nature is disjointed, and every element performs its operations in a different manner, from what it does at present. Battles, revolutions, pestilence, famine and death, are never the effect of those natural causes, which we experience. Prodigies, omens, oracles, judgements, quite obscure the few natural events, that are intermingled with them. But as the former grow thinner every page, in proportion as we advance nearer the enlightened ages, we soon learn, that there is nothing mysterious or supernatural in the case, but that all proceeds from the usual propensity of mankind towards the marvellous, and that, though this inclination may at intervals receive a check from sense and learning, it can never be thoroughly extirpated from human nature.

*It is strange,* a judicious reader is apt to say, upon the perusal of these wonderful historians, *that such prodigious events never happen in our days.* But it is nothing strange, I hope, that men should lie in all ages. You must surely have seen instances enough of that frailty. You have yourself heard many such marvellous relations started, which, being treated with scorn by all the wise and judicious, have at last been abandoned even by the vulgar. Be assured, that those renowned lies, which have spread and flourished to such a monstrous height, arose from like beginnings; but being sown in a more proper soil, shot up at last into prodigies almost equal to those which they relate.

It was a wise policy in that false prophet, Alexander, who though now forgotten, was once so famous, to lay the first scene of his impostures in Paphlagonia, where, as Lucian tells us, the people were extremely ignorant and stupid, and ready to swallow even the grossest delusion. People at a distance, who are weak enough to think the matter at all worth enquiry, have no opportunity of receiving better information. The stories come magnified to them by a hundred circumstances. Fools are industrious in propagating the imposture; while the wise and learned are contented, in general, to deride its absurdity, without informing themselves of the particular facts, by which it may be distinctly refuted. And thus the impostor above mentioned was enabled to proceed, from his ignorant Paphlagonians, to the enlisting

of votaries, even among the Grecian philosophers, and men
of the most eminent rank and distinction in Rome; nay,
could engage the attention of that sage emperor Marcus
Aurelius; so far as to make him trust the success of
a military expedition to his delusive prophecies.

The advantages are so great, of starting an imposture
among an ignorant people, that, even though the delusion
should be too gross to impose on the generality of them
(*which, though seldom, is sometimes the case*) it has a much
better chance for succeeding in remote countries, than if
the first scene had been laid in a city renowned for arts and
knowledge.  The most ignorant and barbarous of these
barbarians carry the report abroad.  None of their countrymen have a large correspondence, or sufficient credit and
authority to contradict and beat down the delusion.  Men's
inclination to the marvellous has full opportunity to display
itself.  And thus a story, which is universally exploded in
the place where it was first started, shall pass for certain at
a thousand miles distance.  But had Alexander fixed his
residence at Athens, the philosophers of that renowned
mart of learning had immediately spread, throughout the
whole Roman empire, their sense of the matter; which,
being supported by so great authority, and displayed by all
the force of reason and eloquence, had entirely opened the
eyes of mankind.  It is true; Lucian, passing by chance
through Paphlagonia, had an opportunity of performing
this good office.  But, though much to be wished, it does
not always happen, that every Alexander meets with a
Lucian, ready to expose and detect his impostures.

I may add as a *fourth* reason, which diminishes the
authority of prodigies, that there is no testimony for any,
even those which have not been expressly detected, that
is not opposed by an infinite number of witnesses; so that
not only the miracle destroys the credit of testimony, but
the testimony destroys itself.  To make this the better
understood, let us consider, that, in matters of religion,
whatever is different is contrary; and that it is impossible
the religions of ancient Rome, of Turkey, of Siam, and of
China should, all of them, be established on any solid
foundation.  Every miracle, therefore, pretended to have

been wrought in any of these religions (and all of them abound in miracles), as its direct scope is to establish the particular system to which it is attributed; so has it the same force, though more indirectly, to overthrow every other system. In destroying a rival system, it likewise destroys the credit of those miracles, on which that system was established; so that all the prodigies of different religions are to be regarded as contrary facts, and the evidences of these prodigies, whether weak or strong, as opposite to each other. According to this method of reasoning, when we believe any miracle of Mahomet or his successors, we have for our warrant the testimony of a few barbarous Arabians: and on the other hand, we are to regard the authority of Titus Livius, Plutarch, Tacitus, and, in short, of all the authors and witnesses, Grecian, Chinese, and Roman Catholic, who have related any miracle in their particular religion; I say, we are to regard their testimony in the same light as if they had mentioned that Mahometan miracle, and had in express terms contradicted it, with the same certainty as they have for the miracle they relate. This argument may appear over subtile and refined; but is not in reality different from the reasoning of a judge, who supposes, that the credit of two witnesses, maintaining a crime against any one, is destroyed by the testimony of two others, who affirm him to have been two hundred leagues distant, at the same instant when the crime is said to have been committed.

One of the best attested miracles in all profane history, is that which Tacitus reports of Vespasian, who cured a blind man in Alexandria, by means of his spittle, and a lame man by the mere touch of his foot; in obedience to a vision of the god Serapis, who had enjoined them to have recourse to the Emperor, for these miraculous cures. The story may be seen in that fine historian[4]; where every circumstance seems to add weight to the testimony, and might be displayed at large with all the force of argument and eloquence, if any one were now concerned to enforce the evidence of that exploded and idolatrous superstition. The gravity, solidity, age, and probity of so great an

[4] Hist. lib. v. cap. 8.   Suetonius gives nearly the same account *in vita* Vesp.

emperor, who, through the whole course of his life, conversed in a familiar manner with his friends and courtiers, and never affected those extraordinary airs of divinity assumed by Alexander and Demetrius. The historian, a cotemporary writer, noted for candour and veracity, and withal, the greatest and most penetrating genius, perhaps, of all antiquity; and so free from any tendency to credulity, that he even lies under the contrary imputation, of atheism and profaneness: The persons, from whose authority he related the miracle, of established character for judgement and veracity, as we may well presume; eye-witnesses of the fact, and confirming their testimony, after the Flavian family was despoiled of the empire, and could no longer give any reward, as the price of a lie. *Utrumque, qui interfuere, nunc quoque memorant, postquam nullum mendacio pretium.* To which if we add the public nature of the facts, as related, it will appear, that no evidence can well be supposed stronger for so gross and so palpable a falsehood.

There is also a memorable story related by Cardinal de Retz, which may well deserve our consideration. When that intriguing politician fled into Spain, to avoid the persecution of his enemies, he passed through Saragossa, the capital of Arragon, where he was shewn, in the cathedral, a man, who had served seven years as a doorkeeper, and was well known to every body in town, that had ever paid his devotions at that church. He had been seen, for so long a time, wanting a leg; but recovered that limb by the rubbing of holy oil upon the stump; and the cardinal assures us that he saw him with two legs. This miracle was vouched by all the canons of the church; and the whole company in town were appealed to for a confirmation of the fact; whom the cardinal found, by their zealous devotion, to be thorough believers of the miracle. Here the relater was also cotemporary to the supposed prodigy, of an incredulous and libertine character, as well as of great genius; the miracle of so *singular* a nature as could scarcely admit of a counterfeit, and the witnesses very numerous, and all of them, in a manner, spectators of the fact, to which they gave their testimony. And what adds mightily to the force of the evidence, and may double our surprise on this occasion, is, that the cardinal himself, who relates the story, seems not to give any credit to it, and consequently cannot be suspected of any concurrence in the holy fraud. He considered justly, that it was not requisite, in order to reject a fact of this nature, to be able accurately to disprove the testimony, and to trace its falsehood, through all the circumstances of knavery and credulity which produced it. He knew, that, as this was commonly altogether impossible at any small distance of time and place; so was it extremely difficult, even where one was immediately present, by reason of the bigotry, ignorance, cunning, and roguery of a great part of mankind. He therefore concluded, like a just reasoner, that such an evidence carried falsehood upon the very face of it, and that a miracle, supported by any human testimony, was more properly a subject of derision than of argument.

There surely never was a greater number of miracles ascribed to one person, than those, which were lately said to have been wrought in France upon the tomb of Abbé Paris, the famous Jansenist, with whose sanctity the people were so long deluded. The curing of the sick, giving hearing to the deaf, and sight to the blind, were every where talked of as the usual effects of that holy sepulchre. But what is more extraordinary; many of the miracles were immediately proved upon the spot, before judges of unquestioned integrity, attested by witnesses of credit and distinction, in a learned age, and on the most eminent theatre that is now in the world. Nor is this all: a relation of them was published and dispersed everywhere; nor were the *Jesuits,* though a learned body supported by the civil magistrate, and determined enemies to those opinions, in whose favour the miracles were said to have been wrought, ever able distinctly to refute or detect them.[5] Where shall we find such a number of circumstances, agreeing to the corroboration of one fact? And what have we to oppose to such a cloud of witnesses, but the absolute impossibility or miraculous nature of the events, which they relate? And

[5] By Mons. Montgeron, counsellor or judge of the Parliament of Paris.

this surely, in the eyes of all reasonable people, will alone be regarded as a sufficient refutation.

Is the consequence just, because some human testimony has the utmost force and authority in some cases, when it relates the battle of Philippi or Pharsalia for instance; that therefore all kinds of testimony must, in all cases, have equal force and authority? Suppose that the Cæsarean and Pompeian factions had, each of them, claimed the victory in these battles, and that the historians of each party had uniformly ascribed the advantage to their own side; how could mankind, at this distance, have been able to determine between them? The contrariety is equally strong between the miracles related by Herodotus or Plutarch, and those delivered by Mariana, Bede, or any monkish historian.

The wise lend a very academic faith to every report which favours the passion of the reporter; whether it magnifies his country, his family, or himself, or in any other way strikes in with his natural inclinations and propensities. But what greater temptation than to appear a missionary, a prophet, an ambassador from heaven? Who would not encounter many dangers and difficulties, in order to attain so sublime a character? Or if, by the help of vanity and a heated imagination, a man has first made a convert of himself, and entered seriously into the delusion; who ever scruples to make use of pious frauds, in support of so holy and meritorious a cause?

The smallest spark may here kindle into the greatest flame; because the materials are always prepared for it. The *avidum genus auricularum*,[6] the gazing populace, receive greedily, without examination, whatever sooths superstition, and promotes wonder.

How many stories of this nature have, in all ages, been detected and exploded in their infancy? How many more have been celebrated for a time, and have afterwards sunk into neglect and oblivion? Where such reports, therefore, fly about, the solution of the phenomenon is obvious; and we judge in conformity to regular experience and observation, when we account for it by the known and natural

6 Lucret.

principles of credulity and delusion. And shall we, rather than have a recourse to so natural a solution, allow of a miraculous violation of the most established laws of nature?

I need not mention the difficulty of detecting a falsehood in any private or even public history, at the place, where it is said to happen; much more when the scene is removed to ever so small a distance. Even a court of judicature, with all the authority, accuracy, and judgement, which they can employ, find themselves often at a loss to distinguish between truth and falsehood in the most recent actions. But the matter never comes to any issue, if trusted to the common method of altercations and debate and flying rumours; especially when men's passions have taken part on either side.

In the infancy of new religions, the wise and learned commonly esteem the matter too inconsiderable to deserve their attention or regard. And when afterwards they would willingly detect the cheat, in order to undeceive the deluded multitude, the season is now past, and the records and witnesses, which might clear up the matter, have perished beyond recovery.

No means of detection remain, but those which must be drawn from the very testimony itself of the reporters: and these, though always sufficient with the judicious and knowing, are commonly too fine to fall under the comprehension of the vulgar.

Upon the whole, then, it appears, that no testimony for any kind of miracle has ever amounted to a probability, much less to a proof; and that, even supposing it amounted to a proof, it would be opposed by another proof; derived from the very nature of the fact, which it would endeavour to establish. It is experience only, which gives authority to human testimony; and it is the same experience, which assures us of the laws of nature. When, therefore, these two kinds of experience are contrary, we have nothing to do but subtract the one from the other, and embrace an opinion, either on one side or the other, with that assurance which arises from the remainder. But according to the principle here explained, this subtraction, with regard to all popular religions, amounts to an entire annihilation; and

therefore we may establish it as a maxim, that no human
testimony can have such force as to prove a miracle, and
make it a just foundation for any such system of religion.

I beg the limitations here made may be remarked, when
I say, that a miracle can never be proved, so as to be the
foundation of a system of religion.  For I own, that otherwise, there may possibly be miracles, or violations of the
usual course of nature, of such a kind as to admit of proof
from human testimony; though, perhaps, it will be impossible to find any such in all the records of history.
Thus, suppose, all authors, in all languages, agree, that,
from the first of January, 1600, there was a total darkness
over the whole earth for eight days: suppose that the
tradition of this extraordinary event is still strong and
lively among the people: that all travellers, who return
from foreign countries, bring us accounts of the same
tradition, without the least variation or contradiction: it is
evident, that our present philosophers, instead of doubting
the fact, ought to receive it as certain, and ought to search
for the causes whence it might be derived.  The decay,
corruption, and dissolution of nature, is an event rendered
probable by so many analogies, that any phenomenon,
which seems to have a tendency towards that catastrophe,
comes within the reach of human testimony, if that testimony be very extensive and uniform.

But suppose, that all the historians who treat of England,
should agree, that, on the first of January, 1600, Queen
Elizabeth died; that both before and after her death she
was seen by her physicians and the whole court, as is usual
with persons of her rank; that her successor was acknowledged and proclaimed by the parliament; and that, after
being interred a month, she again appeared, resumed the
throne, and governed England for three years: I must
confess that I should be surprised at the concurrence of so
many odd circumstances, but should not have the least
inclination to believe so miraculous an event.  I should not
doubt of her pretended death, and of those other public
circumstances that followed it: I should only assert it to have
been pretended, and that it neither was, nor possibly could
be real.  You would in vain object to me the difficulty,

and almost impossibility of deceiving the world in an affair of such consequence; the wisdom and solid judgment of that renowned queen; with the little or no advantage which she could reap from so poor an artifice: all this might astonish me; but I would still reply, that the knavery and folly of men are such common phenomena, that I should rather believe the most extraordinary events to arise from their concurrence, than admit of so signal a violation of the laws of nature.

But should this miracle be ascribed to any new system of religion; men, in all ages, have been so much imposed on by ridiculous stories of that kind, that this very circumstance would be a full proof of a cheat, and sufficient, with all men of sense, not only to make them reject the fact, but even reject it without farther examination. Though the Being to whom the miracle is ascribed, be, in this case, Almighty, it does not, upon that account, become a whit more probable; since it is impossible for us to know the attributes or actions of such a Being, otherwise than from the experience which we have of his productions, in the usual course of nature. This still reduces us to past observation, and obliges us to compare the instances of the violation of truth in the testimony of men, with those of the violation of the laws of nature by miracles, in order to judge which of them is most likely and probable. As the violations of truth are more common in the testimony concerning religious miracles, than in that concerning any other matter of fact; this must diminish very much the authority of the former testimony, and make us form a general resolution, never to lend any attention to it, with whatever specious pretence it may be covered.

Lord Bacon seems to have embraced the same principles of reasoning. 'We ought,' says he, 'to make a collection or particular history of all monsters and prodigious births or productions, and in a word of every thing new, rare, and extraordinary in nature. But this must be done with the most severe scrutiny, lest we depart from truth. Above all, every relation must be considered as suspicious, which depends in any degree upon religion, as the prodigies of Livy: and no less so, everything that is to be found in the writers of natural magic or alchimy, or such authors, who seem, all of them, to have an unconquerable appetite for falsehood and fable.[7]

I am the better pleased with the method of reasoning here delivered, as I think it may serve to confound those dangerous friends or disguised enemies to the *Christian Religion,* who have undertaken to defend it by the principles of human reason. Our most holy religion is founded on *Faith,* not on reason; and it is a sure method of exposing it to put it to such a trial as it is, by no means, fitted to endure. To make this more evident, let us examine those miracles, related in scripture; and not to lose ourselves in too wide a field, let us confine ourselves to such as we find in the *Pentateuch,* which we shall examine, according to the principles of these pretended Christians, not as the word or testimony of God himself, but as the production of a mere human writer and historian. Here then we are first to consider a book, presented to us by a barbarous and ignorant people, written in an age when they were still more barbarous, and in all probability long after the facts which it relates, corroborated by no concurring testimony, and resembling those fabulous accounts, which every nation gives of its origin. Upon reading this book, we find it full of prodigies and miracles. It gives an account of a state of the world and of human nature entirely different from the present: of our fall from that state: of the age of man, extended to near a thousand years: of the destruction of the world by a deluge: of the arbitrary choice of one people, as the favourites of heaven; and that people the countrymen of the author: of their deliverance from bondage by prodigies the most astonishing imaginable: I desire any one to lay his hand upon his heart, and after a serious consideration declare, whether he thinks that the falsehood of such a book, supported by such a testimony, would be more extraordinary and miraculous than all the miracles it relates; which is, however, necessary to make it be received, according to the measures of probability above established.

What we have said of miracles may be applied, without any variation, to prophecies; and indeed, all prophecies are

[7] Nov. Org. lib. ii. aph. 29.

real miracles, and as such only, can be admitted as proofs of any revelation. If it did not exceed the capacity of human nature to foretell future events, it would be absurd to employ any prophecy as an argument for a divine mission or authority from heaven. So that, upon the whole, we may conclude, that the *Christian Religion* not only was at first attended with miracles, but even at this day cannot be believed by any reasonable person without one. Mere reason is insufficient to convince us of its veracity: and whoever is moved by *Faith* to assent to it, is conscious of a continued miracle in his own person, which subverts all the principles of his understanding, and gives him a determination to believe what is most contrary to custom and experience.

I WAS lately engaged in conversation with a friend who loves sceptical paradoxes; where, though he advanced many principles, of which I can by no means approve, yet as they seem to be curious, and to bear some relation to the chain of reasoning carried on throughout this enquiry, I shall here copy them from my memory as accurately as I can, in order to submit them to the judgement of the reader.

Our conversation began with my admiring the singular good fortune of philosophy, which, as it requires entire liberty above all other privileges, and chiefly flourishes from the free opposition of sentiments and argumentation, received its first birth in an age and country of freedom and toleration, and was never cramped, even in its most extravagant principles, by any creeds, concessions, or penal statutes. For, except the banishment of Protagoras, and the death of Socrates, which last event proceeded partly from other motives, there are scarcely any instances to be met with, in ancient history, of this bigoted jealousy, with which the present age is so much infested. Epicurus lived at Athens to an advanced age, in peace and tranquillity: Epicureans[1] were even admitted to receive the sacerdotal character, and to officiate at the altar, in the most sacred rites of the established religion: and the public encouragement[2] of pensions and salaries was afforded equally, by the wisest of all the Roman emperors,[3] to the professors of every sect of philosophy. How requisite such kind of treatment was to philosophy, in her early youth, will easily be conceived, if we reflect, that, even at present, when she may be supposed more hardy and robust, she bears with much difficulty the inclemency of the seasons, and those

---

[1] Luciani, συμπ. ἡ Λαπίθαι    [2] Luciani, εὐνοῦχος.    [3] Luciani and Dio.

416

harsh winds of calumny and persecution, which blow upon her.

You admire, says my friend, as the singular good fortune of philosophy, what seems to result from the natural course of things, and to be unavoidable in every age and nation. This pertinacious bigotry, of which you complain, as so fatal to philosophy, is really her offspring, who, after allying with superstition, separates himself entirely from the interest of his parent, and becomes her most inveterate enemy and persecutor. Speculative dogmas of religion, the present occasions of such furious dispute, could not possibly be conceived or admitted in the early ages of the world; when mankind, being wholly illiterate, formed an idea of religion more suitable to their weak apprehension, and composed their sacred tenets of such tales chiefly as were the objects of traditional belief, more than of argument or disputation. After the first alarm, therefore, was over, which arose from the new paradoxes and principles of the philosophers; these teachers seem ever after, during the ages of antiquity, to have lived in great harmony with the established superstition, and to have made a fair partition of mankind between them; the former claiming all the learned and wise, the latter possessing all the vulgar and illiterate.

It seems then, say I, that you leave politics entirely out of the question, and never suppose, that a wise magistrate can justly be jealous of certain tenets of philosophy, such as those of Epicurus, which, denying a divine existence, and consequently a providence and a future state, seem to loosen, in a great measure the ties of morality, and may be supposed, for that reason, pernicious to the peace of civil society.

I know, replied he, that in fact these persecutions never, in any age, proceeded from calm reason, or from experience of the pernicious consequences of philosophy; but arose entirely from passion and prejudice. But what if I should advance farther, and assert, that if Epicurus had been accused before the people, by any of the *sycophants* or informers of those days, he could easily have defended his cause, and proved his principles of philosophy to be as salutary as those of his adversaries, who endeavoured, with such zeal, to expose him to the public hatred and jealousy?

(14) HC XXXVII

I wish, said I, you would try your eloquence upon so
extraordinary a topic, and make a speech for Epicurus,
which might satisfy, not the mob of Athens, if you will
allow that ancient and polite city to have contained any mob,
but the more philosophical part of his audience, such as
might be supposed capable of comprehending his arguments.

The matter would not be difficult, upon such conditions,
replied he: and if you please, I shall suppose myself Epicurus for a moment, and make you stand for the Athenian
people, and shall deliver you such an harangue as will fill
all the urn with white beans, and leave not a black one to
gratify the malice of my adversaries.

Very well: pray proceed upon these suppositions.

I come hither, O ye Athenians, to justify in your assembly
what I maintain in my school, and I find myself impeached
by furious antagonists, instead of reasoning with calm and
dispassionate enquirers. Your deliberations, which of right
should be directed to questions of public good, and the
interest of the commonwealth, are diverted to the disquisitions of speculative philosophy; and these magnificent, but
perhaps fruitless enquiries, take place of your more familiar
but more useful occupations. But so far as in me lies,
I will prevent this abuse. We shall not here dispute concerning the origin and government of worlds. We shall only
enquire how far such questions concern the public interest.
And if I can persuade you, that they are entirely indifferent
to the peace of society and security of government, I hope
that you will presently send us back to our schools, there to
examine, at leisure, the question the most sublime, but, at the
same time, the most speculative of all philosophy.

The religious philosophers, not satisfied with the tradition
of your forefathers, and doctrine of your priests (in which
I willingly acquiesce), indulge a rash curiosity, in trying how
far they can establish religion upon the principles of reason;
and they thereby excite, instead of satisfying, the doubts,
which naturally arise from a diligent and scrutinous enquiry.
They paint, in the most magnificent colours, the order,
beauty, and wise arrangement of the universe; and then
ask, if such a glorious display of intelligence could proceed
from the fortuitous concourse of atoms, or if chance could

produce what the greatest genius can never sufficiently admire. I shall not examine the justness of this argument. I shall allow it to be as solid as my antagonists and accusers can desire. It is sufficient, if I can prove, from this very reasoning, that the question is entirely speculative, and that, when, in my philosophical disquisitions, I deny a providence and a future state, I undermine not the foundations of society, but advance principles, which they themselves, upon their own topics, if they argue consistently, must allow to be solid and satisfactory.

You then, who are my accusers, have acknowledged, that the chief or sole argument for a divine existence (which I never questioned) is derived from the order of nature; where there appear such marks of intelligence and design, that you think it extravagant to assign for its cause, either chance, or the blind and unguided force of matter. You allow, that this is an argument drawn from effects to causes. From the order of the work, you infer, that there must have been project and forethought in the workman. If you cannot make out this point, you allow, that your conclusion fails; and you pretend not to establish the conclusion in a greater latitude than the phenomena of nature will justify. These are your concessions. I desire you to mark the consequences.

When we infer any particular cause from an effect, we must proportion the one to the other, and can never be allowed to ascribe to the cause any qualities, but what are exactly sufficient to produce the effect. A body of ten ounces raised in any scale may serve as a proof, that the counterbalancing weight exceeds ten ounces; but can never afford a reason that it exceeds a hundred. If the cause, assigned for any effect, be not sufficient to produce it, we must either reject that cause, or add to it such qualities as will give it a just proportion to the effect. But if we ascribe to it farther qualities, or affirm it capable of producing other effects, we can only indulge the licence of conjecture, and arbitrarily suppose the existence of qualities and energies, without reason or authority.

The same rule holds, whether the cause assigned be brute unconscious matter, or a rational intelligent being. If the

cause be known only by the effect, we never ought to ascribe
to it any qualities, beyond what are precisely requisite to
produce the effect: nor can we, by any rules of just reasoning, return back from the cause, and infer other effects from
it, beyond those by which alone it is known to us  No one,
merely from the sight of one of Zeuxis's pictures, could
know, that he was also a statuary or architect, and was an
artist no less skilful in stone and marble than in colours.
The talents and taste, displayed in the particular work before
us; these we may safely conclude the workman to be possessed of.  The cause must be proportioned to the effect;
and if we exactly and precisely proportion it, we shall
never find in it any qualities, that point farther, or afford an
inference concerning any other design or performance.
Such qualities must be somewhat beyond what is merely
requisite for producing the effect, which we examine.

Allowing, therefore, the gods to be the authors of the
existence or order of the universe; it follows, that they
possess that precise degree of power, intelligence, and
benevolence, which appears in their workmanship; but
nothing farther can ever be proved, except we call in the
assistance of exaggeration and flattery to supply the defects
of argument and reasoning.  So far as the traces of any
attributes, at present, appear, so far may we conclude these
attributes to exist.  The supposition of farther attributes
is mere hypothesis; much more the supposition, that, in
distant regions of space or periods of time, there has been,
or will be, a more magnificent display of these attributes, and
a scheme of administration more suitable to such imaginary
virtues.  We can never be allowed to mount up from the
universe, the effect, to Jupiter, the cause; and then descend
downwards, to infer any new effect from that cause; as if
the present effects alone were not entirely worthy of the
glorious attributes, which we ascribe to that deity.  The
knowledge of the cause being derived solely from the effect,
they must be exactly adjusted to each other; and the one
can never refer to anything farther, or be the foundation of
any new inference and conclusion.

You find certain phenomena in nature.  You seek a
cause or author.  You imagine that you have found him.

You afterwards become so enamoured of this offspring of your brain, that you imagine it impossible, but he must produce something greater and more perfect than the present scene of things, which is so full of ill and disorder. You forget, that this superlative intelligence and benevolence are entirely imaginary, or, at least, without any foundation in reason; and that you have no ground to ascribe to him any qualities, but what you see he has actually exerted and displayed in his productions. Let your gods, therefore, O philosophers, be suited to the present appearances of nature: and presume not to alter these appearances by arbitrary suppositions, in order to suit them to the attributes, which you so fondly ascribe to your deities.

When priests and poets, supported by your authority, O Athenians, talk of a golden or silver age, which preceded the present state of vice and misery, I hear them with attention and with reverence. But when philosophers, who pretend to neglect authority, and to cultivate reason, hold the same discourse, I pay them not, I own, the same obsequious submission and pious deference. I ask; who carried them into the celestial regions, who admitted them into the councils of the gods, who opened to them the book of fate, that they thus rashly affirm, that their deities have executed, or will execute, any purpose beyond what has actually appeared? If they tell me, that they have mounted on the steps or by the gradual ascent of reason, and by drawing inferences from effects to causes, I still insist, that they have aided the ascent of reason by the wings of imagination; otherwise they could not thus change their manner of inference, and argue from causes to effects; presuming, that a more perfect production than the present world would be more suitable to such perfect beings as the gods, and forgetting that they have no reason to ascribe to these celestial beings any perfection or any attribute, but what can be found in the present world.

Hence all the fruitless industry to account for the ill appearances of nature, and save the honour of the gods; while we must acknowledge the reality of that evil and disorder, with which the world so much abounds. The obstinate and intractable qualities of matter, we are told, or the observance of general laws, or some such reason, is the sole cause, which controlled the power and benevolence of Jupiter, and obliged him to create mankind and every sensible creature so imperfect and so unhappy. These attributes then, are, it seems, beforehand, taken for granted, in their greatest latitude. And upon that supposition, I own that such conjectures may, perhaps, be admitted as plausible solutions of the ill phenomena. But still I ask; Why take these attributes for granted, or why ascribe to the cause any qualities but what actually appear in the effect? Why torture your brain to justify the course of nature upon suppositions, which, for aught you know, may be entirely imaginary, and of which there are to be found no traces in the course of nature?

The religious hypothesis, therefore, must be considered only as a particular method of accounting for the visible phenomena of the universe: but no just reasoner will ever presume to infer from it any single fact, and alter or add to the phenomena, in any single particular. If you think, that the appearances of things prove such causes, it is allowable for you to draw an inference concerning the existence of these causes. In such complicated and sublime subjects, every one should be indulged in the liberty of conjecture and argument. But here you ought to rest. If you come backward, and arguing from your inferred causes, conclude, that any other fact has existed, or will exist, in the course of nature, which may serve as a fuller display of particular attributes; I must admonish you, that you have departed from the method of reasoning, attached to the present subject, and have certainly added something to the attributes of the cause, beyond what appears in the effect; otherwise you could never, with tolerable sense or propriety, add anything to the effect, in order to render it more worthy of the cause.

Where, then, is the odiousness of that doctrine, which I teach in my school, or rather, which I examine in my gardens? Or what do you find in this whole question, wherein the security of good morals, or the peace and order of society, is in the least concerned?

I deny a providence, you say, and supreme governor

of the world, who guides the course of events, and punishes the vicious with infamy and disappointment, and rewards the virtuous with honour and success, in all their undertakings. But surely, I deny not the course itself of events, which lies open to every one's inquiry and examination. I acknowledge, that, in the present order of things, virtue is attended with more peace of mind than vice, and meets with a more favourable reception from the world. I am sensible, that, according to the past experience of mankind, friendship is the chief joy of human life, and moderation the only source of tranquillity and happiness. I never balance between the virtuous and the vicious course of life; but am sensible, that, to a well-disposed mind, every advantage is on the side of the former. And what can you say more, allowing all your suppositions and reasonings? You tell me, indeed, that this disposition of things proceeds from intelligence and design. But whatever it proceeds from, the disposition itself, on which depends our happiness or misery, and consequently our conduct and deportment in life is still the same. It is still open for me, as well as you, to regulate my behaviour, by my experience of past events. And if you affirm, that, while a divine providence is allowed and a supreme distributive justice in the universe, I ought to expect some more particular reward of the good, and punishment of the bad, beyond the ordinary course of events; I here find the same fallacy, which I have before endeavoured to detect. You persist in imagining, that, if we grant that divine existence, for which you so earnestly contend, you may safely infer consequences from it, and add something to the experienced order of nature, by arguing from the attributes which you ascribe to your gods. You seem not to remember, that all your reasonings on this subject can only be drawn from effects to causes; and that every argument, deducted from causes to effects, must of necessity be a gross sophism; since it is impossible for you to know anything of the cause, but what you have antecedently, not inferred, but discovered to the full, in the effect.

But what must a philosopher think of those vain reasoners, who instead of regarding the present scene of things as the sole object of their contemplation, so far reverse the whole course of nature, as to render this life merely a passage to something farther; a porch, which leads to a greater, and vastly different building; a prologue, which serves only to introduce the piece, and give it more grace and propriety? Whence, do you think, can such philosophers derive their idea of the gods? From their own conceit and imagination surely. For if they derived it from the present phenomena, it would never point to anything farther, but must be exactly adjusted to them. That the divinity may *possibly* be endowed with attributes, which we have never seen exerted; may be governed by principles of action, which we cannot discover to be satisfied: all this will freely be allowed. But still this is mere *possibility* and hypothesis. We never can have reason to *infer* any attributes, or any principles of action in him, but so far as we know them to have been exerted and satisfied.

*Are there any marks of a distributive justice in the world?* If you answer in the affirmative, I conclude, that, since justice here exerts itself, it is satisfied. If you reply in the negative, I conclude, that you have then no reason to ascribe justice, in our sense of it, to the gods. If you hold a medium between affirmation and negation, by saying, that the justice of the gods, at present, exerts itself in part, but not in its full extent; I answer, that you have no reason to give it any particular extent, but only so far as you see it, *at present,* exert itself.

Thus I bring the dispute, O Athenians, to a short issue with my antagonists. The course of nature lies open to my contemplation as well as to theirs. The experienced train of events is the great standard, by which we all regulate our conduct. Nothing else can be appealed to in the field, or in the senate. Nothing else ought ever to be heard of in the school, or in the closet. In vain would our limited understanding break through those boundaries, which are too narrow for our fond imagination. While we argue from the course of nature, and infer a particular intelligent cause, which first bestowed, and still preserves order in the universe, we embrace a principle, which is both uncertain and useless. It is uncertain; because the subject lies entirely beyond the reach of human experience. It is useless; because our knowledge of this cause being derived entirely from the course of nature, we can never, according to the rules of just reasoning, return back from the cause with any new inference, or making additions to the common and experienced course of nature, establish any new principles of conduct and behaviour.

I observe (said I, finding he had finished his harangue) that you neglect not the artifice of the demagogues of old; and as you were pleased to make me stand for the people, you insinuate yourself into my favour by embracing those principles, to which, you know, I have always expressed a particular attachment. But allowing you to make experience (as indeed I think you ought) the only standard of our judgement concerning this, and all other questions of fact; I doubt not but, from the very same experience, to which you appeal, it may be possible to refute this reasoning, which you have put into the mouth of Epicurus. If you saw, for instance, a half-finished building, surrounded with heaps of brick and stone and mortar, and all the instruments of masonry; could you not *infer* from the effect, that it was a work of design and contrivance? And could you not return again, from this inferred cause, to infer new additions to the effect, and conclude, that the building would soon be finished, and receive all the further improvements, which art could bestow upon it? If you saw upon the sea-shore the print of one human foot, you would conclude, that a man had passed that way, and that he had also left the traces of the other foot, though effaced by the rolling of the sands or inundation of the waters. Why then do you refuse to admit the same method of reasoning with regard to the order of nature? Consider the world and the present life only as an imperfect building, from which you can infer a superior intelligence; and arguing from that superior intelligence, which can leave nothing imperfect; why may you not infer a more finished scheme or plan, which will receive its completion in some distant point of space or time? Are not these methods of reasoning exactly similar?

And under what pretence can you embrace the one, while you reject the other?

The infinite difference of the subjects, replied he, is a sufficient foundation for this difference in my conclusions. In works of *human* art and contrivance, it is allowable to advance from the effect to the cause, and returning back from the cause, to form new inferences concerning the effect, and examine the alterations, which it has probably undergone, or may still undergo. But what is the foundation of this method of reasoning? Plainly this; that man is a being, whom we know by experience, whose motives and designs we are acquainted with, and whose projects and inclinations have a certain connexion and coherence, according to the laws which nature has established for the government of such a creature. When, therefore, we find, that any work has proceeded from the skill and industry of man; as we are otherwise acquainted with the nature of the animal, we can draw a hundred inferences concerning what may be expected from him; and these inferences will all be founded in experience and observation. But did we know man only from the single work or production which we examine, it were impossible for us to argue in this manner; because our knowledge of all the qualities, which we ascribe to him, being in that case derived from the production, it is impossible they could point to anything farther, or be the foundation of any new inference. The print of a foot in the sand can only prove, when considered alone, that there was some figure adapted to it, by which it was produced: but the print of a human foot proves likewise, from our other experience, that there was probably another foot, which also left its impression, though effaced by time or other accidents. Here we mount from the effect to the cause; and descending again from the cause, infer alterations in the effect; but this is not a continuation of the same simple chain of reasoning. We comprehend in this case a hundred other experiences and observations, concerning the *usual* figure and members of that species of animal, without which this method of argument must be considered as fallacious and sophistical.

The case is not the same with our reasonings from the works of nature. The Deity is known to us only by his productions, and is a single being in the universe, not comprehended under any species or genus, from whose experienced attributes or qualities, we can, by analogy, infer any attribute or quality in him. As the universe shews wisdom and goodness, we infer wisdom and goodness. As it shews a particular degree of these perfections, we infer a particular degree of them, precisely adapted to the effect which we examine. But farther attributes or farther degrees of the same attributes, we can never be authorised to infer or suppose, by any rules of just reasoning. Now, without some such licence of supposition, it is impossible for us to argue from the cause, or infer any alteration in the effect, beyond what has immediately fallen under our observation. Greater good produced by this Being must still prove a greater degree of goodness: a more impartial distribution of rewards and punishments must proceed from a greater regard to justice and equity. Every supposed addition to the works of nature makes an addition to the attributes of the Author of nature; and consequently, being entirely unsupported by any reason or argument, can never be admitted but as mere conjecture and hypothesis[4].

The great source of our mistake in this subject, and of the unbounded licence of conjecture, which we indulge, is, that we tacitly consider ourselves, as in the place of the Supreme Being, and conclude, that he will, on every occasion, observe the same conduct, which we ourselves,

[4] In general, it may, I think, be established as a maxim, that where any cause is known only by its particular effects, it must be impossible to infer any new effects from that cause; since the qualities, which are requisite to produce these new effects along with the former, must either be different, or superior, or of more extensive operation, than those which simply produced the effect, whence alone the cause is supposed to be known to us. We can never, therefore, have any reason to suppose the existence of these qualities. To say, that the new effects proceed only from a continuation of the same energy, which is already known from the first effects, will not remove the difficulty. For even granting this to be the case (which can seldom be supposed), the very continuation and exertion of a like energy (for it is impossible it can be absolutely the same), I say, this exertion of a like energy, in a different period of space and time, is a very arbitrary supposition, and what there cannot possibly be any traces of in the effects, from which all our knowledge of the cause is originally derived. Let the *inferred* cause be exactly proportioned (as it should be) to the known effect; and it is impossible that it can possess any qualities, from which new or different effects can be *inferred*.

in his situation, would have embraced as reasonable and eligible. But, besides that the ordinary course of nature may convince us, that almost everything is regulated by principles and maxims very different from ours; besides this, I say, it must evidently appear contrary to all rules of analogy to reason, from the intentions and projects of men, to those of a Being so different, and so much superior. In human nature, there is a certain experienced coherence of designs and inclinations; so that when, from any fact, we have discovered one intention of any man, it may often be reasonable, from experience, to infer another, and draw a long chain of conclusions concerning his past or future conduct. But this method of reasoning can never have place with regard to a Being, so remote and incomprehensible, who bears much less analogy to any other being in the universe than the sun to a waxen taper, and who discovers himself only by some faint traces or outlines, beyond which we have no authority to ascribe to him any attribute or perfection. What we imagine to be a superior perfection, may really be a defect. Or were it ever so much a perfection, the ascribing of it to the Supreme Being, where it appears not to have been really exerted, to the full, in his works, savours more of flattery and panegyric, than of just reasoning and sound philosophy. All the philosophy, therefore, in the world, and all the religion, which is nothing but a species of philosophy, will never be able to carry us beyond the usual course of experience, or give us measures of conduct and behaviour different from those which are furnished by reflections on common life. No new fact can ever be inferred from the religious hypothesis; no event foreseen or foretold; no reward or punishment expected or dreaded, beyond what is already known by practice and observation. So that my apology for Epicurus will still appear solid and satisfactory; nor have the political interests of society any connexion with the philosophical disputes concerning metaphysics and religion.

There is still one circumstance, replied I, which you seem to have overlooked. Though I should allow your premises, I must deny your conclusion. You conclude, that religious doctrines and reasonings *can* have no influence on life, because they *ought* to have no influence; never considering, that men reason not in the same manner you do, but draw many consequences from the belief of a divine Existence, and suppose that the Deity will inflict punishments on vice, and bestow rewards on virtue, beyond what appear in the ordinary course of nature. Whether this reasoning of theirs be just or not, is no matter. Its influence on their life and conduct must still be the same. And those, who attempt to disabuse them of such prejudices, may, for aught I know, be good reasoners, but I cannot allow them to be good citizens and politicians; since they free men from one restraint upon their passions, and make the infringement of the laws of society, in one respect, more easy and secure.

After all, I may, perhaps, agree to your general conclusion in favour of liberty, though upon different premises from those, on which you endeavour to found it. I think, that the state ought to tolerate every principle of philosophy; nor is there an instance, that any government has suffered in its political interests by such indulgence. There is no enthusiasm among philosophers; their doctrines are not very alluring to the people; and no restraint can be put upon their reasonings, but what must be of dangerous consequence to the sciences, and even to the state, by paving the way for persecution and oppression in points, where the generality of mankind are more deeply interested and concerned.

But there occurs to me (continued I) with regard to your main topic, a difficulty, which I shall just propose to you without insisting on it; lest it lead into reasonings of too nice and delicate a nature. In a word, I much doubt whether it be possible for a cause to be known only by its effect (as you have all along supposed) or to be of so singular and particular a nature as to have no parallel and no similarity with any other cause or object, that has ever fallen under our observation. It is only when two *species* of objects are found to be constantly conjoined, that we can infer the one from the other; and were an effect presented, which was entirely singular, and could not be comprehended under any known *species,* I do not see, that we could form any conjecture or inference at all concerning its cause. If experience and observation and analogy be, indeed, the only guides which we can reasonably follow in inferences of this nature; both the effect and cause must bear a similarity and resemblance to other effects and causes, which we know, and which we have found, in many instances, to be conjoined with each other. I leave it to your own reflection to pursue the consequences of this principle. I shall just observe, that, as the antagonists of Epicurus always suppose the universe, an effect quite singular and unparalleled, to be the proof of a Deity, a cause no less singular and unparalleled; your reasonings, upon that supposition, seem, at least, to merit our attention. There is, I own, some difficulty, how we can ever return from the cause to the effect, and, reasoning from our ideas of the former, infer any alteration on the latter, or any addition to it.

# SECTION XII

## OF THE ACADEMICAL OR SCEPTICAL PHILOSOPHY

### PART I

THERE is not a greater number of philosophical reasonings, displayed upon any subject, than those, which prove the existence of a Deity, and refute the fallacies of *Atheists;* and yet the most religious philosophers still dispute whether any man can be so blinded as to be a speculative atheist. How shall we reconcile these contradictions? The knights errant, who wandered about to clear the world of dragons and giants, never entertained the least doubt with regard to the existence of these monsters.

The *Sceptic* is another enemy of religion, who naturally provokes the indignation of all divines and graver philosophers; though it is certain, that no man ever met with any such absurd creature, or conversed with a man, who had no opinion or principle concerning any subject, either of action or speculation. This begets a very natural question; What is meant by a sceptic? And how far it is possible to push these philosophical principles of doubt and uncertainty?

There is a species of scepticism, *antecedent* to all study and philosophy, which is much inculcated by Des Cartes and others, as a sovereign preservative against error and precipitate judgement. It recommends an universal doubt, not only of all our former opinions and principles, but also of our very faculties; of whose veracity, say they, we must assure ourselves, by a chain of reasoning, deduced from some original principle, which cannot possibly be fallacious or deceitful. But neither is there any such original principle, which has a prerogative above others, that are self-evident and convincing: or if there were, could we advance a step beyond it, but by the use of those very faculties, of which we are supposed to be already diffident. The Cartesian

431

doubt, therefore, were it ever possible to be attained by any human creature (as it plainly is not) would be entirely incurable; and no reasoning could ever bring us to a state of assurance and conviction upon any subject.

It must, however, be confessed, that this species of scepticism, when more moderate, may be understood in a very reasonable sense, and is a necessary preparative to the study of philosophy, by preserving a proper impartiality in our judgements, and weaning our mind from all those prejudices, which we may have imbibed from education or rash opinion. To begin with clear and self-evident principles, to advance by timorous and sure steps, to review frequently our conclusions, and examine accurately all their consequences; though by these means we shall make both a slow and a short progress in our systems; are the only methods, by which we can ever hope to reach truth, and attain a proper stability and certainty in our determinations.

There is another species of scepticism, *consequent* to science and enquiry, when men are supposed to have discovered, either the absolute fallaciousness of their mental faculties, or their unfitness to reach any fixed determination in all those curious subjects of speculation, about which they are commonly employed. Even our very senses are brought into dispute, by a certain species of philosophers; and the maxims of common life are subjected to the same doubt as the most profound principles or conclusions of metaphysics and theology. As these paradoxical tenets (if they may be called tenets) are to be met with in some philosophers, and the refutation of them in several, they naturally excite our curiosity, and make us enquire into the arguments, on which they may be founded.

I need not insist upon the more trite topics, employed by the sceptics in all ages, against the evidence of *sense;* such as those which are derived from the imperfection and fallaciousness of our organs, on numberless occasions; the crooked appearance of an oar in water; the various aspects of objects, according to their different distances; the double images which arise from the pressing one eye; with many other appearances of a like nature. These sceptical topics, indeed, are only sufficient to prove, that the senses alone

**are** not implicitly to be depended on; but that we must correct their evidence by reason, and by considerations, derived from the nature of the medium, the distance of the object, and the disposition of the organ, in order to render them, within their sphere, the proper *criteria* of truth and falsehood.    There are other more profound arguments against the senses, which admit not of so easy a solution.

It seems evident, that men are carried, by a natural instinct or prepossession, to repose faith in their senses; and that, without any reasoning, or even almost before the use of reason, we always suppose an external universe, which depends not on our perception, but would exist, though we and every sensible creature were absent or annihilated.    Even the animal creation are governed by a like opinion, and preserve this belief of external objects, in all their thoughts, designs, and actions.

It seems also evident, that, when men follow this blind and powerful instinct of nature, they always suppose the very images, presented by the senses, to be the external objects, and never entertain any suspicion, that the one are nothing but representations of the other.    This very table, which we see white, and which we feel hard, is believed to exist, independent of our perception, and to be something external to our mind, which perceives it.    Our presence bestows not being on it: our absence does not annihilate it.    It preserves its existence uniform and entire, independent of the situation of intelligent beings, who perceive or contemplate it.

But this universal and primary opinion of all men is soon destroyed by the slightest philosophy, which teaches us, that nothing can ever be present to the mind but an image or perception, and that the senses are only the inlets, through which these images are conveyed, without being able to produce any immediate intercourse between the mind and the object.    The table, which we see, seems to diminish, as we remove farther from it: but the real table, which exists independent of us, suffers no alteration: it was, therefore, nothing but its image, which was present to the mind.    These are the obvious dictates of reason; and no man, who reflects, ever doubted, that the existences, which we

consider, when we say, *this house* and *that tree,* are nothing
but perceptions in the mind, and fleeting copies or representations of other existences, which remain uniform and independent.

So far, then, are we necessitated by reasoning to contradict or depart from the primary instincts of nature, and
to embrace a new system with regard to the evidence of our
senses. But here philosophy finds herself extremely. em·
barrassed, when she would justify this new system, and
obviate the cavils and objections of the sceptics. She can
no longer plead the infallible and irresistible instinct of
nature: for that led us to a quite different system, which is
acknowledged fallible and even erroneous. And to justify
this pretended philosophical system, by a chain of clear
and convincing argument, or even any appearance of argument, exceeds the power of all human capacity.

By what argument can it be proved, that the perceptions
of the mind must be caused by external objects, entirely
different from them, though resembling them (if that be
possible) and could not arise either from the energy of the
mind itself, or from the suggestion of some invisible and
unknown spirit, or from some other cause still more unknown to us? It is acknowledged, that, in fact, many of
these perceptions arise not from anything external, as in
dreams, madness, and other diseases. And nothing can be
more inexplicable than the manner, in which body should
so operate upon mind as ever to convey an image of itself
to a substance, supposed of so different, and even contrary
a nature.

It is a question of fact, whether the perceptions of the
senses be produced by external objects, resembling them:
how shall this question be determined? By experience
surely; as all other questions of a like nature. But here
experience is, and must be entirely silent. The mind has
never anything present to it but the perceptions, and cannot
possibly reach any experience of their connexion with objects. The supposition of such a connexion is, therefore,
without any foundation in reasoning.

To have recourse to the veracity of the supreme Being,
in order to prove the veracity of our senses, is surely

making a very unexpected circuit. If his veracity were at all concerned in this matter, our senses would be entirely infallible; because it is not possible that he can ever deceive. Not to mention, that, if the external world be once called in question, we shall be at a loss to find arguments, by which we may prove the existence of that Being or any of his attributes.

This is a topic, therefore, in which the profounder and more philosophical sceptics will always triumph, when they endeavour to introduce an universal doubt into all subjects of human knowledge and enquiry. Do you follow the instincts and propensities of nature, may they say, in assenting to the veracity of sense? But these lead you to believe that the very perception or sensible image is the external object. Do you disclaim this principle, in order to embrace a more rational opinion, that the perceptions are only representations of something external? You here depart from your natural propensities and more obvious sentiments; and yet are not able to satisfy your reason, which can never find any convincing argument from experience to prove, that the perceptions are connected with any external objects.

There is another sceptical topic of a like nature, derived from the most profound philosophy; which might merit our attention, were it requisite to dive so deep, in order to discover arguments and reasonings, which can so little serve to any serious purpose. It is universally allowed by modern enquirers, that all the sensible qualities of objects, such as hard, soft, hot, cold, white, black, &c. are merely secondary, and exist not in the objects themselves, but are perceptions of the mind, without any external archetype or model, which they represent. If this be allowed, with regard to secondary qualities, it must also follow, with regard to the supposed primary qualities of extension and solidity; nor can the latter be any more entitled to that denomination than the former. The idea of extension is entirely acquired from the senses of sight and feeling; and if all the qualities, perceived by the senses, be in the mind, not in the object, the same conclusion must reach the idea of extension, which is wholly dependent on the sensible ideas or the ideas of secondary qualities. Nothing can save us from this conclusion, but the asserting, that the ideas of those primary qualities are attained by *Abstraction,* an opinion, which, if we examine it accurately, we shall find to be unintelligible, and even absurd. An extension, that is neither tangible nor visible, cannot possibly be conceived: and a tangible or visible extension, which is neither hard nor soft, black nor white, is equally beyond the reach of human conception. Let any man try to conceive a triangle in general, which is neither *Isosceles* nor *Scalenum,* nor has any particular length or proportion of sides; and he will soon perceive the absurdity of all the scholastic notions with regard to abstraction and general ideas.[1]

Thus the first philosophical objection to the evidence of sense or to the opinion of external existence consists in this, that such an opinion, if rested on natural instinct, is contrary to reason, and if referred to reason, is contrary to natural instinct, and at the same time carries no rational evidence with it, to convince an impartial enquirer. The second objection goes farther, and represents this opinion as contrary to reason: at least, if it be a principle of reason, that all sensible qualities are in the mind, not in the object. Bereave matter of all its intelligible qualities, both primary and secondary, you in a manner annihilate it, and leave only a certain unknown, inexplicable *something,* as the cause of our perceptions; a notion so imperfect, that no sceptic will think it worth while to contend against it.

## PART II

IT may seem a very extravagant attempt of the sceptics to destroy *reason* by argument and ratiocination; yet is this the grand scope of all their enquiries and disputes.

[1] This argument is drawn from Dr. Berkeley; and indeed most of the writings of that very ingenious author form the best lessons of scepticism, which are to be found either among the ancient or modern philosophers, Bayle not excepted. He professes, however, in his title-page (and undoubtedly with great truth) to have composed his book against the sceptics as well as against the atheists and free-thinkers. But that all his arguments, though otherwise intended, are, in reality, merely sceptical, appears from this, *that they admit of no answer and produce no conviction.* Their only effect is to cause that momentary amazement and irresolution and confusion, which is the result of scepticism.

They endeavour to find objections, both to our abstract reasonings, and to those which regard matter of fact and existence.

The chief objection against all *abstract* reasonings is derived from the ideas of space and time; ideas, which, in common life and to a careless view, are very clear and intelligible, but when they pass through the scrutiny of the profound sciences (and they are the chief object of these sciences) afford principles, which seem full of absurdity and contradiction. No priestly *dogmas,* invented on purpose to tame and subdue the rebellious reason of mankind, ever shocked common sense more than the doctrine of the infinitive divisibility of extension, with its consequences; as they are pompously displayed by all geometricians and metaphysicians, with a kind of triumph and exultation. A real quantity, infinitely less than any finite quantity, containing quantities infinitely less than itself, and so on *in infinitum;* this is an edifice so bold and prodigious, that it is too weighty for any pretended demonstration to support, because it shocks the clearest and most natural principles of human reason.[2]   But what renders the matter more extraordinary, is, that these seemingly absurd opinions are supported by a chain of reasoning, the clearest and most natural; nor is it possible for us to allow the premises without admitting the consequences. Nothing can be more convincing and satisfactory than all the conclusions concerning the properties of circles and triangles; and yet, when these are once received, how can we deny, that the angle of contact between a circle and its tangent is infinitely less than any rectilineal angle, that as you may increase the diameter of the circle *in infinitum,* this angle of contact becomes still less, even *in infinitum,* and that the angle of contact between other curves and their tangents may be infinitely less than those betwen any circle and its tangent,

───

[2] Whatever disputes there may be about mathematical points, we must allow that there are physical points; that is, parts of extension, which cannot be divided or lessened, either by the eye or imagination.  These images, then, which are present to the fancy or senses, are absolutely indivisible, and consequently must be allowed by mathematicians to be infinitely less than any real part of extension; and yet nothing appears more certain to reason, than that an infinite number of them composes an infinite extension. How much more an infinite number of those infinitely small parts of extension, which are still supposed infinitely divisible.

and so on, *in infinitum?* The demonstration of these principles seems as unexceptionable as that which proves the three angles of a triangle to be equal to two right ones, though the latter opinion be natural and easy, and the former big with contradiction and absurdity. Reason here seems to be thrown into a kind of amazement and suspence, which, without the suggestions of any sceptic, gives her a diffidence of herself, and of the ground on which she treads. She sees a full light, which illuminates certain places; but that light borders upon the most profound darkness. And between these she is so dazzled and confounded, that she scarcely can pronounce with certainty and assurance concerning any one object.

The absurdity of these bold determinations of the abstract sciences seems to become, if possible, still more palpable with regard to time than extension. An infinite number of real parts of time, passing in succession, and exhausted one after another, appears so evident a contradiction, that no man, one should think, whose judgement is not corrupted, instead of being improved, by the sciences, would ever be able to admit of it.

Yet still reason must remain restless, and unquiet, even with regard to that scepticism, to which she is driven by these seeming absurdities and contradictions. How any clear, distinct idea can contain circumsances, contradictory to itself, or to any other clear, distinct idea, is absolutely incomprehensible; and is, perhaps, as absurd as any proposition, which can be formed. So that nothing can be more sceptical, or more full of doubt and hesitation, than this scepticism itself, which arises from some of the paradoxical conclusions of geometry or the science of quantity[3].

---

[3] It seems to me not impossible to avoid these absurdities and contradictions, if it be admitted, that there is no such thing as abstract or general ideas, properly speaking; but that all general ideas are, in reality, particular ones, attached to a general term, which recalls, upon occasion, other particular ones, that resemble, in certain circumstances, the idea, present to the mind. Thus when the term Horse is pronounced, we immediately figure to ourselves the idea of a black or a white animal, of a particular size or figure: But as that term is also usually applied to animals of other colours, figures and sizes, these ideas, though not actually present to the imagination, are easily recalled; and our reasoning and conclusion proceed in the same way, as if they were actually present. If this be admitted (as seems reasonable) it follows that all the ideas of quantity, upon which mathema-

The sceptical objections to *moral* evidence, or to the reasonings concerning matter of fact, are either *popular* or *philosophical.* The popular objections are derived from the natural weakness of human understanding; the contradictory opinions, which have been entertained in different ages and nations; the variations of our judgement in sickness and health, youth and old age, prosperity and adversity; the perpetual contradiction of each particular man's opinions and sentiments; with many other topics of that kind. It is needless to insist farther on this head. These objections are but weak. For as, in common life, we reason every moment concerning fact and existence, and cannot possibly subsist, without continually employing this species of argument, any popular objections, derived from thence, must be insufficient to destroy that evidence. The great subverter of *Pyrrhonism* or the excessive principles of scepticism is action, and employment, and the occupations of common life. These principles may flourish and triumph in the schools; where it is, indeed, difficult, if not impossible, to refute them. But as soon as they leave the shade, and by the presence of the real objects, which actuate our passions and sentiments, are put in opposition to the more powerful principles of our nature, they vanish like smoke, and leave the most determined sceptic in the same condition as other mortals.

The sceptic, therefore, had better keep within his proper sphere, and display those *philosophical* objections, which arise from more profound researches. Here he seems to have ample matter of triumph; while he justly insists, that all our evidence for any matter of fact, which lies beyond the testimony of sense or memory, is derived entirely from the relation of cause and effect; that we have no other idea of this relation than that of two objects, which have been frequently *conjoined* together; that we have no argument to convince us, that objects, which have, in our experience, been frequently conjoined, will likewise, in other instances,

ticians reason, are nothing but particular, and such as are suggested by the senses and imagination, and consequently, cannot be infinitely divisible. It is sufficient to have dropped this hint at present, without prosecuting it any farther. It certainly concerns all lovers of science not to expose themselves to the ridicule and contempt of the ignorant by their conclusions; and this seems the readiest solution of these difficulties.

be conjoined in the same manner; and that nothing leads us to this inference but custom or a certain instinct of our nature; which it is indeed difficult to resist, but which, like other instincts, may be fallacious and deceitful. While the sceptic insists upon these topics, he shows his force, or rather, indeed, his own and our weakness; and seems, for the time at least, to destroy all assurance and conviction. These arguments might be displayed at greater length, if any durable good or benefit to society could ever be expected to result from them.

For here is the chief and most confounding objection to *excessive* scepticism, that no durable good can ever result from it; while it remains in its full force and vigour. We need only ask such a sceptic, *What his meaning is? And what he proposes by all these curious researches?* He is immediately at a loss, and knows not what to answer. A Copernican or Ptolemaic, who supports each his different system of astronomy, may hope to produce a conviction, which will remain constant and durable, with his audience. A Stoic or Epicurean displays principles, which may not be durable, but which have an effect on conduct and behaviour. But a Pyrrhonian cannot expect, that his philosophy will have any constant influence on the mind: or if it had, that its influence would be beneficial to society. On the contrary, he must acknowledge, if he will acknowledge anything, that all human life must perish, were his principles universally and steadily to prevail. All discourse, all action would immediately cease; and men remain in a total lethargy, till the necessities of nature, unsatisfied, put an end to their miserable existence. It is true; so fatal an event is very little to be dreaded. Nature is always too strong for principle. And though a Pyrrhonian may throw himself or others into a momentary amazement and confusion by his profound reasonings; the first and most trivial event in life will put to flight all his doubts and scruples, and leave him the same, in every point of action and speculation, with the philosophers of every other sect, or with those who never concerned themselves in any philosophical researches. When he awakes from his dream, he will be the first to join in the laugh against himself, and to confess, that all his objections are mere amusement, and can have no other tendency than to show the whimsical condition of mankind, who must act and reason and believe; though they are not able, by their most diligent enquiry, to satisfy themselves concerning the foundation of these operations, or to remove the objections, which may be raised against them.

## Part III

THERE is, indeed, a more *mitigated* scepticism or *academical* philosophy, which may be both durable and useful, and which may, in part, be the result of this Pyrrhonism, or *excessive* scepticism, when its undistinguished doubts are, in some measure, corrected by common sense and reflection. The greater part of mankind are naturally apt to be affirmative and dogmatical in their opinions; and while they see objects only on one side, and have no idea of any counterpoising argument, they throw themselves precipitately into the principles, to which they are inclined; nor have they any indulgence for those who entertain opposite sentiments. To hesitate or balance perplexes their understanding, checks their passion, and suspends their action. They are, therefore, impatient till they escape from a state, which to them is so uneasy: and they think, that they could never remove themselves far enough from it, by the violence of their affirmations and obstinacy of their belief. But could such dogmatical reasoners become sensible of the strange infirmities of human understanding, even in its most perfect state, and when most accurate and cautious in its determinations; such a reflection would naturally inspire them with more modesty and reserve, and diminish their fond opinion of themselves, and their prejudice against antagonists. The illiterate may reflect on the disposition of the learned, who, amidst all the advantages of study and reflection, are commonly still diffident in their determinations: and if any of the learned be inclined, from their natural temper, to haughtiness and obstinacy, a small tincture of Pyrrhonism might abate their pride, by showing them, that the few advantages, which they may have attained over their fellows, are but inconsiderable, if compared with the universal perplexity and confusion, which is inherent in human nature. In general, there is a degree of doubt, and caution, and modesty, which, in all kinds of scrutiny and decision, ought for ever to accompany a just reasoner.

Another species of *mitigated* scepticism which may be of advantage to mankind, and which may be the natural result of the Pyrrhonian doubts and scruples, is the limitation of our enquiries to such subjects as are best adapted to the narrow capacity of human understanding. The *imagination* of man is naturally sublime, delighted with whatever is remote and extraordinary, and running, without control, into the most distant parts of space and time in order to avoid the objects, which custom has rendered too familiar to it. A correct *Judgement* observes a contrary method, and avoiding all distant and high enquiries, confines itself to common life, and to such subjects as fall under daily practice and experience; leaving the more sublime topics to the embellishment of poets and orators, or to the arts of priests and politicians. To bring us to so salutary a determination, nothing can be more serviceable, than to be once thoroughly convinced of the force of the Pyrrhonian doubt, and of the impossibility, that anything, but the strong power of natural instinct, could free us from it. Those who have a propensity to philosophy, will still continue their researches; because they reflect, that, besides the immediate pleasure attending such an occupation, philosophical decisions are nothing but the reflections of common life, methodized and corrected. But they will never be tempted to go beyond common life, so long as they consider the imperfection of those faculties which they employ, their narrow reach, and their inaccurate operations. While we cannot give a satisfactory reason, why we believe, after a thousand experiments, that a stone will fall, or fire burn; can we ever satisfy ourselves concerning any determination, which we may form, with regard to the origin of worlds, and the situation of nature, from, and to eternity?

This narrow limitation, indeed, of our enquiries, is, in every respect, so reasonable, that it suffices to make the slightest examination into the natural powers of the human mind and to compare them with their objects, in order to recommend it to us. We shall then find what are the proper subjects of science and enquiry.

It seems to me, that the only objects of the abstract science or of demonstration are quantity and number, and that all attempts to extend this more perfect species of knowledge beyond these bounds are mere sophistry and illusion. As the component parts of quantity and number are entirely similar, their relations become intricate and involved; and nothing can be more curious, as well as useful, than to trace, by a variety of mediums, their equality or inequality, through their different appearances. But as all other ideas are clearly distinct and different from each other, we can never advance farther, by our utmost scrutiny, than to observe this diversity, and, by an obvious reflection, pronounce one thing not to be another. Or if there be any difficulty in these decisions, it proceeds entirely from the undeterminate meaning of words, which is corrected by juster definitions. That *the square of the hypothenuse is equal to the squares of the other two sides,* cannot be known, let the terms be ever so exactly defined, without a train of reasoning and enquiry. But to convince us of this proposition, *that where there is no property, there can be no injustice,* it is only necessary to define the terms, and explain injustice to be a violation of property. This proposition is, indeed, nothing but a more imperfect definition. It is the same case with all those pretended syllogistical reasonings, which may be found in every other branch of learning, except the sciences of quantity and number; and these may safely, I think, be pronounced the only proper objects of knowledge and demonstration.

All other enquiries of men regard only matter of fact and existence; and these are evidently incapable of demonstration. Whatever *is* may *not be.* No negation of a fact can involve a contradiction. The non-existence of any being, without exception, is as clear and distinct an idea as its existence. The proposition, which affirms it not to be, however false, is no less conceivable and intelligible, than that which affirms it to be. The case is different with the sciences, properly so called. Every proposition, which is not true, is there confused and unintelligible. That the cube root of 64 is equal to the half of 10, is a false proposition, and can never be distinctly conceived. But that Cæsar, or the angel Gabriel, or any being never existed, may be a false proposition, but still is perfectly conceivable, and implies no contradiction.

The existence, therefore, of any being can only be proved by arguments from its cause or its effect; and these arguments are founded entirely on experience. If we reason *a priori,* anything may appear able to produce anything. The falling of a pebble may, for aught we know, extinguish the sun; or the wish of a man control the planets in their orbits. It is only experience, which teaches us the nature and bounds of cause and effect, and enables us to infer the existence of one object from that of another[4]. Such is the foundation of moral reasoning, which forms the greater part of human knowledge, and is the source of all human action and behaviour.

Moral reasonings are either concerning particular or general facts. All deliberations in life regard the former; as also all disquisitions in history, chronology, geography, and astronomy.

The sciences, which treat of general facts, are politics, natural philosophy, physic, chemistry, &c. where the qualities, causes and effects of a whole species of objects are enquired into.

Divinity or Theology, as it proves the existence of a Deity, and the immortality of souls, is composed partly of reasonings concerning particular, partly concerning general facts. It has a foundation in *reason,* so far as it is supported by experience. But its best and most solid foundation is *faith* and divine revelation.

Morals and criticism are not so properly objects of the understanding as of taste and sentiment. Beauty, whether moral or natural, is felt, more properly than perceived. Or if we reason concerning it, and endeavour to fix its standard, we regard a new fact, to wit, the general tastes of

---

[4] That impious maxim of the ancient philosophy, *Ex nihilo, nihil fit,* by which the creation of matter was excluded, ceases to be a maxim, according to this philosophy. Not only the will of the supreme Being may create matter; but, for aught we know *a priori,* the will of any other being might create it, or any other cause, that the most whimsical imagination can assign.

mankind, or some such fact, which may be the object of reasoning and enquiry.

When we run over libraries, persuaded of these principles, what havoc must we make? If we take in our hand any volume; of divinity or school metaphysics, for instance; let us ask, *Does it contain any abstract reasoning concerning quantity or number?* No. *Does it contain any experimental reasoning concerning matter of fact and existence?* No. Commit it then to the flames: for it can contain nothing but sophistry and illusion.

THE PUBLISHERS OF THE HAR-
VARD CLASSICS · DR. ELIOT'S
FIVE-FOOT SHELF OF BOOKS ARE
PLEASED TO ANNOUNCE THE
PUBLICATION OF

## THE JUNIOR CLASSICS
### A LIBRARY FOR BOYS AND GIRLS

"The Junior Classics constitute a set
of books whose contents will delight
children and at the same time
satisfy the legitimate ethical require-
ments of those who have the children's
best interests at heart."

CHARLES W. ELIOT

THE COLLIER PRESS · NEW YORK
P · F · COLLIER & SON